D0913029

Harvard Historical Studies • 168

Published under the auspices
of the Department of History
from the income of the
Paul Revere Frothingham Bequest
Robert Louis Stroock Fund
Henry Warren Torrey Fund

Revolutionary Commerce

GLOBALIZATION AND THE

FRENCH MONARCHY

Paul Cheney

Harvard University Press

Cambridge, Massachusetts · London, England

2010

Library of Congress Cataloging-in-Publication Data

Cheney, Paul Burton.
Revolutionary commerce: globalization and the French monarchy / Paul Cheney.
p. cm. — (Harvard historical studies ; 168)
Includes bibliographical references and index.
ISBN 978-0-674-04726-6 (alk. paper)
1. France—Commerce—History—18th century.   2. France—Economic policy—18th
century.   3. France—Economic conditions—18th century.   4. Economics—France—
History—18th century.   I. Title.
HF3555.C54   2010
381.0944—dc22
2009034950

To Jessie

Contents

Illustrations

Acknowledgments

I NSTITUTIONS CONTRIBUTED quite a lot to the writing of this book, and I am pleased to acknowledge their support and that of the people associated with them. This book began at Columbia University, and many years later I am still benefiting from the advice of David Armitage and Isser Woloch. The Institut National D'Etudes Démographiques (INED) in Paris funded several research trips, and Loïc Charles and Christine Théré have been unstintingly generous colleagues during my visits there. The Queen's University of Belfast provided research funds, and there I would like to thank David Hayton in particular. At the University of Chicago, the Department of History, the Division of the Social Sciences, and the Franke Institute for the Humanities have each supported my research and writing in indispensable ways. Colleagues here providing valuable criticism and support included Fredrik Albritton-Jonsson, Bruce Cummings, Jan Goldstein, Robert Morrissey, and Emily Osborn. Bill Sewell offered particularly detailed, useful comments on the manuscript.

Conferences and seminars provided the occasion for the airing of ideas, some of which proved especially stimulating. In this connection, I would like to thank Bernard Bailyn at Harvard University; Keith Baker at Stanford University; Allan Macinnes and Steve Pincus, who organized a seminar at the Newberry Library; Gabriel Paquette of Cambridge University; the Political Theory Workshop at the University of Chicago, with thanks to Sankar Muthu and Jennifer Pitts; and finally the Probability Seminar at Columbia University, with particular thanks to Eric Wakin. In addition, Hank Clark and Ran Halévi organized Liberty Fund conferences that were the occasion for fruitful, sometimes heated discussion of authors discussed in this book. Many colleagues not named here responded to my work in various ways, and I thank them all.

Antoine and Bénédicte Piron were kind enough to host a perfect stranger making a research visit to Nantes; I am grateful for their hospitality. I would like to thank the editors of *Dix-Huitième Siècle*, *Historical Reflections*, and the *William & Mary Quarterly*, for their permission to include material previously published in the pages of these journals in this book.

Many authors' acknowledgments proclaim the essentially social nature of scholarship, whereas for me it seems a solitary business. I am all the more appreciative, therefore, to have benefited from the encouragement, criticism, and fellowship of Jeff Collins, Joe Green, Tamara Griggs, Edwige Kacenelenbogen, Julia Kindt, Paul Lakosky, Catherine Larrère, Ben Lazier, Allan Potofsky, and Melvin Richter.

My household and its members were in perpetual motion for several years as I made research trips in connection with this book, and we relocated to Northern Ireland so that I could take up an academic post there. During this period, we built up a stock of cherished memories, particularly from a place called the Bloody Foreland, and my seven-year-old son Nicholas now has a dog-eared passport to show for his peregrinations. But prolonged absences on my part and two transatlantic house moves were often less than amusing for my wife Jessie, who kept things together under sometimes strained circumstances. This book is dedicated to her in deepest gratitude for her forbearance, her loyalty, and her sustaining love.

Revolutionary Commerce

Introduction

THOUGH IT IS NOW generally qualified by the adjectives "archaic" or "primitive," the process of globalization in eighteenth-century Europe was considered by those experiencing it to be revolutionary in the most thoroughly modern sense of the term. Contemporary French observers did not use the term "globalization," but referred often to the "advances of trade" *(les progrès du commerce)*, a phrase that evokes both economic growth and the social progress accompanying it. The opening of the East Indian trade and the establishment of a colonial plantation complex that rapidly followed upon the discovery of the Americas were commonly held responsible for millennial social and political transformations on the Continent. Paradoxically, the most significant effects of primitive globalization were believed to be taking place within Europe, and no aspect of traditional society was considered exempt from these changes; we find no shortage of observers who believed that *les progrès du commerce* were responsible for undermining an intimately related set of social relations collectively known as feudalism. In this vein, Guillaume Thomas Raynal began his *Philosophical and Political History of the European Colonies and Commerce in the Two Indies* (1770) with the observation that "there has never been an event so important for the human race in general, and for the people of Europe in particular, than the discovery

1

of the new world and the passage to the Indies by the Cape of Good Hope. From that point forward there began a revolution in the commerce, the power of nations, the customs, the industry and the government of all peoples." Despite the oracular tone, Raynal was not telling his eighteenth-century readers something they did not already know: international best-sellers are not made of such stuff. Rather, he and his collaborators drew upon a historical analysis that was developed in order to describe—and in some senses to master—a revolution that, although already three hundred years old, was not yet complete. The incompleteness of this revolution, and the stakes involved for France in mastering an international scene increasingly dominated by commercial peoples, forms the most basic context for the development of economic thought in eighteenth-century France.[1]

The revolutionary effects of *les progrès du commerce* posed one set of problems for contemporaries and pose yet another for twenty-first-century historians. For enlightened *philosophes,* statesmen, and merchants, *les progrès du commerce* presented an unprecedented set of opportunities for the enhancement of public power and private well-being. At the very same time, the context of international competition and internal social transformations posed distinct risks. When writers such as Charles Louis de Montesquieu, Adam Smith, and Raynal wrote about the destruction of feudal social relations and forms of government by the growth of trade, they were not pursuing purely antiquarian historical interests. Though in some respects fluid, eighteenth-century France remained a hierarchical society organized into status groups called orders: the clergy, the aristocracy, and the third estate. Many believed that this society of orders, with the king and his aristocracy at the head of it, was incompatible with, and would be swept away by, new forms of wealth and economic activity; could France embrace commerce without fully succumbing to its revolutionary effects?

Over the course of the eighteenth century, French economic writers developed a comparative "science of commerce"—note the significance of the phrase in contrast to the more commonly used "political economy"—that was devoted to analyzing the components of economic prosperity. Ancient and modern nations provided examples of the type of economic activities that were carried out in different societies and of their effects upon established governments, status hierarchies, and cultures. On the margins of eighteenth-century economic debates, some believed that France had a capacity for commercial prosperity every bit as strong as the commercial "republics" among its competitor nations, Holland and England. Others believed that an ancient, proudly bellicose monarchy such as France should not get mixed up in the grubby, excessively bourgeois occupation of trade; advocates of republican virtue and austerity believed much the same thing. Between these extremes, the science of commerce provided a historical and sociological method to address how France could rise to the challenge posed to it by primitive globalization: finding a prosperous, politically stable place for itself in an evolving international division of labor.

A central purpose of this book, therefore, is to describe the economic thought of globalization in eighteenth-century France. Though some readers may object to the term "globalization," there is real value in this anachronism at the outset; then as now, transnational economic forces eluded the control of individual states. Like tectonic plates moving slowly and silently underfoot, the changes wrought by the Commercial Revolution and the expansion of Europe's colonial empires were seen as immense and ineluctable and so naturally commanded sustained interest in political, literary, and mercantile circles. It would seem sufficiently ambitious to describe the origin and development of this economic thought, but the dénouement of this story, the collapse of the absolute monarchy in 1789 and the fall in 1792 of the constitutional monarchy that took its place, imposes yet another set of questions. Do these events signify that an organizing question of the science of commerce—how France was to become a modern, commercial monarchy—rested on a false premise and that moderate reform had always been impossible? This weighty question invokes another: what is the relation between the Commercial Revolution, which figured so prominently in the economic writing of the eighteenth century, and the Great Revolution of 1789?

The Treaty of Utrecht (1713) acted as a wake-up call for those who assigned increasing geopolitical importance to questions of trade, and from around this date until roughly 1760, the French developed a science of commerce, the central focus of which was reconciling a new political order founded upon commerce with the peculiarities of France's government, social structure, and customs. After 1748 and the publication of the *Esprit des lois,* the science of commerce sharpened its concepts and methods while strengthening its intellectual authority by persistent reference to Montesquieu, who also sought compromise between old and new types of wealth, social hierarchies, and forms of government.

The science of commerce explored a paradoxical series of developments unleashed by the discovery of the Americas and Europe's subsequent colonial expansion. Shipments of gold and silver were only the first manifestations of historically unprecedented wealth, and it was commonly understood that sugar, coffee, rare woods, cocoa, textiles, and dyestuffs linked a distant colonial periphery to merchants and industries in the heart of the European metropole. In order to ensure a successful symbiosis of domestic industry, colonial plantations, and merchant capital, all agreed that the legal norms associated with "arbitrary" governments (feudal or absolute monarchies) would have to give way to more regular, though not necessarily democratic, forms of government. The cosmopolitan flow of merchant capital, which rendered unimpeachable judgment on rapacious states on a daily basis, as well as the routines of commercial activities and the individual passions associated with them, had a softening effect on governments and manners everywhere. What Albert Hirschman has called *doux commerce* ("gentle" or "sweet" commerce) worked these effects all over Europe and was helping to force the passage from the feudal and the arbitrary to the modern and commercial, whether monarchs and the aristocracy that supported them liked it or not.[2] Commerce was widely believed to be penetrating more deeply than ever before into Europe's political order. As a corollary of *doux commerce,* the interests of productive classes had to be taken more explicitly into account in order to multiply wealth coming from the Americas. The examples of small commercial republics demonstrated that territorial empires' natural impulse to conquest had to be rethought in an age where wealth, and not territory per se, determined the balance of power in Europe.

It is hardly accidental that the development of the science of commerce, which was associated in French government circles and in the Republic of Letters with a moderate path of reform, coincided with an

interval of relative tranquility and prosperity. Despite the critical tone
often taken toward the monarchy by some economic writers, this was a
time of comparative optimism, and justly so: buoyed by its thriving sugar
colonies, France made great strides against its competition, fully exploit-
ing what Perry Anderson has termed the "field of compatibility" between capitalist accumulation and the "nature and programme" of an
absolutist state that remained, however, "irreducibly feudal" because of
its basis in aristocratic and more generally corporate society.[3]

In eighteenth-century France, moderate reform under the sign of commercial monarchy was not so much an illusion as a successful formula
that began to run up against its inherent limitations in the 1760s: the
"provisional coincidence of interests" between the French monarchy
and an expanding world of production and exchange was coming to an
end. The Seven Years' War, which concluded with a massively indebted
France ceding its North American possessions to Great Britain, was in
this respect a prodrome of the final crisis that came in 1789. The impossibility of merely moderate reform was most forcefully articulated by
the Physiocrats, the school of economic thought started by François
Quesnay. Following Quesnay's initial analyses of France's rural economy, which began to appear in the pages of Diderot and d'Alembert's
Encyclopédie in 1757, the Physiocrats directed considerable critical fire
against Europe's colonial-mercantile enterprise. Whereas most French observers had taken colonial commerce as a modernizing force, the Physiocrats argued that a regime based upon slavery, trade restrictions, and
systemic warfare entrenched social relations characteristic of quasi-feudal,
agrarian monarchies. The Physiocratic solution, which extended from
France's rural economy to the organization of its colonial trade, was to
abolish, for the sake of economic liberalism, the whole system of orders,
privileges, and *corps* upon which the monarchy rested: in short, to complete the Commercial Revolution so widely discussed in the Republic of
Letters. The Physiocrats never waged a frontal assault on the French
monarchy—Physiocracy was a movement that originated, after all, in the
halls of Versailles—but as Alexis de Tocqueville rightly observed, the
ensemble of their policies, if enacted, would have left no remnant of the
Old Regime. Although monarchist to the core in their political thought,
theirs was the monarchy of enlightened despotism and not the moderate

or "civilized" monarchy approved by Montesquieu and like-minded followers. As the Revolution later proved, the Physiocratic conception of
sovereignty could easily dispense with a monarch.[4]

From the early 1760s until the watershed of 1789, neither Physiocracy
nor moderate reformism was fully dominant; French economic thought,
like the society surrounding it, remained in a holding pattern, alternat-
ing between two incompatible understandings of the way forward. Parts
of the Physiocrats' social and political vision were debated or even temporarily implemented, only to be weakened or entirely withdrawn in
the face of short-term failure or criticism: the liberalization of the grain
trade (1763, 1764, and 1775), the demolition of the guild system (1776), the
opening up of trade in the West Indies (1765 and 1784), and the abolition
of overseas trading companies (1769) are notorious examples of this pattern. Hesitant policymaking was an expression of a deeper indecision,
since different approaches to reform derived from conflicting social
models and, crucially, attitudes toward the value of history. Clarity, rigor,
and ahistorical generality made Physiocratic "political economy" a more
modern, "scientific" tool of analysis, and in arguing for the superiority
of their system, the Physiocrats criticized Montesquieu and those who
followed his lead as methodologically and politically confused apolo-
gists for the irrational institutions of France's past.[5]

Although unlikely, it is not impossible that the French monarchy,
rather than meeting its violent demise, might have continued muddling
through as it had done in the latter half of the eighteenth century, patch-
ing up the financial strains and social conflicts caused by its failed
struggle for commercial hegemony with Great Britain. In the event, the
absolute monarchy did not survive the financial and political shocks of
1787–1789, which were precipitated by the debts accumulated by France
during the American War of Independence; nor, as it turned out, did the
government designed to take its place. France's constitutional monarchy
has often been described as a worthy if flawed structure built on top of the
smoking volcano of popular sovereignty; revolutionary ideology was destined to push toward successively more direct expressions of democratic
will and demands for social equality much at odds with the structures
and aims of moderate, limited government. However, if we widen the
frame of the inquiry, we better understand the relationship between the
fall of the monarchy and economic thought about globalization.

In addition to finding a stable constitutional order for mainland France, revolutionaries had to establish a new regime in the whole of the French empire. While ensuring the persistence of slavery, such an order had to strike an equitable balance between the economic interests of mainland France and its colonies, which had been diverging in recent decades due to the growth of the sugar islands. No workable compromise involving all of these elements was ever possible, and the terms of the conflict show the degree to which the social and political visions that exploded in what has come to be known as "the affair of the colonies" *(l'affaire des colonies)* preceded the Revolutionary period.

The Revolution did more than simply unleash pre-existing conflicts over the social and political forms appropriate to a modern, commercial French nation; but it is hardly surprising that when the terminal crisis of the absolute monarchy came in 1788–1789, a similar set of questions should reappear with new urgency. The constitution of 1791 instituted stringent qualifications for voting and office-holding in order to preserve property from the leveling tendencies of universal, direct democracy, while the system of slave production received a temporary reprieve in order to guarantee an uninterrupted flow of wealth from the islands. Advocates of these arrangements believed that the Revolution could not survive without prosperity and social order, which effectively meant terminating the Revolution before every revolutionary principle had been brought to its logical conclusion. An incomplete but stable Revolution would have to reconcile itself with the existing social regime on the islands, and within France, as a condition of further progress.

The debate over the constitution of 1791 and the affair of the colonies turned on a set of similar issues about the relationship between property, national prosperity, and an expansive notion of citizenship; both controversies reflected the political choices posed by *les progrès du commerce,* although the affair of the colonies underscores the economic element of both discussions. But what was economics in the eighteenth century?

From Political Economy to the Science of Commerce

"Political economy" and the "science of commerce" were pervasive though not precisely synonymous terms used during the eighteenth century to denote systematic inquiry into the economic processes affecting individuals, communities, and states. Along with *commerce en général* and *commerce politique,* among others, these terms jostled against one another in a rough sort of parity until "political economy," the favored usage of the Physiocrats, began to clear the field in the last quarter of the century. This winnowing was completed with the consolidation of economics into a discipline during the early nineteenth century. From this point onward, the history of economic thought became largely the history of political economy, projecting the related social concerns and scientific conceits of this discipline onto the past. By now, the evidence is so overwhelming as to verge on the commonplace that the history of political economy is biased toward Whiggish narratives cheering the inevitable development of laissez-faire out of mercantilism and tracing the refinement of successively more abstract and scientifically rigorous models of value, growth, and distribution. Historical attention is lavished upon eighteenth-century writers who cut the most plausible figures as precursors of nineteenth- and twentieth-century political economy, and the significance of their work is assessed, accordingly, in these terms. If we understand the history of political economy as a teleological progression from mercantilism to laissez-faire, the material at hand is more or less self-organizing: just situate an author within this teleological arc and affix the label "pre-," "post-," "neo-," or "anti-" as appropriate. In the French case, this explains why the Physiocrats, arch-advocates of the free market and of a deductive model of social-scientific inquiry, have been so thoroughly studied since the nineteenth century, while other thinkers have either fallen by the wayside or been defined purely in relation to this group.[6]

Although saying so risks a kind of nominalism wholly out of place in the study of history, it is true that terminological choices help to determine available perspectives on a phenomenon. Economic inquiry in the century of Enlightenment sprung from a conjuncture of intellectual, political, and economic forces that deserve to be understood on their own terms, apart from two hundred years' accretions on the term "political economy." Using a term unique to the eighteenth century, the "science of commerce," seems a good place to begin. Although they started out as rough synonyms, the "science of commerce" and "political economy" finished, toward the end of the eighteenth century, as rival conceptions about the future of the French polity in a new era dominated by commerce. In order to tell this story and to give it the true weight of its historical significance, I have temporarily set aside concepts that have long colored the intellectual history of political economy. Rather than dwelling on the development of models of value, equilibrium, and productivity, or on traditional dichotomies such as laissez-faire/mercantilism, production/trade, and individual interest/collective interest, this book places into the foreground contemporary thought about competitive pressures, imperial politics, modes of governance, and the related questions of culture and social structure. This thematic reorientation necessitates a consideration of a range of sources broader than those normally used; while the intellectual history of political economy has generally favored the principal witness provided by developed treatises of economic theory and the supporting testimony of published ephemera (pamphlets and journal articles), I shall also enter into evidence the writings of administrators, diplomats, and merchants who thought about France's overseas trade.

A minority of the authors to be examined here were intensely interested in developing abstract economic theory susceptible to broad application, but the majority abstained from such speculation for want of time, inclination, faculty, or need. What held these authors together instead was a common concern over the historical effects of *les progrès du commerce;* the daily preoccupations of merchants in the counting houses of Bordeaux were not those of highly placed ministers at Versailles, but when they wrote about the geopolitics of trade, writers in both places tended to adopt the grandiloquent tone and Olympian perspective characteristic of the wider Republic of Letters. Intellectual exchanges and policy disputes between the cities of the Ponant (the western seaboard of France), Saint-Domingue, Versailles, and Paris were not conducted in the logically rigorous language of the economic treatise, with its increasingly well-defined problems of value, growth, and circulation; instead, conflicting claims about the causes of economic progress, its sociopolitical effects, and the role of government intervention were made in a specifically historical idiom, which appeared in a widely recognized genre of writing: the history of commerce. Once we are sensible to the existence of this genre and come to understand its methods, central categories, and common tropes, a hitherto obscured unity within the economic thought of the eighteenth century emerges. The historical approach to *les progrès du commerce* did not amount to a school of thought like Physiocracy with its charismatic leader, its rigid policy orthodoxy, and its organs of opinion. Nevertheless, the publication of Montesquieu's *Esprit des lois* in 1748 helped to crystallize a hitherto fluid compound; henceforth, the many writers who perceived the epochal significance of France's transformation into a commercial power had a more clearly defined and intellectually authoritative way of speaking about this phenomenon.[7]

The ensemble of recent studies suggests that historians have moved beyond a Whiggish affirmation of present-day economic orthodoxy in order to search out fresh historical problems. Approaches to the history of political economy, nourished in the Anglo-American world by Cambridge School contextualism, therefore deeply inform this book. Of equal importance, on the French side, is the work of Jean-Claude Perrot and those inspired by him, who have consistently pushed beyond canonic textual sources. Simone Meyssonnier and Catherine Larrère reopen the canon and reintroduce a whole range of authors, most notably the circle of thinkers surrounding France's Intendant of Commerce Vincent de Gournay, whose methods and concerns were independent of the Physiocrats. Two recent studies confirm this trend by offering broad syntheses of eighteenth-century French economic thought that mention the Physiocrats but do not assign to them a central role in the developments traced.[8] Across the Channel, historians such as Donald Winch and John Robertson have written groundbreaking studies centering on England, Scotland, and Italy that provide invaluable models for discussing the polemical and comparative national contexts of political economy. Emma Rothschild's study of Adam Smith and the Marquis de Condorcet forcefully demonstrates the warping effects that nineteenth- and twentieth-century economic ideology have had on our view of the whole Enlightenment, in which ideas of commerce played such a central role. Michael Sonenscher's recent work connects the political thought aroused by the interminable financial imbroglio of the French government in the eighteenth century with key elements of Revolutionary ideology. Montesquieu figures prominently in some of these contextualist accounts, in a way that a narrow understanding of what qualifies as the economic thought of the period would have made impossible.[9]

But the virtues and limitations of the Cambridge School approach are of a piece. Early modern economic growth provoked debates about how commerce might supplant other models of political obligation and social organization, and historians working in this tradition have reconstructed this seventeenth- and eighteenth-century political dialogue in luminous detail. We now know more than ever, thanks to the work of historians such as J. G. A. Pocock and Istvan Hont, about how the economic thought of the period was nourished, for example, by republican and jurisprudential traditions. These historians display an imposing command over the mass of second- and third-order thinkers, but their central arguments are usually structured around references to political philosophers such as David Hume, Adam Smith, Samuel Pufendorf, and James Harrington, so that, despite its contextual richness, their work reads like a dialogue between canonic authors; in this colloquy of immortals, problems of international trade become abstract very quickly and with them the underlying conception of capitalism. "Commerce" is treated as one of many political concepts in a historical lexicon and rarely as a set of institutions, practices, or potential antagonisms; the social conditions that dictated the production and distribution of wealth are rarely addressed, and commerce is transposed from a material field into an almost exclusively philological one. Perhaps this is an inevitable consequence of the origins of Cambridge School contextualism in an explicit rejection of what its founders saw as reductive, materialist approaches to history.[10]

This curiously irenic conception of eighteenth-century commercial capitalism is related to a geographically constrained picture of its operations. In this sense, the Cambridge School continues with some older traditions even as it breaks decisively with others. Because of his ongoing interest in the political and economic questions arising out of international trade, the work of Istvan Hont deserves special attention here as a case in point. In his work, examples of intra-imperial exchanges are largely confined to the problem of trade between England, Ireland, and Scotland; a significant source of surplus, slave labor in Europe's plantation complex in the Americas, is left out of his account, as is the method by which a distribution of this surplus that was favorable to the mother country was secured. Among the many discussions of the theoretical rights and wrongs of protectionism and empire, there is no detailed treatment of the Navigation Acts, the cornerstone of the British imperial trade regime. While inequalities between center and periphery clearly enter into Hont's analysis, the focus on European exchanges has the effect of systematically accentuating the consensual rather than the coercive aspects of mercantile expansion. Ireland undoubtedly stood in a colonial relationship to England, but it was not Saint-Domingue, South Carolina, or Jamaica. Hont often emphasizes in his account the development of market models such as Hume's specie-flow mechanism, which demonstrated the futility of sovereign attempts to control foreign trade; these models have more limited application in the wider Atlantic world, where the imposition of labor regimes and terms of trade within empires, and the competition for markets and territories between them, presented a less abstract and benign face. Moreover, while Hont rightly underlines warfare and war debt as the emblematic paradoxes of European commercial development, it is essential to recognize that commercial warfare only became intolerably expensive and politically explosive once it expanded to Europe's colonial periphery—and in particular the Atlantic world.[11]

Classical political economy and the intellectual history that has developed out of it sit uneasily with transnational economic models, whether grounded in world-systems theory or approaches based upon imperial or oceanic units. The most immediately relevant examples of such units are the British Imperial economy; the economy of the Atlantic; or still more narrowly, the French Atlantic world. Although agriculture, industry, labor markets, and the grain trade are subjects of undeniable importance, as principal themes they too easily lead back to nineteenth- and twentieth-century preoccupations over the industrialization of individual nations and the models of value, growth, and distribution employed in modeling this process. The international context in which these sectors functioned exercised an organizing influence on the development of eighteenth-century economic thought and needs to be brought much more explicitly into account.[12]

Once the broader field of the Atlantic world is adopted and some acknowledgment made of the structures that sustained production and exchange in this space, the problem of governance must arise. Colonial societies were often internally fragile and subject to the incursions of imperial rivals; when the economies of these colonies developed beyond a certain point, wealth and newfound political confidence often gave rise to antagonisms with the mother country. The political economy of imperial and oceanic spaces had to contend with the difficulties inherent in both situations. This book does not pretend to offer a developed study of all the institutions that oversaw France's maritime empire, but it is taken for granted that no accurate picture of the economic thought of primitive globalization can dispense with the views of those who conducted foreign trade on a daily basis, ensured France's economic interests in foreign ports and courts, protected trade on the high seas, ensured the governance of the colonies, or developed broader geopolitical strategy. Accordingly, I sound the views of merchants active in the chambers of commerce established in France's port cities, consuls of commerce and diplomats stationed abroad, and finally bureaucrats working in Versailles and in the colonies for the minister of the navy. Broadening the geography and sources for the study of economic thought also expands the sorts of problems it can address.

Toward Synthesis

By temporarily laying aside political economy in favor of the science of commerce, I hope that the social thought of the period will look quite different. But the broadest insights offered here result from squaring this intellectual-historical approach with developments in four other areas of historical research: the economic history of pre-industrial Europe, particularly as it relates to the rise of the economies of the Atlantic world; the history of French absolutism and state formation; intimately connected with the first two, a literature about the spatial organization of capitalist accumulation; and the history of the political thought of Old Regime and Revolutionary France. Set in its proper contexts and furnished with a new range of sources, the study of economic thought can suggest a new synthesis where reigning modes of historical interpretation have falsely opposed political and social phenomena, and hence modes of explanation, to one another. Eighteenth-century economic writers sought to analyze the relationship between the political and social transformations of their times; their self-awareness does not explain every historical problem the period might pose for us, but it is a very good starting point. Sociological and economic research into the eighteenth century not only provides background material to confirm or negate the content of intellectual history but helps us refine our initial questions and take better stock, along the way, of the pressures that shaped contemporary responses to primitive globalization.

The role of foreign trade in the economic history of pre-industrial Europe has never entirely receded from view, but in recent decades a new prominence has been accorded to Atlantic exchanges in explaining the different paths to industrialization among European nations. This new emphasis received its first and most important impetus from world-systems theory and has been much reinforced by the efflorescence of Atlantic history, whether focused explicitly upon the economy or not. A group of new institutionalist economic historians has recently argued the importance of Atlantic exchanges to long-term growth and industrialization, while an econometric study affirmed the proposition that foreign trade acted as a motor of growth for the entire French economy. A case could be made that a study of primitive globalization and the economic thought related to it should take into account the East Indian and Levant trade; while acknowledging that this entire system ultimately hung together, this choice rests on two observations. First, in the eighteenth century, the Eastern (Asian and Levant) trade was in relative decline compared with Atlantic commerce; second, while eighteenth-century observers conceded that the European discovery of the East Indies was instrumental in opening up the world of commerce, they also believed that the winds of social and political change had shifted since the sixteenth century and were blowing stiffly from the west.[13]

Beyond the specifically French example, even formerly skeptical historians have begun to appreciate the "inseparable connections" between foreign trade, the growth of the fiscal-military state, and the encouragement of domestic industry in contrast to more closed national models of economic development. In the colonies, slaves produced sugar, tobacco, coffee, and cotton, while Europeans consumed these commodities or worked them into items of popular luxury; the colonies themselves provided a market for the networks of proto-industrial production that flourished in the hinterlands of Atlantic ports. These related transformations in patterns of work, consumption, and urban living were instrumental in the making of Europe's modern economy.[14]

From the eighteenth century to our own day, attitudes toward France's role in this grand narrative of European economic progress have varied. Recent historical assessments of the French Atlantic economy have been equally changeable, and as in so many other matters, Britain stands as an implicit or explicit point of contrast. One extreme sees the French Atlantic as an inherently infirm economic body further wracked by short-term thinking in government circles and chronic rent-seeking by elites. This pessimistic interpretation underestimates the many strengths of France's overseas trading empire, but it lights upon one important fact: unlike analogous British and Dutch ventures, French crown-sponsored trading companies never overcame their origins in royal patronage networks and remained primarily examples of a risk-averse, rent-seeking type of court capitalism. Against this pessimistic account, another extreme sees the French Atlantic economy adding strength to strength all the way up until 1789. I adopt an intermediate view: despite a solid overall performance, the French economy had fundamental weaknesses to which it finally succumbed in the financial crisis of 1788–1789. The Atlantic economy played a key role in these advances, but it too had structural problems. These included the absence of an American continental base, such as the British possessed in North America, which could provide consumption goods and markets necessary to the ongoing prosperity of island economies. France also relied excessively on reexportation of colonial goods due to limited home demand, which made the country vulnerable to the vicissitudes of demand arising out of competition and warfare. An inability to meet the protection costs of commercial empire was a final, besetting weakness with deep political causes and implications.[15]

As scholars have given a more accurate description of the workings of French absolutism, the mixture of archaism and modernity that characterized the economic domain has come to seem less paradoxical; these developments help to shed light on many of the central concerns of the eighteenth century's science of commerce. The notion of an absolute monarch projecting a unified sovereign will onto a coherent territory through a set of rationally articulated institutions was always myth; indeed, this myth served an ideological function in breaking down the resistance that the elites and corps of French society posed to absolutist rule, and the conflict between theory and practice is a theme that runs throughout this book. Even where historians have conceded this reality, it has often served as only a mild corrective to the view of absolutism as an inherently modernizing and centralizing force. Already in the eighteenth century, Adam Smith had articulated one aspect of what would become a consensus position among liberal and subsequently Marxist historians: the absolutist state represented a modernizing alliance of convenience between crown and mercantile bourgeoisie against their common enemy: noble elites. Later, Tocqueville extended this interpretation, pretending to show how the absolutist state systematically pulverized the institutions of a hierarchical and corporate society, thus paving the way for the ill-fated democratic egalitarianism of the French Revolution. The Tocquevillian view of French absolutism has come under a sustained attack, and it now seems clear that the mismatch between means and ambitions constrained absolute monarchs to work through local elites and corps in order to ensure a steady stream of income and the exercise of power. The absolutist state was modern after its own fashion, rationalizing its administrative forms and the society under its tutelage, but this process was self-limiting given the way selling offices, raising loans, and organizing communities into readily taxable units strengthened oppositional elites and countervailing nodes of local power inherited from France's feudal past.[16]

As a matter of logic, Smith's simple view of a crown–bourgeoisie alliance against the nobility cannot survive revisions to the Tocquevillian interpretation, but one question remains: given these elements of archaism, what was the relationship of early modern state formation to the growth of modern, commercial capitalism? Armed with a more realistic picture of the absolutist state, historians and historical sociologists such as Gail Bossenga, Julia Adams, and Perry Anderson have begun to provide answers. Taken together, their work affirms a set of premises crucial to this book: first, political sociology helped to determine the niche that different early modern European states occupied in the international division of labor; second, in abandoning crude liberal and Marxist sociologies, they open the way for a more accurate assessment of the role of traditional elites and forms of government in the era of primitive globalization; third, while positing a complicated dialectic between the archaic and the modern in the process of early modern state formation, they remain alive to the tensions—and sometimes explosive contradictions— between modes of accumulation and forms of government during this period. Eighteenth-century economic writers explored these issues in their own language, but the science of commerce was fundamentally sociological in its approach to the possibility of commercial monarchy, and nobody who discussed international competitiveness could ignore the French state.[17]

A developing literature on the spatial dimension of capitalist accumulation and state formation helps to put some of these questions into focus. Liberal and Marxist modernization theory often equates the spread of capitalist relations of production with the consolidation of ever-larger national units and, within these units, a process of homogenization that simplifies class relations and breaks down spatial barriers. Thanks to the work of philosopher Henri Lefebvre, Regulation School economist Alain Lipietz, and geographer David Harvey, we now understand much better how the capitalist "production of space" must diverge from this simplified norm.[18] Historians who have given thought to the organization of the capitalist world economy have thus been drawn to spatial metaphors for depicting the flow of goods and the political divisions that helped to determine—and enforce—patterns of unequal exchange. Although much debated, the distinction between core and periphery used by Immanuel Wallerstein remains paradigmatic. In this vein, Giovanni Arrighi explains the rise and decline of early modern commercial empires as cycles of "territorialization" and "de-territorialization," which corresponded, respectively, to "intensive" and "extensive" regimes of accumulation. The Genoese and Dutch preferred extensive trade regimes based upon trading companies, merchant and financier networks that shied away from territorial acquisition, whereas in this account the English and French model concentrated, especially toward the middle of the eighteenth century, on intensive regimes based upon the organization of their colonies into more recognizably territorial, nation-state-like units. These choices were determined by the evolution of protection costs, the possibility of collecting imperial tribute (as in British Bengal), and the need for a more thorough integration of production and exchange within imperial spaces. For example, the slave economies of the Americas could not be maintained on the cheap like mere imperial trading posts: they required heavy internal policing, maritime protection, and a framework of imperial trade that could make these considerable outlays a profitable proposition for the nations that made them.[19]

A set of related economic and political questions led eighteenth-century writers to conceive of primitive globalization in explicitly spatial terms. By overflowing the limits of territorial, "feudal" polities, oceanic exchanges helped to usher in an era where commerce, not conquest, was the principal occupation of states. After mid-century, the realities of empire came more clearly into focus, and some began to rethink the center–periphery divisions that seemed so natural to organizing oceanic space. Did the division of France's own commercial empire into zones of unequal exchange merely reinscribe, and in some senses intensify, the archaism that the rise of commerce was thought to overcome? The Physiocrats envisioned a solution whereby the distinction between center and periphery would be abolished, thereby creating a more recognizably modern nation based upon an even distribution of economic and political rights; others insisted that the context of international rivalry made such a solution impossible and that more supple and heterogeneous—perhaps outwardly anachronistic—models of sovereignty and governance were necessary. During the Revolution, arguments over the form that the French empire should take reproduced and intensified these conflicts, exposing for us how central, in the monarchy's waning days, the problems of economic organization were to competing notions of sovereignty.

These were national and international contexts that shaped a specifically French science of commerce. Primitive globalization touched all other European nations to a certain extent, and a different type of account of eighteenth-century economic thought would examine responses to this phenomenon elsewhere. Cosmopolitanism was an essential characteristic of the Enlightenment, and where intellectual connections were particularly dense, as between eighteenth-century France and Scotland, comparison would lend contrast and strength of composition to the portrait that follows. Here such comparisons are largely set aside in order to pursue the intellectual and political implication of *les progrès du commerce* into the early phases of the French Revolution.

This book is an extended case for the proposition that the study of the economic thought of the Enlightenment, if approached in the correct way, should retain priority for those who are interested in the relationship between ideas and social change during the long eighteenth century. This brings us around to a discussion of the relationship between eighteenth-century economic thought and the political thought of Old-Regime and Revolutionary France. The science of commerce points the way out of the impasse created by the false dichotomy between "social" and "political" interpretations of the Revolution and its origins. Eighteenth-century economic writers were all concerned with France's political structures and the strain imposed upon them by the Commercial Revolution. All the orders in French society were affected—albeit differently—by these transformations, and the common cry for reform that was heard in 1788–1789 is a reflection of this fact. That there is no social referent in these calls for reform that corresponds to the categories of nineteenth-century political economy is hardly surprising. The Achilles' heel of the "social"—that is, Marxist—interpretation of the French Revolution had always been a narrative of events that relied excessively on sociological categories more appropriate to the nineteenth century and its Industrial Revolution than to the Commercial Revolution of the seventeenth and eighteenth centuries. Once it could be established that there was no industrial bourgeoisie whose preponderance in the sphere of civil society necessitated a readjustment in the apparatus of the state, it was a fairly easy matter to point out that, without the requisite social actors, the historical drama could not have been staged as scripted. Although the "social interpretation" was never so pat as this criticism suggested, many revisionists pressed the advantage they gained by pointing out this grave flaw in order to claim that the Revolution was a purely political affair, without material origins of any kind. The stage was set for understanding the Revolution as an event with political causes and outcomes; underlying social changes were relegated to the background as the study of political culture increasingly defined the research agenda for the French Revolution.[20]

That there is no social referent in these calls for reform that corresponds to the categories of nineteenth-century political economy is hardly surprising. That there is no social referent at all is a proposition that deprives politics, as a category of analysis, of any sense. The abstract, voluntarist political discourse that spread toward the end of the Old Regime has been represented as the political pathology of absolutist France; this searching on the level of discourse, which had concrete effects of its own, expressed a profound social reorganization that was under way all over Europe. Economic reformers were trying to straighten out some of the kinks in this process that were peculiar to France, and their fixation on the constitution as the key to France's economic success or failure only demonstrates how intractable many of these problems appeared to them at the time. When the Revolution broke out, the ongoing obsession with forms of sovereignty that writers from Tocqueville and François Furet to Keith Baker observe was not simply a fact of Old Regime politics transposed into a Revolutionary context but of political economy. It was what we would now call primitive globalization, and not industrialization, that posed the greatest challenges for the organization of France's political economy. It is to this process that we need to return if we want to give an accurate account of the relationship between the two revolutions that have always seemed to hold the key to our own modern economic and political life.

CHAPTER 1

Foreign Trade and National Models

IN CLASSIC ACCOUNTS of the development of French economic thought, the first half of the eighteenth century is usually understood as a transitional phase from seventeenth-century, Colbertist mercantilism to the laissez-faire doctrine of the Physiocrats. This era is often, therefore, called the "pre-Physiocratic" or "neo-Mercantilist" period, the better to emphasize this doctrinal shift. If we accept this periodization and these labels, we immediately lose sight of major developments in eighteenth-century economic thought. The contribution of Montesquieu's *De l'esprit des lois* (1748) earned him the sobriquet the "father of the science of commerce," but Montesquieu had little or nothing to say about freedom of trade or guild restrictions, the mainstays of laissez-faire reactions against mercantilist policies; moreover, as we shall see, Montesquieu's influence was strong with economic writers who fell on both sides of this divide. How could he have been so influential if his major contribution did not relate in any way to a dichotomy that was so politically and intellectually central to eighteenth-century economic thought? The answer is obviously that the laissez-faire/mercantilist distinction did not structure Enlightenment economic thought as much as we have come to believe, and it is only by setting this distinction aside that we can fully understand the period in question. Of equal and lasting significance for observers of the French economy were the peculiarities of France's form of government, social structure, and culture; these were issues that arose in an international economic context in which states oriented toward territorial conquest appeared to be losing ground to those devoted to the ostensibly peaceful occupation of trade.[1]

The performance of the French economy—and in particular of its foreign trade, which concerns us most—presents a tantalizing set of contradictions that conditioned much of the thought of administrators and *philosophes* about France's place in the world economy. The period from 1716 to mid-century was in many respects prosperous and dynamic. France was at peace with England until 1740 and had the opportunity to recover from some of the self-inflicted economic wounds of Louis XIV's reign. From 1716 to 1754, France saw a seventeen-fold increase in the total value of goods exported to the Antilles. Overall, the rate of growth in overseas commerce was between 2.4 and 3 times that of Britain during the 1730s and 1740s—a 2.8 percent average annual increase, which is blistering by early modern standards. This impressive growth came at a time when English export growth was mediocre at best. The story is similar if we broaden the time span. From 1700 to 1790, production indices went from 100 to 190 for France, while growing only from 100 to 145 for Great Britain; French exports grew at a considerably faster rate than England's from 1716 to 1787: 2.16 percent per annum versus 1.29 percent. This was not, according to the economic historian Paul Butel, an era of complete British domination but one of "shared preponderance."[2]

Despite these impressive statistics, contemporary observers focused obsessively on the defects of foreign trade, which they linked, not unjustly, to France's fortunes in commercial warfare. The War of Spanish Succession (1701–1712) and the War of Austrian Succession (1740–1748) both represented French humiliations at the hands of the British. These events, and particularly the Treaty of Utrecht (1713), crystallized a pattern in which France was being bested by England in the race for dominance on the scene of colonial commerce. These reversals, moreover, seemed merely the extension of France's seventeenth-century struggles with another small but disconcertingly nimble foe, the Dutch republic.

It was these events, taken together with chronic financial difficulties and a moribund rural sector, that French observers emphasized when they discussed issues of prosperity and international competition.

A number of different factors rendered elite opinion much more sensitive to the faults, as opposed to the sources of real dynamism, in the French economy. By any measure, and as the memoirs solicited from French merchants by the Council of Commerce in 1701 attest, the final years of Louis XIV's reign were, indeed, difficult; since opinion tends to lag behind even momentous demographic, economic, or social changes, it is entirely understandable that this prolonged malaise, in the wake of the Nine Years' War (1688–1697) continued to color French opinion for decades.[3] The speculative bubble that culminated in the disastrous Law episode (1719–1720) did not improve perceptions, although one might argue that, despite the chaos it caused, the mass repudiation of state debt that Law's scheme enabled was an overall benefit for the French economy. In any case, the concepts and accounting categories that lend clarity to the statistics cited above were as yet quite vague. Where clear statistics were conscientiously kept, as in the foreign trade figures compiled by the Office of the Balance of Trade from 1716 onward, they were not widely publicized. Had the average educated Frenchman had the opportunity to look at these figures—and he did not—they may have altered his overall view of France's economic situation. Beyond trade, crucial information on demographics was lacking and, where existent, unduly pessimistic. The state of finances was often a mystery to the crown itself—a state of ignorance that must have generated pessimism independently of the facts in question, and justly so. One telling fact that may partly explain this hiatus between perception and reality is that the overwhelming majority of France's economic writers (61 percent) lived and worked in Paris, far from the centers of France's booming maritime economy, such as Bordeaux, Marseilles, and Nantes. A full one-half of these writers were born in Paris, so that the vitality of overseas trade, which led the commercial revolution in France, may have been beyond their horizon. To this physical distance we must add a degree of cultural alienation between merchants and the Republic of Letters: only five merchants are to be found among over two hundred contributors to Diderot and D'Alembert's *Encyclopédie,* and only 2–3 percent of provincial literary and scientific academy members were drawn from men of affairs. A second set of factors is more psychological than epistemological or sociological but should not be dismissed. As many of these writers emphasized, France was a much larger country than its competitors, blessed with fertile soil, industrious people, and a number of beautiful ports. There seemed no inherent reason a first-rank power should be relegated to second-class economic status. One need only recall the anguished public discourse in the United States in the 1980s, when Japan (another small island nation) seemed poised to dominate the United States economically, to understand this widespread tone of self-recrimination.[4]

Despite these factors, which bulked large, the tone and content of these outlooks on France's economic performance should not be written off as the effects of ignorance, fear, or false consciousness. Despite signs of prosperity, these internal criticisms expressed a basic truth about France's political economy. Writing in *L'Ancien régime et la Révolution* (1856), Tocqueville, who believed that the eighteenth century was a period of unrivaled prosperity, expressed with characteristic clarity the paradox of discontent amidst economic growth: "an opinion that was so commonly held, which was held by such well informed persons, proves at least that no visible progress was being made." An absolute government that could not bring back "public prosperity" because of the "vices of its constitution" and that "hardly did anything but move inside the circle of old routines without creating anything new" was responsible for this situation. Routine, vice, and the looming possibility that France possessed a fundamentally defective constitution formed the analytical core of most of the writings on France's foreign trade.[5]

In the late eighteenth century, France was very much in the running with England but suddenly hit the wall; looking carefully, we can see that many eighteenth-century economists were perceptive about the structural defects that led to this sudden, ultimately catastrophic faltering. Administrators and men of letters were concerned with the articulation of the various sectors of France's economy—agriculture, manufacturing, trade, and finances. While Holland and England profited by the rational and "virtuous" integration of their economies, the larger, potentially more powerful France always teetered on the edge of a downward spiral, fettered by the incoherent relationship between the parts of its economy.

At every juncture, the deficiencies of the French economy seemed to point to the French state, or "constitution"—a capacious term that meant social structure, form of government, and even *moeurs* (customs, manners, or mores). This is why French economic writers passed far beyond simple considerations of the "balance of trade," the supposed concern of "mercantilist" economics, and concentrated instead on the historical, comparative analysis of constitutions.[6]

This eighteenth-century approach is vindicated by the present state of research in economic history. This is by no means an uncontroversial assertion, but economic historians who emphasize the superior readiness for industrialization of England over France in the late eighteenth and early nineteenth centuries cite the problem of integration that was also of interest to the writers examined here. Whether in the relationship of the urban to the rural sectors, of foreign commerce to home manufactures, or the all-important issue of the relation of credit markets to entrepreneurial activity, there is an overall consensus that monocausal factors must be eschewed in explaining England's "takeoff"; instead, the coherent relations of sectors are seen as the crucial issue by those who accept the conclusion that France's own industrialization was retarded by comparison. Even if attention is turned to France's agricultural economy— and France remained a largely agricultural nation well into the nineteenth century—integration remains a key factor. As Philip Hoffmann argues, access to domestic and foreign markets is the single most important factor in explaining increases in agricultural productivity through specialization and capital investment.[7]

I first examine the French response to the close of the War of Spanish Succession and the Treaty of Utrecht in order to give a sense of the specifically historical element in French economic writing. The history of early modern European overseas trade has a dual significance: it was first of all the subject matter of much eighteenth-century economic writing and also the context in which the development of the economic thought of the period must be understood. The next two sections discuss the problem of economic linkage—in other words, the manner in which French observers conceived of the problem of the interrelation of the several parts of the economy, including the role of France's constitution in determining its economic performance. By way of conclusion, I will explore the problem of *moeurs*, which was such a dominant category of eighteenth-century economic thought, although it may strike us now as patently unscientific. These three elements—economic linkage, the constitution, and *moeurs*—provide us with the concepts and contexts of French economic thought that remained central until the Revolution.

The History of Commerce from Carthage to Batavia

The mixed outcome of the War of Spanish Succession (1701–1713) provides a window into the shifting geopolitics of early eighteenth-century Europe and France's struggle to keep up with them. Upon the death of the Hapsburg emperor Charles II, the Spanish crown was to pass into the hands of Louis XIV's younger grandson Philip, duke of Anjou. Fearing the unification of the French and Spanish thrones under the Bourbons, the English and Austrians went to war against the Spanish and French. Louis XIV largely achieved his principal war aims, and the Treaty of Utrecht (1713) confirmed his grandson as King Philip V of Spain— subject to the proviso that the Spanish and French crowns would never rest on the same head. Although Spain no longer belonged to the Hapsburg Empire, it did retain control of all of its American possessions. In the sphere of classic dynastic politics, the war was a victory for France, but other considerations pointed to an uncertain future.

In the late seventeenth century, France was a principal beneficiary of the lucrative trade that Europeans plied in the Spanish New World. Officially at least, all trade flows between Europe and New Spain passed through Seville or Cadiz in annual convoys, and foreign goods were commissioned through Spanish merchants operating in these cities. Profiting from the status of most favored trading nation conferred by the 1659 Treaty of the Pyrenees, in conjunction with its vibrant luxury industry, France held the largest share of the trade passing through Cadiz: 39 percent (17 million livres tournois [henceforth l.t.]) compared with 17 percent (7.3 million l.t.) for Genoa, 14 percent (6.2 million l.t.) for England, and 12 percent (5.1 million l.t.) for the United Provinces. France furnished fully 75 percent of the fabric sent to the New World, and these exports stimulated industry in Brittany, Normandy, and Lyon. France also sent smaller but profitable quantities of paper, books, beaver hats, and lace, industries that kept hands busy in diverse corners of the kingdom. When Spain sent back galleons filled with precious metals, a good deal of it found its way back to France; one estimate puts yearly averages in 1670 at 12 million l.t. worth of gold and silver, and another, from France's diplomatic corps in 1686, puts these returns at 13–14 million. These remittances were made after French merchants had reaped some of their profits in kind as colonial produce or sent silver or gold to their factors in Amsterdam or Genoa.[8]

The commercial provisions of the Treaty of Utrecht were almost exclusively in England's favor, a subject that inspired plenty of anguish among French observers. The Spanish had granted France the *assiento,* or "assignment," of the monopoly privilege to supply the Spanish colonies with African slaves in 1701, but this privilege passed into British hands. In addition to this measure, the British secured the notorious "vessel of permission," which gave them the right to send one ship to trade directly at each of the annual or semiannual trade fairs in New Spain. This ship, which never seemed to run empty, served as the jumping-off point for a century of lucrative contraband trade; the *assiento* did much the same, since it necessarily provided access to the Spanish main for English merchants. The depressing situation this treaty (or rather treaties, signed up until 1716) created for France was summed up in the title of a ministerial memoir of that year, *Geometrical Demonstration of the Imminent Decline of France's Commerce by the Extension of England's Commerce,* which laid out the extent of the disaster in good Cartesian fashion, by presenting a series of theorems and corollaries. The sense of chagrin conveyed in these post-Utrecht documents is palpable and presents a marked contrast to those memoirs written while the war still appeared winnable. At that time, the prospect of the union of the Spanish and French nations under the Bourbon crown inspired optimistic diplomatic maneuvering against British commerce in the Americas. The variety of proposals written during the war all had one aim: to cut England out of the loop of trade in Spanish America by any manner of strategic political alliance—including with Protestant Holland. This diplomatic conniving came to nothing, and as the author of the *Démonstration géométrique* observed, England's newfound access to Spanish America would lead to the "decline of all manufactures in general, of [France's] commerce in the Levant, and the decline in particular of our cloth manufacture." "To what extremity," he continued, "will the kingdom not find itself reduced by the privation of the three greatest parts of its commerce?" Subsequent events partly vindicated this view: the port of Saint-Malo, hitherto the center of French exports to Cadiz and hence to the New World, settled into long-term decline after 1714. That these losses would be recouped in spectacular fashion in subsequent decades by port towns such as Nantes and Bordeaux, whose fortunes grew in tandem with the plantation complexes on France's sugar islands, was unknown to these pessimistic diplomats.[9]

It was in this context of uncertainty and even despair over the prospects for France's overseas commercial enterprises that the *Histoire du Commerce & de la Navigation des Anciens,* by Pierre-Daniel Huet, was published. Huet, like many of the figures we will encounter in this book, combined the role of a functionary (or dependent) of the absolutist state with a presence in the Republic of Letters. In this case, he was the assistant preceptor to the Grand Dauphin under Jacques-Bénigne Bossuet and an early Enlightenment *littérateur* who originally wrote this work at the request of Jean-Baptiste Colbert. Huet was reportedly unsatisfied with this work, and it remained "buried under the dust in his office" until his friends convinced him of the utility of publishing it in 1716. The book was well received, going through multiple editions in the year subsequent to its first publication, and was translated into several languages. It was reprinted at critical junctures over the eighteenth century, including the inauspicious year of 1763, the date of the Treaty of Paris, by which Canada was ceded to the British. Almost simultaneously, in 1717, a revised edition of another of Huet's works, again commissioned by Colbert but not immediately published, hit the shelves. Its full title bears quotation here: *Memoirs on the Dutch Trade, in all of the nations of the world; wherein is demonstrated their manner of conducting it, its origin, their great progress, their possessions and Government in the Indies. How they made themselves masters of all of Europe's Commerce; What are the Goods suited to Maritime Traffic. From where they derive them & the gains that they realize from them.* This work was even more successful than Huet's *Histoire du Commerce* and was periodically republished throughout the eighteenth century. Although it was criticized on occasion for being out of date, the book was successful because it presented a model for how trading empires were built and maintained in the teeth of international competition.[10]

In contrast to the obvious contemporary relevance of his work about Holland, the success of Huet's work on the ancients, from the Deluge to the Roman Empire, demands some explanation. Huet's work barely condescends to speak directly about contemporary issues and is a work of "erudition" rather than "philosophy" in the sense that it is neither synthetic nor polemical but is instead factual and even antiquarian in its approach. In keeping with his scrupulous, erudite method, Huet made only one direct reference to contemporary times, when he compared the Phoenicians to the Dutch, "habitants of an extremely small, sterile and swampy country, encroaching partly on the sea, and defended by continual vigilance and excessive expenses who, nevertheless, by their virtue and industry, have extended their domain to the ends of the earth and today pretend to vie with Kings."[11] This comment was probably intended as a swipe at Louis XIV and his repeated failures to subdue the Dutch and also helps us link Huet's erudite history of ancient commerce to his modern studies. Moreover, it helps to explain why Huet let his manuscripts gather dust until Louis XIV was safely interred.

We can further grasp the interest of Huet's work by noting its future as a source for later authors writing "philosophical" histories of commerce, works that wore their present-minded political concerns on their sleeves. These histories were usually written as a sort of allegory or roman à clef, with England playing the role of Carthage against France's Rome. Comparisons between the Spartans and the Athenians, or between the republican and imperial phases of Rome, served as fundamental points of reference in discussions about the proper role of wealth and luxury in different sorts of polities. In other writings, veiled references to contemporary Europe through the Egyptians, and even the Incans, were not uncommon. This persistent reference to antiquity reflected not only the ongoing quarrel between the ancients and the moderns but the privileged place that antiquity held among eighteenth-century thinkers, by dint of their education. Even though most of these writers were well aware of the differences in technology and social structure that separated the ancient from the modern world, antiquity was in some sense nearer to them than any other epoch, and they often discussed it without any evident sense of rupture. Antiquity also furnished a storehouse of examples for a comparative analysis of regime types and their relation to commerce, which led directly to comparisons with modern commercial societies such as Holland.[12]

Huet, for instance, recounted the history of France's "neighbors and enemies," including the Dutch, "a handful of refugee merchants in a tiny country that could not come even near feeding itself," but whose fabulous wealth nevertheless made them "the oracles of commerce." Huet concluded that their republican form of government was the cause of their prosperity: "Everything is established here in such a manner that neither their lives, their honor, nor their property, depends on any arbitrary power." Behind this analysis lurked an implicit criticism of the "laws . . . maxims and policies" of absolutist France. Like many others, Huet based this analysis on Batavian myth, which considered Dutch prosperity the fruit of their love of liberty—a divine gift to those who showed the audacity to throw off the yoke of the Hapsburg Spanish. Seventy years later, Huet's text was considered sufficiently relevant and controversial that it was recopied for use by the French delegation in Holland, though cleansed of these mildly republican overtones. As Frederic Janiçon explained in 1729, the Dutch were forced to take to the sea—and in particular the Indies—because the tyrannical Spanish crown prevented them from conducting their modest trade at Lisbon. Long-distance trade, reflected an anonymous (and clearly self-interested) advocate of France's own India Company in 1746, was Holland's only means of paying for warfare at the time.[13]

Behind the Batavian myth—which was often the simple corollary of the Black Legend of Spanish Tyranny—was an analysis of the ways in which liberty redounded to the benefit of trade. For Huet, the key lay in the attitude of the state toward its manufacturers and merchants, who were "protected without being constrained." A number of years later, in 1734, the influential Jean-François Melon echoed the same idea in its canonical form: "the greatest and best known of maxims is that commerce asks for only *liberty and protection*." Here the reciprocity between merchants and the state is made clear: a strong state (and in particular its maritime extension) secured a sphere of operation for overseas merchants and trading companies. If commerce were protected and allowed to operate free of arbitrary exaction and other state-imposed constraints, the virtuous churning of this circle would keep riches flowing into the state's coffers.[14]

"Liberty and protection" were increasingly important in a world where capital and labor could flee despotic state action: "it should be taken as an absolutely assured fact that every time COMMERCE is hampered and constrained in a state, it will always withdraw its trade into those countries where it knows it will be the safest and where it will be the most favorably treated." The modern rise of commerce, therefore, contributed to a secular decline in despotism. In Holland, liberty and protection also extended to labor: "the constant protection that is accorded fugitives there . . . [has] contributed much to the increase of commerce and wealth." Huet was hardly unique in observing that the revocation of the Edict of Nantes in 1685, and the subsequent emigration of skilled workers to the Netherlands, allowed the Dutch to compete in cloth production—a sector hitherto dominated by France and the Southern Netherlands. Well after the fact, this self-defeating act of fanaticism was lamented as "the most unfortunate incident of Louis XIV's reign [by which] many of our manufactories were naturalized into foreign countries."[15]

Where Dutch policies created an alloy of power and liberty that was readily convertible into gold, France's government was criticized as a brittle compound of pusillanimity and despotism. The Dutch case, bolstered by the Batavian myth of the Dutch Revolt, indicated that thriving trading empires were largely republican affairs and therefore alien to France. As Batavia was eclipsed by Britannia in the early eighteenth century, republican prosperity shifted to a mixed monarchy. Criticism of France's monarchical institutions was no less persistent for this change, but it became easier to contemplate, by way of a comparative analysis, how to naturalize the virtues of the English constitution in the French context. It also raised the possibility that France need not become republican in order to succeed commercially.

Economic Integration and the State

In 1747, toward the end of the Austrian War of Succession, Etienne de Silhouette, secretary to the duc d'Orléans and future controller general of finance, traveled to England to conduct diplomacy on behalf of the crown. In his moments of leisure, and doubtlessly to secure future advancement, he wrote a lengthy memoir on the finances and international commerce of England in comparison with other major European states: "Observations sur les finances, le commerce, et la navigation d'Angleterre." It circulated widely at the time of its composition and was ultimately reprinted in the *Journal de Commerce* in 1760. In this remarkable memoir, Silhouette linked the success of England's overseas trading empire to the form of its government, its laws, and its institutions, explaining the manner in which republican successes could be replicated in the French monarchy. Along the way, he, like Huet much earlier, developed a theory of how state power served (or failed) to integrate various sectors of the economy. In this memoir, perhaps more than in any single manuscript written prior to the publication of *Esprit des lois,* we see a sustained attempt to relate "the spirit and the principle" of the nation's laws to its commercial prosperity.[16]

By the eighteenth century, writers were used to lauding Oliver Cromwell and his "Famous Act of Parliament," the Navigation Acts of 1651. The Navigation Acts included but were not limited to the following provisions: (a) foreign vessels were prohibited from trade with British colonies, with certain exceptions; (b) foreign vessels were not allowed to bring manufactures or raw goods originating from countries other than their own (this was directed against the Dutch entrepôt; and (c) all ships that flew the British flag had to be of British construction. Silhouette recognized that, however admirable, these acts were successful only because the British economy had the strength and breadth to carry them off. One of their aims, for instance, was to shut foreign merchants out of the British colonies and in so doing to "create a sort of monopoly in order to appropriate the . . . whole fruit [of the colonies] without wanting to let others share in it."[17]

While Silhouette approved of this goal as a general principle, he also observed that Portugal and Spain, "who possess the richest establishments in America and who collect the least fruit," could never do the same. Neither of these countries had a large enough manufacturing base to provide "the manufactured goods that are necessary to their American possessions." Lacking manufactures on the order of France or England, these countries could never hope to gain the profits accruing to trade by

fiat alone. Harsh, incessantly reiterated laws—even capital punishments—
"are and will always be illusory unless the Spanish and Portuguese find
the secret of furnishing out of their own capital and do without foreign
goods." The language is perhaps Machiavellian, but the logic merely
spells out the relationship between manufacture and trade: "[The English]
get from their colonies not only enough [merchandise] for their own consumption, but also enough to sell abroad; this is a product that is in some
way preferable to gold and silver mines: for a state enriches itself doubly
when it is at the expense of nations who could use their wealth in de-
stroying them."[18]

If manufacture was considered a desideratum of commerce, the addition of navigation to this charmed dyad was thought to generate still more
powerful advantages. The term "navigation" denoted much more than
seafaring technique: it could refer to cost-saving shipping technologies as
well as the naval forces that protected merchant fleets. The Dutch furnished the most forceful example of this relation; despite being a postage
stamp–size country that produced little of its own account, Holland
made itself rich trafficking in others' foreign goods. (Some modern-day
historians, it should be said, disagree with this perspective, arguing that
capital-intensive agriculture and a highly productive and flexible consumer goods sector were the keys to world trade hegemony for the
Dutch.)[19] In the following passage, which is worth quoting at length because of its clarity, Pierre-Daniel Huet enumerates all of the advantages
and reciprocal effects that accrue to an efficient transport sector:

> It must be admitted that their fishery, their manufactures and their
> great commerce, have given them all possible advantages to elevate
> their Navy above that of all other nations. But the secret that they
> have found to carry goods by land and sea more cheaply than the
> others, has contributed at least as much; this not only augments
> their commerce, but also, because they can by this means offer and
> furnish their merchandise at a lower cost than all of the other trad-
> ers, other nations gladly use Dutch ships to do their trading insofar
> as the freight costs them less; and because one always finds ships
> ready to depart in Holland to all sorts of countries. . . . Beyond this,
> it is because of the great fidelity and exactitude with which they

render an accounting of everything confided to them. This confidence multiplies their navigation still more considerably and it is also what obliges them to construct a great number of ships.[20]

The golden triangle of commerce, manufacture, and navigation helped the Dutch (and later the English) steadily creep up the supply chain of their competitors and hence appropriate the profits of manufacture, transport, and finance to themselves. Silhouette, having made virtually the same observations as Huet, extended this analysis to show specifically how the Dutch entrepôt function helped them to accumulate capital and merchandise and with them all sorts of other advantages: "Any foreign merchant overloaded with merchandise and pressed for money, finds, in sending his goods to Holland, a Dutch commission agent who falls over himself [to] receive his merchandise, and who advances him two-thirds of the goods' value at the rate of four percent interest per year, until he can find an acceptable sale." In addition to these profits, the Dutch gained on storage, shipping, and the obligatory 2 percent commission.[21]

When multiplied thousands of times over a number years, overseas commerce allowed "the state and the individual [to] enrich themselves from what they are able to glean from other nations." Taken as a whole, it is also a model of how the various sectors of a successful economy worked together to exploit dependent nations, such as Spain, Portugal, and Poland. But was this model appropriate for the French? Looking at England, which appeared to resemble France more closely than the unfortunate Poland, the author concluded otherwise: "the *spirit and the principles of the laws* that concern [their] navigation and commerce differ totally. It is not at all a default of aptitude or discernment on the part of one of these two powers: it is precisely the contrary; what would be advantageous for England, would be the ruin of Holland." This is because Holland is a tiny country that cannot produce its own goods to "trade out of its own capital" and therefore must be completely open to the goods of other countries. England, on the other hand, must subordinate the commerce of other nations' goods to that of its own (including its colonies). Here we are drawn back to the Navigation Acts, which were considered the touchstone of protectionist wisdom and, to a certain point, held up as a model for France.[22]

Reservations about the suitability of the Navigation Acts stemmed from the fact that France was generally judged to be missing one of the elements of the commerce-manufacture-navigation triad that made the Navigation Acts possible and so fabulously successful. On the manufacture side, France's specialization in articles of luxury rather than mass-market manufactured goods was occasionally seen as a liability. In later analyses, when it was not taken as proof of superior French taste, and therefore as an unmitigated good, economists came to see France's emphasis on luxury goods as a result of insufficient home demand, resulting from a skewed distribution of wealth or an autarchic peasant economy. Nevertheless, at the time this bias in production was rarely discussed in any depth.[23]

More significant because more persistent was the gap in navigation due to a relative paucity of French merchant ships and naval power. Long-distance trade was regarded as the most profitable but also the most capital intensive. Beyond this, of course, the American colonies provided a crucial means of import substitution for luxury goods hitherto procured, at the price of bullion, in the East Indies. Even where authors deplored the overly sophisticated consumption habits of the French, they had to concede that, failing a miraculous transformation in French manners, an extensive maritime commerce was necessary to bring luxury goods from the east in French bottoms, so that at least the profits of such excesses would accrue to French merchants. The Ministry of the Navy frequently weighed in on these issues because, until the French Revolution, the direction of the colonies fell to this part of the crown's administration. One observer within the Navy, writing in 1738, declared that "whoever is master of the sea is master of everything," but it seemed that France had fallen permanently behind. The fact was that France, of its own accord, simply did not have the shipping capacity, backed by naval protection, to provide for its own colonies and consequently invited contraband trade on the part of other nations. Such a gap could never be closed by decree, and Silhouette wondered on this account whether provisions similar to the Navigation Acts could be adopted in France. He concluded that "however much this provision could in the beginning be accompanied by some inconveniences, and at first prejudice [our] present commerce, it would necessarily oblige by its consequences

French traders to extend their navigation and their plans [*vûes*] for trade."[24] Such optimism, however, was belied by Silhouette's own analysis and that of virtually every other thinker who approached the problem of how to expand France's trading empire. The reason that the French did not simply build more ships and arm a navy to protect them was not difficult to deduce. Navies were expensive, and overseas trading companies required large amounts of circulating capital to carry on their trade; the charmed manufacture-commerce-navigation triangle was held together, or came unglued, at each of its vertices by the problem of finance. Given this widely recognized problem within the French monarchy, competing answers emerged to the question of what sort of progress could ensure successful trading enterprises.

Commerce, Conquest, and *Police*

While affirming the underlying relationship between constitutional structure and economic prosperity, other observers viewed the English constitution with suspicion, wondering on what terms the English model could be adopted. Whereas the United Provinces of the Netherlands were born during a heroic struggle with despotic Spain, Britain's maritime empire had emerged from the brutal chaos of civil war; political instability and religious intolerance—not a love of liberty—provided the first impetus to Britain's commercial empire. In tracing the origin of the North American colonies, one observer from France's Ministry of the Navy remarked in 1738 that they were "at first nothing but a refuge for fugitives and the banished; the troubles of the Civil Wars sent a great number of Calvinists, Quakers and other types who started to inhabit this lengthy Colony." If the Puritan colonies abroad were the result of royal intolerance and oppression, the parliamentary faction that represented them at home was representative of the disorder inherent in most mixed regimes: "[The Parliament] is led by a party which imperceptibly gains superiority [and] which will sooner or later overturn all that remains of the monarchy. They cry louder than ever the memory of their hero Cromwell and boast of inevitable revolutions." Although Cromwell was universally praised for instituting the Navigation Acts of 1651—and making them stick—his legacy was also deeply suspect. Parliamentary rule, which

Cromwell imposed by regicide and transformed into an irrevocable writ of British liberty, had an anarchic character unseemly to monarchic sensibilities: "The actions and convulsions of England's Government are so extraordinary that they are daily exposed to new incidents." Despite a permanent state of conflict between the Council of Commerce appointed by the king and that of the House of Commons, these bodies found "themselves always united about the Interest of Commerce; this is the only certain advantage that they draw from their mixed government." As much as he appeared to deplore the English system, the author agreed with Voltaire that parliamentary rule—however rowdy—had the virtue of representing commercial interests in a way that monarchy simply could not.[25]

Whether Anglophilic or Anglophobic, French observers shared the widespread belief in the intimate link between the English constitution, its social structure, the manners of its inhabitants, and its commercial prosperity. But most of these authors were economic reformers, not revolutionaries; they would not have willingly traded the stability of monarchy for commercial prosperity if this meant, in turn, assuming the defects they imputed to mixed governments and excessively egalitarian societies. The hazards of the English example, along with their attachment to the institutions and manners of Old Regime France, led these writers to think of ways in which the apparent preeminence of the constitution in commercial questions could be transcended. In this connection, the writings of the abbé Charles-Irénée Castel de Saint-Pierre and Jean-François Melon provide a faithful guide to how these problems were faced, if not precisely resolved, in the economic literature of early eighteenth-century France.

Although he is now relatively obscure, the abbé de Saint-Pierre was a common eighteenth-century type: the well-connected graphomaniac who moved in interlocking circles of the literary salon and upper-echelon government ministers. Saint-Pierre also wrote copiously on economic subjects, but his oeuvre ranged over history, theology, aphorisms, and social advice, as well as far-seeing and (some thought) utopian projects for pan-European political reform. Of all these projects, the most well known was his "Project for Perpetual Peace," a scheme that was frequently dismissed by contemporaries as utopian and which later influenced

Immanuel Kant's writing on the same subject. In praising Saint-Pierre as "the most zealous Frenchman of his time for the public good," Gabriel Bonnot, the abbé of Mably, summed up contemporary judgments of the man and his work. More recently, Saint-Pierre has been praised as a "precocious" economic and political writer during a period of relative quiet between the loss of confidence in Ludovician absolutism and the full flowering of the French Enlightenment in the 1740s and 1750s.[26]

Saint-Pierre's frequently cited *Project pour perfectionner le commerse de France* argued that overseas trade, and particularly that of the Compagnie des Indes, was the most beneficial for France. In this discussion, the negative example of Bourbon Spain loomed large. Like France, Spain had all the natural resources requisite of a wealthy nation, "but fortunately for their neighbors, they are lazy and their poorly constituted government does not encourage them to any commercial enterprise." In summing up these weaknesses, the abbé suggested that the French choose the example of the tolerant, thrifty, and industrious British. The implication of this recommendation was clear: France stood at a crossroads between two different social and political systems, absolutism and moderate government, and had to choose correctly for the sake of its happiness and prosperity.

The abbé, in anticipating the qualms readers might have about his plan, advanced an apparently fatal objection: "you want to change [our military] constitution to make all of us into good Dutch merchants." This complaint followed naturally from the received idea that "the republican constitution is even more favorable to commerce and maritime companies than the monarchical constitution." That the abbé felt obliged to parry this sort of objection shows how deeply ingrained these beliefs were. His responses, in turn, are paradigmatic of the way that economic reformers tried to gently elide the question of the constitution and commerce or even turn it to their advantage.[27]

According to Saint-Pierre, the same qualms were registered a century earlier in England, but it was discovered in short order that military prowess and commerce were complimentary; commercial nations did not become pacific but turned their warrior nobility to the ends of national enrichment. The abbé therefore concluded that the French "can, without disturbing [the] state's constitution, follow the example of the English nation, and succeed in equaling their commerce in less than thirty years." Saint-Pierre conceded that many monarchies had handled their colonies and overseas trading companies badly but denied that their poor management was attributable to the inalterable characteristics of monarchies. Many skeptics believed that monarchies were condemned to poverty since taxes were ceded only grudgingly to monarchs by noble elites who persisted in the conceit that the king could "live of his own" domains, as the expression went. For these reasons, any royally sponsored trading company was apt to be regarded as a scheme for the king to plunder his subjects in order to pay debts. That state-sponsored finance and capitalization schemes (for example, national banks) could not work in arbitrary governments, where the sovereign could raid the coffers at will, was taken simply as an article of faith after the fall of John Law's system in 1720.[28]

Around the same time, French writers expressed the hope that constitutionally based objections could be muted if commerce and finances received what Saint-Pierre termed a *bonne administration* (good administration). The possibility that good administration could trump constitutional differences occupied a central place in Saint-Pierre's argument. At the same time, while a constitutionally neutral good administration occupied such a central aspect of Saint-Pierre's reform project, it remained a hope advanced more by assertion than by argument. It was a case that was continually undercut by the spectacle of France's finances and overseas trading monopolies, whose faults were systematically linked back to the nature of the French monarchy by critics and supporters alike. Jean-François Melon—secretary to John Law and friend to both Saint-Pierre and Montesquieu—also evinced the ambiguities of constitutional economic thought within the context of a reform-minded monarchy.

Jean-François Melon's universally admired *Essai politique sur le commerce* (1734) was written in the same year as Montesquieu's *Considérations sur les causes de la grandeur des Romains et de leur décadence*. Definite proof of their collaboration is difficult to come by, but a common thread in both works was an analysis of the differential effects of the "spirit of conquest" versus the "spirit of conservation" in ancient and modern nations. In the *Réflexions sur la monarchie universelle* of the same year, Montesquieu meditated on the obsolescence of territorial empires dedicated to conquest in an age of commerce. These commonalities suggest at the very least a shared concern over the weakness of the absolutist system, and Montesquieu would certainly have ratified Saint-Pierre's own trenchant judgment: those who believe that in modern times monarchies should devote themselves to conquest instead of commerce are "frivolous minds . . . who have no knowledge of Europe's current situation."[29]

Melon also viewed "conquest" and "conservation" as "mutually exclusive" from the point of view of national manners and therefore for the development of commerce. In this analysis, Melon drew on the examples of Rome, Carthage, Egypt, Alexandrine Greece, and finally Spain. The Spaniards were admittedly "the conquerors of America," but unfortunately for them, the New World "is a thousand times more beneficial to the nations that trade there than those who possess it." Melon emphasized economic changes that transformed the ancient political calculus: the world had changed so much "since Europe has become commercial, that is to say since the discovery of the New World," that the disadvantages in this altered political landscape of the purely military constitution, at the time intimately associated with Europe's monarchies, were only magnified.

While Melon continued to emphasize the broadest context of laws, manners, and institutions when he opposed the spirit of conservation to the spirit of conquest, the terms he used relativized the differences between monarchies and republics. Later in the century, after the outbreak of the Revolution, Antoine Barnave would argue that monarchy was a more commercial and civilized form of government, in contrast to republics, which were necessarily related to bellicose and feudal forms of aristocratic rule. For Melon, the Roman republic and the despotic monarchies of Asia both pursued "military government" to the detriment of "commerce and police"—here *police* and *policé,* which have a common origin in the Greek word *polis* and are synonymous with *civilization* and *civilized,* whose Latin equivalent is *civitas.* Republican Rome pursued conquest instead of "policing itself" and obtaining its subsistence in an "equitable" manner through commerce. The long-term consequences—in the form of the barbarian conquests—were fatal for the later empire. The monarchical despotism of the Turks, had they cultivated the "spirit of commerce and of police, which is inseparable from it," might have overwhelmed even a united Europe.[30]

Melon's discussion of a generic *police* was intended to displace sticky debates over the constitution. Thus, he observed, "the republican spirit counts with pleasure the faults of monarchies; the monarchical spirit counts those of republics and the balance is just about the same." It was for this reason, Melon continued, that England and France managed their colonies "according to virtually the same principles." From this, Melon concluded that "solidity" and the "wisdom of their administration, not the difference between republican and monarchical governments," dictated the success of overseas trading companies, concluding that "administrative corruption and personal interests of the directors . . . pertain to all sorts of governments, because they pertain to human nature."[31]

At the same time, Alexander Pope quipped in his *Essay on Man* (1733–1734): "for forms of government let fools contest / Whate'er is best administered is best." Perhaps the English had more reason to be confident of this proposition than the French; in Melon's case, cracks appeared everywhere in the edifice, if not the foundation, of his argument. In analyzing the question of finances, Melon argued that since Holland had some debt repudiations in its history, "republican debts are no more assured than the others." At the same time, echoing Saint-Pierre, he conceded that only republics can establish "true" banks and that countries without them would remain relatively poor.[32] Similarly, Melon affirmed the importance of Holland's strategic monopolies on certain goods, while arguing that France could do equally well, given similar initial conditions (for example, available capital and exploitable markets). This boast breezily ignored the question of how the initial conditions of Dutch superiority arose. Melon himself admitted that he sought to study the "political interests of Europe, since it has become commercial, that is to say, since the discovery of the New World, *or rather the establishment of the Dutch Republic.*" Melon tacitly acknowledged that Europe's new order did have fundamentally republican origins. *Police,* like civilized monarchy, could not entirely replace the constitution as a category of analysis and comparison. Particularly when it came to the question of finances and their relationship to trade and naval superiority, Europe's republics and mixed monarchies continued to stand as a reproach to absolute monarchies with commercial aspirations.[33]

Finances and Trade

The centrality of finances in the Old Regime threatened at times to crowd out other considerations. On this count, the 1738 memoirist from the Ministry of the Navy complained that such one-sidedness had become a stereotyped criticism of absolute monarchy itself, which, in fact, it had. Later in the century, the Physiocrats would launch an all-out war against what they called the "fiscalism" suffusing French state and society. The Physiocratic criticism was twofold. On the one hand, it referred to a *rentier* mentality that turned the French away from productive pursuits in favor of state bonds, monopoly profits, and sinecures. On the other, it referred to the corresponding intellectual mystification that made it impossible to understand, let alone minister to, the true basis of national wealth in agriculture. Before the Physiocratic assault on fiscalism, virtually every observer attributed France's second-class status in commercial affairs to its failure to get its finances in order; the resulting criticisms of France's finances cut a wide swath through the institutions and social order of the Old Regime. Taken as a whole, their criticisms laid bare "a structure of related impasses"—impasses emphasized as well by Tocqueville—that prevented France's trading empire from expanding its compass to Britannic proportions. On the way, these discussions of finance contributed further to an analysis of the relationship between segments of the economy.[34]

In 1746, toward the end of the War of Austrian Succession, an appellant to the crown for an injection of capital into the Compagnie des Indes posed a familiar question: "why is it that the English and the Dutch, who pay proportionately much more to the state than the French, live at their ease, while the French people, who pay less, are crushed by misery?"[35] The answer to this question had to do with what the author termed the "harmony and concourse [*concours*] of all of the nation's parts, which mutually aid each other, augment their force, tighten the bonds, lend growth to the value of all the productions of the earth and create wealth where there was none."[36] Because of its centrality to this concourse, the author argued that foreign trade, and therefore the Compagnie des Indes, "must be regarded as the soul and the prime mover, not only of maritime commerce, but also of interior commerce, because it furnishes goods to merchants. . . . [T]hey find in it legitimate profits that enrich the state; money employed in commerce is always in circulation, when it is flowing [*vive*] it can never be dear." Such a formulation did not go beyond commonplace notions about the relation between internal and external commerce and the role of specie, but nevertheless constituted a powerful sort of argument: "Money used by the Compagnie des Indes is in perpetual circulation, into which it comes and goes with equal rapidity, never resting, a continual movement that works diligently for the public good; it stirs a multitude of hands and heads busy with commerce."[37]

The "supreme art of finance" enabled this miracle of perpetual motion, maintaining public credit and therefore keeping money, goods, and labor all in a mutually reinforcing circulation. But, observed the author, "nothing is more capable of disturbing this harmony than variations in the value of money . . . that are murderous for commerce." The author's choice of causes for these "murderous" operations is suggestive. "Nevertheless, since these two truthful tableaux are so different as to cause and effect, with France having the same land, the same number of habitants, the same means and the same capacities [as England], resolution of this problem must therefore be found in the difference between their [respective] administrations." Similarly, Charles Dutot, a financier and an opponent of latter-day supporters of John Law such as Jean-François Melon, claimed in 1738 that the French were particularly susceptible to manipulations in the value of money by strapped and unscrupulous monarchs, concluding that "one cannot deny that these diverse variations in money severely disrupt the commerce of a State. One can say to the contrary, with more cause, that without these obstacles our commerce would always be superior to that of our neighbors."[38]

Although Silhouette also had quite a bit to say about France's financial institutions, his take on the problem of finances had its basis in an analysis of England's tax system. Noticing that the more affluent English paid as much or more in taxes than the French, he concluded that it is "less in the taxes themselves, than the manner in which they are apportioned and collected, which impoverishes a nation." In marked contrast to France, taxes in England were "real and not personal," that is to say neither "personal nor arbitrary." The effect of this system, so contrary to that found in a society of orders, was that it left "the individual in complete and entire liberty to promote his industry and labor." Such a system, Silhouette believed, created a nation where people had the incentive to work and to put the fruits of their labor back into circulation, instead of hiding their money from the forces of arbitrary government: "he believes, to the contrary, that it is in his interest to expose his wealth, to increase the opinion of it, if he can, in order to augment his credit, and by this his means and resources." The relation of all of this to commerce is fairly clear: "commerce is the fuel of finance. It procures for the people the means of acquiring wealth . . . [so that they] can pay taxes and make loans to the state." As Silhouette emphasized, the disparity in the maritime forces of France and England, and hence "the riches its commerce produces," were directly explicable in terms of the "resources that [England] finds in her finances and credit."[39]

The preceding should be sufficient to suggest the scope of the problem of finances. They were representative in the sense that they registered all of the defects of the state; in this connection, no greater stigma could be attached to them than the charge of arbitrariness. By the same token, finances were more than a mirror: as the "aliment" and "soul" of commerce, linking all of its respective branches and functions, they acted as a lens that could either magnify or diminish the power of the state to extend to commerce the "liberty and protection" it required.

Imperial Integration: Colonial Products and Territories

This economic logic was true a fortiori in the age of colonial commerce, where "the great enterprises of traders [were] always necessarily mixed with public business." Taken together, the examples of Holland and England provided the raw materials from which were drawn more abstract models of how economies gained coherence and forcefulness in the articulation of their respective parts, all under the aegis of well-ordered finances. However, as Silhouette's memoir reminds us, these speculations grew out of a specific context—the expansion of Europe into the New World and the enormous rewards being reaped by the winners of this contest: "America being in general the source of almost all of the wealth that comes to Europe; and in particular the greater part of England's wealth, we see the necessity and importance of . . . describing the nature of the commerce that is conducted in the new world." In order to understand how France should position itself in this race, Silhouette and others had to raise specifically historical questions about how the Europeans' colonial portfolios were acquired and what should be the optimal relations (be they antagonistic or harmonious) between these colonies.[40]

By the eighteenth century, observers were well aware—thanks to the power of the Spanish example—that not just any empire would do: the respective elements of a nation's colonial holdings had to relate rationally to one another and to the metropole to which they served as satellites. This issue had two dimensions. First, it meant a complementary mix of colonial products that entered into traditional (or prospective) patterns of production and consumption. In more concrete and historical terms, it was impossible to think of the flow of sugar, coffee, cochineal, timber, beef, or even slaves apart from the competition for the production and sale of these commodities between the European powers. Here economics and geopolitics were intimately linked; antiseptic business concepts like "first mover advantage" and "market share" translate back, in the early modern context, into the history of colonial conquest and warfare and were necessarily discussed in these terms.[41]

England's colonial commerce presented what most observers took to be the most successful of trading empires. This superiority did not signify, however, that France should simply ape England's strategies. This followed from the general maxim that "the laws and usages of other nations should not be followed indiscriminately. . . . [T]here are always a great number that should be rejected and that it would be pernicious to imitate." In particular, Silhouette had in mind the ability of American farmers to send some of their produce directly to Europe, in conjunction with the permission they were granted to manufacture goods for their household use, which became a cover for illicit manufactures. In this connection, Silhouette presciently remarked that "the evil can not but grow in consequence, and could someday occasion choler and misunderstanding between England and the Colonies."[42]

Beyond issues of England's policy toward its colonies, Silhouette, among others, realized that the "previous expansion" of the Spanish and English in the Americas had created a specific geopolitical situation into which France had to fit. Silhouette warily eyed the growth of England's North American colonies, worrying about universal monarchy in its modern incarnation: the universal monarchy of commerce. "Nobody could contain them anymore," Silhouette observed, "if they could succeed in appropriating to themselves the whole of America's commerce . . . and it is from the capital of America that they would draw the means to dictate the law to Europe." Discussing France's and England's island colonies, Silhouette correctly observed that France and England were on par with each other, if, in fact, France did not hold the advantage in sugar production. Nevertheless, France had to begin establishing between its island and continental establishments the same powerful linkages, the circulation of goods between colonies—and from colony to metropole—as England had created. France should use Canadian rather than Baltic timber to improve its navy; instead of buying foodstuffs for its sugar colonies from Ireland and the thirteen colonies, it should get them from Canada and Louisiana. Fibers hitherto procured from the East, such as cotton and silk, could be raised in North America in order to provide raw materials for France's textile industry. These goods, in turn, could be sold to Spanish America. The abbé Saint-Pierre expressed the matter in a different but still typical fashion. The idea was to create strategic autarky through colonial expansion and the scientific enterprise of acclimatization: "We have diverse colonies under warm and cold climates and all sorts of regions: thus, there are no sorts of trees, plants and animals that we cannot raise, either in France, or in our colonies. It is only a question of beginning to sow plants and populate them with animals. We have already successfully made attempts with coffee, tobacco and sugar; we only have to make other experiments."[43]

Although Canada had strategic value, political circumstances, and not brute environmental ones, favored French efforts in Louisiana. Silhouette saw great productive potential in its natural resources and therefore envisioned Louisiana as a firewall against complete English dominance in America. If the French were capable of expanding their establishments there, Silhouette projected, they could profit greatly from trade in Spanish America. The English were jealous of Louisiana because "who[ever] masters this colony would make it the depot of contraband trade that . . . would be very advantageous and lucrative." In consequence, the French would form "a barrier between the establishments of the Spanish and the English, preventing them from meeting. If the Spanish and the English ever border each other, the Spanish will find themselves bridled by the English . . . and would receive the law from them."[44]

A universal monarchy imposed upon Spain by the British would constitute a reversal of considerable historical and conceptual importance: it would mean the triumph of a universal monarchy of commerce (a uniquely eighteenth-century fear) over the specifically territorial, dynastic universal monarchy threatened by the Spanish Hapsburgs in the sixteenth century. Silhouette hoped to place France between these powers geopolitically, but this interposition signified a much broader problem in eighteenth-century economic thought. None of the documents that have been discussed—let alone the institutions set up to produce them— are intelligible except as responses to the "new interests for the political system of Europe" that the discovery and commercial exploitation of the Americas continued to generate.[45] In addition to the disadvantages inherent in France's constitution should be added another problem: *moeurs.* In this respect once again, France seemed to be between the extremes of Spain and England; French habits, customs, and manners were less haughty and indolent than those of the Spanish, to be sure, but seemed nevertheless to be maladapted to specifically commercial competition.

Moeurs, the Constitution, and Reform Economics

Montesquieu did not introduce *moeurs* into the conceptual vocabulary of the Enlightenment;[46] he only made more systematic a conceptually loose way of speaking about differences in national character that were believed to express themselves in all sorts of activities, from art, conversation, and politics to sexuality, habits of work, and, of course, commerce.

The idea that *moeurs* had a profound effect on France's economic life was a received opinion by 1748. The widespread emphasis on *moeurs* was not an interpretation in itself about France's fitness for commercial prosperity but a category—one that was so pervasive that any economic analysis with pretensions to relevance had to speak to the relationship between commerce and culture. While it does not follow that the problem was viewed in the same way by every observer, the portrait of French *moeurs* was rarely terribly encouraging from the perspective of economic competition.

André François Deslandes understood the superlative importance of overseas trade to French prosperity and was a direct witness to its operations. Born in Pondicherry, India, into a family of ennobled merchants-turned-directors of the Compagnie des Indes Orientales, Deslandes helped to oversee naval protection of France's merchant marine in his capacity as *commissaire général* of the Navy at Brest and Rochefort. In India and in the Ponant, he had an opportunity to observe closely the mentality and practices of French overseas merchants. Shortly after he quit his post as commissaire—reportedly as a protest against chronic underfunding of the Navy—he published the *Essai sur la marine et sur le commerce* (1743). Jean-Frédéric Phélypeaux, comte de Maurepas and minister of the Navy since 1723, was evidently displeased, and Deslandes's work was placed on a list of banned books. From this point forward, Deslandes applied himself full-time to an already burgeoning career as a materialist philosopher and all-purpose *bel esprit* who could count among his friends Voltaire, the Marquis D'Argenson, Diderot, and D'Alembert and was named by the latter two as a contributor to the *Encyclopédie*. In his *Essay*, Deslandes remarked that Colbert had modeled the Compagnie des Indes on its Dutch and English counterparts, but even so, France's overseas commerce "suffered many gaps and interruptions, especially when it was handed over to individual merchants." Why? The Compagnie des Indes was undercapitalized and corrupt because, as he observed, in an obvious sexual pun, "the French are in a hurry to enjoy [*se hâtent de jouïr*]." He continued: "In general the French fail themselves. They are only touched by the agreeable arts, by arts that simultaneously flatter their taste for sensuality and indolence." Dutot, by contrast, claimed that "activity is not lacking in the French."

Nevertheless, he seconded the opinion that the average Frenchman was hasty and self-indulgent, which led him to seek quick profits in ill-advised deals: "they apply themselves to bad trades [*faux commerces*], because the roads that lead to them appear the most direct, the most abbreviated, the quickest harvest."[47]

The contrast between the improvident, frivolous French and parsimonious, upright Dutch could not have been any greater. Despite their wealth, "in the very bosom of opulence, luxury is ignored." According to the 1738 memoirist, the Dutch succeeded in trade "particularly by their economy, they know so little luxury that their deputies arrive in their assemblies with sacks filled with bread and cheese to avoid the expense of an inn." Moreover, republican manners were not infected by disdain for the picayune details of business affairs, mastery of which is the soul of commercial success. Finally, noble patterns of consumption that informed French taste in general tended to skew demand and production toward luxury goods. The most optimistic prognosis that could be drawn from such observations is that given their temperament—influenced from on high by the aristocracy—French merchants could hope only to participate in high-risk, buccaneering overseas luxury trade *(commerce de luxe)* and not the humbler but ultimately more profitable *commerce d'économie* (the carrying trade) upon which the Dutch burgher had grown fat and the Dutch trading empire so powerful. Most observers judged, moreover, that royal penury and the politics of court favoritism would continue to hobble the success of such ventures (i.e., the Compagnie des Indes) as were left to them by their haughty *moeurs*.[48]

In short, the state of France's economy in relation to its rivals was often viewed as much the outcome of French *moeurs* as of its natural resources, the state of its internal markets, or the larger structures of the world economy. To be sure, much of the discussion on *moeurs* and their relation to commerce not cited in the preceding pages was of a highly general, anecdotal nature that might be dismissed as a sort of cultural white noise. Without being narrow-minded or anachronistic about what qualifies as the economic thought of the period, to enter into our account we should at least expect such discussions on *moeurs* and commerce to pass a certain threshold of analytical ambition; they must posit a functional relationship between cultural norms and, for instance, agriculture, the operation of specific institutions, the production and consumption of certain types of goods, the circulation of money, or patterns of investment. In all of the cases cited above, the analyses of diplomats, administrators, and *philosophes* did precisely this and, in so doing, demonstrated how the ascendancy of noble values influenced France's economic life and therefore the centrality of *moeurs* to eighteenth-century economic thought.[49]

At each juncture in the analysis of the golden triangle of manufacture, commerce, and navigation, crucial issues of France's "constitution" arise. "Constitution" connoted governmental form, but just as frequently, factors deemed inseparable from the overall functioning of the body politic, such as social structure, institutions, and *moeurs,* were subsumed into the term. The sense that all of these things worked together in a complicated, even delicate organic whole meant that reform-minded politicians had to study other countries and their laws from a particular vantage point. Silhouette thought it necessary to "expose summarily the spirit and principle" behind England's laws, adding that not all of these laws could find direct application in France because of "the difference between the constitution of their government and that of our kingdom."[50]

Silhouette's solution, which was to try to make some application of English laws despite the dissimilarity of the two countries, is representative of the way in which many Enlightenment thinkers conceived of the dual nature of economic knowledge. Many liked to invoke a rule-governed universe, in which even the most complicated of bodies, the body politic, operated according to fixed laws that ensured their growth, preservation, or corruption. At the same time, they believed that despite this lawlike regularity, the complexity of human affairs left room for ameliorative action. (Silhouette's invocation of the "spirit and principles" of laws in relation to constitutional forms is suggestive.) One year later, Montesquieu would argue that politicians could overcome the brute force of climate through legislative art. Silhouette's 1747 memoir did not "anticipate" Montesquieu's analysis; it is more accurate to say that a shared question led to a similar approach. Like Silhouette and many of his contemporaries, Montesquieu was interested in the way in which commerce could find a limited but positive role within the seemingly inhospitable environment of monarchical society. Melon drew out the implication of this view when he called for a comparative science of commerce in his *Essai politique:* "nations do not know each other well enough. . . . To examine the progress and the decadence of ancient and modern empires, to penetrate all of the causes, is the highest and most neglected of studies." For Melon, this study was a combination of history, as well as the construction of "general" and "particular" systems "to extend the commerce of our colonies, to simplify the King's taxes, to establish public credit." As Melon observed in reaction to the disorienting array of material that the science of commerce was supposed to organize, "this type of study, which is vague in itself, cannot be brought back into a sufficiently systematic order." In the eyes of many of his contemporaries, it was Montesquieu who achieved this systematic order in his science of commerce.[51]

CHAPTER 2

Montesquieu's Science of Commerce

IN 1764, VOLTAIRE described the mid-century explosion of interest in political economy: "Around the year 1750, France, sated with poetry, tragedy, comedies, operas, novels and adventure stories . . . at last started philosophizing about grain." Although Voltaire denied Montesquieu's role in this sea change with a characteristically dismissive wave of the hand, Melchior Grimm, author of the taste-making *Correspondance littéraire,* dated this turn in intellectual fashion with precision: the publication of Montesquieu's *De l'esprit des lois* in 1748 did more than change intellectual fashion; it "effected a complete revolution in the national mind." For an anonymous author in the *Journal de Commerce,* Montesquieu's contribution was no less seminal: "We are indebted to M. de Montesquieu hardly less for the science of commerce than we are for philosophy and letters." Even those who did not appreciate his approach to the science of commerce lauded the "brilliant dawn" inaugurated by Montesquieu's writings: "The era of the revolution that turned our thinkers to the study of political economy goes back to *M. de Montesquieu,*" wrote the Physiocrat Dupont de Nemours. These appreciations are corroborated by the persistent references to Montesquieu in economic writings well beyond the 1760s.[1]

In his *History of Civil Society* (1767), the Scotsman Adam Ferguson criticized the lazy tendency of historians to telescope long-term social movements into the activity of a founding statesman such as Romulus, or to reduce broadly based intellectual movements to the wisdom of one transcendently wise legislator such as Solon of Athens or Lycurgus of Sparta: "An author and a work, like cause and effect, are perpetually coupled together." But Ferguson was guilty of perpetuating the same myth of the legislator when he idealized Montesquieu as a latter-day Solon: "When I recollect what the President Montesquieu has written, I am at a loss to tell, why I should treat of human affairs." Ferguson's debt was indeed substantial, but his ode is cringe-making partly because of its excessive modesty and deference to intellectual authority. Ferguson and others "treated of human affairs" in original ways we (and they) might not sufficiently appreciate, because the myth of the legislator, which so massively benefited Montesquieu's reputation in the eighteenth century and beyond, obscures our view. When those who followed Montesquieu cited his influence, they often referred, without being precisely aware of the fact, to a broader intellectual movement that the name of Montesquieu only epitomized. Eighteenth-century readers were captivated by a particular book and its contents, and so it is fair to assume that the shape Montesquieu gave to his ideas on commerce speaks to the context in which such an ongoing infatuation was possible.[2]

As a writer, Montesquieu did not set out to write a handbook of economic method; throughout his life, his principal interest remained the problem of despotism and its alternatives. That said, the rise and expansion of commerce in modern post-Roman Europe were central to his concern with despotism. In explaining the decline of the Roman model of conquest and its replacement by a modern system of commerce among compact, peaceful states concerned more with their own conservation than with grandeur, Montesquieu came to terms with a problem that had become salient since the seventeenth century: what was the most appropriate political system for a world order based on commerce rather than on territorial conquest? No single aspect of Montesquieu's system is entirely unique; one can trace aspects of it back to William Temple, Samuel Pufendorf, Niccolò Machiavelli, and Thomas Hobbes, but his synthesis proved uniquely influential in France because it was geared to the particular circumstances of encouraging commerce in the context of a modernized (or "absolute") feudal monarchy.[3]

Montesquieu's initial foray into this problem began in the *Lettres Persanes* (1721). Here, in response to the Law episode (1719–1720), he asks how monarchical societies can make the transition to commercial modernity without falling into despotism. The answer implicit in the *Lettres Persanes* is that such changes are hazardous. Under the regency of the duc d'Orléans, Law's experiments with a national bank and a publicly held overseas trading company ended in a form of despotism as fully pernicious as the autocratic rule of Louis XIV. Montesquieu posed a similar question in the *Esprit des lois* and, bringing to bear his analysis of the nature and principle of different forms of government (monarchy, republic, and despotism), concluded that moderate government was possible for monarchies under the historically novel conditions presented by *les progrès du commerce*. The formula Montesquieu posed was a politics of fusion, envisioning modern forms of commercial life nested within the political and social hierarchies inherited from Europe's feudal monarchies.[4]

Montesquieu's synthesis remained commanding as a science of commerce because it met several requirements simultaneously. First, it was more rigorous than the comparatively loose sociological and historical analysis of commerce that preceded the *Esprit des lois*. It provided a method—a framework for historical reflection and thought experiments— about the interrelation of governmental form, social structure, manners, and wealth creation. Second, Montesquieu was a sophisticated thinker who qualified most of his judgments: he was an advocate of the nobility while admitting that their privileges were inherently "odious"; he admired England's free constitution even as he deplored their harsh and utilitarian manners. Finally and most important, French economic writers returned insistently to Montesquieu because his central problem was their own: the fate of monarchy in modern, commercial society.[5]

Montesquieu did not resolve and abandon earlier problems but rather explored them more deeply in later writings by shifting his emphasis and refining his methods. This explains partly why eighteenth-century observers felt comfortable citing the *Esprit des lois* almost uniquely among his works. At the same time, one can trace the following developmental arc. Earlier writings such as the *Réflexions sur la monarchie universelle* and the *Considérations sur les causes de la grandeur des Romains et de leur décadence,* which were written at the same time and initially published together in 1734, were meditations on the anachronism in modern times of empires based upon conquest. Montesquieu's analysis in these works described how the increased flow of information, people, and goods transformed fundamentally the spatial relations of the world economy and, hence, its geopolitical context; these shifts, as Montesquieu intimated in the *Réflexions sur la monarchie universelle* and *Considérations sur les Romains,* pointed to the dominance of new forms of wealth creation and political organization. This was Montesquieu's history of commerce, which did so much to make his entire oeuvre central to the "philosophical history" developed in the eighteenth century.[6]

Later, in the *Esprit des lois,* Montesquieu deepened his historical analysis of commerce by pairing it with a political sociology. According to Montesquieu, each people had a unique general spirit *(esprit général)* that was a result of several interrelated factors. In a refinement of this line of inquiry, he went on to analyze the role of commerce in monarchical, republican, and despotic societies. The sociology of commerce along with the history of commerce were the central elements of the science of commerce to which later economic writers turned. In Montesquieu's own work, and in that of his epigones in France, these two forms of analysis were applied to the problem of the French monarchy. Although the author of the *Esprit des lois* believed that France was a modern state with modern economic and social structures, the maintenance of a free constitution entailed compromises with its feudal inheritance. The question for Montesquieu, as for others, was to what extent these compromises were consonant with the geopolitical imperatives, including growing colonial establishments, dictated by *les progrès du commerce.* Even during his lifetime, Montesquieu revised the *Esprit des lois* in order to parry the confusions and criticisms generated by his particular solution to the problem of monarchy and commerce.[7]

The New Space of Commerce

The compass was given pride of place in most eighteenth-century explanations of the opening up of the East Indies by Europeans and their eventual discovery and exploitation of the New World. Essential technical, social, and political factors fell by the wayside, but in its simplicity, this explanation usefully emphasized one overwhelming fact: prior to the fifteenth century, Europeans' mastery over maritime space was severely limited and could be extended only by the slow and easily reversible gains of coastal exploration. The ancients' navigational world was organized around seas—the Mediterranean and its satellites—whereas the modern world is oceanic; for eighteenth-century writers, the comparative involution and isolation of the medieval period only sharpened this sense of distinction between the geographical organization of the ancient and modern worlds.[8] Royal mapmaker Robert de Vaugondy's map, printed in the 1757 edition of *De l'esprit des lois* prepared by Montesquieu, conveys a sense of this new and expansive period (see Figure 2.1).

Montesquieu occasionally mentioned the compass, which he credited with the "flight from the coasts," in his account of the passage from antiquity, and such observations were consistent with a deep interest in the technology of navigation. In analyzing the opening up of world trade, Montesquieu also discussed such factors as displacement, keel size, rigging systems, sail configurations, and the proportion of the surface area of the hull to tonnage. But beyond the technical apparatus of navigation, Montesquieu seemed determined to give this phenomenon an interpretation that was at once more concrete and more general, which explains why he reached back to ancient history. The full title of Montesquieu's work on this subject, *Considérations sur les causes de la grandeur des Romains et de leur décadence,* provides insight into the nature of his analysis. Although the opposition of *grandeur* and *décadence* invites us to think of grandeur as a moral quantity in a Machiavellian register, the more basic connotation of grandeur as size is fundamental to Montesquieu's discussion. The first books of the *Considérations sur les Romains* dwell upon the relation of grandeur to power: Rome's initial confinement within a narrow circle was propitious for the development of the military virtue eventually unleashed upon the whole of the known universe. The

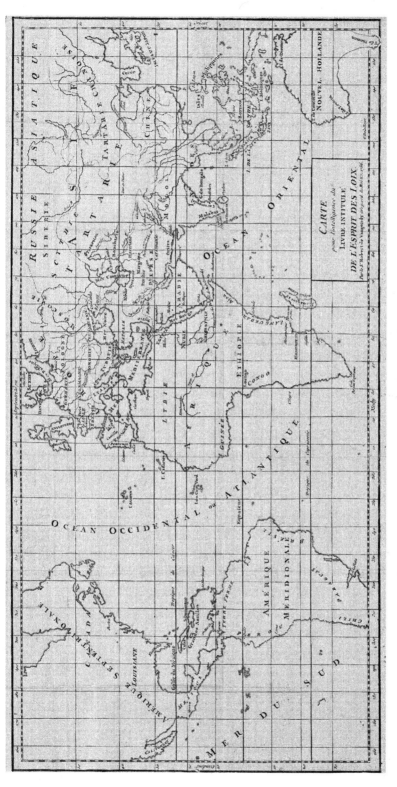

Figure 2.1 The new space of commerce. Map prepared by Robert de Vaugondy, royal mapmaker. The legend reads: "For comprehension of the book entitled OF THE SPIRIT OF THE LAWS." (National Library of Australia.)

expansion of Rome beyond the Italian peninsula and the extension of citizenship to conquered peoples weakened the "spirit of citizenship," so that Rome eventually ceased to form an integrated "ensemble": "the Republic's size [grandeur] was the great evil." In some respect, the *Considérations sur les Romains* can be viewed as a traditional account, related closely to Machiavelli's *Discorsi sopra la prima deca di Tito-Livio*, where the state is conceived of as an organic body inevitably subject to the cycle of growth, decay, and death. Montesquieu never sought to contradict this traditional conception of the body politic but enriched it considerably by describing the secular shifts and discontinuities that changed radically the context in which the life cycle of the state operated.[9]

Whereas the *Considérations sur les romains* explained the rise and dominance of Rome, even in the teeth of opposition from the commercial Carthaginians, its companion piece, the *Réflexions sur la monarchie universelle,* explained the present "moral impossibility" of universal dominion. In the modern age, wealth is the most basic determinant of political strength, and the dynamics proper to commerce dictate the balance of power even where military force is specifically at issue. Spain presented a classic case, for Montesquieu, of this shift. The discovery of the New World and the influx of precious metals should have ensured universal monarchy to the Hapsburgs under Philip II and Charles IV. But as Montesquieu observed, gold and silver were produced commodities, in addition to being signs of wealth, which entailed a threefold loss. First, inflation continually degraded the representative value of precious metals: the more gold and silver Spain produced, the less each additional pound was worth. Second, mining required inputs of capital and subsistence goods, which had to be purchased with ever-increasing quantities of specie devalued by inflation. Third and finally, the decreasing productivity of mines meant that more capital and labor had to be purchased in order to unearth an equivalent amount of metal, further eroding profits. Rome may have sustained its empire with the plunder of its conquests, but the logic of the market prevented the Hapsburgs from converting an analogous windfall in the Americas into universal monarchy.[10]

More generally, Montesquieu, like so many other eighteenth-century writers, demonstrated how fluctuations in the exchange rate between different nations helped to distribute productive advantages—and hence wealth—from rich to poor nations. Countries with active manufacture and commerce drew in specie from abroad, which in turn raised the price of their goods relative to competitor nations. Poorer nations with weak currencies could profit by this imbalance until their growing prosperity put their currency, and hence the price of the labor that went into their manufactures, into line with competitor nations. Whether wealth was conceived of as a sign (in the case of New World specie) or as embodied labor, Montesquieu showed that the dominance of markets meant that power was distributed in a way that differed fundamentally from the old mode of domination by territorial conquest.[11]

As with the circulation of specie, the flow of information in the world of commerce had potentially leveling political effects. Commercial advantage is based partly on informational asymmetries, "all those advantages which intelligent people hold over ignorant ones." Merchants concerned with the rise and fall of internationally traded commodities, foreign currencies, and sovereign debt opened up and perfected channels of communication, creating a situation that rendered the grand enterprises of territorial conquest, which relied on long preparation and a measure of secrecy, increasingly difficult to pull off. Where decisive warfare remained possible, commerce and navigation changed its nature. The Romans, like the French, disparaged the navy relative to the land army, partly because land war depended more on valor and courage rather than on "ruse." But as Montesquieu observed in the *Considérations sur les Romains,* sea power is infinitely more useful in the modern age than it had been in ancient times, and it depended for its conduct on technology and the artisans *(gens d'art)* who mastered and developed this technology, usually within the context of wealthy commercial societies. Technical prowess and wealth were beginning to count for more than the traditional virtues of courage and obedience.[12]

Montesquieu viewed the "communication" of peoples as the essence of the history of commerce, and for him modern commercial society as a whole was defined by a dynamic "flux and reflux" of people, money, goods, and information. Before the compass and the sail made the mastery of oceanic space possible, European merchants were inventing commercial practices to transcend a different sort of spatial limitation.

Money-lending Jews suffered oppression in medieval times, "when one regarded men as land," and invented the letter of exchange in order to move their assets quickly and escape seizure by rapacious princes. In the same way, commercial republics such as Amsterdam and Venice escaped the oppression of territorial empires by trading with "the whole universe" rather than confining themselves to a hinterland controlled by despotic emperors who could choke them off at a moment's notice. The outward thrust of European commercial expansion was preceded by an internal reorganization of commercial space, in which more universal forms of wealth and exchange were designed to help liberty break the territorial confines of despotism.[13]

The growth of "mobile wealth" *(effets mobiles),* which would become so important for later writers such as Antoine Barnave, when he came to explain the difference between "feudal" and "democratic" Europe, helped to undermine the basis of monarchical despotism. A number of causes cured Europe of "Machiavellianism." In a state system characterized by war and the massive fiscal and financial operations necessary to sustain it, financial capital flees despotism. At the social level, monarchs needed to attend more closely to the well-being of their productive classes, who could be expected to work continuously only if they drew some benefit. Just as informational and monetary dynamics had transformed the old modes of warfare and the balance of power from inside out, the rise of mobile wealth was upending the old primacy of agriculture over trade and, with it, the social and political hierarchies of France's military-administrative state. Most present-day economic historians argue that a productive agricultural sector is a desideratum for the development of a capitalist economy, and many eighteenth-century observers would have agreed with this proposition, but here as elsewhere Montesquieu virtually ignored the agricultural sector, probably because he did not see it as a principal source of economic dynamism in the French economy. Montesquieu never argued that commerce outweighed agricultural wealth, only that its very mobility gave it an "advantage over landed wealth" *(fonds de terre).* The old armature that supported landed wealth and power buckled under the monetization of the economy, and mobile capital rendered all forms of wealth, at least potentially, the property of "the whole world." The commercial revolution that swept across western

Europe was proof that the exposure of territorial wealth to mobile capital could have a stimulating effect, but countries such as Poland proved that it was now possible to seize all forms of wealth through the mechanisms of internationalized production and exchange. These peripheral zones would have been better off maintaining a strategic autarky but were instead converted into "colonies" by foreign merchants. If commerce were becoming universal, the distribution of its benefits and drawbacks begged some comprehensive explanation, which Montesquieu sought to give.[14]

The Political Sociology of Commerce

Such were the "great revolutions" in the history of commerce, whose overall effect was to put into play the leveling, cosmopolitan tendencies inherent in exchange. The rise of commerce had the effect of setting strict limits upon the size of empires, making territorial conquest anachronistic, undermining the basis of monarchical despotism, "corrupting" pure *moeurs,* and advancing the arts and sciences wherever they were found. Having observed this, Montesquieu never believed that these great revolutions had an equal effect in all places; when he wrote that "commerce stands in relation [*a du rapport*] with the constitution," he meant the term "constitution" in the widest possible sense, encompassing relatively fixed factors of geography and climate along with historically evolving institutions and forms of government.

Montesquieu was often accused of advancing a species of climactic determinism, following his dictum that "the empire of climate is the first of all empires." Taking this proposition literally, as many of his readers did, one might falsely conclude that a people's penchant for despotism, liberty, penury, or prosperity was fixed once and for all by physical factors. In reality, this proposition signified only that climate (meaning also geographical factors) was chronologically the first of all "empires" because, being closest to nature, it determined human activities and dispositions in the absence of countervailing influences that were the product of history. Taken together, the multiplicity of reciprocally influencing factors made up what Montesquieu called the "general spirit": "many things govern men: climate, religion, laws, governmental maxims, the example of things past, *moeurs,* manners; from which is formed a result-ing general spirit." The balance of forces within this complex varies ac-cording to place and time: "to the degree that . . . one of these causes acts with more force, the others diminish accordingly"; climate domi-nates in primitive and despotic societies, whereas laws and manners take the upper hand in more complex and free ones.[15]

Three aspects of this discussion of the general spirit deserve mention. The first is the methodological holism underlying Montesquieu's politi-cal philosophy. His habit of viewing society as a complicated, evolving totality of laws, institutions, and habits constitutes his central contribu-tion to the science of commerce, well ahead of any specific policies that might be gleaned from his work. Montesquieu believed in the possibility of self-conscious reform, but the very complexity of the general spirit and the self-reinforcing nature of its constitutive elements pointed to the deli-cacy of this task. The legislator must be aware of hidden resistances to change arising from the deep structure given by climate and *moeurs* and alive to the possibility that his reforms may set in motion unintended consequences.[16]

Second, the political sociology of commerce that Montesquieu offers in book 20 of the *Esprit des lois* arose directly out of his analysis of the general spirit and his concern with the problem of despotism and lib-erty. In book 11 of the *Esprit des lois,* Montesquieu enumerates the prin-cipal objects of different states: Rome was directed toward aggrandize-ment while China pursued stability; monarchies tended toward regal glory whereas England took specifically political liberty as its object. Since all persons possessed of a soul ought to be self-governing, repre-sentative government was a desideratum of free government in the strict sense of the term. Having said this, Montesquieu believed that the glory monarchs cultivated was also a species of liberty since its reflection onto the general populace created a "spirit of liberty"; moreover, the limited monarchy that emerged out of "gothic" government ensured valu-able, though not for Montesquieu strictly political, forms of freedom, including customs, municipal franchise, and "civil liberty." For this rea-son, moderate monarchy was one of the best forms of government be-cause it ensured diverse forms of freedom while providing a structure that could resist despotism.[17]

Montesquieu's definition of the general spirit is directly preceded by a series of historical anecdotes that prove that monarchy and republican government are not easily displaced or transplanted where such a change would do violence to deeply held customs and sentiments. Indeed, even the imposition or abolition of tyranny demanded great circumspection. Liberty, for Montesquieu, is also the quality of naturalness: "it is up to the legislator to follow the spirit of a nation, when it is not contrary to the principles of government; for we do nothing better than when we do it freely." Conjuring a people—the French, in fact—"with a sociable disposition, an open heart, a zest for living, taste, an ease in communicating their thoughts which is lively, agreeable, sometimes imprudent and often indiscreet," he concluded that "one mustn't correct for everything" *(il ne faut pas tout corriger)*. These qualities were too pleasing to risk deforming France's general spirit after a model of moral seriousness and political liberty unsuitable to it.[18]

Finally, commerce must occupy a central part of any discussion of the general spirit and the problem of liberty in modern states. The famous final chapter of book 19 (*Esprit des lois,* 19.27) is an extended discussion of the "moeurs, manners and character" of the British nation, a free people blessed with sage laws and a good constitution, both of which guarantee their freedom. Observations on English taxation, colonies, and the domination of individual interests in Parliament make clear the importance of commerce to the English people's general spirit. England was not a "conquering" but a "commercial" nation "freed of destructive prejudices," and from this observation followed a number of positive consequences and invidious comparisons with France. Colonies were established not for the purposes of conquest but for commerce; these establishments were given "their own form of government and this government brought with it prosperity"—with the notable exception of Ireland. England's wealth and maritime vocation helped it maintain a "superior navy," which served as the basis for its outsized political influence in European affairs, which in turn fed a "natural pride" in its own freedom and strength. Although England was not forced to incur the ruinous expense of a land army, an establishment that seriously risked serving as a tool of despotism, its citizens willingly taxed themselves more heavily than France because they knew that these outlays maintained their freedom. These and other reflections on the English general spirit, including Montesquieu's views on English colonial governance, attracted critics and admiring imitators alike, as we shall see when we turn to the works of François Véron de Forbonnais and Georges Marie Butel-Dumont. Although Montesquieu believed that there was a direct and reciprocal connection between Albion's political liberty and the "solid luxury" and "great superabundance" its people enjoyed, he did not believe that England or Holland were the only nations with a general spirit propitious for commerce and liberty.

As Melvin Richter has observed, Montesquieu's comparative method always had something descriptive and normative about it. These two elements should be kept in mind when assessing his science of commerce and the uses to which it was later put. On the one hand, wherever Montesquieu saw the possibility of despotism, moral condemnation quickly followed. This was true even though he was capable of seeing despotism as a coherent system, which, like any organism, had its own principles of conservation, growth, or destruction. Despotic societies were natural and therefore susceptible to analysis, but "natural" in this limited sense did not carry with it the moral approval often ascribed to nature in the eighteenth century; these societies were not good, only comprehensible. On the other hand, like Johann Gottfried von Herder, Montesquieu was a connoisseur of diversity capable of appreciating the sorts of freedom and prosperity that emerged out of varied contexts. It is difficult to reduce to a simple schema the positions that France and England occupied in this descriptive and normative analysis. The virtues and vices of different societies had to be appreciated on their own terms; the very term "general spirit" evokes the holistic, aesthetic judgments Montesquieu called forth. At the same time, individual points of comparison evinced clear trade-offs: England's participatory government more closely approximated the ideal of man as a self-governing political animal that was lacking in France; Montesquieu found the social segregation of men and women in England uncouth and joyless, recalling the seraglio of the *Lettres Persanes* more than the refinement and freedom of France's salon life; and the Romans under the republic may have loved their country more than wealth, but this was solely because, unlike commercial moderns, they were poor and had nothing better to covet than the abstraction of the fatherland.[19]

Directly preceding his celebrated chapter on the English, Montesquieu set out to prove that the monarchical general spirit was favorable to riches. Unlike English society, which segregates women from men, the "conversation of women" *(commerce des femmes)* in French society was a decisive element in the formation of taste at court and in society at large. Citing Bernard Mandeville's *Fable of the Bees,* Montesquieu concluded that frivolous, changing tastes "ceaselessly increase the branches of commerce." The spirit of honor, which animates monarchies, could express itself as vanity or pride, and in the Spanish case, he describes how pride leads to laziness, poverty, and desolation. In France, vanity gives rise to "luxury, industry, arts, fashions, politeness and taste." Just as France possessed an ample share of modern liberty—albeit in forms different from what the English enjoyed—the French also benefited from the *doux commerce* that was transforming Europe. Different general spirits could accommodate and promote commerce, but in various ways; in modern terms, Montesquieu envisioned national forms of capitalism adapted to varied cultures and social structures.[20]

Montesquieu's political sociology of commerce, the kernel of which is found in book 20, is both more general and more specific than the discussion of the general spirit of the previous book. It is more specific in the sense that it serves as the introductory book for an entire section devoted to often highly detailed discussions on trade, finance, taxes, and demographics. (Part 5, comprised of books 20–23, is about one-fifth of the entire *Esprit des lois*). These sections put flesh on the bone of the earlier, more abstract assertions of the centrality of commerce to the general spirit in modern states. But this book also provides a more general method for addressing a vital set of questions. Montesquieu begins by implicating virtually all modern peoples in the moral effects of the rise of commerce, a treatment that recalls the philosophical history of commerce described above and which will also be familiar to readers of A. O. Hirschman's *The Passions and the Interests,* which assigns a central role to *doux commerce,* in furnishing justifications for market society in seventeenth- and eighteenth-century Europe. Commerce "heals destructive prejudices" and "softens manners" *(adoucit les moeurs)* even as it corrupts them. Similarly, while commerce unites and pacifies nations through the channels of trade and communication, it also separates individuals by introducing a petty contractualism into most human relations.[21]

If commerce implicates most peoples, its modalities differ widely according to the national context—in eighteenth-century parlance, the "constitution"—in which it takes place. Montesquieu poses in the broadest manner the following questions about who trades and how: which sorts of regimes are most propitious to commerce; what sorts of commerce are most natural to the peoples of despotic, monarchical, or republican regimes; and what is the proper relation of politics to commerce in different types of states?

In general, Montesquieu was an advocate of economic liberty, a conviction that we can trace back to his personal affairs as a wine grower and merchant. In objecting to a 1725 ordinance limiting the quantity and variety of vine plantings in the province of Guyenne, Montesquieu argued, as he would elsewhere in published works, that the merchant's proximity to the facts and his attachment to profit ensured that he "calculates quite precisely," rendering state intervention redundant or harmful. At the same time, he sought to define economic liberty in a way that transcended individual merchants' interests, so as to understand the purpose of commercial restrictions in different social and political contexts. Montesquieu did not emphasize the function of social coordination that the market performs so much as he did the complementarity of economic with political freedom. The Navigation Acts were the law of the land in England, the home of economic liberty par excellence, and yet this "jealousy of trade" was perfectly consistent with England's thoroughly commercial constitution: "it is in free countries where the merchant finds innumerable obstacles; and he is never less constrained than in despotic countries [*pays de la servitude*]. . . . England harasses merchants, but it is in favor of commerce." In a similar vein, Montesquieu treats the jurisprudence of commerce, asking how laws touching on bankruptcy or debt imprisonment reflect underlying attitudes about commerce and how they affect specific forms of economic activity. Such questions were significant because, as a jurist, he always wanted to relate the dispositions of civil law to deep-seated social practices. Readers of the *Esprit des lois* would find opinions on a range of economic controversies that flared up throughout the eighteenth century, including the value of trade restrictions with colonies, the relative merits of monopoly trading companies, the viability of a national bank in France, the best means of tax collection, and the advisability of currency devaluations. The final chapters of book 20 argue for the limitation of commerce to certain social groups in monarchies. Here we see Montesquieu's sociology of commerce at the service of his politics of fusion.[22]

Commerce in the French Monarchy

The most basic distinction that Montesquieu draws among different forms of commerce is between luxury trade *(commerce du luxe),* which is more suited to the government of one person found in monarchical and despotic states, and the carrying trade *(commerce d'économie),* which is more suitable for republics or "the government of many." Luxury trade concerns goods of fashion and ostentation, befitting nations given to vanity and pride; without saying so explicitly, Montesquieu also implies that the luxury trades generate a high rate of profit. The carrying trade, by contrast, is typified by the Dutch grain trade in the Baltics: low profit margins and high volume necessitate scrupulous attention to bourgeois thrift and honesty, which are rewarded with larger absolute profits over the long term and also ensure access to, and domination of, an expanding web of foreign markets. This distinction was new to Montesquieu, and the coinage *commerce d'économie* quickly entered into currency, often being used thereafter to explain the competitiveness, or lack thereof, of French industry and shipping.[23] Montesquieu would seem to exclude monarchies from the fullest participation in *les progrès du commerce,* since economic advances depend upon "establishments" and "enterprises" not well-suited to the monarchical constitution, including national banks, state-sponsored trading companies, and a class of merchants enriched and schooled by their involvement in the carrying trade. He did not intend this distinction to exclude monarchies from commerce categorically, but he did pose it in order to explain how the alignment of social and political forces—particularly the dominance of bourgeois or noble elites—dictated the position of different states within the international division of labor. Here as elsewhere, the specific conclusions that he draws are less important than the method of analysis he offers.

From a description of the influence of internal social and political factors on external trade, Montesquieu moved to a more explicitly normative discussion of how the internal distribution of wealth preserves or compromises a state's constitution. During the 1750s debate over the possibility of commercially active nobility *(noblesse commerçante)*, the *Esprit des lois* served as a war chest for those who agreed with Montesquieu that the nobility should be banned from commerce. Aristocratic republican thinkers such as the chevalier d'Arcq and the abbé Mably emphasized the corrosive effect commercial activity had on monarchical honor and republican virtue, both of which encouraged in different ways the behavior these polities required of their citizens. In a republic, love of country and a disinterest in material wealth led to acts of patriotic self-sacrifice. In monarchies, the reigning passion was the other-regarding species of self-love called honor; but in seeking out distinction among one's fellow citizens, real or apparent self-sacrifice could call forth recognition in the form of glory. Both republican virtue and monarchical honor, then, ensured that patriotic service to the state would trump the self-interested pursuit of wealth. The discussion in the *Esprit des lois* of the relationship among *moeurs,* commerce, and the constitution gave ample scope for such borrowings during the debate over the commercial nobility, but Montesquieu's principal interest lay elsewhere, with the maintenance of a nobility in modern commercial society that could continue to act as a bulwark against despotism. This argument was rooted in a series of negative observations. Princes should stay away from trade because nothing obliges them to keep their agreements; moreover, when monarchies set themselves up in business, they encourage an extractive form of court capitalism among nobles who become even "more greedy and unjust" than monarchs. Thus, a commercial nobility would come to monopolize the wealth of the bourgeoisie, in addition to lording an "odious" set of privileges over them. Montesquieu, ever sensitive to the feedback between politics and society, insisted that just as the constitution must respect the separation of powers within government, it must also maintain the distribution of wealth among its classes. Far from renouncing commerce, monarchies should ensure that commerce flourishes in a way that reinforces, rather than disturbs, the hierarchies that preserve freedom under a monarchical constitution. The crown should confer nobility upon wealthy merchants, who renounce trade and buy their way into the nobility of the robe *(noblesse de robe);* as administrators and judges, the latter class serves the state by protecting its fundamental laws, ultimately assimilating by seniority into the more ancient military nobility *(noblesse d'épée)*; this class defends the state through military service but also dissipates its fortune and sinks into financial and ultimately social oblivion, thinning its numbers in preparation for new members. Montesquieu may have believed in the "odious" and artificial privileges of the nobility, but he also advocated the cycling of economic and service elites who benefited the state in distinct but complementary ways. Here again we glimpse Montesquieu's politics of fusion, in which he sought to accommodate new classes and types of wealth to older social and political forms. Immediate criticism of the *Esprit des lois* lighted upon the role that Montesquieu envisioned for commerce in a monarchy, whether or not critics explicitly rejected or even understood the politics of fusion that underlay his views.[24]

The abbé Joseph La Porte wondered reasonably enough whether the carrying trade "belonged as much to monarchies as to republics": in a nation of twenty million, characters and talents might vary sufficiently so that some could ply this trade profitably, while others dealt in the luxury trades. It was objectively the case that France produced and traded luxuries and necessities, and Montesquieu, it seemed to La Porte, falsely gave the picture of a nation limited to the production and consumption of high-end baubles. François Véron de Forbonnais exposed the *Esprit des lois* to a lengthy and respectful criticism in his *Extrait du livre "de l'Esprit des lois."* Like Melon and Saint-Pierre twenty years earlier, Forbonnais resisted the fashionable conclusion that France's constitution precluded it from forming wealthy colonial establishments: "England, says the author, gives to the people of its colonies its own form of government, and this government carries with it prosperity; we see great peoples constitute themselves when she sends them thither, even in the forests. Is the privilege of establishing colonies accorded exclusively by the nature of the laws of England?"[25]

Montesquieu's early defenders, Boulanger de Rivery and François Risteau, both explained that distinction between the carrying trade and luxury trade inhered not in the difference between necessary and sumptuary goods, or even in the higher total value of the carrying trade over time, but in the rates of return with which Dutch or English merchants

could satisfy themselves. Risteau and Rivery abandoned the more material notion of luxury as a manufacturing sector in which France's aristocratic culture conferred competitive advantages. Since the French merchant would withhold his capital in many instances where competition
had forced down rates of profit, the French nation as a whole was naturally excluded from lines of business profitably exploited by republican
competitors. As a wealthy Bordeaux merchant and future director of the
Compagnie des Indes, François Risteau probably had self-interested reasons to claim what was advanced as an article of faith among merchants
seeking state protection from foreign competitors: that French merchants had an inalterably higher cost structure than their republican
counterparts, who could serve iron rations to smaller, less exigent crews
of commoner stock. Although information gleaned from his personal
contacts in the Ministry of the Navy gave him cause to believe otherwise,
Montesquieu did not challenge Risteau on this point, and he was by all
accounts satisfied with his friend's refutation of La Porte. He had reason
to be: even as Risteau put luxury manufacture in the shade, he shone a
light on the political sociology underlying Montesquieu's science of
commerce.[26]

Revisions to the *Esprit des lois* responded both directly and indirectly
to critics, and the points of qualification and emphasis Montesquieu introduced in response provide a guide to what he believed essential to his
analysis. "I do not mean to say," he wrote, "that there is any monarchy
that is *totally* excluded" from the carrying trade; conversely, he allowed
that republics were not "wholly deprived" of the luxury trade. These
and other emendations had the effect of softening what, in his initial
treatment, his readers took to be Manichean distinctions between monarchies and republics. At the same time, he took the trouble to reaffirm
the point that differences in their "natures" and "constitutions" determine divergent patterns in the trade plied by monarchies and republics.
In support of this, Montesquieu wrote a wholly new chapter that demonstrated the exceptional character of Holland's carrying trade: in shut-
tling between the southern and northern states of Europe, the Dutch
often carried goods such as lumber and stone whose sale realized no
immediate profit but opened markets while procuring forests and quar-
ries for a tiny, resource-starved nation; similarly, while for individual

entrepreneurs whale fishery was often an unprofitable lottery, the construction and provisioning of ships was profitable to the nation as a whole. Merchants with their eyes on quick profits, seeking to ease themselves into country chateaux and venal offices, do not haul stones and wood, even if these are the building blocks of commercial empire.

Although there is no direct proof that Montesquieu read the criticism by Forbonnais cited above, his revisions for the 1757 edition nevertheless suggest he felt the need to strengthen the distinction drawn, in his history of commerce, between conquest and commerce among ancient empires. Roman Alexandria's trade with the East may have grown, but East and West were not drawn together through *doux commerce* but separated by "ambition, jealousy, religion and hatred" among military rivals. Where the Romans seemed to have extended their commerce in the East, this was only incidental to the closing of overland routes during Rome's struggle with the Parthian Empire (53–39 B.C.E. and during the 60s C.E.). (The Parthian Empire corresponds roughly to modern-day Iran and Armenia.) By contrast, Emperor Mithridates' policy of leaving Greek commercial colonies that he conquered independent, so as to siphon off the proceeds of their trade, enabled the Parthians' unexpected and protracted resistance to the Romans. The Romans, by contrast, destroyed the commercial cities of Carthage and Corinth that they had conquered because they could not imagine that these cities' wealth, whose maintenance would require some degree of political autonomy, could be of real benefit to them. Although Forbonnais denied that France's constitution precluded commercial empire, in the context of the 1750s Montesquieu's new historical examples advanced two provocations. First, imperial Rome, to which France was constantly compared, had difficulty assimilating commerce except in its negative effects: enervating luxury and inequality. Second, empires with the capacity to integrate independent commercial colonies posed an existential threat to conquering peoples with less open political systems.[27]

Paris and the Ponant: Biography in Geographical Perspective

In making these provocations, was Montesquieu thinking of the surprising gains won in America by Great Britain during the War of Austrian

Succession (1740–1748), including the seizure of Louisbourg and an effective blockade of the Atlantic trade? We know from personal correspondence that he worried about the effects such a blockade had on Bordeaux merchants, including the sale of wines from his own estate; after the conclusion of hostilities, Montesquieu fretted about the reestablishment of French commerce in the Americas. The war had proven the capital importance of the Atlantic trade, and while Great Britain maneuvered with disconcerting agility on its colonial periphery, France was entangled in the dynastic, continental warfare that Montesquieu exposed as a dangerous anachronism in the *Réflexions sur la monarchie universelle* and elsewhere.[28]

Having said this, the source of Montesquieu's outlook on the economy remains somewhat mysterious. Five works published over the past one hundred years bear the title *Montesquieu économiste,* and none look into the details of his biography for clues to explain his science of commerce. The same is largely true of an equal number of recent monographs devoting considerable or exclusive attention to the subject. If, as Albert Sorel commented, "the personal life of Montesquieu is uninteresting; in no way does it illuminate his works," it is fitting that so many historians confine themselves to passing references to the trauma of the Law episode or the general context of Anglo–French competition. The details of Montesquieu's life as a landowner, wine merchant, and venal officeholder with a personal stake in the economic and political transformations he analyzed—as in the case of the War of Austrian Succession just cited—are scant enough to suggest a cautious approach to this interpretation. The same may be said of any attempt to contextualize Montesquieu's economic views with respect to the cut and thrust of contemporary political debates—the gold standard among Cambridge School historians of political thought. Unlike Voltaire, Anne-Robert Jacques Turgot, Melon, or virtually any of the Physiocrats who came onto the scene beginning in the 1750s, Montesquieu remained aloof from the debates that would help historians fix his views around definite policy arguments.[29]

One pervasive line of interpretation pairs Montesquieu with Voltaire, the *philosophe* whose travels to England and celebration of the connection between commerce and liberty in the *Lettres philosophiques sur les anglais* (1734) established an agenda of Anglophilic criticism of France during the early decades of the French Enlightenment. In this vein, Montesquieu's own travels to England in 1728–1731 are used to explain the centrality of commerce, and England's system of moderate government, in his political philosophy. While it has the merit of fixing the origin of certain of Montesquieu's views, this interpretation poses two insurmountable difficulties: it relegates the *Lettres Persanes* (1721) and the discussion about commerce and liberty contained therein to prehistory, and it grossly exaggerates his attachment to English culture and institutions. Although, as Louis Desgraves observed, Montesquieu admired the English, he was shocked by their culture and worried that their political system was unsustainably fragile: "his opinion on England is highly nuanced and, in the end, little favorable."[30] Montesquieu puzzled over the relationship between commerce and modern forms of freedom well before his sojourn to England and, after prolonged contact with this country and its institutions, never seriously suggested that France adopt England's political system. Is there a biographical approach that can account for the politics of fusion that underlay Montesquieu's science of commerce?

In *History in Geographical Perspective: The Other France* (1971), Edward Whiting Fox described two discrete social structures within the same nation, the "oceanic" and the "agricultural." From its center in Paris, agricultural France's "military-administrative" state directed its essential functions of extracting peasant surplus and waging wars of territorial conquest. In conflict with this, the "oceanic" society of the Ponant consisted of a network of port cities such as Nantes, Bordeaux, La Rochelle, and Saint-Malo, all oriented toward the Atlantic and its transnational flows; by necessity, these cities had a more open, bourgeois— though not to say democratic—culture, whose commercial success relied on the discussion, pragmatism, and flexibility characteristic of peoples who are self-governing, in contrast to those administered from above. Fox conceived of an active symbiosis of the "oceanic" and "agricultural" communities over the course of the late medieval and early modern periods: commercial cities provided tax receipts so that impecunious monarchs could pursue their territorial ambitions; reciprocally, the interior served as market and productive hinterland for the port cities. Ultimately, the contradictions of these essentially opposed systems came to a head in the late eighteenth century. Fox's thesis, it needs hardly be said, reformulates the historical problem of conquest versus commerce broached by Montesquieu and his contemporaries. Without going into much detail, Fox claimed that elements of Montesquieu's biography—a provincial nobleman with a seat in the *parlement* of Bordeaux and with ties to the "commercial community of Bordeaux and, through it, much of the Atlantic world"—gave him an instinctive understanding of the structures and conflicts described above, perhaps unique among his contemporaries. (There were thirteen *parlements*—sovereign courts, not representative institutions—in France. These exercised various functions, including hearing cases and appeals, intervening in municipal regulation, and registering the king's edicts. Edicts did not become laws of the realm until the *parlements* registered them, and they enjoyed the right of remonstration to the king about laws they found imprudent or unjust. It is this last function that became most controversial in the eighteenth century.)[31]

The evidence is compelling that a life divided between Paris and Bordeaux, with their different sources of wealth, political elites, and cultures, helped to define Montesquieu's outlook and hence the intellectual problems he set for himself. Montesquieu simultaneously played a number of different roles: he was a visitor to the elite Club de l'Entresol in Paris and a founding member of the provincial Academy of Arts and Sciences of Bordeaux; he was a member of Bordeaux's *parlement,* the locus of eighteenth-century opposition to the absolute monarchy par excellence, but at the same time, he was often sent to Versailles because his connections at court commanded influence in resolving their disputes; he was a wine merchant with connections to Bordeaux's merchant elite who had harbored an abiding curiosity about the larger world of commerce connected to that city; at the same time, he was a noble deeply rooted in his region (or *pays*) who invested principally in landed assets and closely defended his feudal privileges. Set out in this way, the set of social connections, political allegiances, and economic activities just described seem like a set of self-canceling oppositions; to the contrary, they formed the elements that Montesquieu wished to combine in order to make France into a forward-looking, commercial nation with a stable social structure and moderate government. This angle is worth pursuing because the purely internal textual evidence of the *Esprit des lois* provides only a limited account of Montesquieu's politics of fusion. The limitation is not one of mass: the final books of the *Esprit des lois* (a great proportion of the total) are devoted to the proposition that France's feudal heritage, in the form of its *parlements* and other "intermediary bodies" should continue to serve as a constitutional and social counterweight to the monarchy. We also have Montesquieu's admission that, however salutary the political effects of the nobility, their privileges are to be counted artificial and inherently odious. However, Montesquieu's discussion is limited because the principal concern of the *Esprit des lois* is to examine the relationship between the nobility and the monarch; he provides a much less developed account, beyond passing mentions in his discussion of luxury and commerce, of the relation he envisioned between the nobility and France's productive classes. In order to answer this question, we turn to a different set of sources.

By dint of his geographical double life, Montesquieu may have been well placed to theorize this synthesis of the "oceanic" and "agricultural" France. The majority of economic writers (61 percent) in eighteenth-century France lived and worked in Paris—which helps to explain pervasive blind-spots in French economic writing, particularly on the subject of foreign trade. An unknown but probably vanishingly small percentage of the remaining 39 percent shuttled as regularly and comfortably as Montesquieu did between the upper reaches of Paris and Bordeaux—or any of the other urban nodes of France's "oceanic" community.[32] His alternation between Paris and Bordeaux was not simply the commute between center and periphery so many Parisians took it to be, but a synthesis of two novel, sometimes conflicting perspectives.

Montesquieu was acutely aware of the distance between the business cultures of Paris and the Ponant: "nobody is stupider in matters of trade than Parisians. These financiers who get rich so easily and quickly think there is nothing so simple as getting richer still." He aimed this withering comment at the Chambre d'Assurances Générales et Grosse Aventures, a private company established in Paris in 1750 with the sponsorship of the controller general of finances Jean Baptiste de Machault D'Arnouville, who wanted to make competitively priced maritime insurance available, particularly in times of war when less highly capitalized or centralized arrangements tended to fail. In the wake of the War of Austrian Succession, England had just passed a law prohibiting its citizens from insuring enemy ships during wartime. During that conflict, only the local *chambre d'assurances* (insurance bureau) of Saint-Malo was able consistently to provide coverage for maritime ventures, which raised the question of France's preparation for a new conflict. However, Montesquieu reasoned, port merchants already drew ignorant and unwary Parisians into unsafe investments in overseas trade. Montesquieu, who had personal experience with the chicanery of insurance agents, believed that merchants would do substantially the same with an insurance company, using local knowledge to cherry-pick safe ventures to be insured by their own local insurance syndicates while packing off the riskiest ventures to Paris to be insured by their *chambre*. The nature of this criticism was twofold. First, as in his 1725 memoir to the intendant of Guyenne in which he criticized an edict limiting vine plantations, Montesquieu argued that local knowledge was almost inevitably superior to designs emanating from the center—in this case, the controller general's office, the hub of centralized administrative control under the absolute monarchy. Second, Montesquieu appealed implicitly to the cultural differences that underlay the distinction between the carrying trade and the luxury trade: Parisians accustomed to high rates of profit and quick, speculative gains could not hope to compete with Ponant merchants whose outlook was closer to Anglo-Dutch norms.[33]

Montesquieu's identification with Bordeaux merchants, including a deep interest in the patterns of international trade, had many possible sources beyond the general fact of his long-standing residence in that city. Choosing a dominant influence from among them would impart a false sense of precision, so what follows must remain suggestive. Montesquieu's estates produced a great deal of wine, and a concerted strategy of land purchases and exchanges over the course of nearly thirty years only increased that amount.[34] Nobles of that region were particularly dependent on the income generated from their vineyards and for this reason often saw directly to the sale of their wines, which frequently went abroad to England and Holland. (Although he does not explicitly say so, we must presume that because Montesquieu sold only the produce of his own vineyards, his activities as a wine merchant did not contravene his strictures against a commercial nobility.) Montesquieu shared a great interest with Bordeaux merchants in the patterns of foreign demand and the vagaries of war, concerns that find concrete expression in his *Spicilège,* a sort of commonplace book of observations and extracts from books and journals such as the *Gazette de Hollande* and the *Gazette d'Amsterdam.* Entries on exchange rates, stock prices, the opening and closing of trade routes, sovereign debt, and population form a continuum of subject matter connecting the prosaic business concerns he shared with Bordeaux merchants to the broader, synoptic view on commerce and history offered in the *Esprit des lois.* He greatly encouraged the Bordeaux Academy to protect the arts and sciences related to navigation and commerce, given the extent of Bordeaux's involvement in foreign trade. In what little that remains of his business correspondence, Montesquieu displays extensive relations in the world of finance and trade, demonstrating familiarity with their terms of art. Whether it was a cause or an effect of his commercial activities, we know from his correspondence with François Risteau and the defense the latter mounted on his behalf that Montesquieu had warm relations with certain segments of Bordeaux's merchant elite.[35]

For all of his mercantile involvements, Montesquieu remained an aristocrat who derived the majority of his income from landed wealth. Estimates of his estate's income at two points—23,000 l.t. in 1726 and 19,000 l.t. in 1756, just after his death—put him squarely in the center of the rich provincial nobility, a segment of the nobility that enjoyed between 10,000 and 50,000 l.t. annual income and comprised just 13 percent of that order. Only 2 percent of the nobility, the super-rich "plutocratic kernel," towered above them. Unlike so many rich provincial aristocrats who dissipated their estates by chasing offices and status at Versailles and in Paris, Montesquieu lived parsimoniously, whether in Guyenne or in Paris. He cultivated his estates carefully and profitably but without any hint of agronomic innovation, letting out his land on a specialized version of the sharecropping lease called the *bail à détroit.* As a seigneur, he showed no embarrassment about pursuing the profitable rights peasants owed their lord, often beginning repossession *(mainmise)* proceedings for surprisingly trivial amounts of money associated with seigneurial obligations due him. None of this evinces economic behavior that is in itself "feudal" or precapitalist: in some respect, Montesquieu and his wife's tightfisted management of their estates was the simple maximization of contractual obligations, seigneurial or not; their deliberate policy of land acquisition aimed at consolidation and expansion manifests a similar economic logic. This was a rational and acquisitive but also traditionally minded form of capitalist agriculture. At the same time, Montesquieu enforced economically marginal privileges, suing poachers who infringed upon his noble hunting monopoly with a surprising tenacity, even vindictiveness. His pedantic insistence on economically meaningless privileges, as when he required his peasants to perform homage, completes the picture of a seigneur keen to assert symbolically the remnants of the feudal order. While he may have denounced noble privileges as "odious" and artificial, he was capable of taking a hardheaded view of their economic and ideological role: "one must regard one's property as a slave; and one must not lose one's slave."[36]

Somewhere between the clashing images of Montesquieu the cosmopolitan Bordeaux wine merchant and the litigious, often punitive lord of the manor at La Brède, we also have the picture of an agricultural capitalist working the land in Guyenne, Bordeaux's hinterland, and thereby linking town and country, or ocean and continent, through the production and sale of wine and other agricultural surplus. In the person of Montesquieu, diversity of outlooks met the rival but also complementary economic systems so characteristic of Old Regime France. A similar complexity was at work in his cultural and social involvements in Paris and Bordeaux.

In Paris, Uzbek, the Persian nobleman of the *Lettres Persanes* who serves as a conduit for so many of Montesquieu's views, encounters a topsy-turvy social world where "liberty and equality prevail": birth, virtue, and success in war count for little, and lackeys command respect because they might well become noble lords some day. Uzbek was exaggerating, no doubt, but his sense of vertigo indicates one of the basic questions addressed in the *Lettres Persanes:* how is it possible to chart a course between the sclerotic world of the seraglio (a symbol for Versailles, the home of the absolute monarchy) and the anarchic social leveling found in Paris, which was caused largely by putting commercial, market relations in the place of more traditional social hierarchies?[37] As

we know, Montesquieu had no use for anticommercial models of aristocratic republicanism, believing that these anachronistic fantasies were
best confined to the pages of Fénelon's *Telemachus*, which described the
lost agricultural paradise of Bétique and its virtuous denizens. Between
the despotism latent in an unrestrained absolute monarchy (the seraglio)
and the despotism that threatened to arise in a social order shorn of distinctions and rank (Uzbek's Paris), Montesquieu sought a *juste milieu*
that could preserve distinctions while accommodating the social dynamism introduced by commerce; this, as we have seen, is the project of
the *Esprit des lois*. We find a similar pattern in Montesquieu's own life.

During the 1720s, Montesquieu was connected to one of the most
influential institutions of the early French Enlightenment, the Club de
l'Entresol, a group that met regularly in Paris from 1724 to 1731 to discuss such topics as government, religion, finance, and trade. Members of
this group included the abbé de Saint-Pierre, whose works on commerce
are discussed in the previous chapter; the marquis d'Argenson, foreign
minister and author of *Considérations sur le gouvernement ancien et
présent de la France*; and Lord Bolingbroke, the British political writer
and moralist. None of the remaining twenty-two members achieved literary fame. They did not have to: aristocrats to a man, most of them were
rich, well titled, and highly placed in government or military circles.
Social rivalry within this group did not take place on the frontier between commoners and noblemen, as was the case in Parisian salons later
in the century, but between the old military nobility and the newer nobility of the sword. Montesquieu could trace his origins to both groups.
The fact that the *parlement* of Bordeaux often called upon Montesquieu
to intervene on its behalf during conflicts with Versailles is a testament
to the ease with which he moved in this rarified world.[38]

In later decades, capitalizing on his fame and gratifying his considerable social appetite, Montesquieu frequented the salons of Mesdames
Tencin, Mirepoix, Du Deffand, Géoffrin, and Dupré, as well as those of
the duchesses d'Aiguillon and de Chaulnes. The tenor and social complexion of these gatherings varied, of course, but as the century wore on
they became more democratic in spirit and were dominated less by aristocratic *bon ton* than by the values of intellectual merit; in these salons, a
new politics of sociability opposed "the hierarchy of the society of orders

and the absolutist state." By every account, Montesquieu fit well into this socially and intellectually stimulating world, as one might expect of somebody who criticized the dreary homosociality of the English scene and caricatured the rigid formalities of Versailles as a form of oriental despotism. Out of these mixed circles, he developed a long-standing and close relationship with Madame Tencin, a woman who, though of noble origins, attached considerable scandal to herself by breaking her convent vows early in life and giving birth to an illegitimate child, one Jean le Rond d'Alembert. Over the course of several decades, Montesquieu protected and subsidized another unlikely friend, quite against the advice of many of his well-heeled friends. The beneficiary in this case was an erudite but louche n'er-do-well from Italy, the Abbé Guasco. In his friendships, Montesquieu conducted himself according to his personal tastes rather than the prejudices of his caste.[39] Where his literary alter ego Uzbek eventually snapped, reverting to the habits of authority and hierarchy of the seraglio back home, Montesquieu was more chameleon-like, adapting himself in Bordeaux and in Paris to an increasingly permeable social order.

Having said this, an examination of Montesquieu's correspondence and his activities with the Royal Academy of Arts and Sciences of Bordeaux demonstrates that there were strict limits to the degree of social leveling Montesquieu would countenance. These limits correspond well with the politics of fusion discussed throughout this chapter. Looking at the biographical details of Montesquieu's correspondents from 1700 to 1731, we see that only three of some 125 of those, where they are known, are merchants, and none issue from liberal but non-noble professions; one letter comes from a peasant, his tenant. Montesquieu did have extensive relations with several members of the Berthelot de Duchy family, but these were financiers on the social ascendant whose past as merchants was quickly receding behind them. We know that Montesquieu did have relationships beyond the cast of judges, ecclesiastics, foreign dignitaries, members of the high nobility, intendants, and other state functionaries that people his correspondence. Many of these relationships, like that between himself and Jean François Melon—fellow Bordelais, author of the *Essai politique sur le commerce,* and founding member of the Bordeaux Academy—may have been local and therefore based on private encounters that because of their nature do not leave much written trace; his friendship with François Risteau appears to have been of this nature as well. But the pattern of his retained correspondence, for much of it is known to be lost, is surely significant. Since Montesquieu saved only certain pieces of his outgoing correspondence by having his amanuensis make a copy or an extract before it was sent, this act of triage speaks to the sense Montesquieu had of the relative importance of his correspondents.[40]

This pattern of social exclusivity extends more verifiably to Montesquieu's activities at the Bordeaux Academy, among the first and most prestigious of France's provincial academies in the century of Enlightenment. The Academy was established by royal patent in 1712, and Montesquieu was elected a member in 1716, giving him the opportunity to present several papers; already by the year 1718, he had been appointed director, ahead of more senior members. Though elected a member of the Académie Française in 1728 and to the Royal Society of London in 1729, Montesquieu continued active participation in the Bordeaux Academy well into the 1750s. For many, membership in an academy—whether provincial, national, or cosmopolitan—conferred social status and intellectual legitimacy, but Montesquieu had need of neither. That he chose to continue his involvement in the Bordeaux Academy, when membership in more prestigious and cosmopolitan academies might have pulled him away permanently from this body, indicates the depth of Montesquieu's regional identification as well as the importance he attributed to this particular institution and its purposes. Two aspects of the provincial academies signaled by their historian, Daniel Roche, help to explain Montesquieu's involvement. First, as Roche demonstrates, while these institutions often had an intellectually progressive, reformist agenda, royal sponsorship and the complexities of local politics meant that they had a necessarily ambiguous relationship to the state. Second, while Roche shows how the provincial academies often replicated the social hierarchies of their host cities, his principal emphasis lies with their democratic character as institutions that deny social divisions and "proclaim a *huis clos* (private domain) equality."[41]

Montesquieu's attachment to the Academy can be seen partly as a variation on the *parlementaire* spirit that lingered in the *président à mortier* well after he sold his office in 1726. Protracted conflicts between the crown's intendant at Guyenne, Claude Boucher, and the Academy, whose membership consisted largely of counselors to the Bordeaux *parlement,* illustrate this dynamic. Montesquieu was only too willing to participate in this tit for tat, having found a nemesis in Boucher since their 1725 dispute over vine plantings. Over the course of Boucher's twenty-three years of service as intendant (1720–1743), the Academy, so normally astute in seeking out patronage, never offered him membership of any sort. His successor, who was more complacent toward municipal authorities, was offered a place almost immediately. In a *parlement* city such as Bordeaux, although academies served primarily as local cultural institutions, they also provided an arena for displaced or extended conflict between the monarchy and the intermediary bodies Montesquieu so cherished.

Although the overwhelming majority of provincial academies studied by Daniel Roche "proclaimed a private domain of equality" in their midst in order to serve their intellectual and reformist goals, the Bordeaux Academy followed a more inegalitarian path. Membership in the provincial academies fell into three categories: associate members, full members, and honorary members. The latter category can be left out of consideration for our purposes since it largely concerns seeking patronage and intellectual luster *extra muros.* "Ordinary" members were full members who usually paid dues and participated in the governance of the academy; associated members presented their findings to the academy and were decidedly of an inferior rank. When full members were concerned about the intellectual qualifications or social status of a postulant, he was relegated to associate membership. An analysis of the data on the membership status of nobles and commoners (*roturiers*) of thirty-three provincial academies evinces a clear pattern: as the total proportion of members from the third estate in both categories (associate and full) increases, the percentage of this group who accede to full membership also grows. The academy of Montpellier had 83 percent total *roturiers,* and 75 percent of its full members were *roturiers* as well. In Arles, the proportions were equally matched at 20 percent each; the port town of La Rochelle was progressive, with an overrepresentation of *roturier* full members relative to total *roturier* members: 67 and 61 percent, respectively. A linear regression on Roche's figures posits the following causal relation: as the total proportion of *roturiers* in all membership classes grows relative to nobles, we would expect to find more *roturiers* in a position of full membership. And this is what we find: for every 10 percent gain in the former, we can expect a gain of 9.8 percent in the latter (see Figure 2.2).[42]

The clear outlier of this group is Bordeaux: where this regression would predict that Bordeaux, with 61 percent total *roturier* membership, would have 54 percent *roturiers* among its full members, it has only 25 percent—a difference of 29 percent. A possible explanation for this noble domination is the fact that Bordeaux was the seat of a provincial *parlement;* if members of these *parlements* viewed the academies as an extension of their oppositional role within the monarchy, it is natural to expect them to guard jealously their power and privileges within this

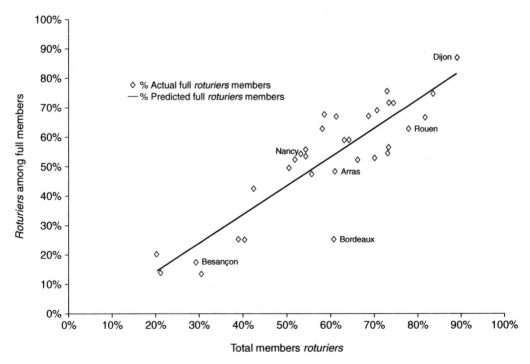

Figure 2.2 Two-tailed regression: total commoner *(roturier)* members against full members. (Figures from Daniel Roche, *Le Siècle des lumières en province.*)

domain. Indeed, Roche speaks of a "parliamentary type" of academy more thoroughly dominated by nobles, and we find some evidence for this in our regression; in six of eight academies established in *parlement* cities, *roturiers* were slightly underrepresented, their ranks being between 6 and 11 percentage points below what we might expect. Bordeaux is by far the most egregious case of *roturier* underrepresentation, at over three standard deviations from the mean, and hence begs further explanation.[43]

Montesquieu played an active role in the Bordeaux Academy for many years. Because of his status as a local noble, his fame as an internationally celebrated man of letters, and his assiduity in finding protectors at court for the Academy, he also played a dominant role, serving as director a total of four times, a distinction shared with him by only one other member over eighty years. He was not shy about exercising his outsized influence, as when he intervened in the process of the election of members, seeking to shape the intellectual and social complexion of the Academy. Despite frequent and sometimes unpleasant conflicts between associate and full members over questions of precedence—in which Montesquieu sometimes ruled against his badly behaved fellow nobles—the Academy maintained its policy of segregating members of the third estate as associates.[44] Montesquieu actively encouraged this policy, or at the very least he countenanced it for a long time, since the slightest reservation on his part would have caused the Academy to change course.

One need not seek too far in Montesquieu's writing to discover the reasons. In one of the few criticisms leveled against England in his famous chapter on the English constitution, he claimed that extremely free states "betray the truth because of their very freedom"; in politicized, democratic societies, "everybody becomes the slave of the prejudices of his faction," making impartial knowledge impossible. More significant are his underlying ideas about the role of hierarchy in a monarchical society, because—after all—French provincial academies did not threaten to erupt into the daily brawl of the English press or the parliamentary proceedings it covered. In many respects, the policy of the Bordeaux Academy fit perfectly the model set out in the *Esprit des lois*. Nobles and members of the third estate rubbed shoulders within an institution that, while not a "private domain of equality," was unquestionably part of new eighteenth-century forms of sociability. Montesquieu clearly be-lieved that the exchange of ideas that took place in the Academy could advance useful knowledge, including the arts and sciences associated with commerce. In this sense, the third estate received a double legiti-mation: the intellectual aims to which their economic activities gave rise received the imprimatur of the Academy, and they were admitted to its ranks as necessary adjuncts in the process of discovery. At the same time, of course, the Academy of Bordeaux obstinately maintained a structure that would not threaten social hierarchy within or beyond its walls.

This politics of fusion, as practiced by the Bordeaux Academy, should be seen as the corollary to Montesquieu's stricture against a commercial nobility. In the context of a society and government dominated by noble elites—since he spoke in the *Esprit des lois* about the whole of France, not about particular regions—Montesquieu argued that the nobility should be banned from commerce so as to preserve the social, eco-nomic, and political balance essential to moderate government. Both commerce and its practitioners needed to be protected from the nobles who exercised such great influence on the nation as a whole. Bordeaux presented quite the opposite case. As a port city with a thriving com-merce, the growing wealth and status of its economic elites threatened to overwhelm the power of the nobles, who drew their wealth and privilege largely from other sources. The very proximity of Bordeaux's haute bourgeoisie to the nobility, into which they often assimilated through the purchase of offices, marriage, or the drawn-out process of social pro-motion known as "living nobly," would serve as an argument for the pres-ervation of artificial distinctions such as were consciously maintained in the Bordeaux Academy. Returning for a moment to Edward Whiting Fox's terminology, if Montesquieu felt it necessary to protect "oceanic" France from the incursions of its "agricultural" elites, a comprehensive politics of fusion made it equally necessary to protect agricultural France from the visibly rising tide of the ocean.[45]

Others of Montesquieu's contemporaries who wrote on the science of commerce—notably, his Bordelais compatriot Jean François Melon and the Abbé de Saint-Pierre, who hailed from Caen—had one foot in "oce-anic" France and the other in its "agricultural" capital, Paris. Perhaps this is why all three authors were precocious in setting France's economic problems in terms of the relationship between commerce and conquest. Montesquieu went the furthest of these thinkers in working through the implications, for France, of the clash of these two systems. The details of his biography give reason to believe, beyond the formidable powers of his intellect, that he was uniquely placed to effect this project of synthesis between old and new.[46]

CHAPTER 3

Philosophical History

ALTHOUGH ONE ANONYMOUS AUTHOR could write in 1759 that "we are no less indebted to Montesquieu for the science of commerce than we are for philosophy and literature," it is helpful to recall that the author of the *Esprit des lois* never described his own economic writings as a "science of commerce." In an era before the consolidation of the social sciences into academic disciplines, and when the meaning of the term "political economy" most familiar to us was only one of many possible appellations for economic science, it is unsurprising to find that many authors self-consciously drew on Montesquieu's methods without consistently attaching the term "science of commerce" to their efforts. Authors working in a tradition they traced to Montesquieu frequently styled their writings as histories of commerce, a genre that became "philosophical" *(philosophique)* during the eighteenth century and came to occupy a central role in the way Europeans explained material and political transformations in their era; Raynal's ten-volume best seller on the subject, the *Histoire philosophique et politique des établissements & du commerce des Européens dans les deux Indes,* was no novelty when it began publication in 1771 but rather merely a popular example of a well-known genre of economic writing.[1]

The term *philosophique* encompassed a set of intellectual dispositions and political attitudes that informed how the history of commerce came to be written in the century of Enlightenment. Philosophical history took a developmental point of view on human civilization, and although attitudes varied about the desirability of Europe's progress toward commercial civilization, authors writing in this mode inevitably sought out the intimate connections among material, political, cultural, and moral aspects of collective life. This approach gave historians, reform economists, and diplomats who examined the workings of the French economy from different points of view and in varying degrees of abstraction a common language in which to argue about commercial policy, from its broadest implications down to highly detailed prescriptions. In its methods, philosophical history often resembled another holistic and developmental science of the eighteenth century, natural history, and indeed these sciences were linked in another way through their common concern with the increase of colonial wealth. The meanings of philosophical history are by no means exhausted by contemporary references to Montesquieu, but there was no more central figure for those who wished to make the history of commerce *philosophique*.

The science of commerce that contemporaries glimpsed in Montesquieu's work was composed of two elements: a political sociology of commerce, laid out in book 20 of the *Esprit des lois;* and a history of commerce, which is narrated systematically in book 21. Readers of the *Wealth of Nations* will be familiar with this division of material, in which the synchronic elements precede the diachronic: in books 1 and 2, Adam Smith explains the principle of the division of labor and the model of value, distribution, and growth that follows from it; in book 3, he moves on to give the history of "the different Progress of Opulence in different Nations," which narrates the decline of feudal social relations and the concomitant rise of commercial society in Europe. Although the historical account in book 3 is frequently ignored by historians and economists who are interested mainly in Smith's contributions to classical political economy and the abstract models taken to be the work's crowning achievements, the analytical and historical sections of the *Wealth of*

Nations were mutually supporting components of an argument against Europe's "mercantile system." Sundering these elements takes Adam Smith out of his eighteenth-century context, where epistemological and polemical considerations would have fairly dictated the presence of both argumentative strategies within such an ambitious polemic. Nevertheless, there is a long tradition of suppressing or ignoring the historical elements of the *Wealth of Nations* at the expense of the simple, elegant description of the market and its self-correcting tendencies offered in the first two books. No matter how subtle, thorough, and repeated their efforts, scholars will probably never reverse this situation entirely.[2]

If the synchronic elements of Smith's analysis came eventually to stand for the whole of his economic thought, Montesquieu's immediate legacy presents the opposite case. The synchronic elements of Montesquieu's analysis—those that facilitated transhistorical comparison between states and made him the father of sociology in the eyes of twentieth-century interpreters such as Raymond Aron—were for his eighteenth-century readers almost entirely subsumed into the diachronic, historical element. This was largely Montesquieu's doing. Even within the *Esprit des lois*—not to speak of other parts of Montesquieu's oeuvre—these elements are not always clearly separated, and there are repeated instances where synchronic sociological comparisons between ancient and modern polities alternate, almost imperceptibly, with diachronic narratives spelling out the effects of the *progrès du commerce*.[3] Eighteenth-century readers took this method of exposition not as a sloppy form of social science but as a form of history rendered more rigorous and philosophical by the use of categories such as *moeurs,* regime type, and the constitution. The history of commerce written in Montesquieu's name was not fundamentally different from the science of commerce, but it did lend itself at times to a sweeping, metahistorical view of things distant from technical discussions of trade, production, or resource allocation. Royal administrators and French diplomats working in foreign ports often combined these very abstract and concrete modes of analysis, a synthesis that helped to shape the formulation of policy in the French commercial empire.

The political meaning of philosophical history is best understood through the criticisms made by eighteenth-century historians of their merely erudite predecessors. "If Cleopatra's nose had been shorter," wrote the seventeenth-century moralist Blaise Pascal, "the entire face of the planet would be different." There were, of course, religious alternatives to this sense of radical historical contingency, for instance in Jacques-Bénigne Bossuet's *Politique tirée des propres paroles de l'écriture sainte* (1709), but Enlightenment thinkers secularized this theological interpretation of historical causation, as when Montesquieu wrote in the *Considérations sur les Romains* that "the world is not ruled by chance, there are general causes, whether moral or physical." If Bossuet's theodicy was one prop of religion undercut by philosophical history, erudition was another. Voltaire depicted ecclesiastical historians, who were the principal bearers of this tradition, as religious obscurantists throwing sand in their readers' eyes, in the form of meaningless facts and arcane bits of narrative lacking any larger pattern. By contrast, the sort of philosophical history that Voltaire called for in the *Essai sur les moeurs* (1741) and the *Nouvelles considérations sur l'histoire* (1744) recuperated history writing by basing it on the study of underlying social structures—here *moeurs* served as Voltaire's catch-all category. In addition to its antireligious (or at least anticlerical) thrust, philosophical history had another characteristically enlightened political overtone: by insisting that deeper, more constant social forces than the passion aroused in Marc Anthony by Cleopatra's nose determined the fate of nations, philosophical history made it possible to appreciate the contribution of the humble classes and their activities to historical progress. David Hume argued that history could be understood scientifically only by setting aside the inherently unpredictable actions of a few great men and looking instead at large groups where the effects of the "universal passions" operating in all individuals manifested themselves clearly and regularly: a paradigmatic case of this, naturally, was commerce.[4]

The opposition between erudite and philosophical history should not be taken to mean that there was a consensus among Enlightenment-era historians as to what philosophical history was precisely. "In reality," writes John Pocock, "the term 'philosophy' was used in a number of ways, not all of which entailed coherent systems of thinking." Nevertheless, the interposition of philosophy into history accomplished two related aims: "'philosophy' denot[ed] both the condition at which history was arriving

and the state of mind in which it should be written and understood." With
the addition of "philosophy," history could be refashioned as a powerful
weapon for Enlightenment thinkers against the church and the barbaric
"feudal" social practices with which it was associated. In this reading,
philosophy and reason became identified with the progress of material and
intellectual civilization, but there were alternative senses of *philosophique*
that also entered into the history of commerce.[5]

In the *Encyclopédie* article entitled "ART," Diderot explained the
aims and methods of a philosophical approach to history, in this case the
history of technology. In keeping with his commitment to valorizing
practical knowledge as a means of social reform, Diderot emphasized
that neither the speculative sciences nor the applied arts could advance
far without the other. This caveat notwithstanding, the editors' preface
to the *Encyclopédie* posited an ascending hierarchy of mental faculties:
memory, imagination, and reason. Since Diderot associated technique
(i.e., "art") with the necessary but inferior faculty of memory, it had to be
put in some relation with reason or philosophy. Diderot wondered how it
would be possible to write the history of trades whose evolution was lost
to posterity: "in these cases recourse must be made to *philosophical* sup-
positions, departing from a probable hypothesis, from some original,
chance event and progress from there to the point where the art has been
perfected." In supplying the missing elements of the historical record,
this method actually improved upon the strictly chronological accounts
found in erudite history:[6]

> In going about things in this way, the progress of a trade [Art] is ex-
> posed in a clearer and more instructive manner than by its veritable
> history, even where it is known. The obstacles that had to be sur-
> mounted to perfect this technique [Art] would be presented in an
> entirely natural fashion, and the synthetic explanation of a trade's
> successive techniques would facilitate the understanding of the
> most ordinary minds, and put tradesmen [Artistes] on the road that
> they should follow to perfection.

The synthetic method had an explicitly didactic—that is to say,
philosophical—purpose: like all historical writing, it was to be descriptive

but with a clarity and order that facilitated understanding and, hence, progress.[7]

In the context of the history of commerce, a philosophical, synthetic method meant less the sort of speculative history condoned by Diderot (and practiced by writers such as Rousseau) than systematic comparisons between Europe's major maritime powers. The philosophical element in Montesquieu's history was twofold. First, philosophical meant not seeing the world as abandoned to chaos or divine providence. Second, Montesquieu's philosophical history was "synthetic" in the sense described by Diderot in that Montesquieu fit his explanations into a clear schema that related events to the relationship between the "nature" and "principle" of a set of well-defined regime types; this approach provided insights into the exact role commerce could be expected to play in different regimes.[8]

The comparative method was, of course, indebted to the political typologies used by Plato, Aristotle, and Polybius, but to the influence of ancient political thinkers must be added natural history. The relationship here is both methodological and political. On the level of sources, we find that Montesquieu's history of commerce is based on ample citations of Pliny's *Natural History*, Strabo's *Geography*, and modern travel narratives—all staples of eighteenth-century natural history. Beyond an overlapping set of sources, most striking is a similarity in method, which is deeper than a discussion of the determinative effects of climate on manners, state forms, or—in the case of natural history—animal morphology. Montesquieu believed in the intimate relationship between natural history and civil history posited by the naturalist and director of the Royal Garden (Jardin du Roi) Georges Leclerc Buffon in his *Époques de la nature*. As Montesquieu told the Bordeaux Academy, "all sciences are related [*a du rapport*] to one another." Both sorts of history attempt to think in holistic terms about the interplay among men, animals, plants, and their surrounding environments; the polity, with its diverse economic and social relationships, is the environment of concern to philosophical historians, whereas natural historians directed their attention to what we would now term an ecosystem. Environments impose physical and moral constraints but are themselves gradually altered by the activity of the beings that inhabit them, which is why both philosophical and natural history are evolutionary sciences that emphasize time-path dependence and reflexive, dialectical patterns of causation. There are numerous accounts of the relationship between the natural and social sciences and in particular the manner in which each borrowed methods from the other. Particularly in the case of economics, however, we find the exchange limited to the borrowing of mere analogies (and authority) from the natural sciences. In the case of natural history and the comparative study of commerce, these inquiries were believed to complement each other.[9]

The writing of Jean-Baptiste Thibaud de Chanvalon demonstrates the political and epistemological ties between natural and philosophical history. Chanvalon was a member of the Academy of Arts and Sciences at Bordeaux who served as director, like his co-member Montesquieu. Beyond the provincial confines of the Bordeaux Academy, Chanvalon was correspondent to the naturalist and geometer René Antoine Ferchault de Réaumur at the Royal Academy in Paris. Chanvalon wrote his *Voyage à la Martinique* after a prolonged stint on that island in 1751–1756, and while in country, he was elected to Martinique's Conseil Supérieur (a body of local notables that consulted with the royal intendants and governors); the *Voyage* contains the musings not of a leisured dilettante but of a state functionary. At the end of his stay, many of Chanvalon's research notes were destroyed in a strong hurricane, but his work was nevertheless read to the Royal Academy and published in 1763, with a long dedication to the Duc de Choiseul, then Minister of War and the Navy. At that juncture, Choiseul was rethinking France's colonial strategy in the wake of the Treaty of Paris and the loss of Canada, and his plans included establishing a colony in Guyana as a continental support for France's sugar colonies in the Antilles. Chanvalon's study apparently contained impressive doses of scientific cachet and strategic economic thinking, and Choiseul awarded him the post of governor of the newly founded colony of Guyana. A series of meteorological and logistical disasters followed: 4,500 of 9,000 white immigrants perished between 1763 and 1765. Chanvalon served as scapegoat for the tragedy; he was briefly imprisoned and fined, and his property was sequestered until Louis XVI pardoned him upon ascending to the crown.[10]

Chanvalon could not have predicted the disasters that followed the ostensible success of his *Voyage à la Martinique,* in which he provided a scientific platform for economic improvements in one of France's premier sugar islands. The proper method to follow, according to Chanvalon, was to study the interrelated history of laws and climate: "the history of the laws of a country is related to the history of its inhabitants and this is almost always related to the history of the soil and climate." Therefore, Chanvalon proposed to "undertake the civil and natural history of Martinique at the same time," adding that "[the] forces and . . . the greatness of the European powers" were principally supported by flourishing agriculture in the sugar colonies. This was an environmental matter, related to the "soil and climate" of these islands but also equally to laws that could guarantee the "felicitous government" that was a precondition for prosperity in these places. Chanvalon considered the manner in which climate, laws, and *moeurs* were related to one another, concluding that the natural and civil history of a place were inseparable from one another: "everything being linked, every spring acting together, to consider them all at the same time, and in all of their relations, is to observe nature's progress along every route." The science of relations *(rapports)* was evolutionary as well; laws related to colonial prosperity should be reconsidered as conditions changed: "laws that are good for growing colonies could be harmful for ones that are already formed."[11]

Although both natural and philosophical history were sometimes purely descriptive, they were just as often linked to the economic aims of the state. Chanvalon, a friend of the naturalists Antoine de Jussieu and Réaumur, devoted his *Voyage* to the duc de Choiseul—a fact that serves to underline the linkage between the colonial-mercantile enterprise and natural history networks. While natural historians described the environmental conditions under which certain plant and animal species thrived, they also experimented with acclimatizing economically useful plants—for example, cocoa, silk trees, coffee, sugar, and tobacco—into less-than-ideal European and American climates. Natural historians hoped, moreover, that the introduction of certain plants and techniques of cultivation would improve native climates, which would aid, in turn, the production of useful crops. By contrast, Martinique as Chanvalon found it was a hot, disagreeable, and impenetrable wasteland because impatient Frenchmen from the metropole ("birds of passage") did not stay long enough to domesticate the island's plants, land, and animals; Chanvalon's description of Martinique's climate was a criticism of French government and *moeurs* overseas.

When acclimatization was broached as a part of philosophical history, it cut with a critical edge. Writing in praise of the English constitution, Voltaire asked why such excellent institutions were not imitated all over the world. His reply provides another sense of the relation of natural to philosophical history—and of the spirit of enlightened reform: "Isn't this the same as asking why coconuts grow in the Indies and don't flourish in Rome? You will answer that coconuts haven't always grown in England, that they only started growing there a short time ago; or that drawing on their example, Sweden has over the last few years grown fruits in other provinces such as Bosnia and Serbia. Then try to plant some yourself." Voltaire's belief that acclimatization was not just a scientific but a political project was more than a passing fancy. Later in the century, as Emma Spary has recounted, scientists associated with the Museum of Natural History (formerly the Royal Garden) claimed that their own experience with plant acclimatization and climate science gave them special insight into acclimatizing the tree of liberty to French soil during the Revolution. How did eighteenth-century writers conceive of the problem of acclimatizing commerce to French soil?[12]

The Chevalier d'Arcq: A Reactionary *Esprit*

In many respects, Philippe-Auguste de Sainte-Foix, the Chevalier d'Arcq, was a perfect example of the downwardly mobile ancient military nobility discussed by Montesquieu in the *Esprit des lois*. D'Arcq might be expected to hold a less sanguine view of the decline of the military nobility than a fellow nobleman who could count his many assets in Bordeaux and its environs. D'Arcq was the natural son of Louis XIV's recognized bastard, the Comte de Toulouse, and had therefore to fight for the recognition of his title. As a member of the military nobility, he enjoyed a brilliant fighting career, but like so many members of his class, he spent himself into oblivion. After giving up his military commission in 1748, he was given a handsome if not luxurious pension of 8,250 l.t. a year by the Duchesse d'Orléans, which he eventually mortgaged and lost. By 1755, he was utterly broke and charged with over 100,000 in debts. He was thus forced to turn to letters, a profession that did not entail the same degree of ostentatious spending as a military career or a life at court. D'Arcq succeeded, but as the *Correspondance littéraire* reported rather unkindly, "M. le chevalier is today at the forefront of tireless writers. . . . [His] works lack intelligence and perspective: his style is lumbering and cold." This critic conjectured with the same lack of charity that "some time ago," d'Arcq, having started off writing novels, "for fear of running out of material . . . has seized upon the history of the world."[13]

Present-day assessments have softened considerably, and questions of intellectual merit aside, it is clear that d'Arcq had a talent for searching out career-enhancing controversy. Before beginning his *Histoire du Commerce* (1758), d'Arcq wrote *La Noblesse Militaire* (1756) in reply to the abbé Coyer's celebrated *Noblesse Commerçante* of the same year, a work that urged the French nobility to overcome its indigence by practicing commerce—a pursuit that would enrich the nation as a whole as well. The frontispiece to Coyer's controversial work shows a nobleman about to board a ship laden with goods. In a heap on the pier lies abandoned a suit of armor, a shield, and an unfurled piece of parchment with the words "titles of nobility" printed on it. With a sweeping gesture of the hand, the noble says (in the caption), "What good is this vain pile of useless glory?" This work was well appreciated by merchants from France's third estate, and the Guyenne (Bordeaux region) Chamber of Commerce addressed a congratulatory letter to Coyer; for its part, the Chamber of Commerce of La Rochelle, believing that Coyer would make a good spokesperson, offered him work as a publicist.[14]

Among many angry ripostes to Coyer's work, that of the Chevalier d'Arcq was the most well known and often reprinted. To formulate his reply, which established him among the standard-bearers in the antiluxury camp among the nobility, d'Arcq drew heavily upon Montesquieu's analysis of commerce and the constitution. D'Arcq enumerated three factors that should be taken into account when determining the role of commerce within specific nations and the distribution of this activity among different social groups: "the location of the country that one wants to render commercial and the resources it has for becoming so. The distinctive character of the people that live there and its genius, which always dictates its means of conservation; finally the form of its Government." This answer could have easily been pulled from chapter 20 of Montesquieu's *Esprit des lois,* and indeed it probably was. In this connection,

Grimm concluded that "Coyer does not need to be refuted; M. de Montesquieu has said enough about it."[15]

But d'Arcq clearly did not believe so. He conceived his *Histoire du commerce et de la navigation des peuples anciens et modernes* as a refutation of Coyer and, crucially, an extension of Montesquieu's *Esprit des lois,* which he regarded as "the most precious work on legislation. This great man has done for the science of government what I propose for the science of history." However, if there was one fault in the oeuvre of "M. le Président," it was that Montesquieu did not bother to write the fine-grained sort of history of commerce that d'Arcq modestly proposed. D'Arcq attributed this fault to high-mindedness, an inability to "see beneath himself the horde of lesser minds." With a keener sense of the dullness of these "lesser minds," and with a more jealous regard for his future reputation, d'Arcq speculated that "perhaps [Montesquieu] would have descended into the historical details, in order to spare himself the reproach of obscurity that has been leveled against him, however unjustly."[16]

However, it was not simply in "completing" Montesquieu's work by giving it the historical embellishment it supposedly lacked that d'Arcq followed in the tracks of his fellow nobleman. He had two goals in mind. The first was to fight against what he saw as the prevailing dogmatism *(esprit de système)* of his time: "History seemed to me the only way to acquire the facts necessary to make sure of the reliability of this inquiry," and in this respect, "a history of commerce and of navigation could be regarded as being somewhat useful." Second, and more important, d'Arcq sought to demonstrate the way that the various "systems" of a state functioned as a whole. According to d'Arcq, these systems were six in number: legislative, regulatory *(police générale),* military, political, financial, and commercial. The proper functioning of the commercial system consisted of "a balance of interior and exterior commerce that is correct, reasoned, and consistent with the situation of the country, its extent, the produce of its soil, with the form of its government and the genius (*génie*) of the nation and relative to other powers." The goal of the legislator and the prince was to moderate the possible defects in each system with an eye toward the better functioning of the whole. For, as d'Arcq concluded, "These . . . systems have between them a relation, a liaison so intimate that the defaults of one can hardly fail to influence the others." The connection with Montesquieu's general spirit *(esprit général)* is immediately evident. "[M]any things govern men," Montesquieu wrote: "climate, religion, laws, maxims of government, the example of things past, *moeurs,* manners, from them comes the resulting general spirit."[17]

However, it is fair to wonder why, if d'Arcq's six systems were conceived as such an intimately related totality, he specifically wrote a history of *commerce.* His decision was attributable, perhaps, to questions of intellectual fashion—"the importance attached to this matter these days." But like so many other authors who wrote about the history of European commerce, the Chevalier took the discovery of the Indies as the central "revolution" of modern times.[18] As he recounts, the discovery of the new world "opened new branches of commerce. Competition and industry were reanimated by commerce. Almost all peoples who at the time had a navy thought only of establishing trading posts and colonies [in the new world]." Contemplating the rise of colonial establishments, d'Arcq lamented that "commerce has become too essential for us, it has an overly intimate relation with every function of government. . . . [T]he spirit of commerce has become the universal spirit among the most powerful people in Europe." Like Montesquieu and Melon, d'Arcq invokes the distinction between regimes of "conservation versus conquest" to explain why a commercial vocation would conflict with the principles of monarchical states, which are bellicose by nature.[19]

Given the centrality of commerce in modern states, it is instructive to notice how d'Arcq handles the ancient epoch in the first two volumes (the only two that were to appear) of the *Histoire du commerce.* D'Arcq's approach differs from that of Pierre-Daniel Huet insofar as his treatment of bygone empires is more transparently present-minded or philosophical than that found in Huet's erudite volume. Thus, the seaborne commercial empires of all the great modern European nations—England, France, Spain, and Holland—variously take the form of ancient Egypt, Persia, Carthage, Phoenicia, Athens, and Sparta. As one might expect, in view of the prevalence of this comparison, England was cast in the role of Carthage. In any case, this reference to ancient republics and commerce was not a purely literary turn. In private correspondence, the Marquis de Mirabeau's brother Jean-Antoine Joseph, who was then working as governor of Guadeloupe, prefaced his own analysis of the ills of France's sugar islands with a discussion of ancient Roman colonies. Similar examples abound in the writings of French diplomats and administrators.[20]

What is more surprising is that France often filled the role of ancient Egypt in this narrative. Voltaire paid extraordinary attention to the Egyptians in his *Essai sur les moeurs,* but it is perhaps more significant that among the topics considered for academy prizes from 1716 to 1786, the prizes offered in the subjects of the history, politics, and commerce of Egypt outweighed those prizes treating similar topics in the British context.[21] Here, as in so much else, d'Arcq had a nose for which intellectual fashions could be peddled successfully at the retail level. Intellectually, d'Arcq was more typical than exceptional, which is why he retains our attention. Whether through conviction or opportunism, the fact that he hitched his literary wagon to Montesquieu is also telling. Moreover, d'Arcq's criticism of Egypt's "commercial policy," which came increasingly to value foreign trade, and the implicit criticisms of France this analysis advances provide a compact summary of d'Arcq's overall thesis and methods.

According to d'Arcq, "the Egyptians kept themselves flourishing for almost eleven centuries." The basis of their wealth and power was a set of laws and institutions that were "the most appropriate to the character of the nation, to the nature of its soil, to its location." Included among these Egyptian institutions, "regulations and particular cares" was an extensive system of canals that was the object of ongoing ministerial concern in the eighteenth century and also the subject of a much-discussed memoir by the abbé de Saint-Pierre. Once again drawing on Montesquieu, d'Arcq contrasts the habits and institutions of the Egyptians with those of the Phoenicians, whose "situation, entirely different"— here d'Arcq is doubtlessly referring to the Dutch—"must in consequence compel the Phoenicians to follow an entirely different path and force them to adopt quite different principles of government."[22]

If d'Arcq's method was modeled closely after Montesquieu's, it also partook of the same slippage, found in the latter's work, between purely descriptive and normative analyses. D'Arcq attempted therefore to ascertain whether the "political conduct" of various nations "respond[s] to the signs of nature's will." D'Arcq's analysis of the proper and lasting basis of state power serves as a case in point. Small size and lack of natural endowments doubtlessly necessitated an emphasis on trade for the Phoenicians and the Dutch. Indeed, as long as it lasted, Dutch or Phoenician trade hegemony also earned them an inordinate share of political influence. But as the Chevalier illustrates in the case of the Phoenicians, the Egyptians were ultimately capable of keeping a solid grasp on power because they possessed a more "natural" basis for it. Moreover, as eighteenth-century observers never tired of pointing out in relation to the Dutch, not even the best government in the world could "prevent the ruin, once neighboring states seized upon the same means that helped establish this type of power . . . means that are now at the disposition of almost all peoples."[23]

Beyond the fact that any nation could learn—as France had under Colbert's stewardship—to compete in the commercial sphere lay the issue of what d'Arcq regarded as the inherent vices of commercial society. In fact, d'Arcq seems to question whether commercial peoples constituted societies in any real sense of the term: "A commercial nation *is nothing but a meeting point* where foreigners and citizens alike meet coming and going, and which is no longer [their] fatherland." It is for this reason, by d'Arcq's account, that the Phoenicians allowed themselves to be conquered by the Persians; since they were concerned merely with wealth, they were just as content to continue as private citizens under Persian domination, paying enough tribute to remain unmolested in the pursuit of private gain. As one might expect, the Chevalier saw commercial people as lacking in courage and in all of the martial arts necessary to procure the safety and glory of a nation. Looking back at the battle of Salamis in 480 B.C.E., in which the Greeks with their three hundred ships had bested a Persian fleet of twelve hundred, d'Arcq observed that "the Greek vessels were manned by warriors; those of the Persians were manned by nothing but merchants, great navigators in truth, but hardly instructed in the arts of marine warfare." Extrapolating from these events with a sad lack of prescience, given the drubbing France received in the Seven Years' War, d'Arcq continued: "one might contemplate what would be the result of a combat between a French and an

English warship today. . . . [T]he French ship would come out the winner." D'Arcq might have noticed that the Athenians, too, were merchants.[24]

As d'Arcq's discussion of ancient Egypt progressed, it served less as a positive model, displaying the benefits accruing to a warlike society of orders that privileged agriculture and internal trade; increasingly, he warned of the dangers to societies—like eighteenth-century France— that turned to foreign trade, indulging in luxury and ease rather than sacrificing themselves in war and virtue. Under the Ptolemaic kings who succeeded Alexander of Macedonia, Egypt's views turned toward foreign trade, resulting in the paradox that while Egypt "had never flourished so brilliantly," at the same time "had she never been so close to her ruin." D'Arcq continues: "Egypt enriched herself more everyday and sunk further into depravity," degenerating into "luxury and softness." Seeking to drive this lesson home, d'Arcq painted the Ptolemaic kings in hues that would have been immediately recognizable to observers of Louis XV's court: "the kings, sadly nursing their lassitude in the depths of their palaces, left their authority in the hands of their ministers.[25] The Chevalier's account of Rome followed the narrative logic of Montesquieu's *Considérations,* which describes a "grand circle" of rise and decline where military strength and virtue were succeeded by luxury and, ultimately, the dissolution of empire.[26] By inscribing this "grand circle" of historical rise and decline more closely into the history of commerce, the Chevalier pursued two related goals: the first, in carrying out his self-appointed task of crowning Montesquieu's *Esprit des lois* with the work of history he felt it lacked, was to place the thematic emphasis squarely where it belonged. Any history that would pretend, as did d'Arcq's, to elucidate the relations between the six "systems of state" must be principally concerned with the history of commerce. D'Arcq's second goal, of course, was to spell out the deplorable consequences of this transformation for modern-day France, to cite alternatives and adduce cautionary examples.

In reading d'Arcq, it is impossible to lose sight of the fact that his *Histoire du commerce* is written in a frankly reactionary spirit, one that regarded with suspicion all of those developments that tended to undermine the basis of monarchy or the nobility that served as its social and political armature. One senses of d'Arcq that his precarious standing among the nobility only sharpened his consciousness of the basis of noble status. It is perhaps for this reason that d'Arcq insisted even more strongly than Montesquieu on the incompatibility of monarchy with commerce; the Chevalier agreed with Montesquieu that the "natural effect of commerce is to lead to peace" but understood this development in a completely negative way. For d'Arcq, peace led inevitably to the decline of empires rather than to their conservation, a deliberate reversal of Montesquieu's and Melon's views on the opposition between the spirit of conquest and the spirit of conservation. Unlike d'Arcq, Montesquieu gave his readers a sense of the trade-offs that came with the *progrès de commerce;* commerce was the scourge of finer sentiment but also served as a brake upon despotism and engendered other forms of freedom. Commercial and warlike societies were simply incommensurable. Nevertheless, both writers insisted with equal consistency that "commerce stands in relation to the constitution." D'Arcq conceived of the monarchy as an equilibrium of social and political forces that was best maintained by emphasizing three principles of national wealth: arms, agriculture, and population.[27]

Taken together, the triad of forces envisioned by d'Arcq, which explicitly excludes manufacture and trade, has a manifestly neofeudal character about it. Although not entirely surprising in view of the Chevalier's commitments, it is worth remarking that, leaving aside his glorification of conquest, the alternative to commercial society that the Chevalier advocated closely resembled aspects of the Physiocratic program that gathered force in the years subsequent to the publication of d'Arcq's *Histoire*.[28] Like d'Arcq, the Physiocrats believed that as a result of Colbert's efforts at catching up with Holland and England, France had abandoned agriculture to its detriment. The crucial difference between d'Arcq and the Physiocrats was, of course, that while d'Arcq supported agriculture for self-consciously conservative purposes, the Physiocrats envisioned an agricultural capitalism that was only one element of a wide program of modernizing reforms. A similar interest in economic reform was shared by Georges-Marie Butel-Dumont, another self-professed follower of Montesquieu's methods.

The Political Geography of Prosperity

Georges-Marie Butel-Dumont was a member of the circle of economists and administrators around Vincent Gournay, France's intendant
of commerce from 1751 to 1758. In his function as a leader of this circle,
Gournay circulated manuscripts and correspondence, presided over a
salon, and encouraged its members to write original works and make
translations of important foreign publications. The pioneering historian of this group, Simone Meyssonnier, argues that the significance of
Vincent Gournay and the circle of economists he assembled lies in their
articulation of a uniquely French "egalitarian liberalism"—a doctrine that
embraced the socially progressive aspects of laissez-faire economics while
at the same time repudiating free-market fundamentalism. For Meyssonnier, "egalitarian liberalism" is the specific difference of French economic
thought stretching from Pierre le Pesant de Boisguilbert to Turgot. Gournay and his circle worked to paint a detailed economic portrait of France,
one that took into account the condition of France's agriculture, finances,
commerce, and manufactures—and also the particular interrelation of
these sectors. To say that the approach of Gournay and his followers was
gradualist in comparison with the more classically liberal Physiocrats is
accurate enough, but emphasis should be placed less on their tentativeness
in matters of policy—for this was not always the case—than on an intellectual catholicism that led them to investigate a wide range of sectors and
national cases in order to understand France's potential role in a new
world economy.[29]

Butel-Dumont's oeuvre should be understood within this context of
a circle of thinkers devoted to reform economics. He was a Parisian of
bourgeois origin trained in the law who came to write a number of different books, mainly on the history and commerce of English colonies in
the Americas and also similar treatises on Louisiana (1753) and even ancient Rome. Because of his writings on European colonial possessions in
America, Butel-Dumont was deemed sufficiently expert to be appointed
secretary of an international commission established to fix the boundary
between French and British holdings in North America "almost without
asking for it"; later he served as censor royal (1755). Unlike the Chevalier
d'Arcq, who used a career of letters as a sort of holding operation against

his declining social position, Butel-Dumont and other members of the Gournay circle combined the *progrès du commerce* with the progress of careers; among this group, the fluid boundary between reform-minded administrative personnel and the Republic of Letters is much in evidence. Several years after this posting, Butel-Dumont wrote the *Théorie du luxe* (1771), a work in which he attempted to cut short the interminable dialogue of the deaf on luxury between metaphysicians and moralists who "were all characters with no acquaintance with administration, or whose studies had no relation to political economy." For Butel-Dumont, the penetration of luxury into Europe's economy and society was an accomplished fact, the complaints of Rousseauists notwithstanding; the essential point for administrators and economists was to help France profit from these transformations.[30]

Butel-Dumont brought this same practical turn of mind to his earlier works on the history and commerce of the English colonies. Accordingly, the principal consideration that brought him to write his *Histoire et commerce des colonies angloises* (originally published in 1754) was "the taste our Nation has acquired for matters of commerce" as a result of England's extraordinary commercial success. It was the colonies, continued Butel-Dumont, "which . . . make the balance of trade lean in England's favor. Today all eyes in Europe are on them."[31] Given the stakes in the commercial rivalry between England and France, England's colonies—including their population, natural resources, and commerce—seemed a natural focal point for Butel-Dumont and his readers.

Butel-Dumont's vision and method went well beyond comparing the social and natural statistics among the several North American colonies. Rather, as Butel-Dumont remarked, other writers seemed to ignore the deeper causes of England's prosperity: "our writers have really neglected the *science of making laws:* it seemed to me that to furnish some ideas on such a pressing matter, would be an act of good citizenship." Writing in his *Histoire et commerce des Antilles angloises* (1757), a pendant piece that followed up on the success of his original work, Butel-Dumont dilated further on his method: "to these various subjects have been added lengthy details on the principal laws, which generally concern the English colonies in the new world. I have tried to elaborate *the spirit of these laws* and to make known the good and evil effects that they have produced."[32]

Two years earlier, he had written that his project could not have been conceived before Montesquieu's writings, since "before le Président de Montesquieu, we could barely cite anybody among us who had delved into the great art of legislation."[33] In the context of the history of commerce, studying the "great art of legislation" provided insight into how the "economical views" of different states were accomplished through "interior administration."[34]

The English colonies in North America provided ideal material for a history of commerce based upon Montesquieu's principles for a number of reasons. The first was the perceived superiority of the English economy over France's. Moreover, since each colony had a different constitution, it presented an excellent comparative context for an inquiry that would further France's "economic designs"—a sort of laboratory of economic success and failure. In short, the colonies provided a rich well of examples of how, with an overall view to prosperity, fundamental laws should be established in relation to a state's population, climate, and external economic and political relationships. For, as Butel-Dumont observed, "the laws of a state make men what they are, industrious or without skills, entrepreneurial or timid, active or passive." Finally, Butel-Dumont shared in the Anglophilia of the period; particularly in respect to the "science of legislation," he believed that "the English are further advanced than other peoples."[35]

The central message that emerges from Butel-Dumont's comparative treatment of the colonies is that freedom from arbitrary government is the cause of material prosperity. While Butel-Dumont was aware of the enormous wealth generated by tobacco and rice production in Virginia and the Carolinas, it is also true that enlightenment, freedom, and prosperity are more clearly etched in the northerly regions of Butel-Dumont's map. Before 1684, for example, New England enjoyed "a state in some respects like the Dutch Republic was before the Stadhouder became hereditary." The independence of the British colonies in New England afforded them, like the United Provinces to which they were compared, a high degree of prosperity until Charles II and James II brought them to heel under the Restoration; then "their progress slowed" until "The charter that William the Third accorded them, reestablished tranquility among them, reanimated their commerce and restored abundance."[36]

Butel-Dumont clearly disapproved of the effects of arbitrary power and was an avid supporter of local general assemblies, in whatever form they took, because they served as a rampart against absolutist despotism. It is for this reason that Butel-Dumont found fault with the handiwork of "Locke and Shaftbury [*sic*]." Although the former would, of course, go on to write in passionate defense of liberty against arbitrary government in the *Second Treatise,* his constitution for the Carolinas "left very little liberty to the people and put them somewhat at the discretion of the Palatine, who . . . was . . . an absolute monarch." Butel-Dumont contrasted the situation in the Carolinas with that of Connecticut, Rhode Island, and, to a lesser extent, Massachusetts, where the people "disposed of all of the authority" through the activity of their assemblies. While Butel-Dumont was cognizant of the migration of powers from local authorities to crown-appointed governors that had taken place in the latter half of the seventeenth century, he was equally convinced that the role representative bodies continued to play in levying taxes, drafting laws, and meting out justice was fundamental to the prosperity of Boston, Massachusetts, and its neighboring colonies, which he painted in golden hues.[37]

Here the contrast between the colonies of New England and Georgia was instructive. Georgia, by comparison, was a penurious, depopulated outpost that never repaid the investments made into it because in Georgia, "constraint has been substituted for the liberty necessary to the formation of colonies." This constraint, in some sense appropriate to this "small military state," established expressly to encroach upon the French and Spanish empires, was also accompanied by an arbitrary form of government, which left "the life and property of individuals" to the tender mercies of local authorities and therefore discouraged industry. Commenting that Georgia's constitution "does not resemble that of other English colonies at all," Butel-Dumont concluded that "the lack of population in this colony results less from its novelty than from the evil constitution of its government." In addition to the incertitude over property that was anathema to commercial pursuits, Georgia's agriculture and population were stymied by another set of laws: "the Commissioners have added new sources of distaste through the system of land distribution that they follow on the lands of their concession." Namely, only male sons could inherit this quasi-feudal property, which was also subject to mortmain. For all of these reasons, of the five thousand souls that had arrived in Georgia between 1732 and 1741, only one thousand remained—the rest fled to the greener pastures of neighboring colonies.[38]

In treating the shortcomings of Georgia's constitution, Butel-Dumont drew on two familiar aspects of Montesquieu's analysis of wealth and politics: first, the potentially deleterious effects that poorly designed laws—more specifically, an unequal distribution of land exacerbated by inheritance laws—could have on population and the incompatibility of despotism with commerce. It should not be concluded from the contrast between the northern and southern colonies, however, that Butel-Dumont intended to write a covertly republican tract against the economic shortcomings of monarchical government. Butel-Dumont, like Montesquieu, wrote against arbitrary government and despotism, but his principal concern was a correct balance of power between colony and metropole within the context of monarchy. His observation on the shortcomings of Georgia, a "small military state," strengthens this impression. In a discussion of the Navigation Acts, Butel-Dumont described the bond of colony and metropole within the British Empire as "a tree with many branches." In his view, one aim of the Navigation Acts was to effect a just division of the surplus arising from colonial production and trade in order to "to make the sap that is carried too abundantly along some of its branches flow back toward the trunk." This is a formulation, seemingly borrowed from Montesquieu's *Persian Letters,* that would be used often in later debates about France's restrictive trading regime, a system that was partly modeled on the Navigation Acts, with its own colonies. Although Butel-Dumont seems to have approved of the general plan, he also observed that because of the inherent dynamism of colonial commerce—a shifting balance of power and mix of commodities—the Navigation Acts were the subject of frequent tinkering on the part of Parliament. These adjustments often failed, however, in coming too late or in erring on the side of constraint. The example of Britain's sugar colonies, and of protectionist attitudes at home, was a perfect case in point that had redounded to France's benefit: "It is in this way that the limits, by which the navigation act restricted for too long the sugar trade, contributed to the growth of sugar plantations in the French Antilles."[39]

Despite the mitigated success of the Navigation Acts, the *Histoire et commerce des Antilles angloises* found in the institutions of colonial governance an effective mechanism for mediating the interests of colony and metropole with a view toward the good of the empire as a whole. Here, as in the *Esprit des lois,* the importance of representative institutions in ensuring a balance of powers bulked large. Butel-Dumont observed that while William III had curtailed many of the local assemblies' responsibilities, the prerogative of fixing the salary of governors appointed by the crown remained with them, who "demonstrate themselves more or less difficult . . . according to the degree to which the governor shows himself disposed toward ignoring the execution of acts passed in England which harass the colonists or threaten their liberty." Placing a Parliament-appointed official halfway in the pocket of local authorities had the effect of preventing "any number of vexations" for the obvious reason that said governor would learn to serve, and to satisfy the interests of, two masters. This utilitarian consideration, Butel-Dumont argued, was simply the expression of an enduring political tradition that preserved liberty through the action of intermediary bodies.[40]

Such was the "spirit of the laws"—a concern for liberty whose practical consequence was to increase Britain's economic and political power by distributing it among its parts—that animated the British colonial empire. While it seems plain enough that he drew heavily on Montesquieu to analyze Britain's economically decisive "great art of legislation," Butel-Dumont was not solely interested in making a comparative "constitutionalist" analysis of the British colonial empire. Indeed, the reader of either *Histoire* comes away with a very lively and detailed portrait of the natural productions, population, trading patterns, and even wildlife of the English colonies from New Hampshire to the Virgin Islands. On some level, this assortment of facts is characteristic of a typical "political arithmetic" that had found purchase since 1690 at the very latest, with the publication of William Petty's *Discourse on Political Arithmetic.* Grimm, for his part, found this work "very useful indeed for the instructive details it contains, which is what makes these types of books worth the price." Where Butel-Dumont's treatment differed was in presenting all of this material—from the most prosaic trade statistics, meteorological data, and information on fisheries—as a totality capable of shedding light on the guiding question of how "the laws of a state make men what they are." A central aspect of Butel-Dumont's presentation was "the history of English colonies," whose vagaries made this history "striking by virtue of the diverse constitutions instituted in these colonies." For Butel-Dumont, historical narrative and comparative constitutional questions were inseparable; insofar as the former influenced the latter, they both had "a rather direct rapport with commerce, which is my object."[41]

Since Butel-Dumont made such lofty claims for both of his *Histoires*—claims that relate directly to his filiation with Montesquieu—it is fair to ask how squarely he met his object. These works were generally well received, and those who commented on them tended to remark on the breadth and fastidiousness of the research that went into them, especially in the English sources, which had remained hitherto untapped. That said, both works, and especially the first, are highly schematized, following the same format for each colony: its establishment first, then geography, natural productions, constitution, and finally its commerce. Moreover, many of the links among these areas of inquiry are left implicit rather than explored in the relentlessly experimental manner of the *Esprit des lois*. In addition to the relationships explored above, Butel-Dumont makes some prolonged observations on the link between religious (in)tolerance and prosperity, and he obviously had a very keen sense of the politics of intracolonial trade—describing at length the operation of natural versus purely historical and political factors in determining a colony's production and trade relations. How, he asked, beyond purely natural factors, which do not seem terribly decisive, did the Carolinas end up producing rice whereas Virginia became the tobacco colony par excellence? Insofar as these relationships helped to define the division of labor between the European states and their colonial satellites, and therefore France's prospects in this sphere, Butel-Dumont delivered as promised. Time-path dependence (as it is now termed) mattered because it would determine France's competitive strategy; Butel-Dumont was not alone in posing these sorts of questions as France lurched toward another conflict with Great Britain.[42]

The writings of d'Arcq and Butel-Dumont provide an example of two economic writers who, by their own admission, were very much influenced by Montesquieu. Both wrote histories of commerce, but as we have seen, the politics that informed their works were diametrically opposed. That an anticommercial nobleman and a reforming economist-administrator both took the *Esprit des lois* as a brief for their respective positions testifies to a great ambivalence over commerce and its consequences that runs through the whole of Montesquieu's work.[43] This fact also helps account for the difficulty historians have experienced in isolating his influence on the science of commerce; at each juncture, it would seem necessary to specify which Montesquieu we are speaking of. But this is true only if the problem is poorly posed. For "internalist" historians of economic thought, this means framing the issue in terms of analytical questions such as monetary theory; for historians of eighteenth-century Europe, Montesquieu's judgments about specific controversies such as luxury or free trade sometimes obscure his real influence. His contribution to the science of commerce was fundamentally methodological, and his approach gained traction because he started from a widely shared set of observations about the transformative role of commerce in European polities.

Postrevolutionary Commerce

Two years after the official start of the conflict between Britain and its thirteen North American colonies, France signed the Treaty of Amity and Commerce (1778) with the newly proclaimed United States. This treaty brought into the open the covert military aid that France had been providing to the colonies in the hopes of punishing Britain for its gains in the Seven Years' War (1756–1763). Moreover, the dispositions of this treaty promised real economic gains for France, by giving it most-favored nation trading status with the United States. In a period of disrupted trade between America and Britain, France hoped to make further inroads into North American markets, with commodities ranging from luxury textiles produced in the metropole to the raw output of France's sugar islands.

Even as this new alliance was being concluded with the nascent United States, doubts arose about the sustainability of the advantages

France had secured in America through the treaty and the sale of arms. Accordingly, the French government worked through its consuls to formulate a commercial strategy for the Americas. Consuls were members of the diplomatic corps who lived in port cities, fulfilling a number of functions for their mother country in support of trade. These could include monitoring the observation of commercial treaties, helping to arrange the provisioning of ships, punishing ill-behaved ships' personnel, smoothing credit arrangements, arbitrating trade disputes, and providing commercial intelligence to the home country. The history of French consuls stretches back to the thirteenth century, but the modern consulate was first established in the Levant in the sixteenth century and was rationalized in 1681 by Colbert. In the context of the American War of Independence, worried consuls hoped to parlay a temporary spike in Franco-American trade into something more permanent "before the peace, that is to say before competition is opened up indiscriminately to every nation, or before preference can be given to England." Indeed, the question of a resurgent American preference for the English loomed large. An anonymous merchant advised his local consul: "Let us not flatter ourselves, they seem attached to us now because they have need of us; [but] they do not like us any more than do the English."[44] (Indeed, these fears were realized: even before the War of Independence ended, Anglo-American trade began to outstrip Franco-American exchanges, and this was only the beginning of a decades-long declension in French trade.)[45]

The author of a 1778 memorandum pushing for the establishment of a network of consuls in the United States framed the problem in terms of knowledge versus ignorance. The French needed a detailed understanding of the United States' economy in the broadest sense, "their population, their productions, their industry [and] all the necessary, useful and agreeable objects of their consumption." Such an undertaking would help them "to understand, appreciate, extend and solidify" their advantages, but France needed more than a source of state-sponsored market research to accomplish this task. Consuls placed in the United States would also "carefully observe its inhabitants; their characters, their desires, their *moeurs* and uncover everything of interest there . . . for the consuls of France and for their policies." Wittingly or not, one candidate for the job of consul invoked the authority of Montesquieu when he described the task of drawing comparisons among the productions, manners, and political systems of the thirteen states as contributing to "the science of every commercial relationship [*rapport*]."[46] Concretely, this call to science meant that France's commercial strategy should be formulated with reference to the broadest sociological context. The Americans were forging novel forms of society and government in the New World that implied specific patterns of consumption and production; what remained to be seen was how the unique relations of French civilization could be linked to these new American forms through trade.

Observing the character, passions, and manners of the Americans as well as the political context in which they operated also meant exploring the ways in which French behavior generated friction in the putatively republican milieu of North America. One writer compared the problem to that faced by social climbers, "whose entry into society depends on their reputation" and whose need for success left little room for error. Because success in any society entailed emulation, French merchants abroad should model their behavior after the "virtuous character of America." But there was ample reason to believe that French merchants were far from virtuous, particularly in their business practices toward Americans. They notoriously exploited their temporary advantage to overcharge for cheaply made commodities and gouged Americans on insurance and freight charges. Concluding pessimistically that "the gratitude that the Americans owe us will not form an indissoluble bond," the author called for heavy surveillance of French merchants. Unless French consuls kept these merchants on a short leash, their abuses might throw the Americans back into the arms of their original oppressors, who were "tyrants, but who share[d] religion, language, habits, *moeurs* and manner of dress with them." Since these sympathies were considered more permanent than the ideology of Franco-American fraternity that prevailed during the war, another consul, perhaps Philippe André Létombe, thought it desirable and necessary to "extinguish liaisons of affinity, blood, religion, laws, *moeurs* and language" with the English that hindered new bonds with France.[47]

Further into the War of American Independence, François de Barbé-Marbois used the same comparative technique in his inquiry into the thirteen American states, this time to find a niche for French luxury goods in the context of a Franco-American alliance of uncertain depth and duration. Barbé-Marbois, best known for arranging the sale of Louisiana to the United States for Napoleon, first arrived in North America in 1779 as the secretary to the French legation in Philadelphia under César Henri, Count de La Luzerne. It is a testament to Barbé-Marbois' political and bureaucratic acumen that he was later appointed intendant of Saint Domingue, France's richest colony. Though Barbé-Marbois' complete works ultimately amounted to some fifteen volumes, two volumes of which included a narrative of his deportation to the French penal colony in Guiana, his most lasting contribution to the world of letters may have been the impetus he gave to Thomas Jefferson's *Notes on the State of Virginia*. Jefferson's work on the *Notes* began as a response to a 1780 questionnaire sent by Barbé-Marbois, in his capacity as secretary, to learned men and dignitaries in each of the thirteen colonies, asking them about geography, climate, fauna, peoples, manufactures, commerce, and finances.[48] Though Barbé-Marbois' biographer speculates that his questionnaire was intended as spadework for a history of the thirteen colonies, his position as secretary to the French legation when he made this request and the use he eventually made of the information suggest that his questionnaire fit into the larger project of calibrating France's commercial strategy in the United States. Like his predecessors in the consular corps, Barbé-Marbois was interested in a broad range of data that could lead to a reliable, scientific analysis of France's commercial relations.

It evidently did not take much penetration to see that the United States, by virtue of its superior natural resources, would eventually dictate the terms of trade and much else to the nations of the Continent; many writers of this period were able to see America's underlying strengths from across the Atlantic, and consuls in the United States also expressed an enthusiasm for the Americans and their political system. As François-Antoine Matignon de Valnais, the French consul in Boston, wrote, "Civilization, liberty, the fertility of their soil, the beauty of their climate seem to call here all the unfortunate peoples of the universe." These views on America and its revolution were reminiscent of the enthusiasm expressed by thinkers such as the Marquis de Condorcet and Jean-Pierre Brissot de Warville. Despite the prospect of American economic and political dominance in the long term, Barbé-Marbois and others saw expanding opportunities in the interim for the trading nations of Europe. Because of its geography and social structure, the United States could not be expected to develop a self-sufficient industrial base for some time. Wide-open spaces, reasoned Valnais, ensured that a class of yeoman farmers would predominate, making industrial labor scarce and expensive: "Even the artisan, who has expatriated himself to come here to exercise his profession, soon abandons it to devote himself entirely to agriculture." Barbé-Marbois explained that in the republican United States, whose residents harbored a particular love of freedom, artisans and laborers were considered little better than domestic servants, a circumstance that augured well for European manufactures.[49]

Though the habit of freedom in the United States created opportunities for Europe as a whole vis-à-vis the United States, Barbé-Marbois was quite naturally most interested in France's place in this new international division of labor. As in Butel-Dumont's work on the American colonies, broad sociological comparisons between the colonies provided the key to his analysis. Like some of the more utopian commentators on the American Revolution in the Republic of Letters, Barbé-Marbois believed that the United States was the newest theater of human progress in its pursuit of equality and political and commercial freedom; nevertheless, he understood that marked differences between regions and states persisted. In particular, social and political inequalities became more pronounced in the South, and it was in these states, which more closely resembled France in their *moeurs,* that merchants could expect to sell French luxury goods. New Englanders guarded their liberty more jealously than did residents of the South; indeed, independent of formal constitutional arrangements, which varied considerably, citizens enjoyed more de facto equality in the egalitarian North than in the neofeudal South. Such cultural differences obviously had political consequences, but the ramifications were also economic: "In the North [there is] more public prosperity, more individual felicity, a pleasant equality [*médiocrité*] and a greater population." This sense of equality stemmed from the ferocity of the Protestant sects that dominated New England. Barbé-Marbois regarded Presbyterians as a group of fanatics, but he appreciated their compensating virtue of detesting "arbitrary government" even more than did their British counterparts, a judgment echoed by his colleague Valnais. This detestation, which reinforced a set of "severe *moeurs,*" contributed, perhaps paradoxically, to a "pleasant equality" in the polity by uniting citizens around "an attitude that proscribes excess." New Englanders worked, saved, and invested to exploit their vast natural resources. Barbé-Marbois concluded that France would have little commerce with these people, except in the unlikely event that corruption and luxury overtook them.[50]

In the South, the situation was considerably different. In addition to finding more planters of French origin (many in South Carolina, a Huguenot asylum after the 1685 revocation of the Edict of Nantes), Barbé-Marbois discerned there a social structure and local character that generally resembled France and its institutions, leading him to conclude that "luxury and inequality of wealth in these states favors our commerce." Since the institution of slavery was symptomatic of larger patterns of inequality and backwardness, France was likely to benefit from its persistence in these states. French traders could compete more easily in an environment where inequality bred lassitude: "Liberty has animated everybody in the North, where everything belongs to those who work. In the South, slavery fetters the activity of the half of mankind." Indeed, in the South, as one consul observed, freemen would not bestir themselves to clear agricultural land but depended instead on slave labor. Even where goodwill and motivation were not lacking, "excessive inequality of fortunes" made it impossible for the poor to launch any sort of enterprise. Instead, surpluses fell into the hands of the rich, whose tastes gravitated toward the luxury goods fashioned for France's own parasitic classes: handsome furniture, porcelain, and fine cloths of every description.[51]

While Barbé-Marbois and Butel-Dumont both examined the thirteen colonies from a comparative point of view, their conclusions differed wildly. Butel-Dumont posed New England as a model to France of the management of a prosperous commercial empire, whereas Barbé-Marbois painted a much starker version of the French monarchy as politically, culturally, and commercially aligned with the despotic slave states of the American South. This difference in outlook can be explained partly by comparing the context of the 1750s with that of the 1770s. With the rise of Turgot to the post of controller general in 1774, and his resignation in disgrace shortly thereafter in 1776, upon the failure of his ambitious program of economic reform, the reformist optimism and intellectual ambition that characterized the Gournay circle in the 1750s was most decidedly dissipated.[52]

Differences aside, what united all of these writers? D'Arcq and Butel-Dumont were at political antipodes, but both insisted on the centrality that foreign trade was assuming in European society and politics; Montesquieu's science of commerce served as a natural methodological basis for their examinations of this problem. The French consular corps in America was an institutional expression of the importance of Atlantic exchanges. Naturally, not everything these consuls wrote was philosophical in the manner of Butel-Dumont or d'Arcq; trade statistics, personnel issues, and legal disputes fill up much of their correspondence and memoirs. But when these servants of the crown addressed problems of competition and geopolitical strategy, their efforts resembled the history and science of commerce so widespread among the *philosophes*. The growth of the European colonies in the Atlantic world and the evolution of their relations with their mother countries became a subject of increasingly heated discussion from the 1760s right into the French Revolution. Before returning to this theme, we now turn to the finances in the French monarchy, a problem that was seen as intimately related to Europe's colonial expansion and the remaking of that continent's domestic political order.

CHAPTER 4

Finances and the Empire of Climate

T HE IMPORTANCE OF ISSUES of taxation and finance in eighteenth-
century France can be conveyed by an image from the Palace of
Versailles. The Hall of Mirrors presents an infinite regress of royal self-
hagiography, representing those deeds that conferred power, glory, and
legitimacy upon the Sun King. Directly opposite the familiar feats of
war, including the invasion of the Netherlands and the conquest of
Franche-Comté, court painter Charles LeBrun depicts Louis XIV's
feats of peace—"encouragements of industry and commerce." Among
these deeds, however, one stands out for the negative manner in which it
is stated: "straighten out the finances" (*L'Ordre rétabli dans les finances*,
1662). That Louis should find it necessary to be depicted as a Hercules
cleaning out the Augean Stables of French finances is one index of the
public unease throughout this period about the system of taxation. The
image was intended to besmirch his predecessors, of course; but given
the fiscal ruin to which Louis XIV's own military ambitions led in the
latter years of his reign, the feats of war and peace on the ceiling of the
Hall of Mirrors create an ironic effect, setting in spatial opposition
the Sun King's contradictory aspirations.

This seventeenth-century image is an appropriate way to introduce
the problem of France's finances in the succeeding century for reasons

that provide insights into the Enlightenment's "philosophical history" of finances. First, no understanding of France's finances could be considered apart from Louis XIV's reign and its aftermath. Louis consolidated the absolutist state and strengthened France's position in the commercial order of Europe, but the underlying weaknesses of this revamped state and its economic apparatus were later exposed during the debt crisis and the fall of John Law and his notorious system in 1721. From this point forward, the relationship of absolute monarchy to modern economic institutions and sound financial management could be regarded only as shaky, if not actively hostile. Second, that matters so picayune as collecting taxes and the borrowing and spending of money worked their way into history painting, the most esteemed genre of academic painting of the period, spoke to the increasing weight of economic problems.[1] During the Age of Enlightenment, history became "philosophical," and the grandest narratives of historical progress were rewritten using commerce as a central analytical category. LeBrun's depiction was thus an early tremor of this later seismic shift in the European historical imagination. Finally, the first two elements combined to give pride of place to the question of finances in many histories that pretended to explain the origin (and ordering) of a new European state system based on the preeminence of trade.

In the domain of finances, France was to lie somewhere between England and Spain, and there was much at stake in just where France stood on a continuum running from free republic to despotism. A central goal of the comparative science of commerce was to determine which virtues—and pathologies—were purely accidental and which were inherent in the regimes or "constitutions" that prevailed in these states. But the problem was not as simple as finding ways that France could better resemble Great Britain. Early French proponents of commerce drew the distinction between territorial empires based upon conquest and commercial empires based upon conservation, ignoring the fact that the heart of Europe's new commercial order lay in international competition and, hence, recurring wars of commerce. That such wars required the massive resources of the fiscal-military state was increasingly obvious; it was equally clear that the state, by its exactions and the dangerous contrivances of finances, often harmed the economic interests it pretended to advance. Some observers suggested that France could defeat England and escape from this impasse by retreating from the seas and returning to a more natural, agricultural economy.

In 1914, Marcel Marion published his *Histoire financière de la France,* an indictment of Old Regime financial mismanagement in five volumes that served to sum up two centuries of almost unrelieved pessimism and disdain. These judgments, which were so widespread that their accuracy is easy to take for granted, have come under criticism during the last twenty-five years; an examination of these findings helps to mark the distance between eighteenth-century perceptions and reality while at the same time throwing into relief the virtues of the approach taken in the eighteenth-century science of commerce, which privileged comparative discussions about the relation between the "constitution" and finances.

A common litany of complaints about eighteenth-century France holds that its subjects were overtaxed while the state was starved of resources due to an irrational and incompetent tax administration. It has now been established that if anything, the French were undertaxed in comparison with England and that the social incidence of taxation did not become less progressive. Indeed, the French state worked hard over the eighteenth century, if not entirely successfully, to eliminate exemptions for its privileged orders. As for administrative incompetence, it appears that while the crown's budgets were not publicized and were often even retrospective affairs, they nevertheless merit a "reasonable confidence." But if overall taxation levels and administrative incompetence are not to blame for the perennial fiscal crises of the eighteenth century, certainly a quasi-feudal patchwork of tax jurisdictions, combined with tax farming, must have resulted in a complicated and therefore inefficient system of tax collection. Once again, new evidence leaves some room for doubt: the "tax efficiency"—a measure of the cost of collecting taxes—was not wildly different in France and England: according to Kathyrn Norberg, collection in France amounted to 7.35 percent of receipts in 1787 and 7.89 percent in 1885. James Riley estimates that in the eighteenth century, French (nonfarmed) taxes cost 13 percent of revenue, whereas in Britain the analogous figure was 10 percent. Riley's figures themselves demonstrate the rationality behind the tax farming system: the most difficult (and hence least efficient) taxes were hired out to others.[2]

If we must disregard the most obvious culprit, royal mismanagement, then such a view only accentuates, a fortiori, the role of expenditures and their inevitable accompaniment, debt. A comparative perspective helps to isolate the problem. By any measure, the outstanding expense of this period, warfare, is mirrored on the balance sheets of each nation. To the extent that they can be measured with any exactitude, expenditures on the War of Austrian Succession and the Seven Years' War were roughly equal for both parties: France spent 1.2 and 1.8 billion l.t. on these conflicts, respectively, while Britain spent 0.8 and 1.7 billion l.t. If the cost of these conflicts in relation to annual government expenditure imparts an accurate sense of the relative financial burdens they imposed, the weight of these conflicts on both sides approaches nearer to equality: the War of Austrian Succession cost both France and Great Britain between five and six years' ordinary government outlay for the period; the Seven Years' War cost France seven years' and Britain between eight and nine years' ordinary government outlay. By every measure, the War of American Independence, in which France was an official participant from 1780 to 1783, was more expensive for Great Britain, costing 1.8 billion l.t. (about seven years' outlay); France spent between 1 and 1.3 billion, or about three years' outlay.[3] Despite these apparent equalities, and the enormous fiscal strains implied by them, Britain managed its finances with considerably more ease, avoiding the constant opprobrium to which France's ministers and financier classes were exposed.

The root of the problem lay in France's inability to support these burdens. Given the fragile but real budgetary equilibrium that France maintained over much of the eighteenth century in its ordinary expenses, extraordinary expenditures (i.e., warfare) meant either new taxes or borrowing—and France had difficulty with both. Of course, borrowing was an expensive proposition for any country, but it was particularly burdensome for France, which consistently paid rates of interest that were about two percent higher than those Britain paid on analogous debt instruments.[4] This fact easily explains the crushing effects that government debt had in France as opposed to Britain, but why did the French pay more than the British?

Most historians agree that the difference has to do with systematic risk—and periodic defaults and partial write-downs of sovereign debt over the course of the eighteenth century attest to the risks lenders faced. According to James Riley, "the crown was too generous in setting the rate of interest on certain government securities (especially life annuities), and the resulting financial pressures made defaults inevitable."[5] These defaults made investors demand, in turn, higher risk premiums. Riley explains this systematic mispricing by cultural factors—financial ministers untrained in probabilities—but some historians throw this conclusion into doubt.[6] In particular, it has been demonstrated that investors did not demand the habitual risk premium for sovereign debt that followed the "Dutch model" (also the English practice) in which loans were floated along with very specific taxes earmarked for their repayment. Buyers of French debt were able to discriminate between comparatively safe and risky debt and demanded a risk premium for the latter, which they received.

What made the overwhelming majority of French debt riskier than British sovereign debt was a series of "constitutional impasses over taxation [that] made partial defaults inevitable." France was the victim of "a political system that completely separated the privilege of spending from the obligation to pay taxes and at the same time left the public enough political power to resist taxation," even though what taxes were approved were collected without excessive expense or chaos. France's monarchy lacked the "legitimacy" that might have "promoted compliance" and a willingness to approve of taxes on the part of taxpayers in the same way that Britain, with its representative institutions, was able to do. The high rate of interest on sovereign debt was an expression of deeper constitutional disorders; these present-day conclusions mesh perfectly with eighteenth-century criticisms of French finances. Issues of taxation were deeply intertwined with many of the causes célèbres of the eighteenth century and helped to play midwife to the rhetoric of liberty and equality that burst forth in the French Revolution. Once again, Tocqueville illuminates the problem: the abuses of French finances were not new; this was, in fact, an old story. What was new were the widespread perceptions of systemic disorder to which these abuses led. As Tocqueville observed in 1856, changes in "government and society" over the previous century had rendered the French "infinitely more sensitive than before" and led even the most conservative classes to demand reform, "without considering that in profoundly changing this part of the government, they were going to bring down all the rest."[7]

Gropingly, economic thinkers and policymakers tried to fit all of the facts that seemed relevant to France's finances into a broad pattern, one that was capable of bringing such seemingly disparate issues as France's aversion to paper money, its systematically higher rates of interest, and finally its motley system of taxation within a unified explanatory scheme. A key to finding this pattern reposed in an analysis of the state finances and commerce at the antipodes of success and failure: on the one hand, Britain, which seemed close to consolidating a universal monarchy of commerce; and on the other, the example of Spain, where the potential deformities of absolutism and despotism created a black legend of their own.

The Black Legend of Spanish Finances

Throughout the eighteenth century, the Spanish monarchy served as a cautionary example for French observers in their attempts to come to terms with the peculiarities of monarchical finances. Criticizing absolutist Spain was an indirect way of evading official censorship in order to communicate to readers the defects of monarchical financial management. After the accession of Louis XIV's grandson Philip V to the Spanish throne in 1700, both regimes were not only monarchical and absolutist but also Bourbon, so this polemical identification became all the more self-evident. Beyond these similarities, which were related to a set of comparable political and social developments (e.g., the consolidation of the absolutist state), the example of Spain, as the ostensible beneficiary of an extended colonial trading empire, also dovetailed with French aspirations and anxieties about France's economic prospects. Spain was frequently depicted as the incarnation of the cursed king Midas, with one observer writing that "Spain, in the middle of its treasures, represents well for us the fate of the king of this fable, who Bacchus favored with the gift of turning everything he touched [to gold]."[8]

Reform movements launched in Spain at mid-century, with the accession of Charles III, provided equally alluring subject matter. When Charles III gave up the crown of the Kingdom of Two Sicilies in 1759 to assume that of Spain, he brought with him leading lights among Naples' reformist *illuministi* and a will to transform the agricultural, commercial, and industrial policies that had led to Spain's seventeenth-century decline. At this point, a system of intendancies resembling France's had been recently installed. This effort had been complemented by the reinvigoration of the council of Castile and the simplification of many of Spain's administrative systems. From this new administrative platform, initiatives that made use of enlightened reform economics were launched to redress gross inequalities in taxation, unproductive patterns of landholding, and an obstructive system of guilds. Trade with the Indies was liberalized with the abolition of the convoy system from Seville. In the narrow but growing sphere of Spanish civil society, patriotic associations were established for the dissemination of economic doctrine and agricultural and manufacturing techniques. Remarking approvingly on these developments, Jean-Baptiste Robinet noted in 1760 that "the science of commerce is not, in Spain, fallow land." For many observers, Spanish reform movements provided a test case for Bourbon reform as a whole.[9]

For these reasons and others, including the overwhelming importance of Spain and its empire as an outlet for French produce, Spain made a compelling object of economic scrutiny. Spain also served as a cautionary example of the risks inherent in colonial expansion. Unreformed monarchies were sorely tested by the unintended consequences of an increasingly globalized economy: "Spain is a proof of the evils that overseas commerce produced," commented one observer, who may well have stood in for tens, if not hundreds, of others who worried about the effects of all of this wealth circulating in an aged body politic.[10] Nowhere was this sclerosis, the perversity of the Midas touch, and its ramifications for France more evident than in Spain's financial system.

The most sustained attempt on the French side to come to terms with the morass of Spanish finances came from François Duverger Véron de Forbonnais, an economist and administrator attached to the circle of Vincent Gournay, who, in addition to several respected treatises, wrote articles on economics for Diderot and d'Alembert's *Encyclopédie*. Forbonnais was born in Le Mans and grew up in an established family of enamelware merchants, serving his apprenticeship with an uncle in Nantes and then deepening his interest in Iberian and more generally international economic questions while working in Spain.[11] There he became acquainted with the works of Bernardo de Ulloa and Gerónimo de Uztariz—eighteenth-century writers who helped provide programs for the reform movements of that century. Forbonnais' contributions to this field are significant because they became the theoretical core of his influential work on the history of French finances. An examination of Spain was therefore the first step in the completion of a broader history and theory of monarchical finances.

Forbonnais' analysis was conventional insofar as he assigned blame to the Spaniards' false view of specie as wealth. Spain was not a naturally poor or corrupt nation, he argued; instead, nature seemed to have favored it with "a great abundance of the richest products . . . vast possessions in the most fertile regions of the new world; inexhaustible gold and silver mines; a powerful navy; an active commerce; good laws; a numerous population; [and] a loyal populace gifted with genius." Such, at any rate, had been the state of Spain until the seventeenth century, when the country fell prey to the illusion of fiscalism. "Finances are justly regarded as the tendons of the state," but, he added, "it is known that tendons are incapable on their own of any movement, that they lose their power, if the substance that nourishes them and vivifies them is exhausted by continual excesses." Moreover, "the disruption of finances decimates agriculture and the arts, while this same ruin, by a vicious circle, precipitates that of finances."[12]

Finally, and most originally, Forbonnais explored the problem of the maldistribution of taxes, which formed the theoretical core of his analysis of France's finances five years later. Spain suffered from an odious system of consumption taxes (the notorious provincial rents) that fell disproportionately on the poor. In violating the all-important principle of distributive justice, these taxes also harmed the industries that functioned as outlets for the nation's labor: "People work either in agriculture, manufactures or in navigation: as long as none of these parts suffers from financial manipulations, taxes will not be too burdensome." Here as elsewhere, Forbonnais was concerned that the production and circulation of wealth be encouraged by a healthy balance of burdens and benefits: "Once a tax is fixed in a reasonable relationship with the means of paying . . . every excess immediately destroys the means of paying the tax, and the mistake is punished by the general decline in every branch of public revenue." The "reasonable relationship" of taxation with work that would ensure economic equilibrium and growth also coincided with norms of distributive justice, but this just equilibrium was generally broken by vices endemic to societies such as Spain and France. In aristocratic countries where commerce was misunderstood and mistrusted, "forced increases in taxes ordinarily fall upon commerce." Commerce is the "least defended part," while in a society of orders, "the rich and powerful, to the contrary, know how to make their cupidity respected under respectable pretexts, and the two parts are rarely counterbalanced." Within the context of reform movements in eighteenth-century Spain, backward finances and the "vicious principles" that underlay them provided a double warning: "every reform is difficult in a large state, because there is no part which is not essentially bound to the others." Related to this difficulty was the intractable problem of the ideological clashes inherent in a large composite state: "there are unfortunately few men among those who call themselves citizens who do not secretly refer to themselves when they proclaim in favor of the general welfare."[13]

Diplomatic assessments echoed Forbonnais' concern with the unequal distribution of wealth in Spain and in particular the social deformities issuing from the hypertrophy of Spain's overseas empire. Writing in 1770, an anonymous French diplomat observed that "The more wealth comes from the new world to Spain, the more it is divided unequally," a process that only exacerbated Spain's natural tendency toward luxury and laziness, the supposed result of its hot climate. This rut was only deepened by workings of a monarchical, despotic state, since "a republican or mixed government would have conducted itself completely otherwise in discovering Peru," distributing the wealth of the Americas more evenly. Instead, "one can see in all of this what the evil effects of despotism can be; when a single man is blinded by his passions in his wrongheaded policies, universal error is brought down upon the entire nation." Among the economic perils that attended American wealth in the hands of Iberian despots, according to this author, were the growth of

ecclesiastical establishments (extra capital was sunk into their endowments); the growth of luxury; the decline of agriculture; and, of course,
imperialist warfare on the Continent—animated by despotic desire for a
universal monarchy. These risks ultimately bankrupted the crown. In
sum, American silver acted as a lens that magnified the faults of despotism because it removed the single effective check on its designs: capital
flight and royal penury.[14]

The relationship between the discovery of the Americas and the constitution of Spain was also the subject of a book-length series of articles
in the *Journal de Commerce* apparently written by Jean-Baptiste Robinet. In a work whose central concerns would be reprised in Raynal's
Histoire philosophique et politique des deux Indes, which began publication ten years later, Robinet applied what he repeatedly described as the
"science of commerce" to the world-historical effects of the discovery and
commercial exploitation of the Americas, "two events which changed the
face of Europe, which are a sort of new creation in the history of the
world." Robinet was typical in viewing Spain in a threefold manner: as a
European nation, as the metropole of an extended territorial and trading
empire, and finally as a vast symbol of the progress of commerce over the
previous three centuries. On this point, Robinet enthused: "I see a part
of the wealth of every nation of Europe in that of Spain." But the varied
significance of Spanish wealth required a supple analysis, one capable of
showing how the "revolution" of the discovery of America reverberated
in different nations: "each nation took part in . . . in accordance with the
situation in which it found itself, in accordance with its character, its industry, the nature and the constitution of its government."[15]

Robinet's analysis of Spanish decline settled on the interrelated effects
of "the constitution of her government" and the "primary cause" of finances. The specter of despotism loomed large in his discussion. "Negli-
gence and infidelity" were the keynote of finances under Philip II and the
costly interlude of the Dutch Revolt. The murderous rioting of unpaid
Spanish troops in Antwerp in November 1576 laid bare the incompetence
and even absurdity of Spain's finances given the vast resources drawn
from Mexico and Peru. Well into the eighteenth century, debts that had
accumulated during this period still hung like a millstone around the
neck of Spanish industries, which faltered under the excessive burden of

taxes levied for debt service. Moreover, taxes were not fixed "except in relation to the needs of finance, and not to the advantage of commerce, agriculture, the arts and the interests of finance *properly understood.*" The ignorance of finances "properly understood" led to an extinction of industry that made American gold and silver mines effectively the property of other European nations, since "industry is incompatible with slavery and flees before the despot."[16] American specie also escaped, flowing to every corner of the European continent from Spain, whose native industry, like rocky, porous soil, could not absorb these riches.

Several years later, Raynal picked up the same theme: "if Spaniards had understood [that] their true interest" reposed in reciprocal trade and industry rather than in fiscalism and colonial domination, they might not have fallen into the "inaction and barbarism" characteristic of despotic societies.[17] Raynal and Robinet suggested that Europeans handled the colonization in the New World according to "the nature and constitution of their government." But they also discerned a pattern of constitutional change. For Raynal, the discovery of the New World accelerated the growth of despotism at home: "The New World was discovered and the passion for conquest engaged every nation. That spirit of aggrandizement was inconsistent with the slowness with which affairs are managed in popular assemblies." Although the discovery of the New World and the growth of the fiscal-military state meant that most European nations were "engaged in enterprises beyond the abilities of the people they have governed," the consequences varied among the nations that undertook these outsized enterprises of colonial domination. A nation with representative institutions, plenty of indigenous commerce, good credit, and modest imperial ambitions would "raise money at an easier rate than an empire, the soil of which is not fertile; which is overloaded with debts; which engages in undertakings beyond its strength; which has deceived its creditors and groans beneath an arbitrary power."[18]

That readers of Raynal were intended to see in Spain a set of dangerous precedents pertaining to France's finances there could be little doubt. Writing in 1775 against Jacques Necker's policies of debt financing, Roche-Antoine Pellissery quoted Raynal, seeing in the latter's observations on Spain "a *tableau vivant* of France's decadence" and inviting his own readers to "give to [them] an application that is relevant to our decadence." Like Spain, France increased its needs for tax receipts by abandoning the "spirit of conservation" and, in consequence, "delivered the state and the citizens to the filthy desires [*désirs empestés*] of the insatiable financier," who destroyed "the equality and good order that constitute good governments." Like so many other observers, Pellissery linked the prosperity of modern nations to their ability to dominate overseas trade but fundamentally doubted the capacity of monarchical nations on this score: "in monarchical states, institutions are generally related to the opinion of ministers; in democratic states, they are dependent on and linked to the constitution of the government: from that, the decadence of Spain under the Philips; from that, the decadence of France."[19]

A potentially awkward aspect of these *tableaux vivants* of monarchical financial decadence emerges at this point. If the nation is an intimately related totality, where diverse factors such as "character, industry and the nature and the constitution of its government" reinforce one another, this view would seem to leave little scope for reform.[20] Locked into a pattern where constitutional form, laws, manners, and institutions all dictated one another, were Europe's monarchies doomed to settle, however slowly, to the bottom of the pecking order in a globalized economy? Eighteenth-century writers saw this conundrum as well and addressed the problem of how to acclimatize commerce into the supposedly hostile climate of monarchy.

The Empire of Climate

In addition to the *Considérations sur les finances d'Espagne,* a second work formed part of Forbonnais' literary debut in 1753, the *Extrait du livre de l'Esprit des lois;* this book consisted of lengthy extracts from Montesquieu's work followed by sometimes highly critical commentary. In this work, Forbonnais bristled at what he viewed as Montesquieu's reflexive Anglophilia, an unshakable preference for England's nominally republican institutions, even where England proved itself more corrupt than France: "The portrait he draws of the two nations in relation to their *moeurs* and to their character, are both of them unsatisfactory. . . . [W]ere the comparison just, I would tremble for my country." Forbonnais took particular exception to the idea that England's constitution made it better suited for establishing prosperous colonies. A deeper source of Forbonnais' quarrel with Montesquieu was that the latter viewed monarchies such as Spain and France as groaning under the "empire of climate," where "everything depends indistinctly on the climate, laws, *moeurs* and habits." In this passage, Forbonnais, like many of his contemporaries, took the notion of the empire of climate in its widest sense as the working of all of those natural and institutional forces that determine the general spirit *(esprit général)* of a nation in a mechanistic fashion. The notion of the empire of climate should be likened to the way the concept of a "constitution" was applied to natural phenomena; in this sense of the term, "constitution" denotes a natural economy or balance of forces that cannot or should not be altered and which operates apart from conscious human intervention. Nevertheless, Forbonnais saw on Montesquieu's part an inconsistent application of the latter's own theories to England. As Forbonnais recognized, Montesquieu did view laws as capable of overcoming the effects and defects of climate, as when he wrote, "Bad legislators are those who have favored the vices of climate and the good ones are those who have opposed them." Somehow, however, only England was given the benefit of the doubt. "For an Englishman," he wrote, "[climate, *moeurs,* and laws] are only partially applicable." France and other monarchies, because they were not viewed as capable of mitigating the empire of climate, suffered by comparison. Within Montesquieu's own oeuvre, this possibility is entirely comprehensible for two reasons. First, he believed that the preponderance of certain forces (such as climate or religion) in the determination of the general spirit changed over time: "to the extent that, in each nation, one of these causes exerts more force, the others cede in their place." Next, he thought that despotic governments were simpler, hence closer to nature, and therefore less resistant to the effects of climate. Clearly, Forbonnais did not believe France to be a despotic nation, while Montesquieu merely exposed the threat of despotism facing France if it did not heed—and improve—its proper constitution.[21]

Although Robinet and Raynal used the empire of climate as a framework for understanding the ills of monarchical financial management in an age of colonial expansion, they also refused to accept the constitution as completely dispositive in matters of wealth and poverty. Despite his periodic railing against the Spanish character, Raynal hoped that "a good form of government may be established, when the true principles on which it is founded shall be once know'n, and the proper means made use of to effect it. The character of the nation is not an invincible obstacle to this change, as it is too generally thought to be." Given Raynal's other pronouncements, how could this be so? In eighteenth-century political thought, laws and *moeurs* stood in an overdetermined relationship: the causal interpenetration between basic social data (*moeurs*) and their institutional expression (laws) leaves a margin of autonomy that is unthinkable if we view the empire of climate in a purely mechanical way. Laws can affect *moeurs* and vice versa, and the canny ruler understands what is in his ameliorative power. Rulers can always try to acclimatize commerce into the hostile climate of a monarchy, in the same way that Voltaire believed it was worthwhile to try to grow coconuts in England; for moderate reformers, this was the very meaning of "philosophy."[22]

For Robinet, the reestablishment of Spanish finances and industry hinged upon the will to reform at the highest levels of the monarchy. Observing that "only revolutions foreign to industry itself are capable of making these sorts of manufactures pass from one nation to another," Robinet made a clear distinction between the "nation"—an interlocking set of relationships, dispositions, and institutions—and its leadership, which was capable, within certain limits, of reordering these fixed relationships. Because "Nations do not reason, [and] they are led or conducted by events that rest in the hands of those that govern them," Spain therefore had to rely on the individual genius of its leaders to coax it out of its economic malaise or to deliver a shock sufficient to lead the economy into a more productive equilibrium.[23]

Montesquieu's famous dictum that "commerce stands in relation [*a du rapport*] with the constitution" did not lay out an unproblematic method for approaching monarchical finances. The polyvalence of the term "constitution" itself was bound to evoke different treatments of this relation, quite independent of shifts in the meaning and usage of the term over the eighteenth century, which also had their effect. On the one hand, the constitution could be taken, as it was in the dictionary of the Académie Française in both 1694 and 1798, in a purely natural or medical sense that is roughly synonymous with the term "animal oeconomy": "Composi-tion. *Form and matter enter into the constitution of a natural body.*" As the century progressed, this naturalistic conception was steadily but not completely overtaken by the alternative notion of the constitution as a written document that formalized political arrangements.[24] The question to be addressed, and which was addressed persistently in relation to France and its principal rival England, was not whether there was a rela-tionship between the state and the economy—this was taken for granted. Instead, it was how the constitution was to be understood as relating these parts. Did "finance properly understood" comprehend a "natural" or "artificial" economy? In the realm of state finances and international commerce, the question was subtle but highly consequential.

Constitution as Nature and Artifice

English finances were an object of perpetual interest for observers across the Channel. In this morality play, republican Britain played virtue op-posite absolutist vice, bringing into stark relief the shortcomings of French institutions. More than any single factor, it was the context of their com-mercial rivalry that caused observers to light upon England, for it was in this sphere that relative strengths and weaknesses were converted into decisive advantages.[25] But if England was able to multiply its advantages due to its formidable fiscal-military apparatus, the improbability of this island nation's story—the very disproportion between its natural means and its present strength—provided lessons, and some hope, for French observers.

In the second half of the eighteenth century, French observers oscil-lated between two views of the relationship of national wealth to fi-nances. One was based in ideas about the connection between govern-mental forms and sound finances, while an alternative view stressed that permanent differences in natural endowments dictated an ultimately greater economic potential for France. Therefore, all of the present dif-ferences between these countries, particularly in respect to overseas commerce, were an effect of the "artificial wealth" that England enjoyed thanks to a ballooning national debt that must eventually deflate or explode.

The history of the development of English finances—in the form that so impressed French observers—was largely the history of the development of "Dutch Finance" in that country, with the accession of William III to the crown in the Glorious Revolution of 1688–1689. The key elements of the Dutch approach in England were the establishment of the Bank of England (1694), the attribution of specific taxes to specific debts, and a "sinking fund" devoted to the amortization of existing loans. These innovations secured the government debt, which had the effect of liberating untold sums for use in commercial ventures and of ensuring low rates of interest. These developments must have seemed the very opposite of France, where complaints were heard routinely of an unmanageable government debt, high rates of interest, and limited capital resources.[26]

However, even as French economists lined up to praise the English system, episodes of war and the inevitable increase in debt left detractors something for which to hope. If England's superior system made it easier to levy taxes, leaving the English people more heavily but less onerously taxed than their French counterparts, the "genius" of this system undermined itself at certain times.[27] Such was the view of Guillaume-Charles Maisoncelle, who argued in 1789 that even if a representative system in which all taxation must be approved was good in itself, its legitimating effects could ultimately serve to weaken the restraining force that public opinion might otherwise exercise on state spending. France, by contrast, faced real limits on its power to tax due to the fact that public opinion was permanently alienated from the actions of the state for lack of representative political institutions: "The monarch, with the appearance of absolute power, is hindered by a thousand considerations that all reduce to the following: the natural desire to prevent discontent." In this context, Maisoncelle reasoned, the French monarchy, unlike the British, was subject to permanent criticism from a public without a constituted voice in affairs of state. Evoking with evident chagrin the habits of restive French *parlements,* whose self-appointed task it was to package free-floating discontent into an effective form of political opposition, Maisoncelle underlined the perhaps excessive efficiency of the British system:

"once they are passed, these fiscal laws will be executed without remonstrances, without oppositions and without trouble."[28]

England's superior commercial strength was connected, with good reason, to the prowess of its navy, which was in turn associated, in a satisfying closure of the circle, with the power of its fisc. The restraining force of public opinion in France, however, meant that "the real power of France will be more limited in its action." Most French observers of Holland and England made successful linkage of these elements the *conditio sine qua non* of national wealth and grandeur; but in a curious reversal, Maisoncelle argued that the delinkage of these elements, and the subsequent political fettering of France's fisc (and the attendant economic drawbacks, of which he was hardly unaware) would ultimately redound to France's advantage. England presently benefited from financial gearing effects, which amplified its economic power, but Maisoncelle found England's "capacity of putting all of its power in contest (*jeu*)" dangerous; with their more limited financial resources, the French were in a far less exposed position, having less to gain but also less to lose, like gamblers at the table.[29]

The theater of this grand contest between England and France was, of course, the New World. Here European nations found "the means to exterminate one another at a distance of four thousand miles" in a monotonous succession of commercial wars brought on by "the progress of navigation and the discovery of a New World." An underlying appeal of Maisoncelle's claims, which is made more explicit in other authors' writings, is that France was at bottom a stronger nation than England because of its larger size and economic basis in agriculture. Therefore, the contest between England and France must be determined in the long run by economic fundamentals, with France emerging victorious. Was territory coming to trump commerce? Once England lost its credit, the source of its "borrowed power," which it must inevitably do, "it will be forced to endure the laws that its rival [France] wishes to impose." Before this impending event, England should be regarded as "supported externally solely by the art of internal administration and by the science of government"—again, a sort of game whose returns must necessarily diminish over time. Britannia would be eclipsed in power by its rival because of the latter's wider, more natural basis of wealth: "doesn't

France have men capable of raising and supporting a more natural edifice, an edifice based uniquely upon national wealth?" Here, the distinction between a "natural" and "artificial" constitution could not have been made more clearly. Another observer, Jacques Accarias de Serionne, framed the matter in terms of the grand contest of colonial commerce and its inevitable complement, war debts. The Austrian War of Succession brought Great Britain to the height of its success, for familiar reasons: "the science of government, the art of administration and the success of wars undertaken exclusively for extending commerce." But pushed beyond their proper measure, "these same causes" would become "the causes of its decadence and destruction" because England was increasingly pushed beyond its "natural power," relying instead on the "artificial power" of credit.[30]

In the event, it was France and not England that sunk under the weight of debts contracted in the grand contest of colonial commerce and warfare; nevertheless, these contemporary analyses were based on a telling set of observations about the state of English finances. Given the extraordinary growth of English revenues and debt since 1688, was it extravagant to believe that Britain may have crossed a critical threshold that put it in jeopardy vis à vis France? Moreover, French observers might also have taken comfort from the fact that France was able to raise more capital in Dutch markets than the British, and to do so more easily.[31] For example, in 1780, the French crown was able to raise 5,000,000 guilders (approximately 7,500,000 l.t.) in Amsterdam while the British were able to raise only one-fifth the sum. Political events helped to determine Dutch openhandedness, but a widespread perception that the British were overextended was also in play. Maisoncelle, for his part, attempted to assemble a set of comparative statistics on the evolution of state revenues over two and a half centuries, all the while complaining that England's figures were necessarily more accurate than those of France. Despite these misgivings, Maisoncelle observed a dangerous convergence, to England's disadvantage, in the absolute levels of taxation in these two nations, whose populations and resources differed so vastly (see Figure 4.1).[32]

Like so many of his countrymen, Maisoncelle deplored the bellicose reign of Louis XIV and its gross accumulation of war debts. "The

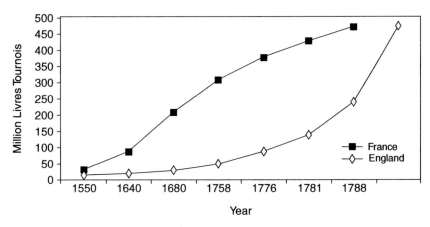

Figure 4.1 De Maisoncelle's revenue estimates for France and England, 1550–1788.

French people at this time were proportionally much more burdened than the English people." Yet, observed Maisoncelle, "things have changed greatly since." It was now England that pursued a "false idea of grandeur" aimed at "a despotism of navigation and of commerce." Although Maisoncelle intended to characterize the policies of an entire century, he was thinking in particular of the period from 1776 to 1788, during which the segment of England's revenue curve bends sharply upward to meet the flattening arc of France's increases. Here, based on a series of calculations on the cost of tax collection and the like, Maisoncelle concluded that during this critical period (the War of American Independence and its aftermath), the "effective rate" of increase in taxation in England had been about twice (128 million l.t.) that of France (67 million l.t.), for an average yearly rate of increase of 10.5 million l.t. in England, compared with merely 5.4 million l.t. in France.[33]

Quite a few years earlier, the anonymous author of "Considérations sur les finances," published in several parts in the *Journal de Commerce* toward the end of the Seven Years' War, had been just as thoroughly convinced that Britain had violated all just proportion between its national product, its population, and its level of taxation. For this author, the ideal, "natural" proportion between taxation and national revenue was 20 percent, a sum this small island nation had completely outstripped. This situation led to a tantalizing set of comparisons with France, "which has exactly twice as many inhabitants, national income and revenues, a territory two-thirds larger, a greater natural produce, more varied, richer and about the same sum of debts."[34]

Writing in 1784, Hilliard d'Auberteuil—by turns a novelist, historian, and economist of the American colonies—painted a similarly alarmist portrait of the evolution of England's finances after the War of American Independence. He believed that up until this point the national debt had been maintained at a sustainable and even economically productive level, at approximately £129 million. D'Auberteuil expresses this relationship rather curiously: "All the loans contracted since William III up until 1776 have served to disassociate (*écarter*) the power and the wealth of the English: [the loans] have provided everybody with the means to pay them, without trouble and without murmuring." By *écarter,* d'Auberteuil signified a positive type of disassociation, one that rendered England's wealth independent of its "natural" or underlying power in much the same way that Maisoncelle would later conceptualize the problem. But Lord North's fateful decision to support a war against the thirteen colonies added another £81 million to England's debt, placing its finances, and hence its power, at a tipping point, especially in relation to France.

How was this so? D'Auberteuil's research disproved the commonplace—also debunked by modern historians—that the French were overtaxed in comparison with the English. Nevertheless, he observed that the English laborer lived in comparative ease and comfort, "while in a rather large part of France, he is almost naked and covered in rags and eats fresh meat only on feast days." Here, d'Auberteuil, like Etienne de Silhouette in 1747, adduced a familiar repertoire of causes relating to the different governments and social structures of France and England: in France, taxes were inequitable between regions, and uneven exemptions and burdens (such as the *corvée,* forced road-building labor for peasants) ensured that taxes were poorly distributed, pulverizing the laborious but fragile classes so necessary to generate national wealth.[35]

Despite this damning tableau, d'Auberteuil believed that "territorial powers" such as France and Spain enjoyed allowed them a wide margin for error in the management of their finances. A commercial nation such as England, by contrast, resembled a fast but fragile thoroughbred running at the upper limit of its performance. In this view, commercial nations that had developed such a tightly functioning relation among the domains of commerce, the military, industry, and finance were able to push their economies to specifically unnatural extremes of opulence. Given the widening gap between England's natural resources and the expansion of national wealth provided by the operation of its government, the art of governance became, in this view, all too dependent on the virtuosity of its leadership. Rather than enjoying a basically propitious constitutional structure that could withstand the normal vagaries of human weakness and error, England's economy resembled a finely tuned piece of machinery with dangerously narrow tolerances: "A bad King or a corrupt Parliament suffices to crush this Kingdom forever."

Territorial powers such as France, however, had constitutions that were less artificial, more in harmony with nature. The upshot of this type of thinking was that by dint of France's superior size, population, soil, and varied produce, "no great efforts of industry and activity are necessary to increase her commerce; all of the branches are budding, so to speak, and susceptible to growth and improvements." Maisoncelle echoed the same opinion, observing (with a hint of Alexander Gerschenkron's "comparative advantage of backwardness" *avant la lettre*) that while behind in comparison with England, France, due to its greater resources, ultimately had much greater and more easily made progress ahead of her.[36]

Inevitably, these predictions were shot through with all of the ambiguity of having been framed within a pattern of understanding that opposed two intimately related categories, "constitutional" and "natural" forces. Thus, Maisoncelle, while asserting the long-term, natural advantages of a "territorial power," was forced to admit "that ultimately the superiority of power rests with the government that reckons (*compter*) the best." Needless to say, the tendencies of an absolutist government, working through a set of inefficient, socially unrepresentative, and geographically particular institutions, militated against such a rational approach to finances. Similarly, while framing his entire discussion in terms of natural versus artificial wealth, as well as "natural" fiscal proportionalities, Maisoncelle was ultimately at pains to decide which force was more powerful: the "empire of climate" (geography, natural resources, and climate itself) or the world of government and artifice (government, institutions, and manners). In the past, "the constitution of its government has not permitted it to give the same advantage to its credit," but the author hoped that by studying England's institutions, "France can appropriate to itself" some practices suitable to its situation and, departing from its superior natural endowments, thereby become "a power more natural, grander, more durable and more solid" than England.[37]

But even as the author of the "Considerations sur les finances" articulated his hopes for France's finances, he was forced, like the abbé de Saint-Pierre and Jean-François Melon, into making a qualification that is telling in its scope. Because they fall prey to the irresistible demands of the king, it was commonly believed that central banks are not suitable for monarchies. Using the familiar analogy of climate to explain the problem of commerce in monarchies, he concluded that, by dint of France's constitution, a central bank "is a foreign plant in France, which every hothouse trick will fail to adapt to this soil." This author moved on to argue—rather weakly—that such a limitation would not sensibly damage France's commercial prospects. Perhaps even more telling is the slippage between nature as climate and the "second nature" of France's institutions, which created an inhospitable environment for such hothouse plants as a central bank.[38] Maisoncelle and others argued that France's latent superiority over England derived from the distinction between "natural" and "artificial" wealth, but there seemed to be every indication that Europe had crossed a threshold in economic history and that France could not do without these "hothouse tricks."

The simple dichotomy so often posed between conquest and commerce (or between territorial and oceanic empires) obscured central features of Europe's new economic order that were laid bare by examination of the problem of finances: warfare, taxation, ballooning debt, and the threat of despotism were systemic risks to which England, Spain, and France were all exposed.

In a world where artificial forms of wealth were coming to predominate and France seemed to be losing dominance because of this shift, it is little wonder that many economists began to think explicitly about the virtues, in the international division of labor, of a natural economy. Not only did such a strategy appear to fit France's natural endowments, but it also—or so the argument went—played to the strengths of its monarchical constitution.

Nobody argued more persistently for a return to natural forms of wealth than the Physiocrats who, beginning in the mid-1750s, advanced a program for righting the French economy that emphasized agriculture over commerce and manufacturing. Although they never argued for economic autarky, as did Rousseau and other republican political thinkers enamored of the fantasy of virtuous and self-sufficient poverty, the Physiocrats did believe that France should reorient its economic views away from the ocean and back to the fertile expanses of its inland empire. But the Physiocrats also rejected the old paradigm of territorial conquest based upon feudal modes of governance; according to them, the mercantile system that served as the armature of France's oceanic empire had only strengthened the anachronistic characteristics of French state and society. This was among their boldest insights, one that complicated the hitherto facile choice between conquest and commerce. The way forward for France was to give up the pretended reconciliation between land and sea and to become an essentially agricultural kingdom, allowing smaller, less resource-rich nations largely to take over France's foreign trade. Such prescriptions had far-reaching implications for the ordering of France's overseas empire, including its relations with competitor nations.

Within France, the Physiocrats envisioned radical measures that set them permanently at odds with Montesquieu and those who took up his mantle in emphasizing France's history, geography, and institutions as the basis for incremental reforms. In turning away from France's feudal past, the Physiocrats sought the political basis for a regenerated French economy in the eternal order of nature; they argued that society and its laws should be understood as an equally immutable subset of this higher natural order. The study of the economy and the legislation that resulted from it should be above all else simple, following the principle of parsimony that served the lodestar for the natural sciences.[39] Such thinking had paradoxical but seductive results when applied to the irrational patchwork of provinces, guilds, monopolistic companies, and sovereign entities that characterized France's incompletely reformed absolute monarchy: in the name of a more natural and rational order, the centuries-long accretion of institutions was to be swept aside by the dictates of an enlightened despot. Appeals to history and a preexistent "constitution"—that is, institutions and ways of doing things that had evolved over several centuries—were dismissed as habits, vested interests, and prejudices, precisely the "empire of climate" examined here. The result was an intellectual polarization over the value of history and of historically oriented economics. Of course, the issue was larger than divergent social-scientific methodologies, since these were conflicting ways of representing the French polity and its economic organization. No school or political tendency can be said to have prevailed in this conflict, which remained in a holding pattern until the fall of the institution that was a central stake in this debate: the monarchy.

CHAPTER 5

Physiocracy and the Politics of History

BEGINNING IN THE 1750S, the French, according to Voltaire, began
to "philosophize about grain," and surely the most widely known
and influential among these new philosophers of grain was court physi-
cian to Louis XV, François Quesnay. After publishing a series of articles,
including "FERMIERS" (1756) and "GRAINS" (1757), in Diderot and
d'Alembert's *Encyclopédie*, Quesnay began to assemble a circle of disciples around him at Versailles who helped to clarify and publicize the
master's new doctrine. By 1758, with the publication of Quesnay's *Tableau
Economique*, the Physiocrats, or *économistes* as they were mainly known,
advertised a bold, complete break with all previous ways of thinking
about the economy. Their claim to novelty was not solely a function of
their belief that the soil was the best guarantee of France's prosperity; in
the late seventeenth century, writers critical of Louis XIV, such as Sébas-
tien Le Prestre Marquis de Vauban and Boisguillbert, had urged a re-
newed emphasis on agriculture, and in the next century a group of im-
provers known as the *agronomes* took this observation as the premise
for a program of research and publicity about improved farming techniques. Instead, the Physiocrats insisted that it was their method that set
them apart, because they were able to establish scientifically what had
hitherto been a matter of mere conjecture and hence put key elements of

their economic doctrine beyond dispute. Most salient among these doctrines was, first, an insistence that only agriculture produced value; all other forms of economic activity, including manufacturing and trade, therefore, were derived from and should remain subordinate to this fundamental activity. Second, individuals' original right of self-preservation resulted in two corollary propositions that served as the basis of every social order in all epochs: the primacy of subsistence arrangements as the foundation and purpose of all governments and the sacred nature of private property. In sum: agriculture, utilitarianism, laissez-faire, and science all hung together in the panoply of Physiocratic claims advanced against their opponents.[1]

As a part of its effort to establish its scientific credentials against those economic methods that preceded it, Physiocracy frequently contrasted itself with history, which it viewed as unscientific. Far from advancing an eccentric viewpoint, the Physiocrats took their authority from the tree of knowledge *(système des connaissances)* discussed in Diderot and d'Alembert's *Encyclopédie,* which advertised itself as the basis for the orderly and enlightened pursuit of knowledge. Francis Bacon's tree of knowledge, which was adopted by Diderot and d'Alembert, shows the epistemic and consequently disciplinary divisions that guided the redaction of the *Encyclopédie* (see Figure 5.1).

In laying out their Lockean, sensualist epistemology, Diderot and d'Alembert divided the mental faculties in a manner designed to reproduce both "the encyclopedic order of our knowledge and its genealogical order": "Thus, memory, reason properly speaking, and imagination are the three different manners in which our soul operates on the objects of its thoughts." Each of these faculties could, in turn, be identified with characteristic intellectual pursuits: "History which appertains to memory; Philosophy which is the fruit of reason; and the Fine arts, which are born of imagination."[2] Voltaire, writing in his *Encyclopédie* article "HISTOIRE," explicitly reinforced the division between history and science by warning his readers that natural history is "improperly called history" because it forms "an essential part of the physical sciences."[3]

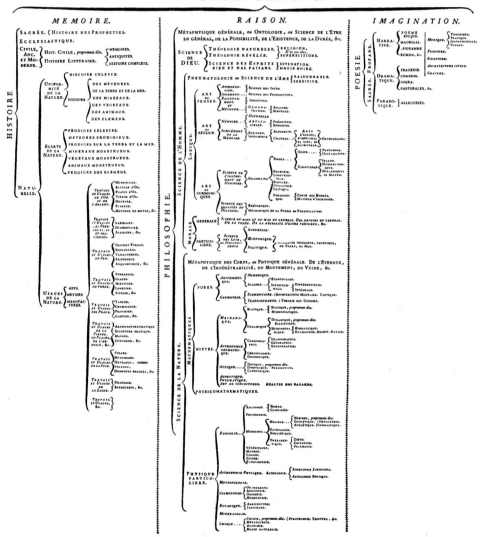

Figure 5.1 The Enlightenment tree of knowledge. From Diderot and d'Alembert's *Encyclopédie,* "Discours Préliminaire." (University of Chicago Library, Special Collections Research Center.)

It is less strange than it may seem at first glance to observe the pre-eminent historian of the French Enlightenment, Voltaire, relegating historians to second-class status in the Enlightenment hierarchy of knowledge. In so doing, Voltaire emphasized the distinction between "erudite" and "philosophical" history. But the Physiocrats chose to ignore this crucial distinction, preferring instead a one-sided emphasis on history in its erudite form as disordered, subject to error, and altogether unscientific. They did this despite the obvious political importance of "philosophical" history and the ease with which it was distinguished, among eighteenth-century thinkers, from merely "erudite" history. The truths the Physiocrats sought were profound and transhistorical, which is why the editors of the *Ephémérides du citoyen* proclaimed that "often history represents nothing but games of chance and grand passions." It was, rather, the "new science" of society that could ensure the founding and propagation of a natural order that served as the cornerstone of Physiocratic doctrine. For this reason, Quesnay explicitly rejected history as erudite, proclaiming that "we do not seek lessons in the history of nations. . . . [I]t represents nothing but an abyss of disorders; historians apply themselves only to satisfying their reader's curiosity: their overly literal erudition does not suffice to shed the kind of light which could illuminate this chaos." Even where a useful and sound "philosophical" history was imaginable, the Physiocrats viewed present-day historiography as bereft of true scientific knowledge: "Unfortunately, the majority of historians," lamented Pierre Samuel Dupont de Nemours, "have satisfied themselves to recount battle stories [and] have disdained these rural details" so loved by the Physiocrats.[4]

The Physiocrats' condemnation of history was clear and frequently reiterated, since it constituted one of the principal advantages they claimed against their opponents. This was not a pure Cartesian epistemology that rejected all facts coming from the external world as inherently unreliable. Quesnay worked hard to establish a firm empirical basis for the figures and ratios in the *Tableau Economique;* however, once the basic data necessary for the *Tableau* were assembled, further recourse to the messy world of history was deemed counterproductive. Because it deduced everything else from the *Tableau,* Physiocracy represented a new "moral and political science" that was simple and "easy to understand, remember and put into practice." Every consequence for the moral and political order (in short, *gouvernement économique*) could be deduced from the very simple set of relations presented in Quesnay's zigzags. Quesnay's *Tableau économique avec ses explications* provides a perfect example, a sort of ideal type, of Physiocratic method: the *Tableau* is first presented and explained; in response to fourteen different economic questions (e.g., relating to the population, the police, taxes, or luxury), the table is simply re-presented, and the reader is told how the fundamental relation (net product and the sole productivity of agriculture) that guides Physiocratic science resolves a multitude of political or economic questions. History, even of the most refined sort, usually introduced distracting facts and false relationships that led to incorrect policies—the very opposite of *gouvernement économique*. Quesnay's approach could not be any different from that of Butel-Dumont or Forbonnais, who believed that the science of commerce had to situate laws within a complex and historically evolving set of relationships.[5]

Dupont de Nemours' *De l'origine et des progrès d'une science nouvelle* (1768) provides an excellent guide to the orthodoxies of Physiocratic thought and how it seized upon Montesquieu's method to mark a contrast with its own. Dupont asked his readers to consider whether, given the state of perfection of the natural sciences, a truly novel science was possible. "What do we lack?" asked his skeptical (and hypothetical) interlocutor, "what don't we know? We measure the heavens and the earth; we measure their revolutions; we calculate their movements; we predict their eclipses." All of these scientific advances, Dupont's skeptic concluded, resulted in an apparently unsurpassable scientific and technical mastery over nature. But if you asked how society should comport itself "so that [it] can be rich, powerful, and flourishing," how would this same skeptic respond, Dupont wondered? The skeptic would reply "'that this is not the object of an exact science, and that this depends upon an infinity of variable circumstances that are difficult to evaluate and disentangle.'" According to the Physiocrats, Montesquieu's inexactitude was the dominant strand in social thought up until the advent of the "new science" of political economy. Even "Montesquieu himself, so worthy to instruct mankind solidly in every respect, has told us that the principles of government must change according to the form of its constitution, without teaching us what is the primitive base . . . of every constitution." Dupont argued that Quesnay, by contrast, had found and explicated "the *physical* laws relative to society" from which all Physiocratic doctrine proceeded and which made historical observation otiose. In so doing, Physiocracy elevated itself to an exact science capable of discerning the "constitutive and fundamental laws of all societies" that were more basic than typologies based upon ephemeral constitutional differences. In this spirit, the abbé Nicolas Baudeau affirmed the Cartesian exactitude of this "philosophical school" whose principles and methods formed a "true science" that ceded nothing "perhaps even to geometry itself."[6]

Physiocratic scientism led to a profound uneasiness toward Montesquieu's historical and comparative method, and well into the 1780s, he entered negatively into the Physiocrats' definition of economics as a discipline.[7] Lacking a firm epistemological basis in "a natural order," this "sublime man" was confined to using "extreme finesse" and the "supreme wisdom of his mind to seek, to invent particular reasons for given cases." However praiseworthy, such accidental qualities of mind as finesse and wisdom could not be relied upon to supply the defects of poor method, unhinged from reasoned speculation about the "physical laws of society." Turning instead to Montesquieu's disciples, who stood safely outside the "President's" halo, Dupont directed jibes against "the scribblers who fashion themselves political philosophers, imagining themselves to be marching in the President's footsteps." The reason he gave for their misdirection reproduced exactly the terms of the tree of knowledge laid out in the *Encyclopédie:* "The habit developed in their childhood to use exclusively their memory has snuffed out the power to make use of their judgment." History, by its association with memory, and not reason or judgment, lay outside of the pale of Physiocratic discourse and method.[8]

It may be objected with justice that the Physiocratic rejection of history relied upon a tendentious understanding of the Enlightenment tree of knowledge and an uncharitable reading of the position that Montesquieu and his followers occupied within this system. As Diderot and d'Alembert observed, the tripartition of the faculties into reason, imagination, and memory set philosophy (i.e., reason) on top, but this did not mean that the several branches of their tree of knowledge did not ideally draw nourishment from the activities of each faculty. "Without a doubt, society owes . . . its understanding to the philosophers," they wrote in the *Preliminary Discourse,* "but neither the one nor the other understand the extent to which they are in debt to memory; it holds the raw material of all of our knowledge; and the works of the erudites have often furnished material for the philosopher."[9]

The most general reason for their dismissive assessment of historical methods in economic inquiry stemmed from Physiocratic scientism. As economists, the Physiocrats were often dogmatic thinkers, sweeping everything before them with the evident sincerity of their reformist, even utopian aspirations. But the Physiocratic allergy to history was intimately connected to another salient aspect of the Physiocratic program: the doctrine of enlightened despotism. Pierre Rosanvallon observes that for the Physiocrats, "absolute despotism signals the possibility of an absolute extinction of politics." The corollary of their "negation of the political" is "a massive repression of history. Time is suspended for the Physiocrats." In keeping with this desire to "repress history," Quesnay systematically opposed the stable, tranquil realm of nature to the chaotic, contingent realm of politics, which is why he sought from the first to discover a set of "perpetual and immutable laws" that could place society above the "governmental disorders" of Old Regime France. The very term *Physiocracy* (etymologically: "rule by nature"), coined by Dupont, registers this aspiration. Turgot's famous demand for "six years of despotism to establish liberty" also epitomized the Physiocratic desire to transcend the vicissitudes of politics through the permanent, unchanging legal structures of enlightened despotism. History and politics stood condemned by the same logic, which is why the Physiocrats attempted to place their system "beyond the bar of merely historical argumentation."[10]

The Physiocrats believed that the political instability of France at mid-century was partly due to political struggles that were fought out in a specifically historical idiom. Most famously, the struggles between the crown and the *parlements* often hinged on opposing claims over the status of "fundamental laws" in France. The *parlements* argued that the "fundamental laws" of the realm left important functions of sovereignty to the intermediary bodies of the monarchy—most notably, the *parlements themselves*—and it was on this basis that they reserved the right to review, or remonstrate against, royal laws that they opposed. Here, of course, Montesquieu's own political theory served as an indispensable source of authority. In their opposition to what they saw as the absolut- ist, centralizing tendencies of the French crown, the Jansenist party of the Paris *parlement* "fortif[ied] itself with the vast historical, ecclesiasti- cal, and juridical erudition of the . . . Jansenist [lawyers]." (Jansenism was a form of Augustinian Catholicism considered heterodox.) Making use of historical arguments, the Jansenist members of *parlement* pre- tended to demonstrate the slide of the French crown into despotism by its negation of traditional liberties and representative institutions. This debate took a public turn in the 1750s with the explosion of the Refusal of Sacraments crisis, in which suspected Jansenist "heretics" were re- fused their final sacraments—and, it was thought, penalized for their re- fractory posture toward the crown in other political matters—in accor- dance with the episodically enforced papal bull *Unigenitus* of 1721. Here, for all of France to see, because the *parlement* printed its remonstrances for public consumption, was the struggle of traditional liberties against despotism. The culmination of this episode was the exile of the Paris *parlement* in 1753, an act that was repeated on a grander scale by Chan- cellor René Nicolas de Maupeou in 1770.[11]

Whenever they had the chance, Physiocrats took sides against the *parlements* and their historical claims, which the Physiocrats saw as em- pirically unfounded and politically reactionary. As the bitter opposition of the *parlements* to the Physiocrats' cherished reforms during Turgot's short career (1774–1776) as controller general illustrates, the Physiocrats were not entirely wrong in their choice of enemies and in viewing his- torical argument as reproducing (and sometimes magnifying) the politi- cal struggles surrounding efforts at economic reform. "Turgot's think- ing was the polar opposite of the *parlementaires*,'" which is partly why his program of reforms, from the liberalization of the grain trade to the suppression of the guilds, ultimately ran aground.[12] An explicitly antipo- litical discourse that opposed politics to nature was meant to furnish a justification for enlightened despotism and its portfolio of reforms, and at the same time to provide a sort of intellectual and political closure that historical argument simply could not.

Nowhere was this antipolitical discourse more evident than in the Physiocrats' attitude toward sovereignty and law. On the issue of sovereignty, the Physiocrats drew upon the theories of Jean Bodin, the sixteenth-century jurist who developed his theory of undivided sovereignty in the context of the French Wars of Religion. Dupont's Bodinian notion of sovereignty can be appreciated in the context of the opposition that the sovereign courts furnished to economic reform efforts in France. Sovereignty must have full authority and sufficient force: "It must also be unique. The idea of several authorities within the same state is nothing but the sheerest absurdity. If they are equal, there is no authority, and nothing less than anarchy would reign. If one among them is superior, that one is the authority, and the others are nothing." The Physiocrats, like Bodin, regarded divided sovereignty as a contradiction in terms and proceeded to argue for the consolidation of the legislative and executive power in the person of a hereditary monarch. Although the upshot of the Physiocrats' view of sovereignty was Bodinian, their views did not originate from identical premises. The Physiocrats derived their principles from a Lockean conception of natural rights and property while explicitly rejecting Locke's theory of limited government. The need for subsistence legitimated property rights, and these rights, in turn, formed the basis for all other liberties. Given their desire to repress politics and history in favor of a stable social order, it is hardly surprising that the Physiocrats sought out a transcendent basis for the laws they announced: "Sovereign authority is not founded in order to *make laws;* for *laws are all made* by the hand of he [God] who created rights and *duties.* . . . [S]overeign ordinances that are called *positive laws,* must be nothing other than the *declaration of these essential laws of the social order.*"[13]

We see from this brief outline how the Physiocrats' attitude toward history, by its association with politics, and specifically toward the political struggles in France at mid-century was of a piece with their more general pronouncements on the subjects of epistemology, metaphysics, law, and sovereignty. Any economic method that used historical comparisons to suggest that different constitutional arrangements naturally implied a variety of legitimate economic policies was bound to offend against the Physiocratic principle that there was but one set of "essential laws" guaranteeing stability and prosperity. Other historical interpretations invited only opposition to the reforms proposed by the Physiocrats. As a corollary to this, the Physiocrats thought that any economics that pretended to use history rather than the eternal principles of reason *(évidence)*, which was itself derived through reason rather than memory, was not "science" at all but an atavism from the days before Quesnay's *Tableau Economique*. Here again, we see a confluence among historical context, social scientific method, and the genre of economic writing. Montesquieu, as the comparative historian par excellence and as a supporter of intermediary powers such as the *parlements*, made a perfect methodological and political target of opportunity.[14]

Physiocratic History of Commerce

Despite these tendencies, which conform to the most routine of the Physiocrats' methodological self-representations, a different picture emerges if we widen the scope of sources to include the full range of Physiocratic writings. By examining, for instance, the articles that appear in the *Ephémérides du citoyen,* the principal organ of *économiste* opinion, a qualitatively different picture of Physiocracy and its attitude toward history and politics comes into focus. Over the twelve years of its publication (1765–1772, 1774–1776, and 1778), 14.4 percent of the 1,550 articles in the *Ephémérides* were consecrated to "historical or exotic demonstration." Indeed, the full title of the journal from 1774 to 1776 (it bore four variants in all) was *Les Ephémérides du citoyen, ou bibliothèque raisonné de l'histoire, de la morale et de la politique.* Despite the Physiocratic obsession with France's agricultural sector, we still find that 3.3 percent and 3.8 percent of the articles were devoted to "colonial problems" and "exterior trade," respectively. Over 20 percent of the journal's articles, then, were devoted to history and colonial commerce, out of seventeen thematic rubrics. Conclusions about the *Journal de l'agriculture de commerce et des finances* are more difficult, but this important eighteenth-century journal manifests the same sustained interest in geography, voyages, and history: 14 percent of 1,280 articles were devoted to these subjects, and another 4 percent were consecrated to colonies, exterior trade, and related categories. If the circle of sources is widened even further to include monographs and articles not intended to provide a theoretical explication of Physiocracy but whose biases are nevertheless manifestly Physiocratic (favoring the liberalization of the grain trade; opposing guild-based restrictions on labor and industry;

opposing "exclusive" merchant companies in the Indies; and, finally, strongly favoring the reform of national manners around the ideology of agrarian virtue), the picture of a science whose rhetorical strategies often ran at cross-currents to its scientific principles emerges even more forcefully.[15]

These findings show how difficult it was, in practice, to maintain the strict identification that the Physiocrats touted between their vision of natural science and their "new" science of society. Moreover, the Physiocrats' willingness to argue on the plane of historical events tacitly conceded the explanatory methods of the science of commerce they pretended to reject. The Physiocratic system is clear, simple, and rigorous in a way that comparative history simply is not; pulverizing their opponents with the hard, crystalline structures of reason was simple enough—and even effective to a certain degree, when it did not create enemies who derided them as a sect. But other forces pulled the Physiocrats in the opposite direction. The Physiocrats always emphasized the importance of public opinion and needed to support one (and at times two) journals to convey their message.[16] In order to accomplish these related goals, they had to speak in a language their readers understood and to address pressing questions in an interesting, varied, and appropriate manner. To do so, the Physiocrats made recourse to every conceivable genre, including fables, travel narratives, novels, philosophical dialogues, poetry, and the very philosophical histories of commerce that they themselves criticized.

The votaries of reason may have locked Montesquieu out the front door with great rhetorical show, but they were secretly forced to let him in the back door in order to apply the tenets of Physiocracy to pressing contemporary questions. Dupont, in a somewhat embarrassed preface to his (narrative) history of the Compagnie des Indes, conceded this methodological difficulty: "The sole merit to which principles and calculations must aspire is that they be founded upon truth, clarity, and that they be conclusive. Narrations permit more rapidity; they are more agreeable to read and write. They come alive like nature and take on her coloring."[17] What is ironic here is that despite their disavowals, the historical consciousness of some members of the sect was very keen, which rendered them capable of explaining the novelty of France's—and more broadly, Europe's—historical position, especially the relationship between the enormous expansion of the world economy and the dissolution of "feudal ties" within European society. Liberated from the procrustean bed of its own antihistorical biases, Physiocracy marshaled vigorous and compelling historical arguments for its central reform propositions. Moreover, these analyses often quite cunningly demonstrated how the abolition of slavery in the colonies, the "de-feudalization" of Old Regime social structures, and the growth of distinctly modern forms of social and political freedom were mutually engendering processes. Conversely, the Physiocrats postulated the relationship between the persistence of mercantile policies abroad and the fettering of social and economic reform at home.

The Physiocrats' history of commerce was devoted principally to exposing their views on *les progrès du commerce,* arguing that the initial effects of colonial commerce were far from progressive; only in its final stages, they believed, could the development of European commerce in the Americas fulfill the promises of the *doux commerce* thesis. It was believed that American commerce actually worked in a historically regressive manner, entrenching feudal social relations and forms of government. For the Physiocrats, the construction of the mercantile system, with "fiscal" and "feudal" government at its center, retarded and, in some cases, reversed the succession of historical stages. This paradoxical reversal continued, by this account, from the sixteenth until the late eighteenth century, when the mercantile system fell of its own weight on the eve of the American Revolution, a victim of its own success in the Atlantic world.[18]

The Physiocratic intervention into the history of commerce took place on two very different but ultimately related analytical registers: the stadial, or four-stages, view of history; and the Physiocratic hierarchy of productive versus unproductive economic activity. The stadial view of history, which was developed in the 1750s and had become commonplace by the 1770s, saw the material conditions of civilization ripening in four successive stages: the hunter-gatherer, the pastoral, the agricultural, and the commercial. The ease with which the stadial view meshed with the narrative of *doux commerce* is plain to see: prosperity, political freedom, and the march of civilization were taken as related processes that had been set in motion during the Age of Discovery and perfected in subsequent incarnations of colonial-mercantile enterprise. This was the case even where observers were capable—as, indeed, many were—of looking European barbarity in the colonies squarely in the face.[19]

Such an understanding of the basis of progress sat uneasily with the Physiocratic hierarchy of productive versus unproductive labor, which took agriculture as the only true source of wealth. How, the Physiocrats might ask, could something so ephemeral and ultimately derivative as commerce (or even manufacture) serve as the organizing principle, let alone the motor, of historical progress? For the Physiocrats, it could not, and a distinctive aspect of their interpretation of the history of European commerce in the Americas was that initially such commerce had regressive economic and political effects. Only in its terminal phase, when the contradictions of the "feudal government" that it encouraged had ripened, did this commercial expansion issue forth as the sort of progress that its earlier partisans had projected. The Physiocratic analysis pointed an accusing finger at the absolutist states that had initially undertaken the expansion into the Americas at the same time as it tried to demonstrate how these empires would inevitably be eclipsed by the forces they had set into motion.

The cornerstone of the Physiocrats' understanding of this historical process was their notion of the evolution of the "fiscal government" as it emerged all over Europe. This regime represented a noxious mixture of backward feudal particularism with all the cupidity characteristic of modern, commercial society. In this connection, the *Éphémérides du citoyen* sketched out the history of the Italian trading republics, which represented the decline of urban, commercial civilizations. "It is in the city-states of Italy," wrote one author, "that the deadly art of modern taxation was born." The pernicious effects of the systems employed in these small, nonagricultural republics were manifold: the sheer number of taxes made them inherently irrational; they generally fell regressively on consumption items; the costs of tax collection made them both inefficient and doubly burdensome; and their incidence on the productive classes put competitively damaging upward pressure on wages. The natural outcomes of these disadvantages were evasion and corruption, which crept into all levels of government. Contrasting this system with the "truly economical constitution" of the *impôt unique* (or single land-tax, the signature Physiocratic tax reform), the author observed that "fiscal government" had "laid waste to Europe and destroyed humankind even in its most fortunate climates."[20]

For the Physiocrats, the deleterious effects of "modern fiscality" resulted from its anachronistic character. For, as Pierre Roubaud observed, it was the quick gains to be found in the Americas and the imperialist ambitions they aroused that gave rise to "unrestrained greed for taxes" typical of modern despotic states. Modern empires, including France, were actuated by a "lust for conquest" whose natural consequence was the fatal "bloating of debt" found among virtually every state with a colonial empire. In effect, ancient forms of feudal government received new impetus from the discovery and exploitation of the Americas.[21]

Beyond the fatal spiral of imperialist war and its attendant debts that the exploitation of the Americas set loose on the Continent, the Physiocrats saw that extractive modes of government developed for colonial rule were reimported to Europe, where they unfolded with their economically and socially destructive logic. Here as elsewhere, the Spanish were taken as both inaugural and representative of this process. Lombardy's decline was therefore laid at the door of the "Spanish fisc" and all of the odium implied by the term. For the Physiocrats, it was the persistence of "feudal government," working hand in glove with modern economic forms (e.g., mercantile empires and the trend toward luxury), that motivated the development of the modern fiscal system in its most notorious aspects: indirect taxes, commercial monopolies, royal patents, and tax farming—in short, the whole system of privilege that constituted the "steel frame" of Old Regime society.[22]

Such a criticism was clearly intended to cut to the quick of Old Regime French society, mutually implicating the worst of the old and new: the privilege and irrational particularism of the former and the burgeoning spirit of gain characteristic of the latter. In his polemic against the exclusive hold on commerce to and from the East Indies enjoyed by the Compagnie des Indes, Dupont de Nemours described the type of parasitic court capitalism such a combination produced: "We have seen how the Company was, by its charter and by the prevailing customs of the Parisians who are its principal shareholders, vastly more inclined to behave like a rentier than a merchant. Here you see what the rentier mentality leads to." Indeed, for Dupont, the manner in which the Compagnie des Indes exploited colonial commerce was not even at issue, since this was only its tertiary function, behind inflating stock values and shoring up the influence of the government.[23]

Next to the speculative value of its shares, the "political notions" of the company also held dear the principle that a share in the Compagnie des Indes constituted a sacred obligation on the part of the state. (In other words, it was viewed as a government bond.) Thus, according to Dupont, a relatively profitless enterprise paid its shareholders dividends at least two-thirds in excess of what was justified by its strictly commercial activities.[24] In this manner, the capital of the company was dissipated, "coldly carved up among [the shareholders]," and subsequently replaced by tax receipts, with no obvious benefits for the crown or for France in general. "This company," complained Dupont, "which was so favored, promptly ate up all of its capital; it only continued to trade through new favors from the King and by onerous pleas to its shareholders, and its credit was sustained through rather dubious manipulations." Here we see the dual linkages between a "mercantile policy" in which the colonies were abandoned to exclusive companies as mere "objects of profit" and the "modern fiscality" deplored by the Physiocrats. On the one hand, as we have just seen, the Physiocrats viewed the company's parasitic relationship with the royal treasury as endemic to this sort of enterprise. On the other, the company used its political clout, bolstered by an exaggerated view of the benefits accruing to France from colonial commerce, to shift protection costs onto the crown and, ultimately, onto France's productive classes. These costs also included, of course, the mounting sums spent over the course of the eighteenth century on wars of commerce and their attendant costs of financing. It would have been impossible for the Compagnie des Indes to keep itself afloat, Dupont de Nemours observed, "had it been left completely in charge of all of its operations. The costs of war and governance would always have ruined it: that is, unless the state had not taken up all of these expenses for the Company." For all of these reasons, exclusive companies had not one but two hands in the till: one to engender the conditions of profitability and the other to pay off shareholders when these profits failed to materialize, as was systematically the case. These enterprises were not the bastions of risk-taking capitalism lauded by the historian Guy Chaussinand-Nogaret in support of his thesis of an economically forward-looking nobility, but examples of corrupt court capitalism that Montesquieu had warned about in the *Esprit des lois,* and which were transparently obvious to other contemporary observers such as Dupont de Nemours.[25]

In this analysis, most Physiocrats laid stress upon the misallocation of society's capital and hence the depressed economic activity that inevitably resulted from France's "mercantile policy"—a charge that would be pressed further by Smith in the *Wealth of Nations.* A central point here is the relationship the Physiocrats posited between colonial commerce, commercial privilege, and the development of "modern fiscality." Such a ratcheting up of fiscal demands and the extractive devices necessary to satisfy them was only intensified by a dialectic of privilege and state penury characteristic of absolutist states, which were compelled to work through the institutions and hierarchies of an ordered society. This is what the Physiocrats meant when they referred, borrowing from David Hume, to "feudal government."

The most sustained Physiocratic attempt to write the history of commerce comes not from the pen of one of the sect's principal theorists—among them Mirabeau, Quesnay, Le Trosne, and Dupont de Nemours—but from Pierre Roubaud, one of Physiocracy's most indefatigable publicists. In 1770, the same year that Raynal began publishing his *Histoire philosophique et politique des . . . deux Indes,* Pierre Roubaud issued the first volume of the *Histoire générale de l'Asie, de l'Afrique et de l'Amérique.* This work deserves close attention because, although there were other attempts in the pages of the *Ephémérides du citoyen,* Roubaud's work is the only attempt to give a comprehensive reading of world history through the lens of Physiocratic economic doctrine.[26]

Roubaud's work, and the Physiocratic doctrine it was based upon, spelled out the implications of Europe's expansion into the Atlantic world by reevaluating the role of commerce in its stadial view of history: commerce, in this telling, did not neatly displace conquest. On one level, Roubaud's *Histoire générale* is a history of commerce like any other, except that it called into question the unalloyed good of *doux commerce.* In this respect, however, it was similar to noble or republican histories of commerce that denounced the eclipse of disinterested civic values in commercial society—here the work of the Chevalier d'Arcq stands out. From the narrowest point of view, the aim of Roubaud's *Histoire gé-nérale* was to condemn the growth of colonial commerce at the expense of domestic agriculture. More broadly, however, his object was to refute the progressive narrative of the history of commerce recounted by thinkers such as Montesquieu and Hume. These narratives were only reinforced by a flood of economic analyses that emphasized the positive reciprocal effects on domestic industry and overseas commercial development secured by restrictive trading regimes imposed by the European metropole on the colonial periphery: for the French, the Exclusive.[27]

Bringing Physiocratic economic and jurisprudential principles to bear on this historical discourse, Roubaud rejected the *doux commerce* thesis, observing in the colonies instead the reign of "the spirit of monopoly and intolerance." Furthermore, Roubaud denied the distinction, dear to partisans of colonial commerce, between the buccaneering Spanish "spirit of conquest" and the innocuous, presumably nonexploitative "commercial spirit," which sought steady accumulation through the unexciting but honest "carrying trade": "It is an error to believe as Montesquieu does that those nations which treated America as an object of commerce were wiser than those [who treated it as an object] of conquest." For Roubaud and others, conquest by army and the bill of exchange amounted to much the same thing, because they proceeded from the same corrupt motives. Roubaud gained rhetorical traction by playing upon the fundamental distinction, posited by Montesquieu and Melon, between commerce and conquest.[28]

The object of Roubaud's work was first of all to chronicle the transformations worked by the Europeans in the New World, whose discovery was regarded as a truly world-historical event by which a "new order of things [was] revealed to the eyes of the universe." Roubaud's conclusions were not inspired solely by the conflicts between England and the thirteen colonies of the 1770s but by the spectacle of discovery and commerce itself. Years before revolutionary tensions boiled to the surface in America, an article in the inaugural issue (1765) of the *Ephé-mérides* explained that during the two and a half centuries since the discovery of the East Indies and the New World, "we have seen by slow degrees astonishing revolutions in the politics, the commerce and the *moeurs* of the French and neighboring peoples." Later economic writers, from Raynal to Smith to Marx, anchored their analysis in similar judgments and in almost precisely the same words. The lines of force that created this "new order" did not move in one direction: "the tidal wave of Old World has swept away the New," wrote Roubaud. "But in the clash of these two great bodies, the strongest could not entirely crush the weaker, without being cracked and broken asunder itself." For another observer, these events had literally turned the world inside out, collapsing the difference between Europe and its peripheries: "Europe is at the ends of the earth, the extremity of the Indies lies in the heart of Europe." In addition to the circulation of peoples and commodities, the interpenetration of core and periphery alluded to here signifies the effects that the civilizations of the Old and New Worlds were having upon one another. Once again, the putatively modernizing effects of *doux commerce* were at issue, and for the Physiocrats, the record demonstrated the tenuousness of this hypothesis. Later, critics of French colonial policy (most especially colonists themselves) would use this intermixing—a political, economic, and even conceptual confusion between core and periphery—to advance their own agendas.[29]

Peruvian society had long been of interest to the Physiocrats because, like China, it presented the spectacle of a society that valued agriculture above mere commerce. In this connection, the Physiocrats had occasion to applaud a set of legal and moral institutions upon which agrarian societies were seen to thrive. (In honoring the "Spartan" rectitude of Peruvian society, the Physiocrats enumerated a curiously bourgeois repertoire of virtues: marital fidelity, cleanliness, industriousness, and education.) For these reasons, preconquest Peruvian society provided material for an "economic novel" to edify eighteenth-century readers. This was true even though contemporary Peruvians—and native Americans in general—had suffered appalling physical and moral transformations since the conquest: "The slaves of the Spanish are nothing more than the shadow of the former Peruvians."[30] This juxtaposition established yet another basis on which to judge the effects of European commerce in the Americas. Far from laying the groundwork for economic progress, the enslavement and destruction of advanced American societies entrenched a sort of backwardness that ran against the grain of stadial progress.

Despite the destructiveness of these initial conquests, Roubaud did hold out hope that the Americas would ultimately develop into the "capital of humanity" from their position of subjugation. Within the context of Europeans in America, such aspirations hinged upon the triumph of the "true" colonial spirit over the "prohibitive, fiscal regime" instituted by some colonial powers, most notably Spain and France. Here, Roubaud's narrative was full of invidious comparisons between the colonial styles of France and Britain. "It has been seen how great the inequality between the forces of the two nations [France and England] were: this difference did not owe its origin to the extent or quality of their land; it was an effect of their governments and *moeurs*."[31]

For Roubaud, the differences between French and English colonization were dictated by the government and *moeurs* of the colonies, which were expressed, in turn, in their respective social structures—all categories, it should be noted, that were completely alien to the *Tableau economique*. First, government had a profound impact on the *moeurs* of colonists sent across the Atlantic. However much, for instance, "The fur trade, and especially beaver pelts, was rather profitable in Canada," the metropole debauched this prosperity with a host of monopolies and taxes, without the compensating benefit of the protection extended to British colonists: "[even] the slave is fed and protected by the hand that oppresses him: France abandoned its colonies to the opposite fate." Such precariousness, which evinced all of the faults of a blind despotism, meant that instead of building a new civilization in Canada, the colonists regressed below the level of an agricultural or even pastoral people: "Far from bending the savages to French customs," Roubaud observed, evoking the contrast between barbarism and civilization that suffused philosophical history, "the French adopted the savage life *en masse*." Here, we see clearly what Roubaud had in view when he emphasized the reciprocal influences that Europeans and Americans were having on each other in the New World.[32]

Roubaud's evocation of "the savage life" was intended to characterize both the backwardness of North American Indians and France's colonial-mercantile apparatus, which valued the ephemeral (and contested) gains of the luxury trade over the eternally self-renewing riches of agriculture: "the English created an agricultural people and the French a hunter-gather people." This lamentable result was both the cause and effect of what Roubaud viewed as the common theme of the entire French colonial effort: the nicety of the regulation imposed by the French trading companies, animated by the spirit of monopoly, put "the French colonies . . . into a state of dilapidation worthy of all of the ministrations of a tutelary government."[33]

It is clear that Roubaud did not view *les progrès du commerce* as contributing inevitably to the civilizing process. He likened the commercial and colonial tactics of the French and Spanish not to the civilizing process of *doux commerce* but to a lapse into "the savage life"—for themselves and the natives alike. For the Physiocrats, the last stage of economic development, which saw the rise of rapacious, buccaneering capitalists as well as the oppressive mercantile apparatus of "feudal government," resembled earlier levels of civilization more closely than later ones. Such an observation does damage to the progressive narratives of Enlightenment that were ubiquitous at the time, especially when we consider how fundamental commerce, and especially European commerce with the Americas, was in explaining this process.

Despite these grim prospects for the Americas and the European nations that held these territories in tutelage, the Physiocrats nevertheless believed that, in the end, Europe's "mercantile policy" laid the basis for its own demise and the subsequent ascendancy of "a truly economic government" or "the constitution of the agricultural colonies."[34]

Since the publication of Véron de Forbonnais' *Encyclopédie* article, "COLONIES," it had become standard to typologize and periodize the styles and stages of colonization, from those of wandering biblical tribes to the establishments of the Greeks and Romans. For Forbonnais, the final historical variety of colony was represented by the European colonies in the Americas: set up by Europeans for their own benefit, these colonies were to be protected but at the price of economic exploitation through the Exclusive—an arrangement also summarized by the term "colonial pact" *(pacte coloniale)*, which was imposed only retrospectively in the nineteenth century. The Physiocrats responded to Forbonnais' typology and its implicit colonial ideology with their own scheme. Mirabeau, for instance, posited the existence of three stages for the

Europeans in America: domination, commerce, and population. This was an analysis carried into the *Philosophie rurale,* a work co-authored by Quesnay and Mirabeau after the latter's conversion to Physiocracy. As Mirabeau explained, succeeding stages could transcend the limitations of the previous ones, though as often as not, European empires such as Spain were stuck in an early stage. France, according to Mirabeau, had a "monstrous" combination of commerce, domination, and population— hardly a ringing endorsement of the monarchy's strategy of reconciling agrarian France with the new world of transoceanic commerce.[35]

As the Physiocratic narrative of eighteenth-century wars of commerce made clear, the spirit of monopoly had given rise to these wars, but only its opposite principle could really claim victory. In the wake of the Seven Years' War, the Physiocrats lamented the lack of true colonists on the ground, claiming that only "a new agricultural militia" would stanch French losses to the British in North America. Drawing on this analysis, Roubaud saw these wars as canceling the powers of monopoly and "feudal government" that had set them in motion in the first place, in a sort of dialectical inversion. The agricultural occupation by the British colonists reinforced their strength against the French, which, in turn, strengthened the colonists' own predilection toward free government, in stark contrast to the French case: "Among the first government was popular: the laws protected them and they were citizens; a military government led the others: they were soldiers, and lived almost everywhere under arbitrary government, much like a military camp."[36]

For the Physiocrats, the superiority of the agriculturally oriented colony determined not only the outcome of intra-European rivalries in the Americas but would ultimately transform the relations of the colonies to their respective metropolises. As early as 1756, Mirabeau presciently concluded what the implications were of the economic maturation of the Americas, "the new theatre of humanity." Through the mutually reinforcing effects of agricultural prosperity and political freedom, the colonies would ineluctably gain strength, and hence independence, vis à vis the metropole: "As for the permanence of [the colonies'] dependence . . . The *new world will certainly shake off the yoke of the old;* there is even reason to believe that this will begin with the strongest and most well-favored colonies. . . . In vain do we rack our brains—whether in London or in Paris—speculating on how to prevent this eventuality." In making these predictions, it seems likely that Mirabeau was influenced by the detailed correspondence he maintained with his brother Jean-Antoine Joseph while the latter served a stint as governor of Guadeloupe (1753–1755). Shortly after his arrival in Guadeloupe, the younger Mirabeau remarked upon the "moral and physical impossibility of the conservation of our colonies"; Mirabeau "searched for the causes of the wrongs I see around me: greed is the principal cause of the small success of these colonies. The policies of European states are the second among them, possibly even the first." Like his older brother, Jean-Antoine Joseph Mirabeau concluded that "America will be lost to us soon."[37]

Looking at the events in British America and projecting forward, Mirabeau and others saw that there was no longer any European power strong enough to dominate the markets of the Atlantic world that their mercantilist policies had, intentionally or not, created. Once they realized this fact, Turgot declared, "the illusion that has deluded our politicians for two centuries will be dissipated." The "new order" of things envisioned by these Physiocratic thinkers sketched out a progressive, emancipationist historical logic that was simply not applicable to the "new order" of Euro-American politics created by Atlantic commerce in its opening phases. Far from simply arriving at the *doux commerce* thesis from a different direction, the Physiocrats accomplished a politically charged form of historical revisionism; the shape that they collectively gave to the history of commerce demonstrated the self-destruction of "feudal government" in one of its most virulent forms: the colonial-mercantile system. At the same time, this revisionist history of commerce demonstrated the long-term fragility of any social and political order that was not based upon the Physiocratic order, and method, of nature.[38]

Territory and Nation

The Physiocratic history of commerce was much at variance with their methods, but it was broadly consonant with the Physiocrats' desire to call the French back to the land. This program was ultimately much more radical, both as social-scientific method and as Old Regime politics, than Physiocratic paeans to rural virtue first appear.

Territory was more than a policy emphasis for the Physiocrats: it was their field of analysis. Most economic models rely at least implicitly on a closed system, a space within which value is thought to be conserved so that the effects of economic processes such as production and exchange can be measured. Bullionism and balance of trade theory take a loosely defined unit called the nation, country, or kingdom, where precious metals or foreign goods flow in and out, and from the rise and fall of these quantities, the effectiveness of trade and monetary policy can be evaluated; the balance sheet defines the business enterprise as a set of assets and liabilities in order to calculate profit. Along these lines, the Physiocrats constituted a space of analysis in order to track the production and circulation of agricultural produce. This closed unit was identified as the "kingdom" or, with increasing frequency as time went by, the "territory." Within the territory, produce could either be consumed productively, in activities that led to economic growth, or unproductively, as in the case of luxury consumption. Resources could be used with varying degrees of efficiency, leaving more or less net produce for consumption or growth. To the degree that goods circulated freely, the territory and its inhabitants were thereby enriched. For bullionists and balance of trade theorists, the only really significant element of this space, from an analytical point of view, is the border: gold and goods flowing in are counted as positive values, while movement in the opposite direction generates negative values. The Physiocrats saw the interior of this space as far more significant, because within it essential processes such as the production, circulation, and transformation of value take place; quite in contrast to their predecessors and contemporaries—or even their followers in classical political economy—the Physiocrats sought to literalize this space through their depiction in an "economic picture," the *Tableau Economique*.[39]

The Physiocratic desire to make France an economically coherent and "legible" space of analysis was not simply a fantasy of Platonic scientific aesthetics or an idle conceit of administrative omniscience. At midcentury, France was still divided into a number of customs zones; outside of a large, relatively free zone of trade known as the "five great farms" created in 1598, most other parts of France were divided for tax and trade purposes into "essentially foreign provinces" *(provinces réputées étrangers)*: twenty-one distinct zones enjoying diverse privileges and exemptions. A limited number of provinces recently incorporated into the monarchy, among them Franche-Comté, Alsace, and Gex, actually traded on freer terms with foreign countries than with other French provinces. Naturally, taxes were paid on goods when they moved from one zone to another, and the addition of transportation costs could halt exchanges altogether by rendering them unprofitable, particularly when heavy or bulky goods moved overland or, in the best of cases, over a still underdeveloped water transport system. As Philip Hoffman has argued, the single most important factor in determining agricultural specialization and growth in Old Regime France was not plot size but the availability and openness of markets, an outcome militated against by France's physical and political divisions. The increasing movement of people and productive processes beyond city walls in the eighteenth century, in order to circumvent the guild regulations intended to restrict the quantity and mobility of skilled labor, only attests to the continued importance of guild privileges over this period. And France's system of taxation, even if it was more efficient than has generally been thought, nevertheless varied considerably not only among regions and cities but also between legal persons and even individual plots of land according to the privileges they enjoyed. Space—whether the distance separating producers and consumers, the limits of labor markets or taxation zones, or the sometimes overlapping spheres of sovereignty—was an economic and political problem in Old Regime France.[40]

The Physiocrats sought to overcome the uneconomic division of space by advocating tirelessly for free markets—laissez-faire, laissez-passer—in the circulation of goods; the abolition of guild restrictions; and the elimination of all tax privileges in favor of a single land tax. To the extent that they converged with absolutist ambitions, including the clear definition of monarchical sovereignty and the amplification of state power through economic growth, Physiocratic policy ideas received episodic encouragement from Louis XV, Louis XIV, and both kings' ministers; but the Physiocratic theory of enlightened despotism went much further than the ad hoc policies of absolutism ever could have hoped, identifying the sovereign with a unified territory whose inhabitants were bound to one another, and the state, through common economic interests. Classical social contract theory such as we see in the work of John Locke finds the origin of society in the right of self-preservation; our self is the one thing we own unambiguously, and that self is projected into the objects of our labor, which are necessary, in turn, to sustain our life. For the Physiocrats, the foundation of the social contract was not property in labor, as we find in Locke and others, but property in land; given the Physiocrats' insistence that agriculture is the sole origin of value, this is to be expected: the social contract is based upon what it preserves and, crucially, what preserves it. But what of the state? Sovereignty is "physically" founded on the land, because it derives from the social contract: "we know that property in land is the basis of all society. Sovereignty is only physically founded upon this." The state provides public goods such as defense, education, and infrastructure, paid for by taxes on net agricultural product. "Co-proprietorship" in this context means first of all the state's claim to a portion of this revenue but also the conjunction of its interests with those of individual landowners: to the extent that landowners prosper, the "co-proprietor"—that is, the state—enjoys a higher revenue.[41] In Physiocratic political theory, rights, interests, and even sovereignty are all resolved into territory and reconciled within this space.

The very coherence of this system enabled a series of claims that were, as Alexis de Tocqueville has observed, quite radical in the context of Old Regime France. The monarchy envisioned in Physiocratic theory had little to do with Montesquieu's politics of fusion or with the moderate reforms proposed by members of the Gournay circle—both of which envisioned a monarchical but commercial France that retained significant elements of its existing social hierarchy and political system. At least formally, Physiocratic political economy could not tolerate trade restrictions of any sort, corporate privileges, civic inequality, or the division of sovereignty. Any of these institutions would upset the reciprocity of rights, interests, and state power within the closed space of the territory, which led Adam Smith to quip: "if a nation could not prosper without perfect liberty and perfect justice, there is not a nation in the world which could ever have prospered."[42]

Physiocratic theory could accommodate foreign trade and colonial establishments only as exceptions. As Dupont de Nemours observed, "every merchant is a foreigner relative to the interests" of agricultural nations. Even where economic writers such as Melon or Forbonnais followed nationalistic conceptions of French grandeur, they welcomed the cosmopolitan dimensions of international trade because competition served as a spur to domestic industry, while the threat of capital flight tempered monarchical despotism. The Physiocrats saw commerce and agriculture, by contrast, as two opposed nations within the same territory: "an agricultural and commercial kingdom unite two nations that are distinct from one another. One forms the essential part [*partie constitutive*] of society attached to the territory that furnishes its wealth and the other is an extrinsic addition that belongs to the general republic of foreign trade, employed and paid by agricultural nations." Dupont de Nemours was no xenophobe, but the supranational dimension of foreign trade gave him pause: "the extent of [international merchants'] profession has no determined limits and no particular territory. Our merchants are also the merchants of other nations."[43] Foreign trade might be beneficial for agricultural nations insofar as it allowed them to direct their capital into its most productive employment, agriculture, while leaving manufacture to others. Implicit in this reasoning was the idea that France had a comparative advantage over its rivals in the domain of agricultural production and that a strategy of import substitution—either through colonial produce or the encouragement of domestic industry—was economically inefficient. But the profits of trade could be conceived of only as a dead loss: when domestic merchants undertook trade, their profits were a transaction cost, a necessary but regrettable dissipation of value or "net produce" that attended the circulation of all goods; foreign merchants' profits were a leakage of value from the territory, and this loss had to be minimized by employing the most competitive carriers. And this was only in the case when goods traded at the natural price dictated by free competition. As their exposé of the "mercantile system" demonstrated, foreign merchants rarely contented themselves with such mediocre profits. Commerce thrived upon the monopolies, privileges, and systems of exclusion that were anathema to the Physiocrats; where the agricultural nation had an interest in opening markets and uniting all parts of the territory through the free circulation of goods, the commercial nation sought to segment and divide the nation in order to capture unnatural profits for itself. On an international scale, colonial trade restrictions and the conquest of markets through commercial warfare were an integral part of this system, reproducing the feudal fragmentation of sovereignty, space, and peoples for the sake of profit.

The Physiocratic diagnosis of the American colonies can be viewed narrowly as an attempt to resolve the difficulties arising out of a rigorous definition of sovereignty and an exclusive theory of value, both tied to the land. But theoretical consistency was far from the primary stake in the question of colonial commerce: in the conflict between the colony and metropole, the Physiocrats sensed a mutually destructive type of social warfare between the productive regions of an empire separated by politics, history, and oceanic expanses. Progress for Turgot, Roubaud, and others meant the encouragement of "agricultural colonies" abroad and the incorporation of these territories, on equal political and economic footing, into the French nation. The geographic separation of colony from metropole places obvious limits on how literally the Physiocratic solution of territorial incorporation should be taken, but the broad significance of this gesture is clear: for the benefit of France as a whole, the Physiocrats wanted to bring the colonies into the space of freedom, exchange, and reciprocity visualized in the *Tableau Economique.*

The space the Physiocrats had in mind, of course, was the nation. Prior to mid-century, *philosophes* and administrators who wrote about questions of colonial political economy used the terms "kingdom," "nation," and even "empire" in loose, generally interchangeable ways. "National commerce" had been used for some time to designate the interests of metropolitan merchants and was taken unreflectively as a synecdoche for the interests of France as a whole. As the century advanced, the French colonies contributed increasingly to the economy of the mother country; with their growth, unequal terms of trade with the metropole came under increasing scrutiny, as did the reflexive identification of the French nation and its economic interests with the metropole.

CHAPTER 6

Center, Periphery, and
Commerce National

W HEN FRENCH ECONOMIC WRITERS including the Physiocrats
speculated about the ultimate fate of Europe's colonial-mercantile
enterprise, they analyzed how peculiarities of social structure, government, and manners influenced France's role in this evolving system; the
science of commerce also provided a means of analyzing nearer-term
geopolitical questions, including the financial, demographic, and military challenges pressing on the French empire. But the prime mover of
this system was profit, and so any substantive discussion among merchants, *philosophes,* and statesmen about the system's structure had to
attend to the division of spoils between metropolitan France and its colonies. In practical terms, this meant debate over the Exclusive, the trading regime established in 1717, when the monopoly privileges in the West
Indies enjoyed by the Compagnie de l'Occident were suppressed and
assigned to the generality of French merchants in a limited number of
port cities. From this point forward, the Compagnie de l'Occident exercised monopoly privileges only beyond the Cape of Good Hope, while
merchants in cities such as Nantes, Bordeaux, Saint-Malo, and La
Rochelle benefited from the exclusive right to trade in the Americas.[1]
The Exclusive was France's answer to England's Navigation Acts of
1651, and like these acts, the Exclusive decreed with some exceptions

that all goods flowing to and from the French colonies must be carried in French bottoms. France, which was a net importer of colonial goods by a great and increasing margin over the eighteenth century, recaptured colonial surplus by selling dear and buying cheaply, charging colonial planters for shipping services in the bargain. There were other formal and informal mechanisms for ensuring a favorable division of colonial surplus for the metropole, including currency and credit arrangements, but the Exclusive was the principle manifestation of this system and came to stand for all the rest.[2]

Over the course of the eighteenth century, this basic element of French commercial policy came repeatedly into question. The problem was twofold. First, in ordinary circumstances, colonial merchants and planters chafed under these restrictions because, by design, the Exclusive raised the prices of their imports and depressed the price of exports—hence, the complaints of the contraband (or "interlope") trade that foreigners, and in particular the English, plied in the colonies. Contraband trade was ubiquitous, but for obvious reasons nobody can be certain of its true extent; anywhere between 10 and 60 percent of colonial produce, and especially sugar, was sold directly to foreigners. Metropolitan merchants lost profits on shipping services, re-export, and often the returns on refining operations located in France, while the crown lost valuable customs duties called the *domaine d'occident,* a tax of at least 3 percent *ad valorem* on goods arriving in France from the Americas. Sugar products were subjected to even higher taxes, assessed on weight, but re-exports of all kinds were exempt. Second, during the disruptions of war, French merchants were incapable of fully provisioning the colonies, and restrictions were often relaxed to allow neutrals to trade in the colonies. In some cases, weakly defended islands such as Martinique actually changed hands for a short period of time—a situation that led colonists to question the basis of their political allegiance to, and economic exploitation by, the French. Metropolitan merchants treated naval conflicts and contraband trade as exceptional, but these were manifestations of competitive pressures bound to arise in a distant colonial periphery. Resistance to this regime—administrative, political, and ideological—was every bit as endogenous to a system of delocalized production, trade, and consumption as were war and contraband.[3]

Merchants' defenses of the Exclusive against the assaults by its opponents are not striking as evidence of intellectual ferment. After request by the directors of the Chamber of Commerce of Saint-Malo in 1758 that their city enjoy the same privileges as other port cities, the Chambers of Commerce of both Nantes and Bordeaux were content to reprint a memoir written on the same subject in 1737—thus sparing themselves the effort of finding new arguments where old ones had succeeded and saving on printing costs at the same time.[4] A wider sampling of these memoirs only confirms the impression made concrete in this instance: as pressure groups working for their own parochial interests and as bodies established by the crown in order to survey and regulate trade, chambers of commerce representing merchants in France's Atlantic ports met a limited number of recurring trade issues with an equally limited repertoire of ideas. The key idea these merchants drew upon was the following: colonies must be useful to the metropole.[5] Like any province, colonies owed political obedience, but on the theory of the "colonial pact," the metropole also had the right to recuperate, with a profit, its expenditures in settling, administering, and protecting the colonies by imposing trade restrictions on them. The diversion of profits to metropolitan merchants would redound to the benefit of France's "commerce national," the interests of which were identified with the nation at large. This was an argument made publicly by Forbonnais in his 1753 *Encyclopédie* article, "COLONIES."[6]

Despite the superficial stability in arguments about the Exclusive over the course of the eighteenth century, important shifts took place underneath the surface. France's Atlantic chambers of commerce would have liked to repeat such arguments as a part of their organized pressure tactics, but as the island economies expanded, colonists were increasingly capable of mounting resistance to the Exclusive of all sorts—passive, active, intellectual, and practical.[7] Moreover, due to a confluence of commercial and geopolitical considerations, the colonists were seconded by ministers and administrators who legitimized and intellectually amplified the colonists' arguments. At issue were empirical questions about capital inputs, consumption goods, shipping capacities, trade circuits, and financial flows, but the debate was conducted on both sides with reference to the familiar question of France's constitution and the commercial structures that best suited it; predictably, Montesquieu's political sociology provided a fundamental referent for interlocutors on both sides of the debate. As the century progressed, however, more radical premises about the dissolving differences between the colony and metropole (or "core" and "periphery" in present-day world-systems theory) found their way into the debate. Even where merchants or administrators fundamentally resisted Physiocratic laissez-faire and the accompanying territorial conception of the French empire, it was apparent that this school had left its mark in sometimes unintended ways. Faced with irresolvable, politically dangerous material conflicts between center and periphery, *philosophes,* merchants, and statesmen reached for new definitions of economic nationhood, which also entailed rethinking old notions of sovereignty and collective interest. Although the merchants of France's chambers of commerce and their representatives did not produce these new ideas, the need to alter their strategies in the face of their opponents testifies to how thoroughly the ground had shifted under their feet—how "rancid," as their opponent Jean-Baptiste Dubuc commented bitterly, old arguments had become. For now, we return to a time when these arguments were fresh, to savor their slow rot over the succeeding decades.

The Discussion in 1701

In 1700, the year that Louis XIV created the Conseil du Commerce (Council of Commerce), he also set out to establish chambers of commerce in France's major port and manufacturing cities. Up until this point, it was only Marseilles and Dunkirk that had established chambers of commerce; other major cities had only *juridictions consulaires* that judged controversies arising from trade, but there were no constituted bodies whose function it was to provide economic information and opinions to the monarch. As a part of this larger administrative effort, and in an attempt to revivify a flagging economy in the wake of the War of the League of Augsburg (1688–1697) and the Peace of Ryswick (1697), the king solicited memoirs from the thirteen provincial deputies to the council. The resulting document provides a remarkably detailed snapshot not only of the state of France's economy at the turn of the century but also of the mentality of its merchant elite.[8]

In all of these memoirs, the passion and lucidity with which the deputies argued for a regime of "liberty" was matched only by special pleading for local privileges and protections. This seeming bad faith was characteristic first of all of a rent-seeking economy but also of an economic mentality where "liberty and protection" were considered complementary rather than contradictory. Given their awareness that other cities were simultaneously advancing their own special claims for liberty and protection to the Council of Commerce, it is understandable that colony–metropole relations were not the exclusive focus of these memoirs. Nevertheless, what was said about foreign trade, and in particular the triangular trade, which was at the time controlled by the Compagnie de la Guinée and the Compagnie de l'Occident, was laden with significance for later debates. As might be expected, merchants hailing from the Atlantic ports objected to the monopoly privileges enjoyed by the Compagnie de l'Occident, which was established by the king in 1664. Where commerce was confined to a charmed circle of merchants associated with the company, these merchants repeatedly underlined the advantages of opening this commerce up to the public.[9]

Clearly, it was advantageous for these groups of merchants to pose themselves as members of a public rather than as a group of individuals who could be viewed as indifferent, or even opposed, to the good of the state. This was especially true in the domain of foreign trade, where cosmopolitanism and the outflow of specie were thought to harm national interests in a way that regional rivalries, however bitter, were not. When contrasted to the enjoyment of exclusive privileges, however, the practice of commerce was nudged rhetorically into the corner of the *public* and the *bien public:* "all these propositions [for individual privileges] are odious and onerous to the state and to the public: each city should have the same liberty: it is to the general and not to the individual good that one must attend." Antoine Héron, deputy of La Rochelle, observed that all policies must lead to the *bien public,* which consisted of taxes paid into the king's treasury; for the king's subjects, increased commerce meant subsistence, "facility and ease." Far from representing the vantage point of self-interested individuals, the deputies of commerce and the nascent chambers of commerce claimed for themselves a special understanding of the *bien public* as an oppressed class that turned the wheels of commerce against the stiff resistance of monopolistic privileges and, crucially, public scorn.[10]

However, when merchants' claims on behalf of the public against privileges were turned against overseas trading companies, the deputies' arguments became considerably more nuanced. Joachim Descasaux du Hally, a deputy from Nantes, argued that in the 1660s, companies of commerce were perhaps necessary because, at the time, ideas of commerce were "completely lost" among the French. The state was therefore obliged to organize these overseas ventures. Moreover, colonies had to be established and protected at great expense.[11] Now, Descasaux argued, old colonies were on firm footing, new colonies were unnecessary, and there was sufficient "enlightenment and competition" among the public to ply this trade on its own behalf. (Without explicitly mentioning the fact, here the "public" meant merchants operating out of a restricted number of Atlantic ports.) Although the argument against privilege appeared general, it was, in fact, subtly modulated: "there is *no longer* need of these privileges"—a qualification that left open the possibility that in other circumstances privileges might indeed be necessary.[12] The other side of the coin—a fact unacknowledged in this memoir, but one that would begin to have consequences as the century wore on—was that the historical conditions that justified the exclusive privileges enjoyed by France's Atlantic ports might well change, giving way to alternative conceptions of the *bien public* and the good of *commerce national.* Before moving on to these shifts, however, we will dwell on the question of how metropolitan advocates defended their exclusive access to colonial markets and produce.

Center–Periphery Relations and the *Police* of Economic Life

Whereas in a purely metropolitan context exclusive trading privileges were seen as subverting the common weal in the name of individual profit, restricting foreign trade in France's colonial periphery was said to bind the colony to the metropole for the public good. As the directors of the Guyenne (Bordeaux region) Chamber of Commerce lamented in 1730, there had formerly been a reciprocal tie between France and the Antilles, with one consuming the surplus of the other: "when this relation was maintained, commerce flourished and abundance reigned; the public enjoyed it and the individual who exposed his fortune and his life to the hazards of the sea profited by it." "But," observed the deputies, "this relation ceasing, commerce must also necessarily cease with it." The decline of this relationship, and hence of France's commerce with the Americas, could be attributed to a number of factors, but the broadest causes related to a lack of will. Island elites did not display the subordination, and even civilization, associated with government on the mainland: "Why let the island be breached and open itself to the enemies and destroyers of commerce who will invade the Island once there is an uprising there?" "The King makes prohibitive edicts," they continued, "why not make them respected?" The answer, for the directors of the Guyenne Chamber of Commerce as for so many others, lay with the supposedly lax government in the colonies: the locals undertook trade with foreigners with the "connivance of [their] superiors who should prevent it." At issue here was whether the king truly exercised his "dominance" over the French Antilles and whether his servants were actually civilizing these far-flung lands by distributing justice fairly and imposing European *police*—a desideratum for commerce in any sort of polity and a fundamental category for contemporary economic writers such as Jean-François Melon.[13]

French laxity, by contrast, supposedly evinced a lack of national pride: "their duty, their conscience and the honor of the nation should oblige them to strictly exclude them [the Anglo-Americans], but isn't it only a sordid greed that blinds us?" Such promiscuous attitudes threatened both "the state and the commerce of our nation." Spain and England, by contrast, "religiously observed" prohibitive laws. Such arguments seem to support the thesis that nationalism—in this case actuated by the desire to catch up economically with other nations—was a cause of economic modernization and growth, but this proposition mistakes cause for effect. These merchants seized upon approved sentiments— "patriotism" or "nationalism"—to shore up arguments arising out of a rather different set of priorities. Rent seekers, from early modern chartered companies to military contractors, have always clothed special pleading in the national interest. But the specious, transparent, and even tawdry reasoning in many of these memoirs evoking patriotic sentiments should erase any doubts about the lines of causation—even where these propositions, when accepted, may have advanced truly national, as opposed to strictly parochial, economic interests.[14]

Without assigning nationalism, then, as a cause of these merchants' views and activities, it is nevertheless true that they viewed America, and particularly the Caribbean sugar islands, as ill defined from the perspective of a profitable *commerce national.* A stricter sense of the nation would serve France's merchants and its national interest. The chambers of commerce repeatedly argued not only that foreigners should be excluded from *commerce national*—this was unsurprising—but that they should be excluded altogether, in imitation of the Spanish, from living in France's colonies. Englishmen or Irishmen living on French islands were regarded as a sort of fifth column for smugglers, whose "close correspondence" with countrymen living elsewhere could only harm national interests. As for contraband trade, the strictest measures were advised in order to make the lesson clear and to enforce a civilizing *police* upon this commerce. One deputy suggested the most draconian measures, noting approvingly that in Paris, five or six lackeys were publicly executed by way of exemplary punishment for breaking street lanterns: "nobody thinks that the death penalty was too severe for maintaining the police, however seemingly trivial the object." Self-interested motives aside, these deputies did have a point: frequently reiterated royal edicts concerning the Exclusive could undermine royal authority *(police)* when they were so regularly contravened in practice. Conversely, repeated interruptions to trade caused by war, vagaries of food provisioning due to weather, and resistance to metropolitan dictates by colonial elites who were steadily "creolized" over the course of the eighteenth century testified to the fluidity of the situation on the ground and the need for a supple commercial policy.[15] Harsh principles and modulated practice can help legitimate the law. By continually asserting the principle of the Exclusive while tacitly allowing for its infraction in cases of necessity, the crown could be viewed more charitably as playing a subtle game intended to keep the colonists within the orbit of its authority.[16]

Nevertheless, in a zone where sovereignty and people shifted more freely, merchants thought it logical to suppose that *commerce national* could be secured for France's exclusive benefit only if the meaning of "national" was well defined—even at the price of severe punishments. A clearer sense of what constituted French versus foreign territory or persons would help staunch the flow of contraband goods in and out of the colonies. All of this is especially true if we take account of the distances between metropole and colony and the multinational, semiprivate character of the settlement of these distant places. In arguing thus, these merchants tacitly invoked the absolutist project of organizing the space of the nation to improve the exercise of sovereign power as well as the production and circulation of wealth. Later in the century, the Physiocrats would extend and clarify this program.

The reformist ideas of the Physiocrats were one thing, the realities of the absolutist state quite another. The economic, administrative, and political rationalization of France led to a dual movement of homogenization and differentiation; the doctrine of laissez-faire, laissez passer, and an impulse to get rid of administrative irrationality led to homogenization, but the expansion of the French state and economy necessitated a carefully ordered and differentiated exercise of authority and space of exchange. France remained a fundamentally corporate society, and monarchs had to work through established elites and institutions in order to exercise their power. Loans for the crown were raised through the intermediary of the Parisian municipality, for instance; royal justice was administered through venal office holders and the corps to which they belonged; and a penurious state often shifted administrative duties onto semi-autonomous local elites. The ambitions of absolute monarchs and the dreams of philosophical partisans of enlightened despotism were clearer, more coherent, and powerful than the comparatively fragile societies on which they were imposed; in this context, a seemingly paradoxical process of homogenization and differentiation makes just as much sense as the doctrine of "liberty and protection." Beyond the specificities of eighteenth-century France, modernization theory, both liberal and Marxist, has also had to come to terms with the fact that "capitalism has always thrived on the production of difference."[17]

What this meant for merchants in France's Atlantic ports was fourfold: First, politically and economically, France's colonial periphery should be more closely identified with the metropole. Second, this identification was not to be confused with equality: the colony–metropole binary was to be asserted even more strongly, with the latter exercising economic and political dominance over the former. Third, both of these aims would be ensured by more sharply differentiating French from non-French territory, commodities, and people in the Americas. Finally, within the islands, this meant the production and enforcement of racial differences in the constitution of the islands' labor force—a proposition seldom contested anywhere. Initially, opponents of the exclusive trading regime rarely questioned the basic distinction between the colony and the metropole, but over the course of the century, everything came up for grabs as colonial wealth and power weighed increasingly in the balance of France's *bien public.*

The Exclusive: Republican and Monarchical Commerce in the Colonies

In the wake of the Seven Years' War and the Treaty of Paris of 1763, France ceded its North American possessions (Canada and Louisiana, respectively) to England and Spain in exchange for those sugar islands that England had occupied during the course of the conflict. This humiliating decision made perfect economic sense at the time but set off a chain reaction. At home, the extraordinary costs of the Seven Years' War led to domestic political crisis and a collective questioning of the profits to be gained from a monopolistic trading regime defended repeatedly throughout the century with blood, iron, and, in particular, royal tax receipts. Within the Ministry of the Navy, this loss set the Duc de Choiseul, the Secretary of State of War and of the Navy, thinking about alternatives to Canada as an American source for raw materials and as an outlet for colonial produce. This quest led directly to Chanvalon and Turgot's disastrous expedition to establish a colony in Guyana in 1763–1765. Furthermore, although colonists were predictably never enamored of the Exclusive, events of the Seven Years' War had a galvanizing effect on their opposition to this policy. Guadeloupe and Martinique prospered during the brief time that the English controlled them during the conflict, and the inability of the French crown to protect its overseas possessions only underlined the fact that, far from representing a social pact with reciprocal rights and responsibilities, the metropole–colony relationship amounted to simple economic exploitation. Conversely, the fact that the colonists of Martinique and Guadeloupe put up so little resistance to their English invaders contributed materially to France's difficulties during the Seven Years' War; France's commercial policies toward the islands created this soft underbelly in the French commercial empire, which only amplified colonists' sense of resentment.[18]

This unnerving spectacle led the crown to rethink, from their foundations, the laws governing colonial commerce, and most particularly the Exclusive. As a first step, Choiseul appointed Jean Dubuc as the first secretary *(premier commis)* of the Bureau des Colonies. Dubuc was a native of Martinique and a plantation owner who had initially traveled to France to serve as a deputy of commerce for that island to the Royal Council of Commerce. Whether Dubuc was appointed to this post despite his family's participation in the 1727 revolt of St. Domingue or because of it is an interesting if unresolved question; an answer would shed light on the relative importance Choiseul assigned to the colonial and metropolitan lobbies and to the level of provocation he intended by Dubuc's appointment. In any case, Dubuc's intelligence, diligence, and connections on both sides of the Atlantic were sufficient recommendations to this post. For the purposes of initiating a dialogue with the maritime chambers of commerce, Dubuc submitted a memoir entitled *On the Extent and Limits of Prohibitive Laws on Foreign Commerce in Our Colonies,* which was read in the Council of Commerce on 9 April 1765; it argued that the colonies, and in particular Martinique, were suffering economically from a lack of slaves because French merchants could not supply them in sufficient quantity or quality. Consequently, Dubuc argued, the Council of Commerce should legalize the import of slaves (and a limited number of other commodities) by non-French nationals and also allow for the direct export of some colonial products, such as syrups and rum *(tafias).* The latter measure, Dubuc claimed, would serve as a spur to colonial production by raising the prices of colonial goods, which were depressed by the exclusive privileges presently enjoyed, in theory, by French merchants.[19]

This memoir was circulated to the chambers of commerce of France's maritime cities, which coordinated a series of detailed and vigorous replies; Dubuc had struck a nerve. The Nantes Chamber of

Commerce complained that Dubuc's memoir was "read in the Council of his Majesty," which lent it a false air of authority, concerning as it did "a project that will decide the fate of Commerce and—this is not an exaggeration—of *the state with which it is intimately linked.*"[20]

Sensing the seriousness of the threat posed by a change of commercial regime, these chambers of commerce drew on their best authority: Montesquieu. Because these colonies were established at the initiative and expense of the mother country, their dependence dictated the subordination of trade to the economic and political goals of the metropole. "It is a fundamental law of Europe," Montesquieu explained, "that all commerce with a foreign colony is regarded as a pure monopoly. . . . It is still widely understood that the commerce established between metropoles does not entail such permission for the colonies, which always remain in a state of prohibition." Such, in skeletal form, was the underlying justification and practice of the Exclusive. The author of Saint-Malo's response to this seditious memoir began by quoting the passages just cited, emphasizing for his audience the "fundamental laws" that were to guide colonial trading policies: the economic benefit of the metropole should prevail over that of these new and dependent societies.[21]

Taking into account their interests and his prestige, the elective affinities of the Atlantic chambers of commerce with Montesquieu are not terribly surprising; they did not quote Forbonnais, for instance, who laid out this logic approvingly, whereas Montesquieu merely described it. Questions of authority aside, the way Montesquieu's ideas were used went far beyond the opportunistic insertion of a few key sentences on the Exclusive here and there in order to give these memoirs polish and credibility. Montesquieu provided, to borrow the words of Bernard Bailyn, a "logic and grammar" for people on both sides of the debate. His intellectual authority explains why Hilliard d'Auberteuil devoted long forensic passages to disproving the idea that the *Esprit des lois* should be used as a brief against colonial interests; instead, d'Auberteuil plausibly argued that Montesquieu's whole approach supported the idea of readjusting colonial legislation to changing circumstances. The author of the Saint-Malo memoir stated simply that permission for foreigners to enter colonial ports would be the ruin of French trade because neither French shipping services nor its manufactures could possibly withstand open competition.[22] This writer did not cite any statistics in favor of this opinion but instead appealed to "facts" and "nature" as opposed to the "dogmatic reasoning" *(raisonnemens sistêmatiques)* of the Physiocrats. "Our laws and our *moeurs* condemn our navigation to be two times more expensive than that of the people of the Baltic states of Europe and it is the first proof of the fact that we cannot support competition with them." Here, of course, the author is referring to the carrying trade *(commerce d'économie)*, which, given "the sobriety of these people supported by their laws," produced in these more austere northern types a greater vocation for this sort of trade than that found among the extravagant French.[23]

Extending Montesquieu's analysis of the role of the carrying trade in republican versus monarchical states, the author also drew on the famous taxonomy of the form and principle of governments to strengthen his case. Transforming the potentially abstract discourse of *moeurs* into a specifically economic argument, this author asked why French shipping was persistently costlier than Dutch or English services. "Our *moeurs* come next. . . . In a monarchical government, whose principle is honor," novices cannot rise through the ranks to become captains. In other countries, where the principle of honor provides no obstruction, "commerce itself trains its own captains." So, for training purposes, we find "a multitude of officers on our ships . . . who demand treatment superior to that of sailors and earn higher salaries." The principle of honor thus drives up costs, which the colonial pact had to offset.[24]

Beyond the obvious attractions to metropolitan merchants clinging to valuable privileges of Montesquieu's formulations on the subject of colonial commerce, both sides in the battle over the Exclusive ranged over the same terrain of ideas. This explains why Montesquieu is the only author who is either quoted directly or alluded to indirectly by interested parties on both sides of the issue, whether they hailed from France's chambers of commerce or were administrators in the Ministry of the Navy. All of the interlocutors in the debates in the 1760s basically accepted the premise of colonial dependence embodied in the Exclusive. Opponents of a strictly enforced Exclusive, however, suggested that "prohibitive laws" should be loosened in order to adapt them to "circumstances of the times" and concluded by citing Montesquieu that "the essential point is to favor and support commerce 'whose effect is wealth, the effect of wealth luxury and that of luxury the perfection of the arts.'" To this commonplace of *doux commerce* theory, proponents of the Exclusive replied with the subtler—and also more historically contingent—argument that excessive wealth tended toward the demise of commerce: "If the state of indigence smothers commerce at its birth, the very height of wealth is its grave."[25]

To establish this point, they drew on the example of the Spanish trading empire familiar to readers of the *Esprit des lois*. Although Montesquieu's argument is complex, two elements deserve attention because they are frequently recycled in these memoirs. The first is the somewhat commonplace emphasis on the incompatibility of luxury with the carrying trade; these concerns often dovetailed imperceptibly with the contention that colonies should remain dependent—a status incompatible with endlessly multiplying commercial wealth.[26] Next, as we have also seen, Montesquieu observed the paradoxical, impoverishing effect that the production of precious metals had on Spain. Ignoring the crucial distinction between fictional and real wealth, the Saint-Malo memoirist established a link between the Spanish paradox of abundance and the situation of the French Antilles since the end of the Seven Years' War. The influx of foreign goods during the late war depressed their price in the colony and increased their consumption, and here is where the paradox came in: "There you have it: from this point of view they were quite wealthy. But if the metropole is in an opposite situation, if it only sells its surplus at a low price, and if it pays dearly for what it requires, the balance is destroyed; it has to abandon the Colony that it has established for its commerce, because it cannot support it." Trade policy had to balance the real wealth of colony and metropole in order to prevent one society from ruining the other.[27]

When this debate spilled over the banks of official correspondence into the wider valley of public opinion, partisans on both sides turned no less to the *Esprit des lois* as a source of slogans, examples, and concepts. Sensing its target, the *Journal de l'agriculture, du commerce et des finances* published an article entitled "Letter on the opinion of the author of the SPIRIT OF THE LAWS concerning the colonies," signed "M. de l'Isle" but written, in fact, by François Quesnay, in whose name so many criticisms of Montesquieu were launched.[28] By this time, Montesquieu had been dead eleven years, so we can be certain that this polemical shot on behalf of the colonies ("de l'Isle") was aimed at the metropolitan lobby. Even as he refuted the reasoning behind Montesquieu's alleged support of the Exclusive, Quesnay used the language of Montesquieu's political sociology; the effect—as with the Physiocratic history of commerce— was to affirm the importance of the science of commerce while helping to transform the terms of the debate on colonial commerce.

The first distinction Quesnay posited was between a "republic of merchants" (i.e., Holland and England) and an "agricultural empire" (potentially, at least, France). Within these basic regime types, "the sovereign, the state, the nation and the traders that practice external commerce must be distinguished" when weighing the potential social conflicts that might arise from colonial commerce. The trading post *(colonie de comptoir)* typical of the Dutch in the East Indies posed very few conflicts, since in the home country the sovereign was nothing but a ruling committee of businessmen. To this type Quesnay opposed the "Carthaginian constitution" of the company establishment *(colonie des compagnies),* where even commerce within the metropole is regulated by, and submitted to the interests of, trading monopolies—not to speak of the forsaken interests of the colonists themselves. Here the author plainly had in mind England; but once again Quesnay, as so many others, deferred to habitual assumptions about France's ability to conduct a thriving overseas commerce. Despite the internal opposition of interests generated by commercial privileges, England as a whole managed to benefit by this commerce due to the extraordinary profits accruing to trade. By contrast, the example of the "Carthaginian constitution cannot serve as a model for monarchical empires, whose politics and commerce are quite opposed to the carrying trade." For his penultimate ideal type, Quesnay looked to New Spain, which served as a source of raw goods (principally gold) for merchants and trading companies. The problem here lay with the fact that "all of these arrangements are completely separated from the interests of the nation which is part of the metropole"—which was painfully evident on the Iberian Peninsula, bereft as it was of agriculture and manufactures of its own.

Finally, Quesnay turned to the "agricultural colony" beloved of other Physiocrats and described by Roubaud in his *Histoire générale.* Here,

Quesnay extended Montesquieu's comparative political sociology in an attempt to transcend the apparently inevitable conflict of economic interests between colony and metropole. As a good theorist of enlightened despotism, Quesnay argued that in a monarchy there could be no legitimate distinction between these parties, because all parts of the nation were united under the authority of the sovereign: "this distinction could only be current in the government of a *merchant republic,* where it is merchants who constitute the metropole, the state and the nation, and where these merchants are themselves the owners of the land and the products that grow in the colonies." Because both colony and metropole enjoyed the same sovereign protection and benevolence, such structural inequalities could not be made a matter of law. Behind these constitutional arguments lay the notion—quite contrary to the chamber of commerce's representations—that for economic purposes the colonies and metropole should be a homogeneous space of economic exchange, with no artificially imposed economic or legal inequalities to hinder or otherwise distort economic activity. Whereas monarchical government had typically been associated with the persistence of heterogeneous legal norms—and hence the inevitable economic backwardness of these regimes—for once the "monarchical empire" cut a more modern figure than the commercial republic.

Beyond the novelty of posing the monarchical state as organically better suited for nurturing certain kinds of economic and political equality than a republic, the interest of these analyses is that they demonstrate the insufficiency of purely economic arguments for what we would now probably reduce to a question of economic policy: whether the Exclusive should be retained in the French colonies in America. Proponents of the abolition of the Exclusive had plenty of laissez-faire economic arguments on their side, which they advanced with varying degrees of cogency. What this debate shows is that none of these arguments could convincingly be made in a vacuum: the manner in which Atlantic markets, and empires, were said to function was always refracted through the problem of regime type. Nobody was more radical than Quesnay in proposing a "monarchical empire," which implied abolition of the whole system of hierarchies, spatial divisions, and privilege the French monarchy was based upon; still others responded to similar pressures to reimagine the relationship between center and periphery.

The Branch and the Trunk: The Fruits of Colonial Growth

By the outbreak of the Seven Years' War in 1756—that is to say, even before the feisty (and successful) defense of their privileges in 1765—the
directors of France's chambers of commerce were able to claim with en-
hanced authority the centrality of colonial commerce to France's economy as a whole. It was a sort of keystone that upheld the entire edifice of
agriculture, manufacture, commerce, and consumption: "it is enough to
observe that cotton alone," which was not yet a colonial export of tower-
ing significance, "supports a world of workers in the realm." A deputy in
Nantes described at length the reciprocal linkage effects that multiplied
the production and consumption of goods on both sides of the Atlantic.
The increasing importance of foreign trade to the French economy is a
thesis substantiated by present-day economic historians. Exterior trade
represented between 1 and 1.5 percent of France's gross national product
in 1715 and between 4.5 and 5.5 percent in 1791; it was responsible for between 14 and 27 percent of France's industrial production as a whole and
between 6.5 and 7.5 percent of all growth in the national economy. Beyond these figures, modern economic historians—like the deputies of
Nantes—have come to regard the Atlantic trade as a leading sector of the
eighteenth-century economy.[29]

The importance of colonial trade in the metropolitan economy served
here and elsewhere as an argument for protecting France's exclusive access to colonial produce and for preserving an increasingly rich captive
market for French goods. But carried to a certain extreme, the argument
had an unintentionally subversive potential, as when the Nantes deputy
concluded at one point that "colonial commerce has become such a considerable object that one may affirm that it is the principal branch, and
might be the trunk, of the whole realm's commerce." Elsewhere, defenders of the Exclusive regime argued that the exploitation of the colony was
justified on utilitarian grounds by the superior size of the mother country; colonies were referred to in seventeenth-century English as "plantations" and the capital invested in them, by eighteenth-century French
writers, as the *germe* or seed. Georges-Marie Butel-Dumont pictured the
colony–metropole relation in terms of a tree and its branches, defending
trading restrictions as a salutary means of drawing away excessive sap

(riches) from the branches. Plants have the tendency to grow, however; this is why, in defending the Exclusive regime, the deputy of Nantes moved from regarding commerce as an important branch or seed to conceding that it might indeed be the weightiest element of *commerce national*: the trunk. This reversal of roles, which was made plausible by increasing contribution of colonial trade to France's wealth, was eagerly seized upon by critics of the Exclusive regime, even within the royal administration itself.[30]

The most substantial weakening of the Exclusive came in the form of a decree issued by the king's council on 30 August 1784. This decree was both a political and economic response to the War of American Independence (1776–1783); absent some recalibration of the economic relations between center and periphery, it was feared that a similar uprising might upset the French empire. This was particularly true because during the inevitable disruptions of war, French colonies were supplied by neutral ships, and the crown wished to prevent political upheaval by preserving the economic status quo. As a part of the 1778 Franco-American Treaty of Amity and Commerce, a mitigated form of the Exclusive was put into effect on the islands, and the policy was a political success. Much in contrast to their behavior during the Seven Years' War, islanders mollified by a modified Exclusive made a concrete difference in the American War of Independence, supporting instead of passively resisting French efforts. The 1784 decree was a signal to metropolitan merchants that France would not reimpose trade restrictions as completely as it had after previous conflicts. This new system of regulation—ultimately softened due to pressure from metropolitan merchants—established free ports around France's sugar islands and allowed for the importation of basic goods (wood, grains, cattle, etc.) and the exportation of colonial produce (syrups and *tafias*) in foreign bottoms. This last item was of major significance; in 1770 alone, France exported 5,777,747 gallons (worth around 5 million l.t.) of molasses, the main ingredient in rum production, to the thirteen colonies of British North America. In the preamble to the 1784 decree, the Marshal de Castries observed that the king needed "to reconcile the agricultural growth of his colonies in America with the general extension of the commerce of his kingdom." Like the merchants of France's Atlantic ports writing eighty-four years earlier against the monopoly privileges enjoyed by the Compagnie de l'Occident, the crown was now arguing that evolving economic conditions—here, "the agricultural growth of [the king's] colonies"— made it necessary to "temper" the regime of the Exclusive. in order "to maintain in a *just equilibrium* of interests that should mutually favor each other."[31]

The deputies of Nantes, Bordeaux, Saint-Malo, La Rochelle, and Bayonne among others resisted the king's prescriptions, of course, but tacitly accepted the argument that much had changed, economically speaking, in the colony–metropole relation: the "branch" had very possibly become the "trunk," so new ways of justifying the same relationship of dependence had to be invented. Here again, the basic issue was whether the metropole had the right to impose the Exclusive because, on so many occasions, it had failed in its corresponding obligation to provide the capital (mainly slaves) and consumption goods without which the colonies would languish. The deputies of France's Atlantic chambers of commerce repeatedly drew up inventories and ship lists intended to refute the colonists' insistent claims that they were being starved of these basic necessities. As the eighteenth century progressed, the growth of Guadeloupe, Martinique, and particularly Saint-Domingue only made this question more pressing. Jean-Baptise Dubuc, the former first secretary in the Ministry of the Navy who launched the debate of 1765, challenged on this basis a fundamental premise of the colonial pact. Perhaps the colonies were created "by and for" the metropole, Dubuc argued, but a colony is a "sum of culture" and not a "sum of land." Over the course of the century, Saint Domingue and Martinique had grown rich, but this was in spite of metropolitan merchants' capital and entrepreneurial activities, not thanks to them. Indeed, the largest boost to Martinique's sugar production came with the occupation by the British from 1761 to 1763, when large numbers of slaves were brought in. The implication of Dubuc's argument was that in assessing its trade policies toward the colonies, the crown should think more about productivity and capital inputs (culture) than about sovereignty and the right of metropolitan exploitation that flowed from it (land). Changing forms of wealth required a different set of political and economic arrangements, in the same way that "conquest" was repudiated by most observers from the 1730s onward in favor of "commerce" (or conservation). In this connection, the Marquis de Mirabeau's brother Jean-Antoine Joseph observed that if Guadeloupe's *créole* population were granted fuller rights, they would cultivate their land more sagely and productively than at present—all to France's benefit, including easier defense against the English.[32]

This type of thinking was the drift of later proposals to open up the southern part of Saint Domingue to foreign merchants who could provide subsistence goods and slaves in order to lift it out of its chronic under-development. Upon his arrival and installation as the governor general of Saint-Domingue in 1789, the Marquis de Chilleau issued a decree opening up southern ports to foreign merchants. (It was reversed by the crown shortly thereafter on the grounds that it exceeded his authority.) The members of the Chamber of Agriculture of Cap Français were more pleased with Chilleau's initiative than was the crown, since they hoped that the same facility would be extended to them in the northern part of the island; in their praise, they contrasted the profit motive that underlay *commerce national* with the imperative to "extend cultivation and give rise to prosperity to which it [Saint-Domingue] has always been called," but which "exclusive privilege" put out of reach. Here, the colonists opposed *commerce national* to "culture" because the former undermined the latter through exclusive privileges. The colonies owed their enormous eighteenth-century growth not to the Exclusive but to infractions against this regime: all Dubuc and others sought, in effect, was a legalization for the conditions of the colonies' optimal growth. The colonies and indeed the entire French nation (not just the commercial part of it) would be better off if Saint-Domingue, Martinique, and other islands could build up their "culture," even if this meant using foreign capital and goods. Dubuc ventured the opinion that due to the type and magnitude of these colonies' wealth, they deserved to be considered "integral parts" of the French state, not mere satellites. Perhaps colonists were even more deserving of consideration than certain parts of the mother country, since the islands were home to "more usefulness, more enlightenment, fewer people and fewer knaves." Dubuc concluded with the radical observation that "it therefore would actually be truer to say that Bordeaux, Nantes, Le Havre & c. were formed by the Colonies, than that the Colonies were formed by the Metropole."[33]

French merchants were unwilling to concede the policy demands made by colonists and their supporters in the royal administration but were forced by the sheer fact of this growth onto different ground. The manner in which they refuted their critics in this crucial period between 1784 and 1789 is therefore revealing. Charles Lemesle—a self-styled "old man from the Médoc" but in reality a wealthy merchant and the director of the Guyenne Chamber of Commerce—described, in his response to Dubuc's *Le Pour et le contre,* "an immense chain that links the Colony to the Metropole": "ships are the bridges by which France and its Colonies seem to touch one another: how delicious this harmony is, Sir!"[34] Although Lemesle invoked a great chain of being that linked the colony to the metropole in ties of dependence, elsewhere he affirmed the observation made in 1756 by the deputies of the Guyenne Chamber of Commerce. All types of commerce are "tightly linked," he argued: "it is a tree where all of the branches nourish one another, mingle and grow together: *but American commerce is the principal trunk* where sap is made that carries both ornament and fecundity to all of the extremities.[35] Here, America is placed at the center, where it had formerly been in the periphery. Elsewhere, Lemesle did not privilege America and its produce in this striking fashion; rather, in order to refute Dubuc's assertion that the colonies had built up the metropole, Lemesle relativized France's (and Europe's) position even further. According to Lesmele, Dubuc and other colonists had made the mistake of placing the colony in the center, where the metropole had once stood. Such a reversal, according to Lemesle, masked the full complexity of the world economy: "you have certainly not measured this circle whose center is everywhere and whose circumference extends to the ends of the earth." When this "old man from the Médoc" reaches for theological metaphors for God's omnipresence to describe the decentered world of global capitalism, it seems evident that the shifting reality of markets had begun to elude habitual modes of expression.[36]

In this altered world, where old questions of preponderance and dependency could no longer be settled easily with reference to the metropole's superior size, wealth, or centrality in the world economy, a different set of principles were called upon to bring order to *commerce national:* "it is merely a question of the general interest of commerce, that is to say, of the interest of the nation; from this grand principle derive all of the relations between the colony and the metropole." According to Lemesle, this interest was verified with reference to a "national outcry" that called for the reestablishment of the Exclusive for the good of the nation. The justness of his reasoning was ratified in the "tribunal of the nation": "what is more, we write under the eyes of the nation, and we write for the conservation of national wealth." Another critic of Dubuc, the Chevalier Deslandes, put the matter in a similar way: a general appreciation of what was good for *le commerce national* required a common perspective beyond the colony–metropole division: "let us set aside all dogmatism (*esprit de système*) Let's be Frenchmen and patriots."[37]

By *esprit de système* Deslandes might, of course, have meant dogmatic economic or political views such as those advanced by the Physiocrats, but in practice he meant anything too closely associated with either the immediate economic interests of the colonial planters or a too dogged insistence that the size, splendor, and economic weight of the colonies entitled them to political equality. "The colonists are without a doubt subjects of the King like everybody else," wrote the deputy of Le Havre; "they deserve the same treatment, but in reasonable and admissible things." What was unreasonable or inadmissible? It was the demand that colonists should purchase goods as cheaply as possible, if this meant recourse to foreign merchants. Indeed, Deslandes himself—like so many other supporters of the Exclusive—conceded that the English sold goods in the French colonies more cheaply than the French merchants themselves. What could balance the scales and make this seeming exploitation of an increasingly large and productive segment of France's population acceptable? (As Lemesle himself conceded, after all: "some sort of reciprocity is necessary.") What, in a word, could make this *commerce national* based upon the Exclusive truly "national" in the range of interests it reconciled? The simple assertion of common nationhood—a call to patriotism and a respect for law—was one answer. These arguments crowded in where the older material justifications, backed by organic metaphors, strained to the point of breaking.[38]

The final years of the Old Regime saw a ratcheting up of voluntarist political discourse as the contradictions of the absolutist state mounted: will replaced justice or rationality where the latter two solutions produced more conflict than they resolved. In Keith Baker's account, the discourse of justice was largely a juridical one, conforming to the notions of reciprocity, hierarchy, and historical tradition befitting a society of orders. In opposition to this, the discourse of reason found the basis for the social order in nature, beyond the contingencies of politics and history. This is the ideology of enlightened despotism, whose purest expression Baker saw in the doctrine of the Physiocrats. Rushing in to take the place of these incompatible visions of society and the institutional conflicts they generated was the doctrine of political will. In this context, it is clear that the "public opinion" and "general interest" invoked by merchants eager to elide conflicts between colony and metropole were a produced, not a found, artifact. François Furet diagnosed a similar pathology in the social thought during the autumn of the Old Regime, arguing that the French constantly groped for a "political vision of society" because they could not envision individuals reconciling their interests in the marketplace or any other institution operating apart from the state. But Furet assigned a different role for the Physiocrats in his analysis of French political culture; though François Quesnay and his followers tried to depoliticize the economy and the market by assimilating it to nature and reason, their doctrine of enlightened despotism only magnified the role of the state and, hence, of specifically political will. Pierre Rosanvallon describes this memorably as the "return of the repressed": in search of a fixed order of nature to replace the vicissitudes of political will, they put despotism and sovereign proprietorship in the service of laissez-faire. In place of an organic constitution resembling the "animal oeconomy" with its capacities of self-correction, the Physiocrats insisted upon a constitution, in the much more modern sense of the term, as a fixed imposition of the rational will. Whereas Baker and Furet viewed the growth of voluntarism as having a "specifically political content" without any "discrete sociological referent," here we see economic conflicts with discrete social referents (acknowledged, moreover, on all sides) being papered over by voluntarist claims. In the context of metropolitan and colonial conflicts of interest, the problem was that the voluntarist solution cut both ways: "the law is nothing but a chain that links the interest of each individual with the general interest. The general interest of the colony and the metropole are but one; they can't be divided without leading to the tyranny of the metropole or the independence of the colony." How, then, to re-establish this chain of interest to avoid looming conflicts, for which the American War of Independence provided such a frightening pattern?[39]

Increasingly, metropolitan merchants argued that the extension of credit balanced the scales. Although French merchants did charge more for goods than their English rivals, only "national" merchants extended credit, which allowed colonists to find capital at the right time to expand their operations. Credit implied a special and reciprocal relationship between colonial planters and metropolitan merchants that justified the larger context of commercial restrictions. This ignored, of course, the stark reality of the exploitation of planters by merchants through credit. Indeed, Dubuc argued that the colonies were better off with the cash-and-carry system established between them and foreign smugglers: it forced them to live within their means. The irony here is, of course, that this renovated argument for the Exclusive presupposed the operation of the Exclusive itself. Only in a context where foreign trade was made illegal would it be impossible for English, Dutch, and American merchants to extend credit.[40]

What this recourse to tautology suggests is that by the late 1780s, habitual ways of thinking about the relation of France's metropolitan center to its colonial periphery had broken down. Everybody agreed that a prosperous *commerce national* was a beneficial thing, but there was little consensus about what, finally, was to be comprehended by this term. Over the course of the eighteenth century, *commerce national* became more politically invested: protagonists on both sides described the space of Euro-American exchanges in more starkly voluntarist terms, terms that transcended natural hierarchies of parent to child, head to body, or trunk to branch. While clinging to old economic interests and arguments, the deputies of France's Atlantic chambers of commerce were nevertheless pushed by the logic of economic developments, and by the ingenuity of their colonial interlocutors, into rethinking their place—and reinscribing their privileges—in the world economy.

Progress and Privilege

Thus far, only the chambers' rearguard actions have come into view, but merchants were also capable of taking stock of the political opportunities presented to them by *les progrès du commerce*. In response to the king's decree of 11 July 1788 asking for advice about how to organize the Estates General, France's chambers of commerce waged an organized campaign to secure separate representation for merchants among the third estate deputies in the run-up to the Revolution. On this head they advanced three related claims: commerce now occupied a central and historically novel position in all European states; those involved in foreign trade were best suited to offer advice on pressing economic matters; and finally, anachronistic privileges fettered commerce while excluding from political representation the very classes upon whose economic activity and insight France depended.

The terms of Nantes' initial call to arms of 23 July could have been taken from the pages of Raynal's *Histoire des . . . deux Indes* itself: "the discovery of the two Indies has completely changed the politics of the European powers . . . and has directed the views of diverse governments toward the growth of commerce." Montpelier alluded specifically to the new importance of "arts and industry" rather than "arms"—commerce versus conquest—in fixing the balance of power between states. At the time of the last Estates General in 1614, virtually every chamber emphasized, commerce was only in its infancy, so the old forms of representation conformed to the seventeenth-century social landscape of agriculture and aristocratic domination. Nantes, Lille, and Saint-Malo explicitly emphasized the establishment of colonies as decisive historical changes while others referred to pivotal "revolutions" in foreign and especially maritime commerce that necessitated new forms of representation.[41] Unsurprisingly, merchants imagined themselves uniquely suited to understand what Saint-Malo called "the science of the interests of commerce" and therefore believed themselves specially placed to help France cope with debt, bad economic conjuncture, and its ongoing rivalry with England. Picardy's chamber commented impertinently that if the king had listened to merchants rather than to "financiers and capitalists," he might have avoided the source of the present troubles: useless wars and the taxation that accompanies them. More revealing, perhaps, is the account many chambers gave of the emergence of commerce out of feudalism and of the challenges that merchants, usually described as a class, faced in a society still organized around privilege. Amiens told a familiar story of *doux commerce,* recounting the rise of a "new class" that had "softened manners" among the French and enriched their cities: "their fathers [who] were nothing but serfs or vassals, have become free and independent" through commerce. Low origins had inculcated this class with a solid work ethic and also given them special insight into the problem of privilege: "the ravages of monopoly, the inconveniences of privileges, the exploitation of certain taxes, the prejudice of the prohibition of ports . . . in a word, all the obstacles that hinder communications and bind (*emmaillotent*) commerce." Connecting privilege and commercial stagnation to immediate political concerns over the representation of the third estate, La Rochelle concluded: "it is time to remove the stigma of feudalism from France and to count for something."[42]

The chambers defended the Exclusive by using the voluntarist rhetoric of nationhood that was becoming increasingly pervasive in the 1780s. This fact does not so much explain the success of the metropolitan lobby as it underlines a set of related phenomena: the escalation of the social struggle between colony and metropole, the delegitimization of the Exclusive regime that institutionalized it, and the elusiveness of a solution based upon truly shared economic interests. Much in contrast to their defense of exclusive trading privileges, when it came to establishing their right to representation in the Estates General, the chambers drew the connection between commercial restrictions and the vestiges of the feudal order. A prosperous France required a rational social order premised upon the political freedom of its productive classes and the fullest possible emancipation of markets and industry. The contradiction in the chambers' positions can be ascribed to hypocrisy or to willful blindness. There was plenty of both to go around, as we shall see in the next chapter, when debates about colonial commerce were refracted through the problem of slavery.

Another way of seeing this contradiction is that the chambers' responses only reflected a broader indecision about the future of the French polity in the wake of *les progrès du commerce*. The chambers advanced the widely shared premise that history had placed commerce at the center of European states and societies. The merchants' call to "remove the stigma of feudalism" and the manner in which they joined this to a far-reaching criticism of France's political economy recall nothing so much as the Physiocrats' anticorporatism. In this vein, chambers advanced reform propositions on subjects as varied as taxation, canal building, *corvée* labor, and internal customs duties, suggesting at all times the need to renounce individual and corporate interests in order to shape a more rational, progressive, and prosperous national economy. At the same time, French merchants posed themselves as the arch enemies of dogmatism *(esprit de système)*—their code for Physiocratic laissez faire and other radical reforms. Montpelier congratulated France's chambers of commerce for charting a course between "the illusions of personal interest and the false charms of the spirit of system." Like many other Frenchmen, many of whom were advocates of a politics of fusion or of moderate reform, these merchants believed in the possibility of a compromise between France's commercial future and the hierarchies, institutions, and practices inherited from its past. The Revolution put paid to this illusion.[43]

CHAPTER 7

L'Affaire des Colonies and the
Fall of the Monarchy

OVER THE COURSE OF THE EIGHTEENTH CENTURY, *philosophes,* administrators, and merchants struggled to understand the political threats posed to France by primitive globalization; awareness of these threats was sharpened by the increasingly conflict-ridden relationship between the European core and its colonial periphery, as well as by the financial strain that arose when economic competition took a military turn. The final verdict on the monarchy's ability to reconcile its feudal, corporatist heritage with the imperatives of participating in Europe's new commercial order came in two successive stages: first, with the bankruptcy of 1788 and the ensuing Revolution of 1789; and second, with the fall of the monarchy in 1792 and the proclamation of the Republic.

Between the monarchy's initial and terminal crises, members of the newly established National Assembly sought to give the Bourbon monarchy a more modern social basis and constitutional framework. Socially, this entailed sweeping away the remains of France's feudal regime and dissolving its corporatist structures; constitutionally, this meant establishing a representative and limited government. Over the past thirty years of historical writing, the failure of this project has been cast in almost exclusively political terms, as the collision of two mutually incompatible models of sovereignty: on the one hand, the limited and divided government cherished by moderates; and on the other, the Jacobin model of sovereignty advanced by more radical revolutionary elements. For historians such as François Furet and Keith Baker, Jacobinism was merely the obverse of the absolute monarchy's theory of sovereignty. While political authority no longer emanated from the monarch, it would retain its essential unity of purpose and direction as the expression of the general will of the people. In this interpretation, deep roots in the absolutist political culture of the Old Regime made the triumph of the Jacobin theory of sovereignty inevitable, but the practical dilemma of finding a sufficiently pure instance of this general will in a diverse nation of twenty-five million could never be resolved. As demands for political unity and virtue became more exigent, France became increasingly divided, and the Revolution, by this logic, was bound to skid off course. Although undoubtedly a political failure of grand proportions, the collapse of the constitutional monarchy in fact had its roots in contrasting social visions that were developed in France over the course of the preceding century in response to *les progrès du commerce.* The precise nature of this failure becomes evident upon examination of the process of constitution making against the backdrop of *l'affaire des colonies,* a controversy in the early stages of the Revolution about the fate of the sugar-producing slave societies on France's colonial periphery.

Most observers believed that slavery, a central element of France's Old Regime in the colonies, could not be swept aside immediately without dire economic and geopolitical consequences. Saving the revolutionary project at home therefore required a moderate approach to social and constitutional questions in the colonies. But the explosive consequences of this choice on both sides of the Atlantic demonstrate that the moderate path of reform, followed by preference or default over the course of the eighteenth century, was now blocked.

Financial crisis precipitated the great Revolution of 1789. In the wake of the American War of Independence, the king found himself in straitened financial circumstances and, unable to get traditional elites to agree on a slate of urgently needed fiscal reforms, suspended payments to the treasury on 16 August 1788, effectively declaring bankruptcy. One impasse led to another: the king decided to summon the Estates General to engage in a national process of consultation, reconciliation, and reform, and in the ensuing conflicts he soon lost control. Eventually the Estates General settled the mantle of national sovereignty upon itself, and in assuming the title of the National Assembly, it also took responsibility for the nation's financial crisis, which remained a central preoccupation over the following months.

The events of 1787–1789 were both a repetition and culmination of a pattern that had been developing over the course of the eighteenth century and one that was recognized by contemporary analysts of colonial commerce: war, fiscalism, and political crisis. In the War of Spanish Succession, the War of Austrian Succession, the Seven Years' War, and finally the War of American Independence, major European states increasingly vied over the spoils of each other's colonial establishments. In these wars of commerce, which naturally shifted their focus to Europe's colonial periphery, the possibilities of quiet, steady accumulation thought to be inherent in trade were transformed into urgent questions of national prestige and even survival, which helps to explain the great sums invested in them.

Warfare accounted for France's budgetary woes over the course of the eighteenth century. As Michel Morineau has demonstrated, ordinary budgets remained in a fragile equilibrium with expenses, but the crown's powers of taxation could never keep up with the recurring expense of war; the resulting budgetary overhang led to mounting debts, and by the late 1780s, debt service accounted for 50 percent of the crown's budget, eliminating all room for maneuver. After the War of Austrian Succession, naval expenses doubled to around 11 percent of the crown's annual revenue, while the proportion devoted to land forces shrank, from around 30 percent in the 1720s and 1730s to 17 percent in the 1780s. During the War of American Independence, all budgetary restraint was abandoned, and from 1778 to 1783 naval expenses averaged 158 million l.t. per annum—well over 30 percent of the annual revenue. In peacetime, the costs of garrisoning, patrolling, and administering France's colonial possessions also grew, so bloated budgets did not automatically snap back into form with the cessation of hostilities. Although France prevailed over England in the American War of Independence, perfidious Albion soon had sweet revenge: because the crown had avoided raising taxes during the war, when the bill ultimately came due in 1787, it was enormous, and few were inclined to pay without receiving concessions. The protection costs of France's commercial empire ratcheted up domestic conflicts among the state, creditors, and taxpayers over their rights and obligations, manifesting yet another revolutionary potential of the *progrès du commerce*. France could no longer afford to maintain itself simultaneously as a territorial and as a sea power.[1]

It may be objected with some justice that the crown might have put itself in a position to assume the latest round of protection costs and bring France's century-long investment—its struggle with Great Britain to control Atlantic markets—to fruition. Had the crown managed, with more success than it experienced in the preceding decades, to impose universal forms of taxation by eliminating geographical, corporate, and individual exemptions, more money would have flowed into the treasury, with less distorting effects on the economy. In order to legitimize and administer such taxes, the crown would have been obliged to establish new institutions, since existing bodies that approved taxes—*parlements* and provincial estates—were genetically ill disposed to such a project. The "provincial assemblies" advocated by the Physiocrats and proposed by Turgot and later Charles Alexandre de Calonne were designed for this purpose and were accordingly rejected as an end-run around established political liberties. Further counterfactuals would serve only to underline the improbability of a successful resolution of the crown's financial crisis.[2]

Given the actually and potentially revolutionary effects of the *progrès du commerce,* it is surprising to find how little connection is posited between the Commercial Revolution and the Great Revolution of 1789. This lacuna can be explained in two ways. First, since the 1980s, revisionist scholarship of the French Revolution has made "materialist" explanations largely a no-go zone for *bien pensant* historians. Second, contemporaneously, the rush of events from 1789 onward precluded much sustained reflection upon the origins of the Revolution. Antoine Joseph Barnave stands out as one notable exception. A young *grenoblois* lawyer who quickly vaulted to the heights of revolutionary leadership and who ended his career on the scaffold for his connivance with Marie Antoinette, Barnave has often been maligned as embodying the hypocrisies of the Revolution itself: liberal, even radical at the outset, Barnave, along with many other ex-Jacobins who followed the same trajectory, eventually came to defend a constitution with strict voting qualifications, the basis of a regime devoted to the protection of property. By late 1791, this meant the defense of the constitutional monarchy against calls for a republic. Barnave was given the sobriquet *monsieur double visage* by his enemies and naturally fought these charges bitterly during his career. In the mirror of twentieth-century scholarship, Barnave also presents a Janus face.[3]

Barnave explained the Revolution as the result of a process much discussed in the preceding decades of the eighteenth century: the rise of commerce and the development of mobile assets at the expense of landed wealth and power. In his *Introduction à la Révolution française,* written in the interval between his arrest in August 1792 and his execution in November 1793, Barnave depicted 1789 as the culmination of the democratization of a monarchical state that had developed, alongside a mercantile and industrial bourgeoisie, as a third force against the power of a feudal, land-holding aristocracy. Little wonder, then, that Marxist historians such as Jean Jaurès and Albert Soboul quote Barnave in support of their interpretation of the Revolution.[4]

Ironically, Barnave later emerged as something of a political hero to many of the same revisionists thought to have demolished the Marxist interpretation. In the wake of the king's ill-advised flight to Varennes, so these accounts go, this "tragic hero" and the "last of the Revolution's moderates" defended the constitutional monarchy. (During this period, the Jacobin club, in which Barnave was an active member, split: republican elements remained within the club, and advocates of a constitutional monarchy formed the "Feuillant" party.) But there is more than present-minded elegy toward moderate eighteenth-century liberalism in these accounts. For these historians, the doom of the constitutional monarchy and many of its defenders objectifies the difficulty of a liberal society emerging out of absolutist traditions. More broadly, revisionists take the defeat of moderate monarchism as an object lesson in the perennial threat that statist ideologies—absolutist, Jacobin, or Marxist-Leninist, which they tend to see as genetically related—pose to the freedoms enjoyed in civil society.[5]

If Marxists and revisionists alike have turned to Barnave, they have generally ignored or downplayed the one element of his career that might reconcile their conflicting interpretations: his activities and writings as the spokesman for the Comité des Colonies. The Committee, like the majority of the Assembly, supported slavery, the deprivation of political rights from free men of color, and a restrictive trading regime between the French metropole and its colonies. Jaurès' explanation here was sociologically weak and reductive: according to him, Barnave was merely executing the demands of a newly dominant capitalist bourgeoisie, liberal universalism notwithstanding. Barnave, however, was a noble and a lawyer without any direct commercial or industrial investments and was certainly innocent of all entrepreneurial activity. On the revisionist side, the response has largely been one of tactical silence, with few citations to the speeches he made in his capacity as spokesman and no discussion of how Barnave's ideas on colonial trade and governance might touch on his domestic political views. François Furet, uniquely, is forthcoming about Barnave's work on the Comité des Colonies but tells at best half the story when explaining Barnave's views as the fruit of a principled moderation.[6]

The shared fate of the French constitutional monarchy and its colonial empire—implosion and conflagration, respectively—begs more thorough analysis. The same can be said about the relationship between the moderate monarchism that became increasingly doomed over the course of 1791 and the *affaire,* in which Barnave and other prominent Feuillants played a determinative role. That Feuillantism is a common term in these dual crises is hardly fortuitous. The suitability of monarchy and its attendant social forms was a central theme among *philosophes* and economists who attempted to find a place for France within a world order organized around commerce. So it is hardly surprising that the politics and social conditions of France's richest colonial possessions should figure prominently among the impasses to be dealt with along the troubled path to a liberal, constitutional monarchy. Barnave's struggle to save the constitutional monarchy was not only contemporaneous with his efforts to establish a durable regime in the French colonies. Those elements of Barnave's thought that Furet rightly identifies as enduring problems of modern liberalism were present in both debates: sovereignty, representation, social stratification in modern societies, the nature of executive power, and the distinction between active and passive citizenship. (The constitution of 1791 relegated about one-third of adult males to "passive" status, which gave them equal civil rights but deprived them of the right to vote.) In contrast to the domestic scene, the colonial context demanded that the abstractions of sovereignty and liberty be squared immediately with questions of geopolitics and profit. The effect was to underline the infelicities of the constitution of 1791 and to put their social significance into focus. To take only the most notorious example, the deprivation of political rights from free men of color could not but invoke the distinction between active and passive citizenship. The *affaire* amounted to a searching if failed attempt to impart a functioning regime on France's sugar islands, even as these colonies were roiled with internal conflict and threatened with foreign invasion. The success of any regime hinged on a working, consistent definition of the French empire, as well as some sense of what sort of social structure *(régime social)* was appropriate to it. In facing this problem, Barnave and other members of the Assembly were confronted with the economic and political realities that were the result of prior developments in the French Atlantic, as well as the insistent demands of planters and merchants, who exerted considerable pressure to have things resolved to their profit and political satisfaction.[7]

Nation and Empire

Searching discussions of empire are most striking in eighteenth-century France by their absence. Although throughout the eighteenth century administrators and *philosophes* used the term "empire" to refer to France's colonial establishments and their relationship to the crown or the metropole, the concept itself was rarely questioned. It is hard to imagine, for example, a French counterpart to David Armitage's *The Ideological Origins of the British Empire,* a work that argues for the centrality of empire to British nationhood and self-understanding. One possible explanation is that from an economic, social, or juridical standpoint, there never really was a French empire in the British sense. It is more accurate to say that although France had colonies or "establishments" that were loosely spoken of as belonging to an empire, the political traditions of the absolutist state were sufficiently flexible to accommodate them juridically without inciting too much reflection. Social regimes and legal systems that were manifestly different did not prevent colonies such as New France and Saint-Domingue from remaining incorporated within the monarchy just like any other *généralité*. Little distinguished the bureaucracy of France's colonies from the home provinces except that a military governor served alongside, and often in competition with, the crown's intendant. In any case, replication and conflict of authority were typical, and what differences did remain between colony and metropole were not anomalous given the pervasive reality of institutional variety under the Old Regime. Nor was the colonies' political status bound to break the flexible mold of absolutism, since the existence of representative institutions or consultative bodies varied considerably in mainland France; the questions of sovereignty and legislative independence that pressed upon the British empire were simply not capable, in the French context, of provoking too much sustained discussion of empire. The one great exception to this state of affairs was the Exclusive, which came under an increasingly bitter and politically significant attack toward the end of the Old Regime. When the Physiocrat François Quesnay criticized the Exclusive, he proposed to substitute what he regarded as the quasi-feudal structure of the French empire with a more rational "monarchical empire." Here, "monarchical" was not intended to modify "empire" but to abolish it: in becoming "monarchical" according to Quesnay's particular definition, France and its possessions would cease to be an empire in any contemporary understanding of the term. Before 1789, principles of reform created strange ideological bedfellows, as between Physiocrats and slave-holding colonists, both of whom pushed for laissez-faire in the interest of truly national prosperity. After this date, the permutations of interest and ideology became even more complicated, posing the gravest of challenges to a constitutional monarchy with aspirations to modernity.[8]

In 1789, France was reorganized into eighty-three administratively identical departments, an act that set the standard against which future deviations could be measured. By accepting and, indeed, pushing for representation within the Assembly, colonial deputies implicitly placed the islands within this newly homogeneous national space; the decision to seek representation was therefore controversial among colonists and remained a point of recrimination between them. This is why, when discussing matters of concern to them, the Corresponding Society of French Colonists Residing in France—commonly known as the "Club Massiac"—spoke of the "regeneration of the French empire" instead of the French nation. This formulation was precisely the opposite of Quesnay's *empire monarchique:* "empire" gave more breathing room for the application of principles at variance with the Revolution than did "nation," but this tactical ambiguity nevertheless left many unresolved questions.[9]

In December 1789, in the wake of the August 1789 slave uprising in Martinique, the National Assembly reluctantly turned to pressing colonial issues and debated putting together a committee for colonial affairs. Several deputies denied that the Assembly even had jurisdiction over the French colonies, and in this connection the argument of Louis-Elie Moreau de Saint Méry, native of Martinique, jurist, academician, and author of the encyclopedic *Description . . . de Saint Domingue* (1797), was paradigmatic: the "dissemblance" between colony and metropole meant that the former could not make the latter submit to legislation formulated in the Assembly. But as Pierre François Blin, master surgeon and deputy from Nantes, observed, nobody had really begun at that point to study "colonial theory" *(la théorie de la colonie):* even if this "dissemblance" were universally granted, which it seemed to be, there was much room for debate about what sorts of relationships should direct a "regenerated" French empire. For Blin, irreducible differences in *moeurs* and economic interests meant that the colonies could not be understood as "provinces of the same empire." Blin described the colonies as "allied powers" that could not be submitted to the same form of government, as was logical for the "contiguous provinces" on the Continent. Liberal noble and soon-to-be émigré François-Alexandre-Frédéric duc de La Rochefoucauld-Liancourt argued later but in a similar context that "without a doubt the colonies are parts of the Empire, but they are distinct ones; *they are united to the metropole without being an integral*

part of the same body. They are separate bodies, whose linkages and reciprocal relations have their own unique principles." La Rochefoucauld-
Liancourt gave force to this opinion by pointing out that the crown had
originally denied representation to the colonies in the Estates General
and that the National Assembly did not bother to send its decrees to the
islands for enforcement. Colonists from the northern part of Saint-
Domingue, refusing to take part in an independence movement that
would ultimately be put down by the Constituent Assembly, expressed
their desire to remain part of the "French empire" but stressed the fact
that "the conditions necessary for [its] existence demand that [the col-
ony] not be assimilated to the other provinces."[10]

It is telling that partisans on all sides of the *affaire* had to repeat and
reformulate the view that the colonies were not to be regarded as simple
provinces of the nation but required "particular principles" suited to the
conditions of their existence. Since the assertion of particularity went
against the entire drift of the National Assembly's reform efforts for
France, which sought liberty through equality and uniformity, particularity was the subject of obsessive justification. This position was en-
shrined early on, in the Assembly's first (8 March 1790) decree on the
subject of metropole–colony relations. Differences of climate, *moeurs*,
and economic output made the colonies "peculiar entities," which were
not to be assimilated into the "national body" or unified with each other.
However abstract this discussion might have become, constitution making in the French empire always boiled down to finding a set of compromises on political and economic rights that ensured that the sugar islands remained a profitable joint enterprise linking center and periphery.
Most participants in this debate took the underlying economic purpose
of "colonial theory" as read, even if the means to that end remained elu-
sive. Advocates of the slave system and of the denial of rights to free men
of color *(gens de couleur)* blamed the machinations of negrophiles in the
Société des Amis des Noirs for this failure, but this reading was both
self-serving and partial.[11]

Most versions of the "colonial theory" offered up during the *affaire*,
and more broadly during the period 1789–1792, foundered on a similar
set of contradictions; the question of political rights for free men of color
in the French colonies was only the most explosive manifestation of this

phenomenon. A rigorous notion of empire was a tardy entrant in the field of French political ideas and was seized upon almost exclusively to settle the political economy of metropole–colony relations. The case for empire was not only adventitious; it flew directly in the face of the revolutionary principle of national sovereignty, with its implicit demands of consistency and equality. Nevertheless, those who resisted the implications of national sovereignty in one domain (such as civil and political rights for blacks) were not averse to demanding them in another, as when some colonists demanded representation in the Assembly or called for freedom of trade on the grounds of a common right to property within the nation. This was not mere opportunism but followed the binary logic of "incorporation or independence" that was the drift of thinking about the colonies in the late eighteenth century: colonies should either be brought into the fold of nationhood as equal "allied provinces" or be granted independence as mature societies. Against the radical threat posed by national sovereignty and its complementary economic forms, the architects of "colonial theory" argued the virtues of moderate reform, the need to respect economic, cultural, and geographic differences within the French empire. Strategic and economic considerations made this line of reasoning as attractive as it was, ultimately, untenable.

The *Régime Social* of the Colonies

By 23 September 1791, the date of Barnave's final speech on the subject in the Constituent Assembly, virtually every issue surrounding the constitution of the French empire had been assimilated to the question of political rights for free people of color in the colonies. The Assembly's first decree of 8 March 1790 granted partial legislative autonomy to the colonies. "External" matters, meaning the trading regime between France and its colonies, were to be left to the metropole, while "internal" affairs, the code word for the status of slaves and people of color, were to be left to the colonies. All legislation emanating from the colonies had to be approved by the crown, and the king would still have a governor in place to exercise special executive powers, particularly in matters of trade and justice. At the same time, the decree of 8 March guaranteed that legislative initiative on the subject of civil and political rights for slaves and free people of color would always remain with the colony. However, the instructions that Barnave and his colleagues in the Committee issued on 28 March to accompany the earlier decree pretermitted to mention—either by way of inclusion or exclusion—free people of color among those who were to be consulted in primary assemblies on the islands: "any" property-owning male over the age of twenty-five could vote in these assemblies. Whether by error or by intention, the Committee set the stage for eighteen months of struggle over the question of rights accorded to free men of color. On 11 October of the same year, the National Convention took the trouble to reaffirm the legislative initiative of the colonies on "internal" matters at the same time as it denounced independence movements that had developed in Saint-Domingue. A second attempt to reaffirm legislative initiative on matters of race, from 7–15 May 1791, resulted in a surprising reversal in favor of free men of color. The victory was in reality minuscule, since it granted political rights only to free people of color born to both a free mother and a free father, but the symbolism of granting the vote to 5 percent of free people of color was sufficiently intolerable as to send opponents into apoplexy and reactionary elements in the colonies, particularly in Saint-Domingue, into full resistance. On 23 September 1791, the National Convention, buying into the widely held notion that the 15 May decree encouraged the slave uprising that began on 22 August, attempted to restore order by revoking the decree.

Pierre-Victor Malouet, a long-serving colonial administrator under the Old Regime, best captured the significance of the debate over free men of color. His long experience, in combination with his habitual moderation, eventually led to high-level postings in the Ministry of the Navy under Napoleon and under the restoration of the Bourbon monarchy. In addition to serving various posts in Saint-Domingue (1767–1774) and in Guyana (1776–1778), Malouet, a friend and close associate of Raynal, became a plantation owner on Saint-Domingue by marriage, a fact that probably explains his membership in the Club Massiac as well as his frequent interventions in the *affaire*. (Indeed, although Malouet was not a member of the Committee, like other interested nonmembers he attended numerous meetings.)[12] Malouet's analysis was a straightforward application to the colonial question of Montesquieu's political principles:

"government should be related to its principles and its means." Any new law, even when in conformity with justice and reason, is to be counted "bad" if it "attacks the principles and supports of the social structure (*régime social*)." This meant that the social structure of the colonies was not to be gainsaid by questions of justice: "What are the principles of the colonial regime (*régime colonial*)? What are the means of cultivation in our colonies in the torrid zone? The slavery of blacks." Political liberty and a system of free labor belonged to the people of Europe by dint of its climate and history. Those who would extend these benefits to the colonies fatally misunderstood the nature of colonial society and by extension the wealth that flowed from it: "one must not set upon the same basis or submit to the same theory two regimes which are not only different, but absolutely contradictory." The Chamber of Commerce of Bayonne worked from the same premises when it argued that the sugar islands had a "[social] system incompatible with the social and political state of France" and that abolitionists "seek to make a harmful revolution coincide with a salutary one." Moreau de Saint Méry, a man perfectly at ease with his own prejudices and expert in exposing his colleagues' high-minded hypocrisy, asked: "Do you imagine that the constitution that you have just given to France will suit the colonies? You must then renounce your wealth and trade, or declare frankly that the Declaration of the Rights of Man is not applicable to the colonies."[13]

Malouet himself claimed that colonial establishments were essentially "vicious" because of slavery, commercial warfare, and the corrupting influence of luxury. Nevertheless, the Europeans in general, and the French in particular, were stuck with their colonies and had to find some way to make them work: "colonies and their products are the *first link* in this chain [of industry] and one cannot break this link without causing the general subversion of public wealth." A nation cannot be composed of incompatible social structures, but this was possible within the empire envisioned by advocates of slavery and an exclusive trading regime between France and its colonies. What is left implicit by Malouet, and what was of great significance in all of the discussions about the form this empire was to take, was that colonial commerce had become an integral part of Europe's social structure. The "chains" mentioned by Malouet could be conceived of as conduits of value or as the interlocking elements in a worldwide division of labor, but they were also constraints imposed by the need for consumption and accumulation nourished from overseas. Malouet's comments proved prescient when riots over sugar shortages erupted in January 1792 and helped to radicalize the revolutionary agenda.[14]

Malouet's reservations echoed familiar economic, moral, and political debates about the value of colonial commerce that had run since at least the mid-eighteenth century. Perhaps this is why Jean-Baptiste Nairac, the special deputy sent by the Chamber of Commerce of La Rochelle to Versailles, feared a growing wariness within the Assembly toward commercial interests. Nairac wanted merchants—and, to the extent possible, colonists—to create a concerted lobbying campaign to sew the connection in people's minds between the interests of Atlantic commerce and the economic well-being of the whole nation. Otherwise, Nairac observed, their special pleading would be "destroyed by *national* principles." In previous decades, critics of the Exclusive threw into doubt the easy conflation of *commerce national* with the activities of Ponant merchants. Fearing that this ideological battle had been won, memoir after memoir circulated by these merchants stressed the importance of colonial commerce and asserted that between six and eight million Frenchmen depended on this trade for their livelihood. Barnave, in his first report to the Assembly on 8 March 1790, argued that it was "bizarre bad faith" not to understand the importance of the colonies or to "pretend to separate the prosperity of *commerce national* from the possession of our colonies." At this moment, he continued, "all aspects of our *social existence* are intimately linked and combined with the possession of a booming trade (*grand commerce*) and with that of the colonies." Indeed, Nairac emphasized that no plausible political strategy could deny the ugly realities of colonial slavery; the importance to France of the colonial commerce simply outweighed humanitarian considerations. In fine, the fate of the colonies was the fate of the Revolution, however mutually contradictory their principles.[15]

External and Internal Governance

A common topos of eighteenth-century histories of commerce was that the center of continental Europe had been inalterably changed by the productive activity taking place in its colonial periphery. At the same time, it was widely understood that while European colonies were different from their mother countries in important respects, their cultural, economic, and political ties added up to a relation of parentage between them. In order to save the social structure of the colonies and all this implied, the French empire was to be based upon the all-important distinction between their "external" and "internal" regimes. But this distinction was rendered politically fragile by the realities just described; the Assembly and the pressure groups ranged around it were frequently incognizant of this fact and hence impotent in the face of it. Attempts to arrange the economic, juridical, and political structures of the colonies foundered on this makeshift division of sovereignty.

To the extent that historians have discussed the issue, it has been generally thought that the metropolitan merchants and planter-colonists put away their differences over terms of trade in order to enter into an unholy alliance for the preservation of slavery. This was, of course, their hope, since priority belonged to the production of surplus over its mere division. This explains why Jean-Baptiste Nairac fairly delighted in Honoré-Gajnol Mirabeau's abolitionist stance in the Assembly on 30 November. Abolitionism stood no chance in the Assembly, Nairac reasoned, but the appearance of this specter, however insubstantial, was sufficient to throw terrified colonists into the arms of commercial cities, whose representatives might even be invited to sit in the Club Massiac.[16]

Colonists' actions at the outset of the Revolution lend color to Nairac's observation that only a good shock to the system, such as the threat of abolitionism, could bring them into an alliance with metropolitan interests. In response to two meteorological crises—one in Saint-Domingue, which damaged food crops, and the other in France, the terrible winter of 1788–1789, which threatened to do the same—a number of colonial governors, working in concert with local assemblies, gave temporary permission for the entry of foreign flour, biscuits, and other foodstuffs into the sugar islands. At first, these permissions fell within the provisions of a "mitigated" Exclusive, established by a decree of 1784, which had relaxed trade restrictions on islanders, allowing them limited access to non-French markets. Soon, however, the scope of these permissions grew, which put the governors and local assemblies at odds with the king's intendants and Comte de La Luzerne, Minister of the Navy. Most dramatically, Marguis de Chilleau, governor of Saint-Domingue, issued an ordinance on 9 May 1789 allowing foreign slaves and foodstuffs to enter three ports in the poorer, southern part of that island for a period of five years. Chilleau was fired for his impertinence soon enough, but the cumulative effect of all this promiscuity could not be undone: by the summer of 1789, "an almost total liberty [of trade] reigned," and the local institutions that had abetted this situation, the *conseil supérieur* of Saint-Domingue and various colonial assemblies, began to take freedom of trade as an early acquisition of the Revolution itself. Barbé-Marbois, former secretary of the French legation in Philadelphia and now intendant of Saint-Domingue, opposed Chilleau on the grounds that the latter had exceeded his authority as governor in issuing his decree unilaterally. Beyond his purely legal reasoning, Barbé-Marbois used the same political and economic arguments in favor of the Exclusive that colonists and metropolitan merchants set forth as the justification for their union. Such was the colonists' collective commitment to these principles that once Chilleau's decree was revoked on 29 June and Barbé-Marbois attempted to restore the Exclusive, they began a systematic campaign of vilification and slander against him. In October 1789, he fled the island of Saint-Domingue to avoid being lynched.[17]

Against these facts on the ground, colonists and their deputies in France pledged their allegiance to the logic of the colonial pact and the trade restrictions it justified. Whereas colonists and their advocates within the royal administration had spent the previous twenty-five years arguing that the true benefit to France of its colonies could be harnessed only by loosening trade restrictions, they now asserted somewhat implausibly that "the colonies would be crushed by free trade" and that it was only enemies of the Revolution who spread the false rumor that the colonists wanted to abolish the current trading regime. The present situation called for patriotism, a short-term renunciation of egotistical interests that would pay long-term dividends: "French colonists enrich your country. She will enrich you in turn." The strain is evident in these repeated calls to patriotic unity with the metropole, which recall earlier attempts to supply the defects of interest politics with the rhetoric of political voluntarism. Perhaps this is why the colonists at Bordeaux followed up their stirring, patriotic call to cease all meddling with the

Exclusive with the modest suggestion that the islands be allowed to buy building materials and provisions directly from New England. Saint-Domingue had patriotically sacrificed its forests in the process of developing a plantation complex for the benefit of the mother country, but an "attentive providence has placed a storehouse of provision close to our colonies [i.e., in North America]." Recurring questions of reciprocity within a national community and the optimal strategy for economic prosperity were never far below the surface. The French empire was being built around the notion that the colonies were not to be "assimilated" or "incorporated" into the mother country, but discussions of economic justice and prosperity had to assume something of this sort.[18]

Because of the difficulty in settling the differences between colonists and metropolitan merchants, the Club Massiac established a small "special commission," consisting of members of the Club and their opposite numbers among the extraordinary deputies sent by commercial and manufacturing cities. The proceedings of this commission, which sat for four months in early 1791, show how tenuous the distinction between an "interior" regime belonging to the colonies and a purely "exterior" regime defined by metropolitan control of trade flows really was—even if the Exclusive was taken as a premise of these discussions. The merchants' deputies pointed out that effectively policing foreign trade concerned an "infinity of objects which would seem to belong to the interior regime of the colonies, which in fact bear upon the commerce of the metropole and vice versa." For example, who would judge in matters of debt imprisonment or in cases of dubious goods? Justice and police belonged ostensibly to the "interior" regime, but the nature of their commercial relations spoke, again, to the necessary imbrication of metropole and colony. Despite its superficial clarity, this distinction actually made little sense and could not, therefore, dictate much of substance about colony–metropole relations. For their own part, the colonists believed that metropolitan merchants merely wanted to leave the door open to external meddling. In the event, both parties hewed to a cynical *attentisme* when it came to the constitutional instruction that the Committee was drawing up for the colonies: neither would commit to the precise boundary between "external" and "internal" in the hopes that the Committee would decide in a manner that favored their economic interests. But this wrangling usually remained behind the scenes: as Barnave observed to his fellow committee members, "for a good outcome, we must speak with one voice." Publicly, merchant and colonists proclaimed their alliance, based upon unfree labor and unfree trade, against the "philosophical" opinions that supposedly dominated the Assembly.[19]

Dupont du Nemours had a slightly less philosophical Committee and Assembly in view when he addressed the mismatch between the ostensible economic ends of France's colonial establishment and its political basis: "your colonial system," he chided them, "had always been pitiful and it has only become more so in the last several years." Though a Physiocrat, Dupont's views were moderated during his tenure in the Bureau de Commerce, and he did not advocate pure laissez-faire for the islands. He preferred free exit of colonial goods, with restrictions on the importation of most merchandise to the colonies, with the exception of timber and foodstuffs, as the colonists at Bordeaux had proposed. Underlying the "pitiful" economic and political state of the French empire was the Assembly's break with the doctrine of a "one and indivisible" nation, which made impossible a community of reciprocal interests based upon shared rights and economic prosperity. Absent some remedy, Dupont warned the Assembly, the colonies would justly demand their independence: "you are walking on hot coals covered by ashes." The Assembly quietly ignored Dupont's warnings in order to reimpose the status quo, but their complacency did not betoken a lack of activity, as attested by the Committee's efforts to draft a constitution for the colonies.[20]

By all rights, the Assembly should never have attempted such a task, even if the resulting "instruction" was merely an advisory document. Speaking to the Assembly on 8 March 1790, Barnave proposed the distinction between internal and external regimes, assuring the colonists as a consequence that France would "receive from [the colonies] themselves instructions on the type of governmental regime that would suit their prosperity." This nod toward independence was calculated to appease colonists, who were strongly represented in the Committee and behind whom stood the formidable lobbying apparatus of the Club

Massiac. No more than nine months later, members of the Committee found themselves preparing their constitutional instruction with the full cooperation of colonial deputies such as Moreau de St. Méry, whose views hitherto leaned toward independence. In the interval, there was no change in the basic issues, but political conjuncture favored some sort of action: as arguments favorable to the cause of free men of color gained traction in the Assembly, it seemed increasingly wise to establish the colonies' constitutional order. Definitive action would put the colonial question beyond the reach of the much-feared "second legislature," which was to assume power once the king accepted the constitution, which he eventually did in September of 1791. This gesture of submission, even in so weak a form as cooperation with an "instruction," also helped to mollify an Assembly that was growing increasingly alienated by independence movements brewing in the colonies.[21]

Short-term tactical considerations aside, the need to circumscribe colonial independence, along with a desire to guarantee order and prosperity within the French empire, favored intervention into multiple aspects of the colonies' social structure through a constitutional instruction. Addressing Chabert de la Charrière, a deputy from Guadeloupe who had broached the question of "constitutional laws on trade" that were to be embodied in this document, Barnave interjected that there could be no such thing, since trade policy was "a mere instrumentality" subject to change. More basic according to Barnave was the fact that the new constitution would consecrate the "destruction of the nobility." Once this destruction was achieved, the trades would prosper because nobility "will no longer take any more men away from useful professions. We will therefore have, as a result of our geography and resources, a dominant navy and then we won't have any more need of prohibitive laws."[22] Social structure was the long-term determinant of prosperity, beside which terms of trade were a fleeting consideration. At the same time, the Assembly wanted to subcontract the one aspect of the empire's social structure that it could not "call by its true name"; this they accomplished through the fictional distinction between the internal and external regimes of the colonies.[23]

The instruction that did emerge was, as one critic put it, "immense; it contains the whole organization of our colonies, interior regime, exterior regime [and] regulatory laws." This document in 255 articles ranged over the judiciary, military, composition of primary assemblies, and local administration, sometimes in pointillist detail, as when it dictated what forms of dress were prohibited in primary assemblies or the minimum age (twenty-five years) for a court clerk. The Committee's discussion in camera reveals why it produced such an obsessively detailed document. Relations between the metropole and the colonies had to be given a solid social basis by dint of careful constitutional design. For instance, by adjusting the property qualification to take greater account of the mobile wealth found among merchants and artisans in the cities of Saint-Domingue, Barnave sought to reinforce social elements with "a more metropolitan mindset." Elsewhere, he suggested cutting down the number of members in the colonial assemblies, reasoning that in a society where "one is more absorbed in private than public matters," a large body would be subject to chronic absenteeism and therefore a debilitating political lassitude.[24]

When it came to differentiating colonial from metropolitan affairs, members of the Committee were more businesslike than ideological. Barnave at one point asked whether "one could distinguish a tribunal ruling over interior affairs from one judging external matters." There was general disagreement about whether this was possible in principle, but the result found in the constitutional instruction was a pragmatic compromise that would have eluded the Committee had its deliberations concerned the racial distinctions for which the interior–exterior division was created. In the midst of a discussion on taxation and the distribution of military expenditures, Barnave proposed that "each colony pay for the maintenance of its fortifications." In objecting to this arrangement, Moreau de St. Méry perhaps unwittingly exposed the fiction of a French empire composed of a metropolitan center and a number of semi-independent colonial satellites. Martinique, he explained, was not an "agricultural or commercial colony" generating its own surplus and capable of economic and military self-sufficiency, "but a rampart of the Antilles," whose fortifications cost 12 million livres: "[Martinique] will request that all those who profit by it support it as well." Ultimately, the instruction specified a system of "fixed contributions" that would subsidize fortifications of this sort, thus effecting a system of redistribution among the colonies, dictated from the center. Here again, pragmatism trumped the principle of self-administration and local consent for taxation.[25]

A detailed reading of the final instruction shows how limited the colonists' interest in constitutional autonomy really was at that point, unless it was focused on the question of "the status of persons." Even here, when principles found in the French constitution were congenial to colonists' ideas about the social structure necessary for prosperity and order, the instruction adopted them wholesale and without the least embarrassment. Although the colonists fought the application of the French constitution (and hence the declaration of rights) in the colonies tooth and nail, the instruction explicitly embraced at its core "the *constitutional* abolition of privileges, of orders, of the feudal regime, of monastic vows." Elsewhere the instruction proclaimed, along with the Declaration, the equality of all citizens before the law and abolished all privileges and inequality in matters of justice. One might say that the only questions of "status of persons" the instruction did not proclaim upon in frank imitation of the French constitution were those based on racial distinctions. In this spirit, Moreau de St. Méry observed—gratuitously, since the issue was not under discussion—"the Jews that remain in some of the colonies should share the fate of those in France."[26]

The Committee's instruction proclaimed, "Saint-Domingue is part of the French Empire," and hence governed by a mix of "national powers" coming from the center and "particular institutions" legislated locally, but this never added up to a coherent theory of sovereignty. Late in the Committee's deliberations (5 May 1791), Barnave, Malouet, Moreau de St. Méry, and others could still not agree on a fundamental question: is the division of sovereignty between parts of the French empire theoretically possible?

The compromise they worked out was a standoff between competing ideas and interest groups, which could at any moment push to their advantage this flexible boundary between "particular institutions" and "national powers"—all in the name of political and economic necessity. This partly explains why a workable constitutional order for the French empire permanently eluded the Assembly.[27]

The Assembly was nevertheless encouraged in its labors by the example of the British Empire—oddly, it might seem, given the successful rebellion of Britain's North American colonies over issues of taxation and trade. The intrusion of the British in the "interior" affairs of the Americans after the Seven Years' War had caused the loss of the Americas and was therefore a "rich source of useful lessons" (presumably negative) for the French, according to Blin, the deputy from Nantes. On the positive side of the ledger, Blin adduced Ireland, a move that may now seem off-key, given our picture of Ireland as the perennial victim of metropolitan exploitation. But the reference was not entirely perverse: partly as a result of the War of American Independence, Ireland was granted an independent parliament in 1782 and partial admission into the English navigation system and so stood as an example of enlightened imperial reform, however compulsory the gesture. As readers will recall, Blin was an opponent of colonial representation in the Assembly, so the Irish solution of an independent colonial parliament checked by metropolitan executive authority, in the person of the governor at Dublin Castle, presented for him "nothing which can shock good sense and reason." [28]

For others in the *affaire*, the Americans provided a model of ingenious constitutional design that favored liberty and moderation. Revisionist scholarship on revolutionary ideology has always implicitly or explicitly relied upon a comparison between a moderate American Revolution and an inherently radical French Revolution; the former respected property, individual liberty, and local autonomy, while the latter was illiberal, statist, and inexorably centralizing—even totalitarian—in its single-minded pursuit of equality. The positive attention lavished by revisionist historians upon revolutionary moderates, or *constitutionnels*, is explained by the latter's advocacy of an American-style constitution as an alternative to the egalitarian tendencies of radical Jacobinism. The same logic attracted members of the Assembly in search of a constitution for the French empire to the American example. [29]

By his own account, the English colonies, and in particular the United States, served as a guide to Barnave during the whole unfortunate *affaire des colonies*. Barnave argued that the English had managed the division between internal and external regimes to the best advantage of both colony and metropole, all the while curiously failing to mention the American Revolution. In his speech of 23 September 1791, Barnave underlined that local control of the interior regime was imperative to the maintenance of slavery.[30] Members of the Club Massiac accepted this logic, and in their discussions with the extraordinary deputies from the Ponant, made the relation to the American constitution even more explicit:

> New England is in the exact same situation with its states as is France with respect to its colonies: their declaration of the rights of man begins, as does France's, *that all men are born and remain equal in rights,* and yet slavery exists almost everywhere, as it does in France.
>
> How could the Congress make this general principle agree with particular exceptions? It is by leaving to each state internally the laws pertaining to its blacks, and to only subject the parts [i.e., states] to the general interest of all; by means of this political organization, slavery is tolerated in some states, prohibited in others, without the central legislative body violating the universal principle of liberty and equality.[31]

Although the logic is strained, the goal is clear: some sort of compromise had to be found between the universal principles of the Revolution and the laws necessary to preserve the social structure in diverse corners of the empire. The nation manifests uniformity; empire, diversity. Without speaking its name, merchants, colonists, and other advocates of the slave system reached for federalism as a solution to the incompatibility between French universalist nationalism and the demands of commercial empire. Naturally, promoters of this sort of political organization did not insist so much upon the conceptual rigor of their solution—how could they?—as they did the self-evident superiority of the American constitution, "the freest on the planet," born of "sage philosophy." The facts on the ground hardly impeached this judgment in their eyes. Rather, they gave a living example that the federalist syllogism worked despite glaring inconsistencies among its premises; or, as Guadeloupe deputy Chabert de la Charrière put it, "you will be less astonished by the laws of our colonies in consulting the constitution of Carolina or Georgia, which are provinces cultivated by slaves."[32]

In treating the colonial question, the Assembly, its Committee, and the interest groups orbiting around these bodies all hesitated between two fundamentally incompatible versions of the metropole-colony relationship. The first version brought the colonies within the compass of the nation, where the distribution of rights and the organization of economic exchanges were judged by the regulative ideal of universality and equality. The Physiocrats had proposed something similar in previous decades in order to overcome conflicts between mainland France and its colonies. Despite an almost unanimous refusal to concede that the colonies could be incorporated within the nation, the challenge of giving the colonies a constitution fitted to their social structures and the need to impart a rational plan of governance upon the empire made the pull of Jacobin solutions irresistible. While it is counterintuitive to say so, these plans took the same attitude to sovereignty as had Quesnay in suggesting an *empire monarchique*. The second version rejected the Jacobin logic of incorporation as too radical and as one whose application (in the case of free trade and the abolition of slavery) would lead either to colonial revolt or to de facto independence. Between incorporation and independence lay the imperial solution, one that was sometimes likened to American-style federalism. Like the Constitutional Monarchy ratified in 1791 and just as quickly lost in 1792, the imperial solution was conceived as a way of terminating the Revolution and giving it a solid institutional basis, from which further progress toward the ideals of the Revolution could be made. It remains to explore the common sources of these illusions, principally in the thought of Antoine Barnave.

The Colonies and the Constitutional Monarchy

On 15 July 1791, Barnave asked the Assembly: "are we going to terminate the Revolution, or are we going to restart it?" The ostensible occasion of this speech was a debate in the Assembly over royal inviolability in the proposed constitution. But the king's recent (21 June 1791) capture at Varennes, after an unsuccessful attempt to meet enemies of the Revolution across France's eastern border at Montmédy, put into question the fate of the king and of the monarchy itself. It was the first time that republicanism became a serious force in revolutionary politics—effecting the conversion to the cause, for instance, of the Marquis de Condorcet and Jean-Pierre Brissot de Warville. Beyond the clearly incumbent issues of executive authority and constitutional provisions for judging the king, Barnave dwelled on the threat that republicanism posed to the very basis of society: property. In abolishing the feudal regime, the Revolution had earned itself numerous allies among the people, "but what night of the 4th of August lies in the future, if not one directed against property?" In a carefully coded swipe at critics of the property qualifications in the constitution, Barnave added: "does there remain any other aristocracy to destroy, save that of wealth?" Republicanism threatened to restart the Revolution in the name of "metaphysical maxims" such as equality and democracy.[33]

Barnave's case against republicanism in France was both circumstantial and historical and turned on the role of conquest in modern, commercial societies. Like many writers on the subject before him, Jean-Jacques Rousseau and Montesquieu being the most immediately relevant, Barnave believed that this form of government was inappropriate for a geographically large and populous nation such as France. Barnave tended to emphasize this circumstantial case to audiences sympathetic to republicanism, as when he defended himself before the Revolutionary Tribunal on 28 November 1793: "I have always believed that republican governments were the most noble and the most fitted to the nature of man." Historically, he argued that republics were becoming anachronistic among the commercial peoples of Europe, who were animated more by the passion of self-interest than by either virtue or reason. The latter are, according to Barnave (following the abbé de Mably), immoderate, "conquering passions" *(passions envahissantes)* while self-interest, in commercial societies, leads naturally to moderate, "conservative passions." Barnave used this natural history of the passions in commercial society, doubtless familiar to readers of Mandeville, Hume, Montesquieu, and Smith, to derive two salient political consequences.[34] First, the people in modern, commercial societies are more attached to their private interests than to the direct expression of public virtue in the political sphere. Because the accumulation and enjoyment of property requires stable institutions, order is just as necessary as liberty—a fact that may at times justify the sacrifice of certain forms of equality and political participation at the altar of bourgeois tranquility. A second consequence is that modern polities should be organized not for war and

conquest, which is the shared destiny of republican and despotic regimes, but for peace, conservation, and international equilibrium:
"commerce forms a large class of people who are lovers of peace abroad,
tranquility at home and an established government." The type of modern state that delivered these benefits was the "civilized" or "organized"
monarchy.[35]

Barnave believed that the English and, perhaps counterintuitively,
American constitutions provided a model for an organized monarchy.
Most important, as we see from Barnave's *Introduction* and other writings, it is not sufficient simply to replace landed, aristocratic wealth with
mobile, bourgeois wealth in order to secure freedom. In a large territorial nation such as France, this succession, however historically inevitable, posed significant problems of order; only a centralizing monarchy
could, in this context, provide unity and a plausible counterweight to
the residual power of the aristocracy. In this sense, the diffuse power
of the "laborious classes" was to be concentrated in the person of the
monarch. But in any territorial empire, the natural seat of monarchical
power is the army; the political quietism and immaturity of the productive classes could not, in Barnave's view, form a reliable bulwark against
the monarchical tendency toward conquest abroad and despotism at
home. The people threatened to be enslaved and impoverished by the
strong monarch and army so generously funded with their newly created
wealth.[36]

Two essential elements emerge from this brief account of Barnave's
thought. First, the "organized monarchy" he had in mind was a complicated machine, an outlook on government that he relentlessly contrasted
with the simple, "metaphysical" notions circulating among republicans.
Like the Jacobins he came to oppose, Barnave believed fervently in the
virtues of centralization, but in contrast to them, he also thought that free
government was basically limited government, which demanded elaborate mechanisms that could set the conquering passions found in different branches of government, or segments of society, against one another
in order to neutralize them. Second, therefore, Barnave saw the need for
an intermediate, moderating force against the despotic tendencies of
the modern monarchy—a solution similar to the politics of fusion advocated by Montesquieu.[37]

The question for Barnave was how to "introduce an aristocracy into the machine of government without creating a nobility in the nation," since the landed aristocracy with the venal offices, *parlements,* and hereditary privileges upheld by Montesquieu could hardly be expected to serve as an intermediary between the crown and the people in the new regime. He justified his answer, property, in terms similar to those of Emmanuel Joseph Sieyès, author of the agenda-setting *What Is the Third Estate?* (1789). Sieyès believed that in a society characterized by the extensive division of labor, the functions of voting and government should be reserved for the educated and economically independent but not juridically privileged classes. Barnave believed that the constitution should introduce an aristocracy of property, allotting political liberty and the job of government to the "easy and enlightened" members among what he called the "mercantile and bourgeois aristocracy." This class would defend equally against the despotic pretensions of the monarch and the anarchic levelers among the people. In the course of the debate over the constitution in the summer of 1791, Barnave and Malouet contrived a speech in which the latter would attack the constitution from the right in order to make it more palatable to centrist deputies. A highly restricted franchise was necessary to the defense of property, Malouet argued, since "property is often irreconcilable with the fullest extension of liberty." Like Barnave, Malouet believed that for most people the free enjoyment of property was more useful than political liberty. He also attacked the "abstraction" and unrealism of republican theories, citing instead the need for a just equilibrium of power in order to guarantee "natural and civil" rights. In contrast to the reality of the French social structure and the constitution that stood in relation to it, Malouet condemned the dangers of the doctrine of popular sovereignty and the general will: "simple and rude people [are] dangerously misled by this declaration [of the rights of man and citizen] which you immediately retract in your constitution because you have felt it necessary to observe and to recognize inequalities in rights." In the course of the same debate, Barnave was no less emphatic about the irrelevance of democratic theory to France, arguing that pure democracy could only subsist, as it had in ancient Greece, at the expense of complete slavery for the vast majority. Modern society must admit the principle of representation, and monarchies must allow for a principle of aristocracy, even if these requirements seem to contravene popular sovereignty and notions of equality that lay at the heart of the revolutionary project: "it is not enough to want to be free, one must know how to be free." [38]

Knowing how to be free meant giving a durable form to the revolutionary project—"terminating the revolution"—even where the process of consolidation and institutionalization entailed compromises with revolutionary principles. In mainland France, a "bourgeois aristocracy" would serve as the intermediary force in a social structure based upon property, keeping the laboring forces in check. In Saint-Domingue, the need for order was all the more imperious, given a lopsided population: "subordination, which is the very essence of the colonial regime," Barnave wrote, "cannot exist without an intermediary class between that which is occupied with cultivation and that which must be called to the administration of public affairs." Here, the "intermediary class" was not a privileged group—quite to the contrary: 30,000 free men of color would suffer the deprivation of political rights in order to maintain an artificial racial prejudice against 450,000 slaves, even though this "moral means" of keeping order in Saint-Domingue was both "artificial" and wrong. In mainland France, Barnave argued that centuries of aristocratic domination rendered the *moeurs* of the laboring population unfit for the immediate enjoyment of full political rights, even though they were just as responsible for the production of mobile wealth as the "bourgeois aristocracy" that was to hold them in tutelage. For Barnave, a self-described believer in eventual slave emancipation, the same gradualist logic applied in the colonies: in both cases, universal principles were trumped by slowly evolving historical circumstances and social utility. [39]

Opponents of political rights for free men of color repeatedly underlined the analogy between the situation in mainland France and in the colonies, and in so doing gained political advantage from their opponents' hypocrisy. In his speech of 23 September 1791, which led to the deprivation of what little had been granted to free men of color on 15 May, Barnave made his case uncomfortably plain: the Assembly was collectively working, by a sort of conspiracy of silence, to deprive 600,000 black slaves of all species of right. Why, then, was the Assembly so solicitous of the political rights of "a handful of individuals" in the colonies when three million Frenchmen were deprived of the same rights by the distinction between active and passive citizenship?[40]

It is unsurprising that Barnave criticized his opponents in the *affaire* in precisely the same terms as he criticized his political opponents at home, given the analogy between these two situations. He laid the blame for the *affaire* at the door of the Physiocrats, who "contributed much to the disasters in the colonies," and criticized this group of "fanatics, sectarians [and] enthusiasts" in terms familiar to readers of Alexis de Tocqueville's *L'Ancien régime et la Révolution*. Tocqueville, it will be remembered, castigated the Physiocrats for their complete lack of respect for the past, their excessive rationalism, and their indifference to political liberty and believed that they incarnated the radical dogmatism *(esprit de système)* of the Enlightenment that had caused the Revolution to degenerate into violence. Everywhere in his personal notebooks and his speeches before the Assembly, Barnave defined political wisdom by the "experience" and "respect for circumstances" that the Physiocrats swept aside in favor of "simple ideas": "indefinite liberty of commerce, LAISSEZ FAIRE, LAISSEZ PASSER; in consequence, no guilds, no monopoly companies, no colonies, no customs, no barriers and no distinction between the interior and exterior." While Barnave admitted with evident conviction that these principles were "in themselves grand and generous," he argued with equal heat that the realities of international economic and political competition precluded their full and immediate application. This was a matter, he and others believed, of national survival.[41]

Between metropole and colony there was a relationship of analogy and dependence. They both maintained their social structures through intermediary classes and the judicious deprivation of rights—hence the analogy. Dependence stemmed from the fact that colonial commerce enabled prosperity and limited government where the peculiarities of France's geography made "organized monarchy" difficult to achieve and maintain. As a large territorial empire, France was inherently given to agriculture and, hence, political domination by the "equestrian and feudal" aristocracy. However, with its long coastline and commodious harbors, France had an equally strong vocation for overseas trade and the industry it nourished. Like Montesquieu, Barnave envisioned a compromise between oceanic and territorial, agricultural France in the name of preserving freedom against despotism. Wherever it appeared, the growth of commerce contributed to "popular power," making "democratic revolution inevitable." At the same time, while absolute monarchs had traditionally protected the bourgeoisie and other members of the "laborious classes" from the aristocracy, these same monarchs had the tendency to debauch commercial prosperity with the formation of monopoly companies, confiscatory taxation, and a lust for territorial conquest. Given these circumstances, Barnave believed that trade was a particular necessity in France, since only it could bury the last vestiges of aristocratic power in an agrarian nation; it would also keep the conquering spirit of the monarch, which as a large nation France could not do without, in check. Barnave also believed that, in a nation so influenced from top to bottom by aristocratic *moeurs*, industry would "keep the people busy and moralize them," thus saving France from the worst of revolutionary excesses.[42]

Barnave made the case that it was not just commerce in general that could ensure these benefits to France but specifically colonial commerce. Historically, colonial commerce had brought economic progress to France, which was otherwise hobbled by a stationary agricultural economy and the trappings of feudalism at home. In this respect, France differed from England; while the latter had of course benefited from colonial commerce, England seemed, on Barnave's account, to have more internal physical and cultural resources to sustain the growth of commerce and industry. In a nation where aristocratic habits and institutions would not disappear overnight, external trade and the cultural forces it brought into play would remain crucial sources of social change. Furthermore, Barnave argued that in a large, heterogeneous society characterized by inequalities, "the unity of an empire can only be maintained by certain things that belong to the masses," including the symbolic figure of the king but also, significantly, a common source of wealth in the colonies. For Barnave, a truly modern revolutionary project of "liberty, equality and unity" could be accomplished only through expanding prosperity and work. The liberal revolution at home required the continual flow of wealth from the colonies and the continuation of their illiberal social structure. This is perhaps why Barnave insisted, in his *Introduction,* on the linkage between the colonial question and that of the monarchy.[43]

Dénouement

In early 1791, the provincial assembly at Cap Français voted a subscription to raise a bust in honor of Antoine Barnave, "défenseur de la colonie," in recognition of the legislation he had helped to shepherd through the Assembly, which was so congenial to their interests. This touching commemorative gesture never came to fruition: on 22 August 1791, encouraged by revolutionary ideology and strengthened in their cause by conflicts among the elites on the island, the slaves of Saint-Domingue rose up. Plantation owners were murdered or fled while their property—fields, sugar mills, and slave quarters—was put to the fire. Barnave and his fellow committee members' defense was evidently inadequate. On 10 August 1792, almost exactly one year after the colonies erupted in full-scale revolt, the monarchy fell, and officials of the newly proclaimed French Republic arrested Barnave, the self-appointed defender of the constitutional monarchy. He was executed in November 1793.[44]

Barnave, along with some self-interested advocates in the colonial and merchant lobbies, frequently tied the survival of the Revolution to that of the colonies because of the wealth they generated. Jaurès himself adduced one of the clearest cases of this influence, when popular protests in Paris over high sugar prices in January 1792, directly caused by the slave uprising in Saint-Domingue, strengthened the hand of radical Jacobins against moderate monarchist elements in the National Convention. By this time, modest Parisians counted sugar among the daily necessities worth fighting for, and its absence, like the shriveling of profits from colonial trade as a whole, had destabilizing effects. Historians such as R. R. Palmer and Bailey Stone have made broad arguments that foreign conflict helped to "revolutionize" or radicalize the Revolution at home. Continental warfare has always bulked large in these sorts of accounts, but the importance of the colonial theater has more recently come into focus. The great powers quickly saw the opportunities that the Revolution presented them in the Caribbean, and England's entrance into the colonial fray was a particular threat. France's enemies alternately took sides with slaves and counterrevolutionary royalists, stoking internal tensions that ultimately led to civil war and the collapse of the colonial economy. Although some contemporaries argued that colonies and the monarchy stood and fell together, for us the case is not so much weak as circumstantial; judging it requires imagining a complex—though it should be said highly unlikely—counterfactual: what if slave revolt had not erupted in the colonies? The very least one can say is that the symbiosis between metropole and colony had lost any obviously stable political and economic basis by 1791.[45]

Moreover, the moderate paths charted by constitutional monarchists at home and advocates of a racialized regime in the colonies were destined to failure for similar reasons. In the wake of the king's flight to Varennes, the popular movement came to believe that the "bourgeois aristocracy" lauded by Barnave would do anything, including cover up the crimes of a proven traitor to the nation, in order to save a socially biased, undemocratic, and inegalitarian constitution. In addition to the active/passive distinction, which agitated so many among the urban poor, the Assembly's tergiversations over the abolition of feudal property deeply alienated the peasantry from their new masters in Paris.

On 4 August 1789, members of the Assembly offered up their privileges for destruction in a bonfire of the vanities that lasted deep into the night. But in their follow-up decree of 10 August, which proclaimed the "complete destruction of the feudal regime," the Assembly provided clarifications that show that their orgy of self-abnegation led to some serious regrets. Fearing that the abolition without compensation of illegitimate "feudal" property would delegitimize all forms of property, onerous "redemption fees" were imposed upon peasants who wished to be released from feudal obligations. These amounted to between twenty and twenty-five years' worth of annual dues, a rate that often put emancipation entirely out of reach. In the meantime, until the new regime could be firmly established, peasants were expected to pay existing taxes (including church tithes) and even submit to seigneurial courts. Alexandre Lameth, a future member of the Committee, close friend of Barnave, and a plantation owner, drew the connection between the Assembly's equivocal abolition of feudalism and the need to settle the colonial question. In both cases, the Assembly was called to action by events on the ground in the summer of 1789: within France, the war on the *châteaux* threatened France's agricultural economy by spreading disorder in the countryside; abroad, a slave insurrection in Martinique beginning in August threatened lucrative colonial production and trade. Lameth and the Assembly as a whole hoped that quick action would halt the spread of misguided egalitarianism on both fronts: "our determination on this subject is a sure way of dissipating the error of the people," who might demand either emancipation from slavery or an immediate end to the seigneurial regime.[46]

Those who were excluded by the constitutional monarchy could not be so easily dissuaded of their errors, given how unevenly distributed the benefits to moderation seemed to be. In the colonies and at home, the core principles of the Revolution made moderate compromises with France's history, geography, and *moeurs* seem "timid and inconsistent," thus rendering them politically untenable and in the final analysis explosive. This is why events on the ground—whether in the countryside, the city, or the plantation—so often dictated events and principles in the Assembly.[47]

Although Barnave complained ceaselessly about the crimes of the uncompromising republican regime that would ultimately put him to death, aspects of his historical thesis found even clearer illustration later in the facts of the Napoleonic episode. In his *Introduction,* Barnave argued that only foreign trade, because it relied on the more fundamentally democratic forces in society, could moderate the despotic tendencies of monarchs in large territorial empires. When the restoration of monarchy did occur in France, it came in the form of Napoleon Bonaparte, who brutally depoliticized the public sphere and reoriented collective values around the principles of military conquest and state service. Napoleon even reinstituted a form of feudal property in the empire in order to support his marshals and members of his newly established nobility. All of this was quite the opposite of the modern "organized monarchy," nurtured and balanced by colonial trade, that Barnave had in mind. Barnave was no longer available for the task, but Benjamin Constant wrote a fitting postscript to this story. In his coruscating polemic against Napoleon Bonaparte, *De l'esprit de conquête et de l'usurpation* (1814), Constant described the consequences of Napoleon's usurpation: material "deprivation and suffering"; intolerance of political dissent among militarized public officials, for whom "opposition is disorder"; and the diversion of talent away from the arts and learning. Constant, who shared many of Barnave's intellectual influences and preoccupations, saw all of these consequences issuing from the "gross and disastrous anachronism" of a modern society devoted to warfare in "an age of commerce."[48]

The sudden collapse of Atlantic trade after the uprising in the colonies in 1791 led to a profound reorientation of the French economy, which culminated in the "Continental System," by which Napoleon tried to blockade the entire continent of Europe and fix terms of trade to France's advantage. Though intended to inflict pain upon the British, the primary consequence of the blockade was to revalorize, even if it did not reinvigorate, the agricultural sector and also to effect a massive involution of the French economy. In the space of a decade, France became more territorial and agrarian than it had been in over half a century; this was the regression to agrarian-military despotism feared by Barnave and observed by Constant. Perhaps ironically, at the same time, cut off from the Atlantic trade and forced to live off of its continental resources, France reoriented its industry geographically along the Rhenish axis where it remains to this day; updated its textile and metallurgical technology; and began to explore more seriously the energy sources that would ultimately fuel its path to an industrialized economy. The era of primitive globalization, oriented around an Atlantic economy and anxiously analyzed in the eighteenth-century science of commerce, was over. After the Napoleonic interlude, the French economy began to look more recognizably like the one envisioned by nineteenth- and twentieth-century political economy.[49]

Notes

Index

Notes

Abbreviations

MANUSCRIPT SOURCES

A.D.   France: Archives Départementales
      ChC   Chambre de Commerce
      Ch-Mar   Charente Maritime
      L-Atl.   Loire Atlantique

A.N.   France: Archives Nationales (Paris, CARAN)
      A.E.   Affaires Etrangères

M.A.E.   France: Ministère des Affaires Etrangères (unless otherwise specified, Quai d'Orsay, Paris)
      C.P.   Correspondance Politique
      M.D.   Mémoires et Documents

PRINTED SOURCES

AP   France, *Archives parlementaires de 1787 à 1860; recueil complet des débats législatifs & politiques des chambres françaises* (Paris: P. Dupont, 1862).

EL   Montesquieu, Baron Charles de Secondat, *De l'esprit des lois* (citations from OC).

HI   Guillaume Raynal, *A Philosophical and Political History of the Settlements and Trade of the Europeans in the East and West Indies,* 2nd ed., trans. F.R.S. J. O. Justamond. (London, 1783).

OC   Montesquieu, *Oeuvres complètes,* ed. Roger Caillois, 2 vols. (Paris: Gallimard, 1951).

OC (Voltaire Foundation)   Montesquieu, *Oeuvres complètes,* eds. Ehrard, Volpilhac-Auger, Larrère, et al. (Oxford: Voltaire Foundation, 1998–).

WN   Adam Smith, *An Inquiry into the Nature and Causes of the Wealth of Nations,* ed. Edwin Cannan (Chicago: University of Chicago Press, 1976).

Introduction

1. On "archaic globalization," and for a succinct summary of the risks attaching to it, see C. A. Bayly, *The Birth of the Modern World, 1780–1914: Global Connections and Comparisons* (Oxford: Blackwell, 2004), 27 and 92–96. Guillaume Raynal, *HI*, 1:1. Adam Smith's discussion of the decline of feudalism through commerce comes in *WN*, book 3, especially chap. 3. Montesquieu's view of this process is taken up in chap. 2.

2. Albert O. Hirschman, *The Passions and the Interests: Political Arguments for Capitalism before Its Triumph*, 2nd ed. (Princeton, NJ: Princeton University Press, 1996), 59–62. The phrase *doux commerce* never appears in Montesquieu's *EL*, a key text for Hirschman in his reconstruction of the *doux commerce* thesis; but it was of course widely held that commerce softened manners and government.

3. Perry Anderson, *Lineages of the Absolutist State* (London: Verso, 1977), 41.

4. On "provisional coincidence": ibid. The mid-century turning point for the French colonial empire is commonly recognized; see Olivier Pétré-Grenouilleau, "How Did France Enter and Play its Role in the Atlantic? State and Maritime Traders: From Clashes to Compromise (ca. 1580–1830)," in *Atlantic History: History of the Atlantic System, 1580–1830*, ed. Horst Pietschmann (Göttingen: Vandenhoeck & Ruprecht, 2002), 285; and Julia Adams, *The Familial State: Ruling Families and Merchant Capitalism in Early Modern Europe* (Ithaca, NY: Cornell University Press, 2005), 188. For views on the Physiocrats, see Alexis de Tocqueville, *L'Ancien régime et la Révolution* (Paris: Gallimard, 1967), book 3, chap. 3: "all of the institutions that the Revolution would irrevocably abolish were the object of [the Physiocrats'] attacks."

5. Jean-Claude Perrot discusses this holding pattern in *Une Histoire intellectuelle d'économie politique* (Paris: Presses Universitaires de France, 1992).

6. For a general discussion, see Mark Blaug, "On the Historiography of Economics," *Journal of the History of Economic Thought* 12, no. 2 (1990). Blaug distinguishes between "doxological," "rational reconstruction," and "contextual" approaches; the latter two, because of their internalist approach, tend more toward the Whiggism discussed in the text. In the French case, this trend was first established by the editorial labors of Eugène Daire, whose *Collection des principaux* established the lineage between the Physiocrats and classical political economy and also defined their predecessors as "pre-physiocrats." Eugène Daire, ed., *Collection des principaux économistes*, 15 vols. (Paris: Guillaumin, 1840–1848). The monumental editorial work of Gustave Schelle is much in the same vein. This tradition of defining French economists against the Physiocrats was continued by George Weulersse. See Georges Weulersse, *Le Mouvement physiocratique en France de 1756 à 1770*, 2 vols. (Paris: Félix Alcan, 1910); *La Physiocratie à la fin du règne de Louis XV, 1770–1774* (Paris: Presses Universitaires de France, 1959); and *La Physiocratie à l'aube de la Révolution, 1781–1792* (Paris: EHESS, 1985). For a statement on the need to push beyond the dichotomies that have structured the history of French economic thought, see Antoine Murphy, "Le développement des idées économiques en France (1750–1756)," *Revue d'histoire moderne et contemporaine* 33 (1986): 1–2.

7. Discussions of genre can be found in Vivienne Brown, "Decanonizing Discourses: Textual Analysis and the History of Economic Thought," in *Economics and Language,* ed. Willy Henderson and Tony Dudley-Evans (New York: Routledge, 1993); and by the same author in *Adam Smith's Discourse: Canonicity, Commerce, and Conscience* (London: Routledge, 1994). For a discussion of history in Adam Smith, see J. Salter, "Adam Smith on Feudalism, Commerce and Slavery," *History of Political Thought* 13, no. 2 (1992).

8. Jean-Claude Perrot, *Une Histoire intellectuelle d'économie politique;* Simone Meyssonnier, *La Balance et l'horloge: La genèse de la pensée libérale en France au XVIIIe siècle* (Paris: Editions de la Passion, 1989); and Catherine Larrère, *L'Invention de l'économie au XVIIIᵉ siècle: Du droit naturel à la physiocratie* (Paris: Presses Universitaires de France, 1992). The two recent "non-Physiocratic" studies are Henry C. Clark, *Compass of Society: Commerce and Absolutism in Old-Regime France* (Lanham, MD: Lexington Books, 2007); and John Shovlin, *The Political Economy of Virtue: Luxury, Patriotism, and the Origins of the French Revolution* (Ithaca, NY: Cornell University Press, 2006). Shovlin makes an explicit point of sidelining Physiocracy (3).

9. Donald Winch, *Riches and Poverty: An Intellectual History of Political Economy in Britain, 1750–1834* (Cambridge: Cambridge University Press, 1996); and by the same author, *Adam Smith's Politics: An Essay in Historiographic Revision* (Cambridge: Cambridge University Press, 1978); John Robertson, *The Case for the Enlightenment: Scotland and Naples, 1680–1760* (Cambridge: Cambridge University Press, 2005); Emma Rothschild, *Economic Sentiments: Adam Smith, Condorcet, and the Enlightenment* (Cambridge, MA: Harvard University Press, 2001); and Michael Sonenscher, *Before the Deluge: Public Debt, Inequality, and the Intellectual Origins of the French Revolution* (Princeton, NJ: Princeton University Press, 2007).

10. Foundational works in this tradition include J. G. A. Pocock, *Virtue, Commerce, and History: Essays on Political Thought and History, Chiefly in the Eighteenth Century* (Cambridge: Cambridge University Press, 1985); and Istvan Hont and Michael Ignatieff, eds., *Wealth and Virtue: The Shaping of Political Economy in the Scottish Enlightenment* (Cambridge: Cambridge University Press, 1983). On the anti-Marxism of Cambridge School contextualism, see Steve Pincus, "Neither Machiavellian Moment nor Possessive Individualism: Commercial Society and the Defenders of the English Commonwealth," *American Historical Review* 103, no. 3 (1998): 708–711.

11. Istvan Hont, *Jealousy of Trade: International Competition and the Nation-State in Historical Perspective* (Cambridge, MA: Harvard University Press, 2005). The Navigation Acts are mentioned four times in the introduction (36, 53, 113, and 115) and once in the main body of the text (245). Nowhere is there any discussion of the concrete provisions of these Acts. Slavery is mentioned three times: twice in the footnotes as political slavery (chap. 7) and once indirectly in a reference to black shipbuilders, presumably slaves, in North America (255). The American constitutional system is discussed at length in chap. 7, but there are few and only glancing references to America and American trade or production elsewhere.

12. On the transcendent importance of empire to understanding the Atlantic world, see Trevor Burnard, "Empire Matters? The Historiography of Imperialism in Early America, 1492–1830," *History of European Ideas* 33 (2007). See also Emma Rothschild, "Global Commerce and the Question of Sovereignty in the Eighteenth-Century Provinces," *Modern Intellectual History* 1, no. 1 (2004).

13. World-systems approaches include Immanuel Wallerstein, *The Modern World System,* 3 vols. (New York: Academic Press, 1974–1980); and Fernand Braudel, *Capitalism and Civilization, 15th–18th Century,* 3 vols. (Berkeley: University of California Press, 1985–1992), esp. vols. 2 and 3. The New Institutionalist view is articulated in Daron Acemoglu, Simon Johnson, and James Robinson, "The Rise of Europe: Atlantic Trade, Institutional Change and Economic Growth," *American Economic Review* 95, no. 3 (2005). For a sectoral analysis of the French economy, see Guillaume Daudin, *Commerce et prospérité: La France au xviiie siècle* (Paris: Presses Universitaires de l'Université Paris-Sorbonne, 2005), on foreign trade in general and growth: 210 and 223; on the dynamism of the Atlantic trade: 225; for the relative decline of Asian and Levant trade: 226. For further affirmations of the importance of the Atlantic trade to France, see Paul Butel, "Succes et déclin du commerce colonial français, de la Révolution a la Restauration," *Revue économique* 40, no. 6 (1989): 1086. For a highly skeptical view about the importance of Atlantic trade, see Pieter Emmer, "The Myth of Early Globalization: The Atlantic Economy, 1500–1800," *European Review* 11, no. 1 (2003). Emmer concentrates too heavily, in my view, on what he sees as the inferior mass of eighteenth-century trade flows.

14. The convert to foreign trade and empire is Patrick K. O'Brien, "Inseparable Connections: Trade, Economy, Fiscal Sate, and the Expansion of Empire, 1688–1815," in *Oxford History of the British Empire,* vol. 2, ed. P. J. Marshall (Oxford: Oxford University Press, 1998). For an important recent synthesis, see Robin Blackburn, *The Making of New World Slavery: From the Baroque to the Modern, 1492–1800* (London: Verso, 1997), introduction, chaps. 9 and 12. Blackburn assigns great importance to the role of racial ideology and its relationship to the forms of civil society characteristic of the capitalist mode of production, but these are not of immediate concern to the thesis developed here.

15. A summary of all the pessimistic accounts can be found in James Pritchard, *In Search of Empire: The French in the Americas, 1670–1730* (Cambridge: Cambridge University Press, 2004), esp. chaps. 4, 5, and 9. The comparison of French to British and Dutch trading companies comes from Adams, *The Familial State,* chap. 6. On the wildly optimistic side, see Jean-Pierre Poussou, "Le dynamisme de l'économie française sous Louis XVI," *Revue économique* 40, no. 6 (1989): 974; and L. M. Cullen, "History, Economic Crises, and Revolution: Understanding Eighteenth-Century France," *Economic History Review* 46, no. 4 (1993): 640. Paul Butel also sees few clouds on the horizon until 1789: see "Succes et déclin du commerce colonial français, de la Révolution a la Restauration." More nuanced views can be found in Sylvia Marzagalli, "The French Atlantic," *Itinerario* 23, no. 2 (1999); and Pétré-Grenouilleau, "How Did France Play Its Role in the Atlantic?" Despite the loss of the British North American colonies in 1776, British trade with North America quickly exceeded preconflict levels. See Jacques Godechot, "Les Relations

économiques entre la France et les Etats-Unis de 1778 à 1789," *French Historical Studies* 1, no. 1 (1958).

16. Adam Smith, *W.N,* book III, chap. iii; Tocqueville, *L'Ancien régime et la Révolution,* book 2, chaps. 3–4. For revisions to the Tocquevillian view, see David Parker, *The Making of French Absolutism* (London: Edward Arnold, 1983); William Doyle, *Venality: The Sale of Offices in Eighteenth-Century France* (Oxford: Clarendon Press, 1996); Gail Bossenga, "City and State: An Urban Perspective on the Origins of the French Revolution," in *The French Revolution and the Creation of Modern Political Culture,* vol. 1, ed. Keith M. Baker (Oxford: Pergamon, 1987); and by the same author, *The Politics of Privilege: Old Regime and Revolution in Lille* (Cambridge: Cambridge University Press, 1991); and Hilton Root, *Peasants and King in Burgundy: Agrarian Foundations of French Absolutism* (Berkeley: University of California Press, 1987).

17. Anderson, *Lineages of the Absolutist State,* 40–41; Adams, *The Familial State,* 16 (on corporatism and patrimonial rule) and chap. 6 (for comparative insights). For a subtle discussion of the role of corporate institutions other than trading companies in eighteenth-century French capitalism, see Gail Bossenga, "Protecting Merchants: Guilds and Commercial Capitalism in Eighteenth-Century France," *French Historical Studies* 15, no. 4 (1988).

18. For a criticism of liberal modernization theory, see Charles Tilly, "Did the Cake of Custom Break?" in *Consciousness and Class Experience in Nineteenth- and Twentieth-Century Europe,* ed. John Merriman (New York: Holmes-Meir, 1980). Tilly is responding to Eugen Joseph Weber, *Peasants into Frenchmen: The Modernization of Rural France, 1870–1914* (Palo Alto, CA: Stanford University Press, 1976). The classic of Marxist modernization theory is Barrington Moore, *Social Origins of Dictatorship and Democracy: Lord and Peasant in the Making of the Modern World* (Boston: Beacon Press, 1967). On the "production of space," see Henri Lefebvre, *La Production de l'espace* (Paris: Editions Anthropos, 1974); and Alain Lipietz, *Le Capital et son espace* (Paris: François Maspero, 1977), 19–25. A good summary of Lefebvre's ideas, particularly in relation to the problem of state formation, can be found in Henri Lefebvre, "Space and the State," in *State / Space: A Reader,* ed. Neil Brenner, Bob Jessop, and Martin Jones (Malden, MA: Blackwell, 2003). For further reflections on state formation, see Nicos Poulantzas, "The Nation," in the previous volume; John Ruggie, "Territorriality and Beyond: Problematizing Modernity in International Relations," *International Organization* 47, no. 1 (1993); David Harvey, *The Limits to Capital,* new and updated ed. (London: Verso, 2006), chap. 12; and by the same author, *Spaces of Capital: Towards a Critical Geography* (London: Routledge, 2001), chap. 7: "Capital: Factory of Fragmentation."

19. For the existence of center–periphery relations within the center, see Braudel, *Capitalism and Civilization, 15th–18th Century,* 3:35–42. Giovanni Arrighi, *The Long Twentieth Century: Money, Power and the Origins of Our Times* (London: Verso, 1994), 218–222. Alain Lipietz also discusses the process of territorialization and de-territorialization in *Mirages and Miracles: The Crises of Global Fordism* (London: Verso, 1987), 54–59, within a wider criticism of crude center–periphery theory, 48–60. For challenges to world-systems theory, and in particular the dominant relationship of the center in

developing capital-intensive methods of production, see Sidney W. Mintz, *Sweetness and Power: The Place of Sugar in Modern History* (New York: Penguin Books, 1985), introduction. The problem of space has recently been incorporated into studies of the French Atlantic world: Kenneth J. Banks, *Chasing Empire across the Sea: Communications and the State in the French Atlantic, 1713–1763* (Montreal: McGill-Queen's University Press, 2002).

20. See, in particular, Georges Lefebvre, *The French Revolution: From Its Origins to 1793* (New York: Columbia University Press, 1962), 6–13. Lefebvre emphasizes both the importance of the Atlantic trade and, from a Marxist perspective, the complexity of eighteenth-century social relations and the conflicts to which they gave rise. At the same time as revisionist historians dismantled the narrative of the rise of an industrial bourgeoisie and its inevitable capture of the state, cognizant Marxists were busy reworking their own views. An early expression of this was Perry Anderson's *Lineages of the Absolutist State.* Later, Geoff Eley and David Blackbourn argued that capitalist social relations could and did subsist in nineteenth-century Europe without the bourgeois capture of the state insisted upon by older varieties of Marxism. Their brief was to demolish the *Sonderweg* thesis by proving that nineteenth-century Germany was a liberal (i.e., capitalist) society despite the continued political dominance of aristocratic elites. These historians used Gramscian Marxism to dismantle the very same notion of bourgeois revolution memorably denounced by Furet as the "Jacobin catechism"—even citing Furet approvingly in the bargain. See *The Peculiarities of German History: Bourgeois Society and Politics in Nineteenth-Century Germany* (Oxford: Oxford University Press, 1984), 53–55 (on bourgeois revolution) and 169n (for Furet). Wallerstein is chastised for a similarly crude sociology in his world-systems theory, which insists upon bourgeois dominance, in P. J. Cain and A. G. Hopkins, *British Imperialism: Innovation and Expansion, 1688–1914* (London: Longman, 1993), 57.

1. Foreign Trade and National Models

1. Georges Weulersse, *Le Mouvement physiocratique en France de 1756 à 1770* (Paris: Félix Alcan, 1910), 1:20–29. See also Antoine Murphy, "Le développement des idées économiques en France (1750–1756)," *Revue d'histoire moderne et contemporaine* 33 (1986). The mercantilist/laissez-faire dichotomy was only used, in a highly partisan way, beginning in 1763. See Lars Magnusson, *Mercantilism: The Shaping of an Economic Language* (London: Routledge, 1994), 25.

2. On recovery and peace, see Joël Félix, "The Economy," in *Old Regime France, 1648–1788,* ed. William Doyle (Oxford: Oxford University Press, 2001), 13–25. For comparative statistics, see Paul Butel, *L'Economie française au xviiie siècle* (Paris: SEDES, 1993), 12, 80–87. See also François Crouzet, "Angleterre et France au XVIIIe siècle: Essai d'analyse comparée de deux croissances économiques," *Annales E.S.C.* 21 (1966): 254–291, which is a source for some of Butel's statistics. On export growth, see Guillaume Daudin, *Commerce et prospérité: La France au xviiie siècle* (Paris: Presses de l'Université Paris-Sorbonne, 2005), 219. For all of these growth figures, we should take into account that France was starting from a smaller

base than England and that per-capita income and per-capita trade still remained superior in England in 1788, despite French gains.

3. Perceptions of the French merchants are discussed at greater length in Chapter 6. See also Warren C. Scoville, "The French Economy in 1700–1701: An Appraisal by the Deputies of Trade," *Journal of Economic History* 22, no. 2 (1962).

4. The first public airing of trade statistics came in 1791, with M. Arnould, *De la balance du commerce et des relations commerciales extérieurs de la France dans toutes les parties du globe, particulièrement à la fin du règne de Louis XIV et au moment de la Révolution,* vol. 3 (Paris: Buisson, 1791). The closest thing to a systematic assessment of population statistics came in 1778, with M. Moheau, *Recherches et considérations sur la population de la France (1778),* ed. Eric Vilquin (Paris: Institut National d'Etudes Démographiques, INED, 1994). For authorial statistics, see Christine Théré, "Economic Publishing and Authors, 1566–1789," in *Studies in the History of French Political Economy: From Bodin to Walras,* ed. Gilbert Faccarello (London: Routledge, 1998), 242. See also Daniel Roche, *France in the Enlightenment* (Cambridge, MA: Harvard University Press, 1998), 152. On intellectual and mercantile elites, see Daniel Roche, "Négoce et culture dans la fin du XVIIIe siècle," *Revue d'histoire moderne et contemporaine* 25 (1978): 376–382. Kindleberger acknowledges the importance of trade to France's eighteenth-century successes, but the title of the chapter that contains these reflections is telling: "France, the Perpetual Challenger." See Charles P. Kindleberger, *World Economic Primacy, 1500–1990* (Oxford: Oxford University Press, 1996), chap. 7, esp. 109–113.

5. Alexis de Tocqueville, *L'Ancien régime et la Révolution* (Paris: Gallimard, 1967), book 3, chap. 4. Tocqueville, it should be said, did not believe in the now commonly accepted post-1770 downturn in the French economy.

6. Daniel Roche also emphasizes the lack of connection among France's agricultural, manufacturing, and commercial sectors, which individually had their own latent dynamism in the eighteenth century but were never quite brought together. Roche tends to cast these questions in spatial terms. Roche, *France in the Enlightenment,* chap. 5, esp. 142–143.

7. The most comprehensive statement of this view, and one that has the merit of taking into account the scholarship by critics of modernization theory and its extensions in economic history, is by Maxine Berg and Pat Hudson, "Rehabilitating the Industrial Revolution," *Economic History Review* 45 (1992). In many ways, Berg and Hudson reassert the relevance of David Landes, *The Unbound Prometheus: Technological Change and Industrial Development in Western Europe from 1750 to the Present* (Cambridge: Cambridge University Press, 1969), which also lays emphasis on factors of sectoral integration (see 51). For a highly pessimistic account of France's path to industrialization, particularly in respect of its credit markets and entrepreneurial activity, see the comparative study by Clive Trebilcock, *The Industrialization of the Continental Powers, 1780–1914* (London: Longman, 1981). On the other side of this question, Robert Aldrich summarizes the "revisionist" economic history of France's path to industrialization, which seeks to narrow the differences between France and England in the nineteenth century, in "Late Comer or Early

Starter? New Views on French Economic History," *Journal of European Economic History* 16, no. 1 (1987). See also Philip T. Hoffman, *Growth in a Traditional Society: The French Countryside, 1450–1815* (Princeton, NJ: Princeton University Press, 1996).

8. Michel Morineau, *Incroyables gazettes et fabuleux métaux: Les retours des trésors américains d'après les gazettes hollandaises (XVIe–XVIIIe siècles)* (London and Paris: Cambridge University Press and Maison des sciences de l'homme, 1985), 269 (trade figures) and 302 (bullion returns); Albert Girard, *Le commerce français à Séville et Cadix au temps des Habsbourg; contribution à l'étude du commerce étranger en Espagne aux XVIe et XVIIe siècles* (Bordeaux: Féret & Fils, 1932), 341–365 (on French textile industry).

9. On the War of Spanish Succession, M.A.E., C.P., Espagne (1716), vol. 326, f. 392v. Even after the War of Austrian Succession (1740–1748), the diplomat M. de La Borde opined ruefully that "A long experience has taught us only too well how destructive to France the advantages that they have derived from this treaty have been." A.N., A.E., B^{III} 361 (1748), "Mémoire sur le Commerce concernant differentes Puissances de l'Europe," 5r. The Chamber of Commerce of Nantes collected a dossier of Spanish complaints against the British on account of the *assiento*, in the hopes that these grievances might eventually lead to a reversal. A.D., L-Atl., C 747 (1713 and 1723). For a more detailed discussion of the effects of Utrecht on contraband trade in the Antilles, see Jacques Petitjean Roget, *Le Gaoulé* (Fort de France: Société d'histoire de la Martinique, 1966), 500; A.N., Commerce et Industrie, F^{12} 647 (1716), *Démonstration géométrique de la chûte prochaine du Commerce de France par l'agrandissement du Commerce des Anglois.* See also A.N., F^{12} 643, "Mémoire du Conseil de Commerce sur le nouveau traité conclu et signé entre l'Espagne, et l'Angleterre le 14 Décembre 1715"; M.A.E., C.P., Espagne 243 (1713), "Effets de l'union de la France et de l'Espagne"; M.A.E., C.P., Espagne 326 (1716), "Mémoire du Conseil de Commerce sur le Commerce avec l'Espagne," ff. 389r–396v. For diplomatic conniving, see M.A.E., C.P., Espagne 148 (1705), "Mémoire sur le commerce d'Espagne et sur celuy d'Amérique," by Helvétius; M.A.E., C.P., Espagne 147 (1705), "Mémoire sur la société de commerce proposée entre la France, l'Espagne et la Hollande," by Helvétius; M.A.E., C.P., Espagne 149 (1705–1706), "Raisons pour lesquelles la France et l'Espagne doivent former une société de commerce à l'exclusion de l'Angleterre," ff. 212r–217v; M.A.E., C.P., Espagne 217 (1712), "Observations sur le Commerce de Castille, dans lesquelles on propose une nouvelle forme, qui puisse estre à la Satisfaction de la France, l'Angleterre et de la Hollande," 168r–172r. In a secret mission of 1706, the diplomat Helvétius tried and failed to come to an understanding with the Dutch republic. M. Van der Bijl, "De Franse politieke agent Helvétius over de Situatie in de Nederlandse Republiek in het Jaar 1706," *Historish Genootschap* 80 (1966). On "privation," see "Démonstration géométrique," f. 2r. On Saint-Malo's decline, see Henri Sée, "The Ship-Owners of Saint Malo in the Eighteenth Century," *Bulletin of the Business Historical Society* 2, no. 4 (1928).

10. Pierre-Daniel Huet, *Histoire du Commerce & de la Navigation des Anciens* (Amsterdam: Humbert & Mortier, 1716), avertissement and preface; Pierre-Daniel Huet,

Mémoires sur le commerce des Hollandois, 3rd ed. (Amsterdam: Villard & Changuion, 1718). "In general he does the Dutch Nation a great deal of honor. . . . In representing her as the wisest and most prudent in Europe . . . perhaps even there is a bit of excess in all of the praise he gives them." For contemporary views, see Jean Le Clerc, *Bibliothèque ancienne et moderne: Pour servir de suite aux Bibliothèques Universelle et choisie* (Amsterdam: David Mortier, 1717), 7:415 (for quote) and 5:455–461 (on competition). For other scholarship on the importance of comparative economic thought in the early modern period, see Joyce O. Appleby, *Economic Thought and Ideology in Seventeenth-Century England* (Princeton, NJ: Princeton University Press, 1978), chap. 4; and François Crouzet, "Les Sources de la richesse de l'Angleterre, vues par les français du xviiie siècle," in *De la supériorité de l'Angleterre sur la France: L'économie et l'imaginaire xviie–xxe siècle* (Paris: Librarie Academique Perrin, 1985).

11. Huet, *Histoire du Commerce & de la Navigation des Anciens,* 34.

12. Among authors who cite Huet directly, see, for instance, André François Boureau Deslandes, *Essai sur la marine et sur le commerce, . . . avec des remarques historiques & critiques de l'auteur* (Amsterdam: François Changuion, 1743); Jean-François Dreux du Radier, *Eloge historique de la Navigation, où l'on parle de des causes, de son origine, de des progrès & de ses desavantages* (Paris: Lambert, 1757); Philippe-Auguste de Sainte-Foix Chevalier d'Arcq, *Histoire du Commerce et de la navigation des peuples anciens et modernes: Ouvrage divisé en deux Parties; dont la premiere contient l'Histoire politique du Commerce des Anciens: & la seconde, l'Histoire générale du Commerce chez les Peuples modernes,* 2 vols. (Amsterdam: Desainte et Saillant, 1758); Hubert Pascal Ameilhon, *Histoire du Commerce & de la Navigation des Egyptiens sous le regne des Ptolémées. Ouvrage qui a remporté le prix de l'Académie Royale des Inscriptions & belles lettres* (Paris: Saillant, 1766). Montesquieu himself used Huet as a source but posed a number of criticisms. On their relation, see especially Catherine Larrère, "Montesquieu et l'histoire du commerce," in *Le Temps de Montesquieu,* ed. Michel Porret and Catherine Volpilhac-Auger (Geneva: Droz, 2002). The interpretation offered here of Huet differs substantially from Larrère's. On eighteenth-century views of antiquity, see Chantal Grell, *L'Histoire entre érudition et philosophie: Etude sur la connaissance historique à l'age des Lumières* (Paris: Presses Universitaires de France, 1993), 133. See also Chantal Grell, *Le Dix-huitième siècle et l'antiquité en France: 1680–1789,* 2 vols. (Oxford: Voltaire Foundation, 1995), in which the author discusses in more depth classical education in the eighteenth century.

13. Huet, *Histoire du Commerce & de la Navigation des Anciens,* preface, chap. 1. Textual note: in the archive of the Ministère des Affaires Etrangères reposes a highly abridged manuscript version of Huet's text, dated 3 April 1777 (long after Huet's death) and "recopied and reviewed" by L. C. De Colins (M.A.E., M.D., Hollande, vol. 72, ff. 298r–361v.) Here and there (e.g., f. 305r) one finds additions, not in the original text, intended to blunt the force of Huet's "republican" analysis of commerce. F. M. Janiçon, *Etat present de la republique des Provinces-Unies et des pais qui en dépendent* (1729–1730), 4th ed. (The Hague: Jean van Duren, 1755), 1:13, 390. On the Compagnie des Indes, see A.N, Colonies, F³ 46 (1746): "one cannot admire

enough that, crushed by a War which threatened them with Servitude, they had the courage to establish their commerce even in the middle of this war; it was the only means of supporting the costs."

14. Huet, *Histoire du Commerce & de la Navigation des Anciens,* preface. Jean-François Melon, *Essai politique sur le commerce* [1734], in *Economistes financières du dix-huitième siècle,* ed. Eugène Daire (Geneva: Slatkine, 1971), 673.

15. On capital flight, see Melon, *Essai politique sur le commerce* chap. 1. On the revocation, see Helvétius, "Mémoire sur la société de commerce," 331v–336r. This observation was exaggerated. Emigration from the Southern Netherlands was earlier and more significant, and the Dutch textile industry, judging by its decline during the early eighteenth century, did not benefit as much as supposed from this influx of human capital. Jan de Vries and Ad van der Woude, *The First Modern Economy: Success, Failure, and Perseverance of the Dutch Economy, 1500–1815* (Cambridge: Cambridge University Press, 1997), 673. Deslandes, *Essai sur la marine et sur le commerce,* 157. See also Janiçon, *Etat present,* 20–38. Janiçon, a French refugee naturalized into the Netherlands, gloats over this fact at length, all the while condemning the effects of arbitrary government on commerce. His work sold well in France.

16. M.A.E., M.D., Angleterre (1747), ff. 207r–249v; quote on f. 220r (see also 213v). The document can also be found in France's Bibliothèque Nationale: Manuscrits Français, no. 12162. The same memoir was printed, with minor revisions, in the *Journal de Commerce* in 1760. Michaud, *Biographie Universelle, Ancien et Moderne* (Paris: Delagrave et Compagnie, 1843), 39:341–342. See Pierre Clément, *M. de Silhouette Bouret: Les dernières fermiers généraux* (Paris: Didier et Compagnie, 1872), 75–91, for details of Silhouette's trip. Clément falsely believed (p. 28) that the document was never printed. That this memoir was reproduced without comment indicates the extent to which (a) the ministerial manuscripts used as a source for this book were part of the mainstream of Enlightenment opinion and (b) the lapse of time between the War of Austrian Succession and the Seven Years' War did not fundamentally alter the economic problems that were considered relevant. In addition to his official qualities, Silhouette was a well-known *littérateur* who translated Alexander Pope and wrote a number of popular travelogues. Silhouette's tenure as the controller general of finances during the Seven Years' War was initially successful but ultimately came to grief.

17. Silhouette, *Observations sur . . . Angleterre,* f. 227v–228r.

18. Ibid., f. 228r–v (on punishment) and f. 224r (on English colonial wealth). On the role of Machiavellianism in mercantilist economics, see Lionel Rothkrug, *Opposition to Louis XIV: The Political and Social Origins of the French Enlightenment* (Princeton, NJ: Princeton University Press, 1965), 460 passim.

19. There is a historiographical controversy on this point. Historians such as de Vries and Van der Woude, cited in note 15, highlight the development of a capital-intensive primary (agricultural) sector, backed by efficient transport and energy production (peat, wind, water), as the basis for Dutch prosperity. With the exception of transportation costs, all contemporary accounts ignore these factors. Jonathan Israel does not dismiss the contributions of the primary and secondary sectors to Dutch

prosperity but tends rather to highlight the function of the state in helping to capture the high-profit overseas trading routes, which in turn greased the wheels of the Dutch manufacture and intra-European trade. Jonathan Israel, *Dutch Primacy in World Trade, 1585–1740* (Oxford: Clarendon Press, 1989).

20. We might add to Huet's analysis that constructing a great number of ships decreases costs, which only adds to the advantages enumerated in the text. Huet, *Mémoires sur le commerce des Hollandois*, 51. For more on transportation costs, see Charles Irénée Castel Saint-Pierre, abbé de, "Project pour perfectionner le commerse de France," in *Ouvrajes de politique* (Rotterdam: Jean Daniel Beman, 1733), 204. As the century progressed, fisheries came to be viewed as the cornerstone of both nations' prosperity, their "Peruvian silver mines." The income was viewed as attractive not only because it was directly generated but also because of the fisheries' function as a "nursery of sailors," who then contributed to Dutch naval might.

21. Silhouette, "Observations sur . . . Angleterre," f. 221v.

22. Ibid., f. 221v (on comparison) and f. 220v (on the spirit of the laws, emphasis added).

23. A.N., B^{III} 436 (1738), f. 81.

24. According to Silhouette, "the Merchant marine is in England 3 or 4 times greater than in France. We count in Great Britain or its colonies seven thousand large or small sea-going vessels employed in commerce" (ibid., f. 214r). Merchants in France's chambers of commerce ritually complained, for their part, of a lack of sailors. See, e.g., A.D., L-Atl., Series C, vol. 615, 1744. On capital requirements and profit, see Deslandes, *Essai sur la marine et sur le commerce*, 156. Capital intensive it was, but as to its long-term profitability, see chapter 1 of Robert Forster, *Merchants, Landlords, Magistrates: The Depont Family in Eighteenth-Century France* (Baltimore: Johns Hopkins University Press, 1980), which throws this generally accepted idea into question. On import substitution, see Silhouette, "Observations sur . . . Angleterre," f. 230v. On luxury consumption, see Saint-Pierre, "Project," 259. This argument was common and shows a certain pragmatism in the face of the problem of luxury consumption. See also Silhouette, "Observations sur . . . Angleterre," f. 226r. On mastery of the sea, see A.N., B^{III} 436 (1738), f. 61; see also A.N., F^3 46 (1746), "Mémoire sur la Compagnie des Indes," f. 9v/15. On the consternation caused by the capture of merchant vessels during the War of Austrian Succession, see A.N., F^3 46 (1746), "Mémoire sur la Compagnie des Indes," f. 43v/24 passim. For a closer analysis of the complaints of the directors of France's Chambers of Commerce, and for more on contraband trade in general, see Chapter 6 of this book. On the Navigation Acts, see Silhouette, "Observations sur . . . Angleterre," f. 215v.

25. For a discussion of universal monarchy in relation to Britain's debt, see John Robertson, "Universal Monarchies and the Liberties of Europe," in *Political Discourse in Early Modern Britain,* ed. N. T. Phillipson and Quentin Skinner (Cambridge: Cambridge University Press, 1993); Istvan Hont, *Jealousy of Trade: International Competition and the Nation-State in Historical Perspective* (Cambridge, MA: Harvard University Press, 2005), chap. 3; A.N., B^{III} 436 (1738), f. 43 (on the colonies' origins), f. 46 (on "convulsions"), and f. 49 (on mixed government). For Voltaire's views, see Voltaire, *Lettres philosophiques* (Amsterdam: E. Lucas, au Livre d'or, 1734), letters 8–10.

26. Immanuel Kant, "Idea for a Universal History with a Cosmopolitan Purpose (1784)," in *Political Writings,* ed. Hans Reiss (Cambridge: Cambridge University Press, 1970). Mably is cited in Keith Michael Baker, "A Script for a French Revolution: The Political Consciousness of the abbé Mably," *Eighteenth-Century Studies* 14, no. 3 (1981): 253. Jean-François Melon, Dutot, and Voltaire also cited him frequently. Saint-Pierre was a regular guest in the salon of Mme. Dupin, whose husband Claude was an officer in the finance ministry and an important writer on economics in his own right. For modern assessments, see Jean-Claude Perrot, *Une Histoire intellectuelle d'économie politique* (Paris: Presses Universitaires de France, 1992), 40. Lionel Rothkrug links the emergence of the French Enlightenment with the efflorescence of critical models of economic thought during the discontented final years of Louis XIV's reign. Rothkrug, *Opposition to Louis XIV.*

27. Saint-Pierre, "Project," 225.

28. Ibid., 243.

29. Ibid., 252.

30. Melon, *Essai politique sur le commerce* 690, including quote in previous paragraph.

31. Ibid., 679 (on reciprocal faults) and 684 (on corruption).

32. Ibid., 751.

33. Ibid., 703, emphasis added. Alexander Pope, An *Essay on Man Address'd to a Friend* (London: J. Wilford, 1733-34), epistle 3.

34. A.N., B^{III} 436 (1738), f. 50. To wit: "that Absolute Monarchies neglect [commerce] . . . because however able and well-intentioned the ministers are they are too occupied with current affairs [i.e., making ends meet on a strained treasury] to enter into the vast detail that the protection of commerce requires." This subject is treated in more depth in Chapter 4. For an excellent discussion of the Physiocrats in the context of "fiscalism," see Herbert Lüthy, *La Banque protestante en France de la révocation de l'Edit de Nantes à la Révolution,* 2 vols. (Paris: Service d'édition et de vente des publications de l'éducation nationale, S.E.V.P.E.N., 1961), vol. 2, chap. 1. The phrase "structure of impasses," is taken from Emmanuel Le Roy Ladurie, *The Peasants of Languedoc* (Urbana: University of Illinois Press, 1976), 297. (Ladurie uses it in the context of France's agricultural economy.)

35. A.N., Colonies, F3 46 (1746), f.7r/9.

36. Ibid., f.14v/23. See also f. 25v/45: "heureuse harmonie."

37. Ibid., f.7r/9 (on misery), 14v/23 (on "concourse"; see also f. 25v/45, on "heureuse harmonie"), 12r-v/19–20 (on circulation), and f. 9v/13 (on continual movement). The author also emphasizes, as do many others, the training that sailors receive on merchant ships, which are, in turn, protected by the navy.

38. Ibid., f. 14v/23; Charles Dutot, "Réflexions politiques sur les finances et le commerce [1738]," in *Economistes financières du dix-huitième siècle,* ed. Eugène Daire (Geneva: Slatkine, 1971), 796. This work was written as a response to Jean-François Melon.

39. Silhouette, "Observations sur . . . Angleterre," f. 219r-v. Silhouette estimated that England was able to spend 80 million livres a year during the War of Austrian Succession, whereas France was capable of mustering only 47 to 48 million. See also A.N., B^{III} 436 (1738), f. 16; and Deslandes, *Essai sur la marine et sur le commerce,*

xvi–xvii. Each of the "four propositions" that Deslandes' entire book is based upon states the relationship among finance, naval power, and national wealth.

40. On the mixing of private and public affairs, see *EL*, 20.4. On the centrality of American wealth, see Silhouette, "Observations sur . . . Angleterre," f. 210r.

41. The verdict on Spain in the documents under examination is unanimously negative. See, e.g., A.N., B^{III} 436 (1738), f. 28; Silhouette, "Observations sur . . . Angleterre," ff. 223r–v; A.N., F³ 46 (1746), f. 7v/9; and Deslandes, *Essai sur la marine et sur le commerce*, 161–162. Voltaire is the only contemporary who, to my knowledge, challenged widely held opinions about the Iberian-American decline. See Voltaire, "Observations sur MM. Lass, Melon et Dutot; sur le Commerce, le Luxe, les Monnaies, et les Impôts [1738]," in *Oeuvres Complètes* (Paris: Antoine-Agustin Renouard, 1819), 26:146–147. More recently, see Henry Kamen, "The Decline of Spain: A Historical Myth?" *Past and Present*, no. 81 (1978); Jonathan Israel's reply, "Debate: The Decline of Spain: A Historical Myth?" *Past and Present*, no. 91 (1981); and finally David R. Ringrose, *Spain, Europe, and the "Spanish Miracle," 1700–1900* (Cambridge: Cambridge University Press, 1996).

42. Silhouette, "Observations sur . . . Angleterre," f. 229r (on laws) and 232v (on Anglo–American relations).

43. Ibid., f. 248v (on English monopoly) and f. 223v (on Canada). Although Silhouette wrote in the context of the War of Austrian Succession, he still had in mind the reverses suffered by France from the Treaty of Utrecht: "The French profit more than any other nation from the commerce of the Spanish in America (through Cadiz), [and] it is up until now the principal source of gold and silver that enter into the Kingdom. It would be difficult for the French to maintain themselves in a wealthy and flourishing state, if this source came to dry up completely, or if the English succeeded in appropriating this commerce almost entirely, as they have done in Portugal." This statement accounts for much of the official concern revolving around trade in Spanish America to be found in the archive of the Ministère des Affaires Etrangères. Saint-Pierre, "Project," 232–233.

44. Silhouette, "Observations sur . . . Angleterre," f. 236r.

45. Ibid., f. 227r. See also A.N., B^{III} 436 (1738), f. 61; and Melon, *Essai politique sur le commerce*, 704, 721. Of course, all of this is only a prelude to Guillaume Raynal, *Histoire philosophique et politique des etablissements & du commerce des Européens dans les deux Indes*, vol. 7 (Amsterdam: 1773–1774), which was a best seller of the eighteenth century.

46. For a discussion of *moeurs* as a political category in eighteenth-century France, see Georges Benrekassa, "Moeurs comme 'concept politique,' 1680–1820," in *Le Langage des lumières* (Paris: Presses Universitaires de France, 1995). On *moeurs* in the context of nationalism, see David Bell, "The Unbearable Lightness of Being French: Law, Republicanism and National Identity at the End of the Old Regime," *American Historical Review* 4, no. 4 (2001).

47. Deslandes, *Essai sur la marine et sur le commerce*, 169–170, 180, 188; Dutot, "Réflexions politiques sur les finances et le commerce [1738]," 900. Both Dutot and Deslandes use the curious phraseology *se manquent à eux-mêmes*; since Dutot's well-known text was earlier, one wonders if this is not an example of the innocent

plagiarism so characteristic of the period. For biographical details on Deslandes, see Rolf Geissler, *Boureau-Deslandes; ein Materialist der Frühaufklärung* (Berlin: Rütten & Loening, 1967), 15 (on his work as commissaire and friendship with d'Argenson); J. Macary, "L'Esprit encylopédique avant l'*Encylcopédie:* André François Deslandes," in *Transactions of the Third International Congress on the Enlightenment,* ed. Theodore Besterman (Oxford: Voltaire Foundation, 1972), 975–979 (on other associations).

48. A.N., F³ 46 (1746), f. 7r/9. Invitations to the nobility to engage in overseas and wholesale trade without fear of derogation were reiterated by the French monarchy from at least Richelieu onward, to little avail and to the despair of many would-be reformers. For a contemporary discussion favorable to these laws, see Dutot, "Réflexions politiques sur les finances et le commerce [1738]," 904–906; and l'Abbé Coyer, *La Noblesse commerçante* (London: Duchesne, 1756). Roturier merchants were necessarily interested in these questions, as a dossier on the subject kept by the Chamber of Commerce of Nantes attests. See A.D., L-Atl., Series C, vol. 695 (1669–1780), Noblesse du Commerce en Gros, Cotte 2, no. 25. For further discussion, see Chapters 2 and 3.

49. For an excellent discussion, see Richard Whatmore, *Republicanism and the French Revolution: An Intellectual History of Jean-Baptiste Say's Political Economy* (New York: Oxford University Press, 2000), introduction.

50. Silhouette, *Observations sur . . . Angleterre,* f. 213v.

51. Melon, *Essai politique sur le commerce,* 755–756 (on the study of history) and 765 (on systematic order). On the legislator, see *EL,* 14.5.

2. Montesquieu's Science of Commerce

1. Voltaire, "GOUVERNEMENT, dans Dictionnaire philosophique," in *Oeuvres Complètes* (Paris: Garnier Frères, 1879), article BLE ou BLED (Grain); Friedrich Melchior Grimm, *Correspondance littéraire, philosophique et critique par Grimm, Diderot, Raynal, Meister, etc.,* ed. Maurice Tourneux, 16 vols. (Paris: Garnier Frères, 1877-1882). 3:267 (15 August 1756), quoted in Georges Weulersse, *Le Mouvement physiocratique en France de 1756 à 1770* (Paris: Félix Alcan, 1910), 1:24. Here is Voltaire's dismissal of Montesquieu as an economic thinker: "Montesquieu had no knowledge of the political principles relative to wealth, to manufactures, to finance or commerce. These principles hadn't been discovered yet. . . . It would have been as impossible for him to write Smith's *Wealth of Nations* as Newton's *Principia Mathematica.*" Quoted in Louis Althusser, *Montesquieu, la politique et l'histoire* (Paris: Presses Universitaires de France, 1959), 57. "*De l'Esprit des Loix,* premier extrait," *Journal de Commerce* April (1759): 85–86. Dupont de Nemours is quoted in Weulersse, *Le Mouvement physiocratique,* 1:26, original emphasis.

2. Adam Ferguson, *An Essay on the History of Civil Society* [1767], ed. Duncan Forbes (Edinburgh: Edinburgh University Press, 1966), 66 and 120.

3. A masterful synthesis of seventeenth-century currents is found in Istvan Hont, *Jealousy of Trade: International Competition and the Nation-State in Historical Perspective* (Cambridge, MA: Harvard University Press, 2005), esp. chap. 1.

4. A now classic account of the Law episode can be found in Thomas E. Kaiser, "Money, Despotism and Public Opinion in Early Eighteenth-Century France: John Law and the Debate on Royal Credit," *Journal of Modern History* 63, no. 1 (1991). The interpretation of the *Lettres Persanes* as a roman à clef denouncing despotism under Louis XIV and then under the regency of the duc d'Orleans, with special emphasis on the machinations of Law, is advanced with particular force by J. L. Carr, "The Secret Chain of the *Lettres Persanes*," Studies on Voltaire and the Eighteenth Century, *SVEC* 55 (1967); and Claude Dauphiné, "Pourquoi un roman de sérail?" *European Review*, no. 574 (1977). These are cited in Theodore Braun, "'La Chaîne Secrète': A Decade of Interpretations," *French Studies* 42, no. 3 (1988). Larrère goes so far as to argue that the Law episode and the threat of despotism it posed is the guiding thread of Montesquieu's analysis in the *Esprit des lois* itself: see Catherine Larrère, "Montesquieu économiste? Une lecture paradoxale," in *Montesquieu en 2005*, ed. Catherine Volpilhac-Auger (Oxford: Voltaire Foundation, 2005). The thesis that Montesquieu advanced a politics of fusion is argued, without using this term, in two works by Céline Spector: *Montesquieu, les "Lettres Persanes": De l'anthropologie à la politique, Philosophies* (Paris: Presses Universitaires de France, 1997); and *Montesquieu: Pouvoirs, richesses et sociétés* (Paris: Presses Universitaires de France, 2004), esp. 259–267, "Capitalisme et féodalité."

5. On noble privileges, see *EL*, 11.6. On English manners, Montesquieu says, "Money here is cherished above all else; honor and virtue very little." Montesquieu, "Notes sur l'Angleterre," in *OC*, 1:878.

6. On the simultaneous composition of the *Réflexions sur la monarchie universelle* and *Considérations sur les Romains*, see Robert Shackleton, *Montesquieu: A Critical Biography* (Oxford: Oxford University Press, 1963), 150–151. Paul Rahe does an excellent job of exploring the thematic unity of these works but makes a rather speculative argument, without the aid of new documentation, that Montesquieu intended to publish these two works along with *EL*, 11.6, "On the English Constitution," as a separate treatise. Paul Rahe, "The Book That Never Was: Montesquieu's *Considerations on the Romans* in Historical Context," *History of Political Thought* 26, no. 1 (2005).

7. "Sociology" and "political sociology" are, of course, anachronisms, but they best capture the analysis I am trying to describe in contrast to Montesquieu's historical narrative. Montesquieu's contemporaries would have lumped these concepts together as *histoire philosophique* or the *science du commerce*. For this usage, see Raymond Aron, *Les Etapes de la pensée sociologique* (Paris: Gallimard, 1967), 43; and Melvin Richter, "The Comparative Study of Regimes and Societies," in *The Cambridge History of Eighteenth-Century Political Thought*, ed. Mark Goldie and Robert Wolker (Cambridge: Cambridge University Press, 2006). Michael Sonenscher also traces a developmental arc from the earlier *Considérations sur les Romains* and the *Réflexions sur la monarchie universelle* to the later *Esprit des lois*. Stated briefly, he sees the novel problems of the *Esprit des lois*, as they relate to commerce, as turning on the question of representation in a monarchy and the justification of inequality. The latter I simply do not see as being a controversial issue for Montesquieu, and the former receives an extensive treatment in order to bring Montesquieu into line

with his overarching discussion of Sieyès, for whom representation was a central problem. Michael Sonenscher, *Before the Deluge: Public Debt, Inequality, and the Intellectual Origins of the French Revolution* (Princeton, NJ: Princeton University Press, 2007), chap. 2, esp. 134, 150, and 152.

8. On the compass, see Jacques Accarias de Serionne, *Les Intérêts des nations de l'Europe développés relativement au commerce* (Leiden: Elie Luzac, 1766), 380; François Véron de Forbonnais, "COLONIES," in *Encyclopédie*, ed. d'Alembert and Diderot (1753); and Honoré Lacome de Prezel, *Les Progrès du commerce* (Amsterdam: 1761), 18. On expanded European commerce, see *EL*, 21.21.

9. On the compass, see *Considérations sur les Romains*, book 4; *OC*, 2:88. On shipbuilding, see *EL*, 21.5–6. On expansion and decline, see *Considérations sur les Romains*, book 9; and *OC*, 2:117–118. On Montesquieu's interest in Machiavelli, see Shackleton, *Montesquieu*, 152, and bibliographical references in note 7. Andrivet and Volpilhac-Auger emphasize the influence of Bossuet on Montesquieu's *Considérations sur les Romains* in their introduction, but the notes and commentary of their edition give further valuable references to Machiavelli. Patrick Andrivet and Catherine Volpilhac-Auger, "Introduction," in *Considérations sur les causes de la grandeur des Romains et de leur décadence*, ed. Catherine Volpilhac-Auger and Jean Ehrard (Oxford: Voltaire Foundation, 2000). Vanessa de Senarclens emphasizes the rupture between Montesquieu and humanist historiography in *Montesquieu historien de Rome: Un tournant pour la réflexion sur le statut de l'histoire au XVIIIe siècle* (Geneva: Droz, 2003), 24–30.

10. On the economics of specie, see *Réflexions sur la monarchie universelle*, *OC*, 2:30–32 (section 16); and *EL*, 21.22. The discussion in both works recycles observations made in an earlier unpublished work: Montesquieu, "Considérations sur les richesses de l'Espagne [1728]," *OC*, 2:9–18.

11. For the classic treatment, see Hont, *Jealousy of Trade*, chap. 3, on the Scottish debate.

12. On informational asymmetry, see *EL*, 21.6; territorial conquest, *Considérations sur les Romains*, book 21, *OC*, 2:193; and the army over the navy, *EL*, 21.13. A modern study confirms the superior status of the army relative to the navy and hence the preference of the upper nobility for the former: James Pritchard, *Louis XV's Navy, 1748–1762: A Study of Organization and Administration* (Montreal: McGill-Queen's University Press, 1987), 64–65. A number of authors have commented on the role that the rise of commerce plays, in Montesquieu's *Considérations sur les Romains* and elsewhere, in producing the radical rupture between the ancient and modern worlds. See Senarclens, *Montesquieu historien de Rome*, 77–83; Georges Benrekassa, *La Politique et sa mémoire: Le politique et l'historique dans la pensée des lumières* (Paris: Payot, 1983), 53; and James W. Muller, "The Political Economy of Republicanism," in *Montesquieu and the Spirit of Modernity*, ed. David W. Carrithers and Patrick Coleman (Oxford: Voltaire Foundation, 2002).

13. On "flux and reflux," see *EL*, 21.5; Jews, *EL*, 21.20; and expanded trade, *EL*, 20.6.

14. On Machiavellianism, see *EL*, 21.20; productive classes, *EL*, 23.15; landed wealth, *EL*, 22.15; globalized assets, *EL*, 21.21; and Poland, *EL*, 20.23.

15. *EL*, 21.4.

16. An admirably clear discussion of Montesquieu's methodological holism can be found in Althusser, *Montesquieu, la politique et l'histoire,* 46–49.

17. On the objects of states, see *EL,* 11.5; self-government, *EL,* 11.6; and liberties under gothic government, *EL,* 11.8.

18. On transplantation, see *EL,* 21.2–3; on naturalness and the French character, *EL,* 19.6.

19. Richter, "The Comparative Study of Regimes and Societies." See also Melvin Richter, "Introduction," in *Montesquieu: Selected Political Writings,* ed. Melvin Richter (Indianapolis: Hackett, 1990).

20. The Mandeville reference comes at *EL,* 19.8.

21. Albert O. Hirschman, *The Passions and the Interests: Political Arguments for Capitalism before Its Triumph,* 2nd ed. (Princeton, NJ: Princeton University Press, 1996), 70–80. On "destructive passions," see *EL,* 20.1. The phrase "destructive prejudices" also arises earlier in the discussion of the English *esprit général* at *EL,* 19.27.

22. Montesquieu, "Mémoire contre l'arrêt du Conseil du 27 Février 1725 portant défense de faire des plantations nouvelles en vignes dans la Généralité de Guyenne," in *Oeuvres Complètes de Montesquieu,* ed. André Masson (Paris: Nagel, 1950), 3:267. On "jealousy," see *EL,* 20.7; and obstruction of trade, *EL,* 20.12.

23. See, for instance, during a debate within the Guyenne (Bordeaux region) Chamber of Commerce on French shipping to the Baltics, which turned on the viability of *commerce d'économie:* one director within the Chamber of Commerce observed that: "the ordering of our classes contributes (*le régime des classes y concorut*) to our higher costs." A. D. Guyenne, C 4348 pieces 51 and 54, May 1783 (quotation in piece 54).

24. It is not anachronistic to speak of "classes" when discussing Montesquieu's political sociology of commerce; he uses the word "classes" or "class" when dividing groups according to their economic function. See, e.g., *EL,* 2.2, 13.14, 27, and esp. 22.18. Later, Turgot would adopt the vocabulary of economic classification wholesale in his 1766 *Réflexions sur la formation et la distribution des richesses.* On court capitalism, see *EL,* 20.19; the distribution of wealth, *EL,* 20.19–20; and an open elite, *EL,* 22.20. For a similar set of restrictions on commerce in an aristocracy and the need to encourage commerce in a monarchy, see *EL,* 5.9. Montesquieu's vision of an open elite is mentioned briefly in Sonenscher, *Before the Deluge,* 103 and 105. On aristocratic republicans and the debate over the commercial nobility, see, inter alia, John Shovlin, *The Political Economy of Virtue: Luxury, Patriotism, and the Origins of the French Revolution* (Ithaca, NY: Cornell University Press, 2006), 58–65. Mably's anticommercial views are discussed in Johnson Kent Wright, *A Classical Republican in Eighteenth-Century France: The Political Thought of Mably* (Stanford, CA: Stanford University Press, 1997), 57–64.

25. Abbé Joseph de La Porte, *Observations sur l'Esprit des loix,* 2nd ed. (Amsterdam: Pierre Mortier, 1751), 182–196; quotation on 185. Boulanger de Rivery's *Apologie de l'Esprit des loix* is reprinted in the same volume with de La Porte's *Observations.* (see 128–130 on profits). François Risteau's *Réponse aux observations sur l'Esprit des loix* is reprinted in Montesquieu and Octavien de Guasco, *Lettres familières du président*

de Montesquieu, baron de la Brède, à divers amis d'Italie (Florence: 1767), part 2; on profit, see 110–127. These and other details are found in Shackleton, *Montesquieu,* chap. 17. François Véron de Forbonnais, *Extrait du livre de l'Esprit des lois* (Amsterdam: Arkstée & Merkus, 1753), 197–198, original emphasis. Forbonnais quotes from *EL,* 19.27.

26. On Montesquieu's approval of Risteau, see *Oeuvres Complètes,* ed. André Masson (Paris: Nagel, 1950), 3:1381–1382 (letter to Risteau, 19 May 1751); and Montesquieu, *Oeuvres posthumes* (Paris: 1798), 243n. Between 1734 and 1738, Montesquieu learned from an intendant of the Navy, Michel Bégon, that just as many sailors were on board in French and Dutch long-distance routes and that rations were the same. Montesquieu, *Spicilège, OC* (Voltaire Foundation), 13:559–560 (item no. 633), written in Montesquieu's hand. Dating by editors. For a discussion of intellectual justifications of the luxury trade, see Michael Sonenscher, "Fashion's Empire: Theories of Foreign Trade in Early Eighteenth-Century France," in *Innovation and Markets in Eighteenth-Century France,* ed. Robert Fox and Anthony Turner (London: Hambleton Press, 1998). Sonenscher discusses Risteau's defense of Montesquieu, particularly insisting upon the latter's approval, but instead of describing the way in which Risteau's defense sidelines luxury manufacture, he argues that Risteau's treatment has the effect of emphasizing the importance of luxury trades. Sonenscher, *Before the Deluge,* 170.

27. On monarchical commerce, see *EL,* 20.4; Dutch trade, *EL,* 20.6; and Roman Egypt's trade, *EL,* 21.16. *EL,* 21.12, is a new chapter devoted to Mithridates' conflict with Rome. *Considérations sur les Romains* contains ample references to Mithradites, especially in book 7.

28. Tim Blanning sees the separation of continental and colonial spheres in the War of Austrian Succession, and its negative consequences for France, as a harbinger of the Seven Years' War. T. C. W. Blanning, *The Pursuit of Glory: Europe, 1648–1815* (New York: Viking, 2007), 574. On the economic effects of the war, see Shackleton, *Montesquieu,* 206; *OC,* 2:1084–1085, in "Dossier de l'esprit des lois"; and Montesquieu and Guasco, *Lettres familières,* 22, letter to abbé Guasco in Paris, 1742. On the importance of the Americas, see ibid., 98–99, letter to le Grand Prieur Solar in Malta, 7 March 1749.

29. Joseph Oczapowski, "Montesquieu économiste," *Revue d'économie politique* 5 (1891); Nicolaï, "Montesquieu économiste," *Revue économique de Bordeaux* 16 (1904); Charles Jaubert, *Montesquieu économiste* (New York: B. Franklin, 1970); Joseph Lagugie, "Montesquieu économiste," in *Révolutions en Aquitaine, de Montesquieu à Frédéric Bastiat* (Bordeaux: La Fédération, 1990); Joseph Lagugie, "Montesquieu économiste," *Actes Acad. Bordeaux* sér 5, vol. 15 (1992); and Larrère, "Montesquieu économiste? Une lecture paradoxale." The monographs in question are Claude Morilhat, *Montesquieu: Politique et richesses* (Paris: Presses Universitaires de France, 1996); Spector, *Montesquieu: Pouvoirs, richesses et sociétés,* and by the same author, *Montesquieu et l'émergence de l'économie politique* (Paris: Champion, 2006); Henry C. Clark, *Compass of Society: Commerce and Absolutism in Old-Regime France* (Lanham, MD: Lexington Books, 2007); and finally Sonenscher, *Before the Deluge.* Spector and Morilhat, it should be said, are philosophers, so this

particular line of inquiry is not necessarily germane to their work. Albert Sorel, *Montesquieu* (Paris: Hachette, 1889), 6. For the classic statement on Cambridge School contextualism, see Quentin Skinner, "Meaning and Understanding in the History of Ideas," in *Meaning and Context: Quentin Skinner and His Critics,* ed. James Tully (Princeton, NJ: Princeton University Press, 1988), esp. 57–67.

30. Let a limited number of references stand for tens, if not hundreds. On Voltaire's discovery of England, see Daniel Roche, *France in the Enlightenment* (Cambridge, MA: Harvard University Press, 1998), 140–141; on Montesquieu, see Shackleton, *Montesquieu,* 284; and tying these two authors together is Rahe, "The Book That Never Was," 50–60. Louis Desgraves, *Montesquieu* (Paris: Mazarine, 1986), 243–246.

31. Edward Whiting Fox, *History in Geographic Perspective: The Other France* (New York: W. W. Norton, 1791), chap. 3 (on two societies) and 78 (quotation).

32. An analysis of Montesquieu's notarial acts proves conclusively that Montesquieu, while in the west of France, resided principally in the city of Bordeaux and not at his family chateau at La Brède. Jean Max Eyland, *Montesquieu chez ses notaires de La Brède* (Paris: Delmas, 1956), 51–63.

33. *OC,* 2:1083–1084, in "Dossier de l'Esprit des lois." On chicanery, see *Correspondance, OC* (Voltaire Foundation), 18:26–27: Jacques Lamude to Montesquieu, 22 February 1720. The Chambre d'Assurances Générales et Grosse Aventures was established initially with a capital of 4.5 million l.t. drawn from 1,500 stockholders; a subsequent issue of stock pushed the capital to 12 million as the Chambre moved into house insurance. On Machault and the war context, see François Véron de Forbonnais, *Elemens du commerce,* 2nd ed., 2 vols. (Leiden: 1754), 2: chap. 7. A modern survey of the actual practices of Paris-based maritime insurance companies seems to undercut Montesquieu's criticisms, but there is no way to prove or disprove his assertions of what amounts to insider trading. See John G. Clark, "Marine Insurance in Eighteenth-Century La Rochelle," *French Historical Studies* 10, no. 4 (1978): 577. See also Henri Sée, "Notes sur les assurances maritimes en France et particulièrement à Nantes au xviiie siècle," *Journal Historique du droit français et étranger* série 4, année 6 (1927): 291, cited in Clark, "Marine Insurance."

34. Upon Montesquieu's death, one of his many vineyards had 458 hogsheads (approximately 24,000 imperial gallons) of wine on hand: "the produce of none but a very large vineyard." Shackleton, *Montesquieu,* 204. On land acquisition, see Eyland, *Montesquieu chez ses notaires,* 98–111.

35. For a sampling, see Montesquieu, *Spicilège,* vol. 13, *Oeuvres Complètes* (Oxford: Voltaire Foundation), items 39, 227, 238, 326, 350, 393, 438, 441, 472, 497, 517, 552, 573, 590, 608, 615, 633, 663, 726–727, 731, and 740–741. On the encouragement of the Bordeaux Academy, see Montesquieu, *Correspondance, OC* (Voltaire Foundation), 18:307, letter to Issac Sarrau de Boynet, May 1727. Montesquieu's Bordeaux friendships are not well documented, however, in his surviving correspondence—a genre of writing to which he attached comparatively little importance. René Pomeau, "Montesquieu et ses correspondants," *Revue d'histoire littéraire de la France* 82, no. 2 (1982): 183.

36. Attempts to locate all of the sources of Montesquieu's income and to establish their relative proportions have frustrated all of Montesquieu's biographers. For income

estimates, see Shackleton, *Montesquieu,* 207–208. For noble income distributions, see Guy Chaussinand-Nogaret, *The French Nobility in the Eighteenth Century: From Feudalism to Enlightenment* (Cambridge: Cambridge University Press, 1985), 52–53. The classic study of declining noble family fortunes is Robert Forster, *The House of Saulx-Tavanes; Versailles and Burgundy, 1700–1830* (Baltimore: Johns Hopkins University Press, 1971). In addition to one-half of the crop—the usual payout to the landlord under a sharecropping lease *(métayage)*—the *bail à détroit* also shared gains in livestock. On this subject, see Montesquieu, *Correspondance, OC* (Voltaire Foundation), 18:lxxxix, editor's introduction; and Eyland, *Montesquieu chez ses notaires,* 103–104 (on land acquisition) and 90 and 93 (on homage). On poachers, see Jean Barennes, "Montesquieu et la braconnage à La Brède," *Revue historique de Bordeaux* 5 (1912). For a discussion that delinks capitalism from technological innovation and rational means of exchange (including bookkeeping methods), see Fernand Braudel, *Capitalism and Civilization, 15th–18th Century* (Berkeley: University of California Press, 1985–1992), 1:245–290 and 2:315 (on technology) and 2:302–305 (on exchange). On the symbolic relation of game laws to feudalism, see John Markoff, "Violence, Emancipation, and Democracy: The Countryside and the French Revolution," *American Historical Review* 100, no. 2 (1995). On property as a slave, see *OC,* 2:1290, in "Mes Pensées," no. 1128, cited in Eyland, *Montesquieu chez ses notaires,* 85.

37. *Lettres Persanes,* letters 88 and 98 from Uzbek. *OC,* 1:263 and 276–277.

38. Nick Childs, *A Political Academy in Paris, 1724–1731: The Entresol and its Members* (Oxford: Voltaire Foundation, 2000), chap. 14 (on Montesquieu's participation) and chap. 2 (on noble conflict). On missions to Versailles, see Jean Dalat, *Montesquieu magistrat,* 2 vols. (Paris: Lettres modernes, 1971–1972), 1: au parlement de Bordeaux.

39. Quotation from Dena Goodman, *The Republic of Letters: A Cultural History of the French Enlightenment* (Ithaca, NY: Cornell University Press, 1994), 5. See Shackleton, *Montesquieu,* on increasing democratization and Montesquieu's salon habits, 178–190; and Guasco, 190–193.

40. The details of this census, including the biography, are culled from *Correspondance, OC* (Voltaire Foundation), vol. 18.

41. On Montesquieu's academic activities, see Shackleton, *Montesquieu,* 20–26, 85–89, and 210–217. See also P. Barrière, *L'Académie de Bordeaux, centre de culture internationale au xviiie siècle (1712–1792)* (Bordeaux: Bière, 1951). Daniel Roche, *Le Siècle des lumières en province: Académies et académiciens provinciaux, 1680–1789* (Paris: Mouton, 1978), 1:185–210 (on social composition) and 1:392 (quote).

42. My data source is Roche, *Le Siècle des lumières en province,* 2:282–287 (tables 13–18).

43. On the "parliamentary type," see ibid., 1:200. Here are the residuals for the cases of under-representation, in ascending order of magnitude: Arras, -.06; Besançon, -.06; Metz, -.07; Rouen, -.08; Pau, -.11; and Bordeaux, -.29. This says, for instance, that Arras had an actual percentage of *roturier* membership six points below what the model would predict, whereas Pau was eleven points less and Bordeaux twenty-nine. The figures for cases of *roturier* over-representation are Dijon, .05; and Nancy, .08. Standard deviation of residuals: ±.09

44. See Barrière, *L'Académie de Bordeaux,* on directorships, 42; court protection, 26–28; and the election of members, 51–53.
45. Montesquieu was conscious of the growth of this wealth in Bordeaux in particular. See Montesquieu, *Correspondance, OC* (Voltaire Foundation), 18:307, letter to Isaac Sarrau de Boynet, May 1727. On the strategies of assimilation into the nobility by the merchant bourgeoisie, see Paul Butel, *Les Négociants bordelais, l'Europe et les îles au XVIIIe siècle* (Paris: Aubier, 1996), 325–335.
46. Melon wrote his major statement, the *Essai politique sur le commerce,* in 1734. Saint-Pierre's *Project pour perfectionner le commerse de France* was written in 1733.

3. Philosophical History

1. "*De l'Esprit des Loix,* premier extrait," *Journal de Commerce,* April 1759, 85. On the evolving names of political economy, see Philippe Steiner, "Commerce, Commerce Politique," in *Commerce, population et société autour de Vincent Gournay (1748–1758),* ed. Loïc Charles and Christine Théré (Paris: INED, forthcoming).
2. On the historical sections of the *Wealth of Nations,* see Istvan Hont, *Jealousy of Trade: International Competition and the Nation-State in Historical Perspective* (Cambridge, MA: Harvard University Press, 2005), chap. 5; J. Salter, "Adam Smith on Feudalism, Commerce and Slavery," *History of Political Thought* 13, no. 2 (1992). On distortion of Smith, see, among others, Donald Winch, *Adam Smith's Politics: An Essay in Historiographic Revision* (Cambridge: Cambridge University Press, 1978); and Emma Rothschild, *Economic Sentiments: Adam Smith, Condorcet, and the Enlightenment* (Cambridge, MA: Harvard University Press, 2001), introduction.
3. "Montesquieu's sociology is characterized in the final analysis by the incessant interplay of what one can call synchronic thought with diachronic thought." Raymond Aron, *Les Etapes de la pensée sociologique* (Paris: Gallimard, 1967), 65; see 27–43 for a discussion of Montsquieu's political sociology.
4. Voltaire had particularly in mind the monks of the Benedictine order of Saint-Maur. Chantal Grell, *L'Histoire entre érudition et philosophie: Étude sur la connaissance historique à l'age des Lumières* (Paris: Presses Universitaires de France, 1993), 217–218. As Grell and others point out with some relish, Voltaire was not above plundering the erudite histories or writing the sort of event-centered political histories he criticized. "Perhaps one day we will see the same thing happen to history writing that has happened in the sciences [*la physique*]. New discoveries have buried old systems. One would like to understand the human race in the same significant detail that serves today as the basis for natural philosophy." Voltaire, "Nouvelles considérations sur l'histoire [1744]," in *Oeuvres historiques,* ed. René Pomeau (Paris: Gallimard, 1957), 46–49, quote on 46. David Hume, "Of the Rise and Progress of the Arts and Sciences [1742]," in *Essays Moral, Political, and Literary,* ed. Eugene F. Miller (Indianapolis: Liberty Classics, 1985), 112–113.
5. J. G. A. Pocock, *Barbarism and Religion* (Cambridge: Cambridge University Press, 1999), 2:17 and 20. Edward Gibbon is the most noteworthy example here.
6. Further discussion of this hierarchy comes in chapter 5. This political stance comes out very clearly in Diderot's article "ENCYCLOPEDIE" in the *Encyclopédie* itself:

"I say a *society of men of letters and of skilled workmen* for it is necessary to assemble all sorts of abilities." Translation from Keith M. Baker, ed., *The Old Regime and the French Revolution,* vol. 7, *University of Chicago Readings in Western Civilization* (Chicago: University of Chicago Press, 1986), 75. For further discussion of the political significance of the role of the arts in the *Encyclopédie,* see Hélène Vérin, "Les Arts, l'homme et la matière dans l'*Encyclopédie,*" in *La Matière et l'homme dans l'Encyclopédie,* ed. Sylviane Albertan Coppola and Anne-Marie Chouillet (Strasbourg: Klincksieck, 1998), 276.

7. Diderot's solution recalls the conjectural history presented by Rousseau in the "Discours sur l'origine de l'inégalité:" "such was, or must have been, the origin of society and laws"; Jean-Jacques Rousseau, "Discours sur l'origine et les fondemens de l'inégalité parmi les hommes [1755]," in *Oeuvres complètes,* ed. Bernard Gagnebin and Marcel Raymond (Paris: Bibliothèque de la Pléiade, 1964), 3:164. The term *philosophique* denoted both an epistemological clarity, reforming zeal, and—at least among some—sexual libertinism. See Robert Darnton, *The Forbidden Best-Sellers of Pre-Revolutionary France* (New York: Norton, 1996), introduction.

8. Bertrand Binoche, *Introduction à De l'esprit des lois de Montesquieu* (Paris: Presses Universitaires de la France, 1998), underlines the importance of the rise of commerce (90–91).

9. Montesquieu, *OC,* 1:57, "Discours sur les motifs qui doivent nous encourager aux science (1725)." Compare to Georges Louis Leclerc comte de Buffon, *Les Epoques de la nature, classiques de l'histoire des sciences* (Clermont-Ferrand: Paleo, 2000), premier discours. For these citations and this general point, see Denis de Casabianca, "Le Sens de l'esprit: Les sciences et les arts, formations du regard dans L'Esprit des Lois" (PhD diss., Université Aix-Marseille I, 2002), 224–229. Numa Broc, "Peut-on parler de géographie humaine au xviiie siècle en France?" *Géographie* 78, no. 25 (1969), also discusses Montesquieu and natural history. On borrowings between natural sciences and economics, see Philip Mirowski, *More Heat Than Light: Economics as Social Physics, Physics as Nature's Economics* (Cambridge: Cambridge University Press, 1991), introduction; and I. Bernard Cohen, *Interactions: Some Contacts between the Natural Sciences and the Social Sciences* (Cambridge, MA: MIT Press, 1994), chap. 1.

10. Archives de l'Académie des Sciences, Paris, Dossier biographique: CHANVALON, 39–40. The details of Chanvalon's ordeal are recounted in the editor's preface to Jean-Baptiste de Thibault Chanvalon, *Voyage à la Martinique, contenant diverses observations sur la physique, l'histoire naturelle, l'agriculture, les moeurs de cette isle, suivi des "Moments perdus ou Sottissier"* (manuscrit inédit), ed. Monique Pouliquen (Paris: Karthala, 2004). See also Emma Rothschild, "A Horrible Tragedy in the French Atlantic," *Past and Present* 192 (2006) and Marion F. Godfroy, "La Guerre de Sept ans et ses conséquences atlantiques: Kourou ou l'apparition d'un nouveau système colonial," *French Historical Studies* 32, no. 2 (2009).

11. Jean-Baptiste de Thibault Chanvalon, *Voyage à la Martinique, contenant diverses observations sur la physique, l'histoire naturelle, l'agriculture, les moeurs, et les usages faites en 1751 et dans les années suivants. Lu à l'academie Royale des Sciences en 1761* (Paris: Claude J. B. Bauche, 1763), 30 and 5.

12. Ibid., 26–30. Chanvalon's criticism is taken up almost word for word by Pierre Poivre in the context of the Ile de France (present-day Mauritius). Voltaire, "GOUVERNE-MENT, dans Dictionnaire philosophique," in *Oeuvres Complètes* (Paris: Garnier Frères, 1879), 19:296–297. On natural history networks, see Emma Spary, *Utopia's Garden: French Natural History from Old Regime to Revolution* (Chicago: University of Chicago Press, 2000), chap. 2, esp. 96–98. On acclimatization, see Lisbet Koerner, *Linnaeus: Nature and Nation* (Cambridge, MA: Harvard University Press, 1999); Richard Drayton, *Nature's Government: Science, Imperial Britain, and the "Improvement" of the World* (New Haven, CT: Yale University Press, 2000); and Richard H. Grove, *Green Imperialism: Colonial Expansion, Tropical Island Edens, and the Origins of Environmentalism, 1600–1860* (Cambridge: Cambridge University Press, 1995), chap. 5, esp. 119–216 on the Physiocrat Pierre Poivre, intendant of the Ile de France. See also 247–255 for some fine discussion of Bernardin St. Pierre's "Rousseauist" synthesis. For a rich portrait of scientific institutions in the French Antilles, see James E. McClellan, *Colonialism and Science: Saint Domingue in the Old Regime* (Baltimore: Johns Hopkins University Press, 1992), chap. 9, esp. 152–156, on acclimatization of cochineal from continental Spanish possessions into Saint-Domingue. On the tree of liberty, see Spary, *Utopia's Garden*, 132–149.

13. Friedrich Melchior Grimm, *Correspondance littéraire, philosophique et critique par Grimm, Diderot, Raynal, Meister, etc.*, ed. Maurice Tourneux, 16 vols. (Paris: Garnier Frères, 1877–1882), 3:516.

14. A critical reassessment is found in François Moreau, ed., *Dictionnaire des lettres françaises au XVIIIe siècle* (Paris: Fayard, 1995), which refers to d'Arcq as "an accomplished writer: novelist, *philosophe*, economist and historian" (81–82, article "D'ARCQ"). There has been a surprising recrudescence of interest in d'Arcq. See John Shovlin, "Toward a Reinterpretation of Revolutionary Antinobilism: The Political Economy of Honor in the Old Regime," *Journal of Modern History* 72, no. 1 (2000); and Jay M. Smith, "Social Categories, the Language of Patriotism, and the Origins of the French Revolution: The Debate over *Noblesse Commerçante*," *Journal of Modern History* 72, no. 2 (2000). On Coyer's life and works, see Frederic C. Green, *Eighteenth-Century France: Six Essays* (New York: Frederick Ungar, 1964), 70–110. On the controversy between Coyer and d'Arcq, see Ferdinando Galiani, *La Bagarre: Galiani's "Lost" Parody*, edited with and introduction by Steven Laurence Kaplan (The Hague: Martinus Nijhoff, 1979), 178–185; and F. E. Sutcliffe, "The Abbé Coyer and the Chevalier d'Arcq," *Bulletin of the John Rylands Library Manchester* 65, no. 1 (1982). On appreciation of Coyer in Bordeaux, see A.D., Gironde, Series C 4263, Register of Correspondence, 16 July 1757. On La Rochelle's overtures, see A.D., Ch-Mar, ChC La Rochelle, Dossier 12, Correspondance Divers, part E: Demandes de collaboration à des journaux ou à des ouvrages-envois. Details of d'Arcq's financial dealings, including a string of lawsuits involving money and constant attempts to secure patronage, come from his private papers in the Bibliothèque Nationale de France, Manuscrits Français, 33001–33002. For other aspects of his life, see Sutcliffe, "The Abbé Coyer and the Chevalier d'Arcq"; and Jean-Pierre Brancourt, "Un théoricien de la société au XVIIIe siècle: Le chevalier d'Arcq," *Revue Historique* 250 (1973).

15. Philippe-Auguste de Sainte-Foix Chevalier d' Arcq, *La Noblesse militaire, ou le patriote françois* (1756), 7. Compare to *EL*, 20.1, 2, 4, 7, 10, 21, 22, and 23. Grimm, *Correspondance littéraire*, 3:207. In this connection, Jay Smith observes that Montesquieu's "ghost hovers over the text of *La Noblesse militaire*." See Smith, "Social Categories," 359.

16. Philippe-Auguste de Sainte-Foix Chevalier D'Arcq, *Histoire du commerce et de la navigation des peuples anciens et modernes: Ouvrage divisé en deux parties; dont la premiere contient l'histoire politique du commerce des anciens: & la seconde, l'histoire générale du commerce chez les peuples modernes* (Amsterdam: Desainte et Saillant, 1758), 1:xlv, xxxix, and xli. Despite d'Arcq's claims, in fact, book xxi, chaps. 4–21 of the *EL* deal extensively with ancient commerce. There is more material on the history of commerce in the *EL* than on any other historical subject, save feudal law.

17. The *Annonces, affiches et avis divers* seized on this aspect of d'Arcq's argument in making its judgment: "the author is interested in showing the usefulness of history for all of the political matters that are supposed to be a matter of discussion, demonstrating that the lessons that result from history are the surest means to arrive at the political, economic, military and civil sciences. This truth, which has always been understood, has never been contested except by those philosophers who rail against historical studies. *Annonces, affiches et avis divers;* also known as *Affiches de province* (Paris: 1752–1784), 1758:73. D'Arcq, *Histoire du commerce*, 1:xxvii.

18. D'Arcq, *Histoire du commerce*, xlvii–xlviii. The term "revolution" is applied here in its modern, progressive sense, rather than in its older, more literal signification of a return to a previous order of things. On the novelty of this distinction in the eighteenth century, particularly as it attached to the economic transformations in the Atlantic world and their effects on absolutist states, see Reinhart Koselleck, *Critique and Crisis: Enlightenment and the Pathogenesis of Modern Society* (Oxford: Berg, 1988), 160, 176–187. See also Keith Michael Baker, *Inventing the French Revolution: Essays on French Political Culture in the Eighteenth Century* (Cambridge: Cambridge University Press, 1990), 203–209.

19. D'Arcq, *Histoire du commerce*, 1:xlvii–xlviii and liii. On conquest and commerce, see Jean-François Melon, Essai politique sur le commerce, in *Economistes financières du dix-huitième siècle,* ed. Eugène Daire (Geneva: Slatkine, 1971), chap. 10. Compare chap. 9 of the *Considérations sur les causes de la grandeur des Romains et de leur décadence (OC,* 2: 116–120) to D'Arcq, *Histoire du commerce*, 1:16–17. For more on the relation between Melon's and Montesquieu's thought, see Eluggero Pii, "Montesquieu e Véron de Forbonnais. Appunti sul dibattito settecentesco in tema di commercio," *Pensiero Politico* 10, no. 3 (1977).

20. André-Boniface-Louis Riqueti Jean-Antoine Joseph Mirabeau, 10 January 1754 from Guadeloupe, Musée Paul Arbaud, Aix en Provence, France, Fonds Mirabeau, 23:35–36.

21. On Voltaire and Egypt, see Jerome Rosenthal, "Voltaire's Philosophy of History," *Journal of the History of Ideas* 16, no. 2 (1955). The discussion of academy prize competitions is based on my analysis of Antoine-François Delandine, *Couronnés Académiques* (Paris: Cuchet, 1787). The compiler of this work points out with a

perverse sort of defiance in his *discours préliminaire* that "This work is dry but easy, it only takes some grit to undertake it, this is why it hasn't been done."

22. D'Arcq, *Histoire du commerce,* 1:51–52 and 69. The parallel with the Dutch is made entirely evident later in the text, when d'Arcq characterizes the Phoenician system of government: "The several cities of Phoenicia seem to have been as many states, independent of one another and without any liaison between them except what a common interest in profit and defense led them to establish." D'Arcq added, in a slur against the British form of government characteristic of convinced monarchists, that the Carthaginian (i.e., English) form of government "is subject to frequent revolutions, especially in a commercial state"; 1:80–81. On canals, see Charles Irénée Castel Saint-Pierre, abbé de, "Project pour perfectionner le commerse de France," in *Ouvrajes de politique* (Rotterdam: Jean Daniel Beman, 1733).

23. D'Arcq, *Histoire du commerce,* 1:44 (on nature's will) and 1:71 (on Dutch ruin). On the problem of nature and law giving, see Alberto Postigliola, "Forme di razionalità e livelli di legalità in Montesquieu," *Rivista storica della filosofia* 1 (1994), 73–109.

24. On the nation as a "meeting point," see D'Arcq, *Histoire du commerce,* 1:274 (emphasis added). D'Arcq exaggerates the disparity. The proportions were closer to four hundred Greek ships and eight hundred Persian ships. This battle is recounted in Thucydides, *History of the Peloponnesian War,* book 1. On the Seven Years' War, see D'Arcq, *Histoire du commerce,* 1:189. Compare to *Considérations sur les Romains,* chaps. 9 and 10. One critic, in taking d'Arcq to task for his loose treatment of the facts ("when he lack facts, he supplements them with his own reflections"), unintentionally draws a parallel to Diderot's account of philosophical history. Jacques Accarias de Serionne, *Les Intérêts des nations de l'Europe développés relativement au commerce* (Leiden: Elie Luzac, 1766), 372.

25. D'Arcq, *Histoire du commerce,* 2:62–65. Here we find more proof of d'Arcq's sensitivity as a sounding board. His reference to Louis XV's voluptuousness was somewhat precocious, given the libel literature that evolved over the next couple of decades. See Robert Darnton, *The Literary Underground of the Old Regime* (Cambridge, MA: Harvard University Press, 1982), 29–36 and 199–208. See also Sarah Maza, *Private Lives and Public Affairs: The Causes Celèbres of Prerevolutionary France* (Berkeley: University of California Press, 1993), 180–181. Among a number of other works, Maza discusses a later (1782) libel, *Les Fastes de Louis XV.*

26. D'Arcq, *Histoire du commerce,* 1:5. Compare to the *Considérations sur les Romains,* chap. 18: "The Romans succeeded in commanding all peoples, not only by the art of warfare, but also by their prudence. . . . Once all of these virtues dissipated under the emperors, the art of war remained with them, with which they conserved all they had acquired, despite the tyranny and the weakness of their princes: but once corruption sunk even down to the militia, they became the prey of all other peoples." (See also chap. 10.)

27. "A warlike Carthage would never have failed, because the military spirit always necessarily works for the general interest, for which *conservation* is always the principal object. A commercial Carthage couldn't save itself because the commercial spirit always works toward individual interest, in preference to all others"; D'Arcq, *Histoire du commerce,* 2:268. Quotations are from *EL,* 20.2 and 4. The

incommensurability of ancient and modern value systems is emphasized in Vanessa de Senarclens, *Montesquieu historien de Rome: Un tournant pour la réflexion sur le statut de l'histoire au XVIIIe siècle* (Geneva: Droz, 2003), 101. On arms, agriculture, and population, see D'Arcq, *Histoire du Commerce,* 2:201–202; see also 1:152 for a statement of the same three principles.

28. D'Arcq's *Histoire* and Quesnay's *Tableau Economique* were both published in 1758. For more detail on the Physiocratic critique, see Chapter 5. For contemporary thinking on this problem, see Victor Riqueti Marquis de Mirabeau, *L'Ami des hommes, ou traité de population,* nouvelle ed. (Avignon: 1758), 1:136–139. François Quesnay explicitly praises the Egyptian model two years later in "Tableau économique avec ses explications," in *Oeuvres économiques complètes et autres textes,* ed. Christine Théré, Loïc Charles, and Jean-Claude Perrot (Paris: INED, 2005), 1:440.

29. Simone Meyssonnier, "Le Libéralisme anti-capitaliste du XVIIIe siècle en France," in *L'Amérique et la France: Deux révolutions,* ed. Elise Marienstras (Paris: Publications de la Sorbonne, 1990). The full-fledged study on the Gournay group is Simone Meyssonnier, *La Balance et l'horloge: La genèse de la pensée libérale en France au XVIIIe Siècle* (Paris: Editions de la Passion, 1989). For a more recent examination of the Gournay circle, see Loïc Charles, "La Liberté du commerce des grains et l'économie politique française (1750–1770)" (Thèse pour le doctorat, Université Paris I Panthéon-Sorbonne, 1999). Charles discusses the social strategies of Gournay circle writers at length.

30. For these details and others, see Charles, "La Liberté du commerce," 128–130. The quote comes from Butel-Dumont's correspondence. The memoirs for this commission can be found in France and Great Britain Commissioners of the King and Queen, *Mémoires de Commissaires du roi et de ceux de Sa Majesté britannique, sur les possessions & les droits respectifs des deux Couronnes en Amérique; avec les actes publics & pièces justificatives* (Paris: Imprimerie Royale, 1756–1757). Georges-Marie Butel-Dumont, *Théorie du luxe, ou Traité dans lequel on entreprend d'établir que le luxe est un ressort, non seulement utile, mais même indispensablement nécessaire à la prospérité des états* (n.p.: 1771), ix.

31. Georges-Marie Butel-Dumont, *Histoire et commerce des colonies angloises dans l'Amérique septentrionale: Où l'on trouve l'état actuel de leur population, & des détails curieux sur la constitution de leur gouvernement, principalement sur celui de la Nouvelle-Angleterre, de la Pensilvanie, de la Caroline, & de la Géorgie* (London: 1755), 6–11.

32. Quotes are from, respectively, Butel-Dumont, *Histoire et commerce des colonies angloises,* emphasis added; and Georges-Marie Butel-Dumont, *Histoire et commerce des Antilles angloises* (n.p.: 1757), vii–viii, emphasis added.

33. Butel-Dumont, *Histoire et commerce des colonies angloises,* xiv.

34. Butel-Dumont, *Histoire et commerce des Antilles angloises,* viii–ix.

35. Butel-Dumont, *Histoire et commerce des colonies angloises,* 3. Butel-Dumont's Anglophilia did not preclude a certain realism about the English and their imperial pretensions: "English ambition, though it is turned entirely toward commerce, is not for all that any less unjust or insatiable, like all ambition." Butel-Dumont, *Histoire et commerce des Antilles angloises,* vii. It seems a bit awkward to speak of

Anglophilia in the context of intermittent Anglo-French warfare, particularly since Butel-Dumont had this commercial rivalry specifically in view. We have an account of this complicated relationship between Anglophilia and Anglophobia in Josephine Grieder, *Anglomania in France, 1740–1789: Fact, Fiction, and Political Discourse* (Geneva: Droz, 1985). In a review of *Napoleon and the British* by Stuart Semmel, David Bell remarks on how our difficulty in accepting this seemingly paradoxical state of affairs is a reflection of how narrow and chauvinistic our own political culture has become. See David Bell, "Violets in Their Lapels," *London Review of Books*, 23 June 2005.

36. Butel-Dumont, *Histoire et commerce des colonies angloises,* 108 and 113.

37. Ibid., 284–285. Butel-Dumont confounded the terms "arbitrary" and "absolute"— which he also used as a synonym for "despotic" or despotism, a form of "Machiavellianism that forms the principles of absolute government"; ibid., 117. Melvin Richter, "Le Concept de despotisme et l'abus des mots," *Dix-huitième siècle* 34 (2002), distinguishes helpfully between these concepts and also discusses the political significance of mixing them. On Boston, see Butel-Dumont, *Histoire et commerce des colonies angloises,* 112.

38. Butel-Dumont, *Histoire et commerce des colonies angloises,* 325 and 334. Presumably, Butel-Dumont is referring to the white population in these statistics.

39. Ibid., 138. Here, as in the reference to the implications of Georgia's inheritance laws for colonial growth and development, Butel-Dumont appears to be drawing from his reading of Montesquieu's *Lettres Persanes*—even though the *EL* appears to be the major point of departure. Note, in connection with the Navigation Acts, the lexicographic and thematic similarities with *Lettres Persanes,* letter 121: "On peut comparer les empires à un arbre dont les branches trop étendues ôtent tout le suc du tronc et ne servent qu'à faire de l'ombrage." In letter 119 of the same group on population, Montesquieu describes the deleterious effects of the law of primogeniture. On sugar, see Butel-Dumont, *Histoire et commerce des colonies angloises,* 139. For confirmation on this point, see Sidney W. Mintz, *Sweetness and Power: The Place of Sugar in Modern History* (New York: Penguin Books, 1985), 39. For further explanation of France's trading regime with the Americas—a set of laws that, taken together were referred to as "the Exclusive"—see Chapter 6 of this book.

40. Butel-Dumont, *Histoire et commerce des Antilles angloises,* 147–148. "This practical consideration enters without question into the motives that commit the Parliament to respecting this prerogative. The protector of the legitimate liberty of the members of the nation that it represents, in whatever part of its dependence they might reside, it has always avoided following the representations of the Lords Commissioners of Trade and Commerce"; Butel-Dumont, *Histoire et commerce des Antilles angloises,* 148. Lords commissioners of trade and plantations ("lords of trade") were crown-appointed "place-men" generally favorable to metropolitan mercantile interests.

41. Grimm, *Correspondence littéraire,* 2:466. On narrative, see Butel-Dumont, *Histoire et commerce des colonies angloises,* xii–xiii.

42. For favorable criticism, see *Annonces, affiches et avis divers,* 1754:202. See also the cited review in *Correspondence littéraire* (2:466 and 4:25). Grimm's initially hostile review, which he later recanted, can be attributed to the mass of information

Butel-Dumont presented: "[Yet] another work on commerce. . . . This history is rather dry, poorly written and without principles. Since the public has given a favorable reception to some good works that have appeared on the subject of commerce, the same thing happens here as in other areas of history [*littérature*]: once good minds turn themselves toward an object with some attentions, mediocre intellects appropriate the subject and bury us under a pile of useless books." Grimm, *Correspondence littéraire,* 2:449. On the situation before the Seven Years' War, see, e.g., "Vûes politiques & economiques d'un voyageur," *Journal Oeconomique,* March 1754–February 1755, esp. July 1754, 87, on the Carolinas.

43. On the question of Montesquieu's ambivalence, see Chapter 2. See also Elena Russo, "Virtuous Economies: Modernity and Noble Expenditure from Montesquieu to Caillois," in *Postmodernism and the Enlightenment: New Perspectives in Eighteenth-Century French Intellectual History,* ed. Daniel Gordon (London: Routledge, 2001), 67–70. Pierre Manent sees in Montesquieu's ambivalence an affirmation that commerce is the regime of liberty but one that reigns at the expense of ancient models of virtue, which, in both the Greek and Christian account, represented a fulfillment of human nature: "With respect to the old law that oppresses nature, the new regime affirms it. However, the *ancien régime* presupposes a certain understanding and affirmation of nature that is necessarily mingled with the law, with respect to which the new regime aims at being pure liberty that no natural finality [i.e., ancient virtue] can jeopardize. Modern consciousness negates the ancient regime of life under the law in the name of nature and at the same time it negates nature in the name of liberty." Pierre Manent, *The City of Man,* ed. Thomas Pavel and Mark Lilla, trans. Marc A. LePain, *New French Thought* (Princeton, NJ: Princeton University Press, 1998), 48–49.

44. A.N., A.E., B III, 441 (1778), "Considérations sur le commerce de la France avec les Etats-Unis" ("before the peace"). Two other problems were solved by an expansion of Franco-American trade: the islands received needed wood and provisions more cheaply, and the turnaround time for merchants' capital was reduced by sending goods to the United States, which increased overall profits. See A.N., A.E., B III, 441 (1778), "Fragment sur le commerce intérieur des Isles Françaises et sur leur commerce extérieur avec la France et les Etats-Unis de l'Amérique." Fear of eventual open competition was rife. See also M.A.E., M.D., Etats-Unis, 2, "Considérations politiques sur le commerce de la France avec les Etats-Unis de l'Amérique," 53r. On "flattering ourselves," see M.A.E., M.D., Etats-Unis, 2 (1777), 44r (24 July). For an introduction to the organization of the two main repositories holding Ministry of Foreign Affairs documents pertaining to the United States, see Waldo G. Leland, *Guide to Materials for American History in the Libraries and Archives of Paris* (Washington, DC: Carnegie Institute, 1943); and Abraham P. Nasatir and Gary Elwyn Monell, *French Consuls in the United States: A Calendar of Their Correspondence in the Archives Nationales* (Washington, DC: Library of Congress, 1967). On the early history of the consulate, see James Donnadieu, *Les Consuls de France* (Paris: Recueil Sirey, 1928), 13–19. On consular duties, see Peter P. Hill, *French Perceptions of the Early American Republic, 1783–1793* (Philadelphia: American Philosophical Society, 1988), 13–19.

45. French exports to America averaged 11,480,000 l.t. per year from 1781 to 1783 and declined to a yearly average of 3,217,000 l.t. from 1786 to 1789. British exports, by contrast, rebounded from a nadir of 816,000 l.t. in 1778 to 20,848,000 l.t. in 1781. For the figures on Franco-American and Anglo-American trade as well as figures on Great Britain, see Jacques Godechot, "Les Relations économiques entre la France et les Etats-Unis de 1778 à 1789," *French Historical Studies* 1, no. 1 (1958). For the figures on France, see Ambroise-Marie Arnould, *De la balance du commerce et des relations commerciales extérieures de la France, dans toutes les parties du globe, particulièrement à la fin du règne de Louis XIV, et au moment de la révolution* (Paris: Buisson, 1795), vol. 3, table 4.

46. On careful observation, see A.N., A.E., B III (1778), "Considérations sur le commerce de la France avec les Etats-Unis." On "every commercial relationship," see A.N., A.E., B III (1783), "Mémoire: Etablissement d'un consul général dans les Etats-Unis d'Amérique." "Market research" does not diminish the importance of this sort of information, which was crucial to any useful understanding of France's present or future competitive position. A call for detailed research can be found in A.N., A.E., B III, 441 (1778), "Mémoire sur les Etats-Unis de l'Amérique septentrionale, le commerce qui s'y fait, et celui qu'on y peut faire," which discusses the different qualities of French and English cloth and the uses to which they could be put in different regions of the United States.

47. On the comparison between French merchants and social climbers and on slippery French trade practices, see A.N., A.E., B III 441 (1783), "Second mémoire: Etablissement d'un consul général dans les Etats-Unis d'Amérique." Such exploitative practices by merchants were criticized everywhere in this group of documents. See A.N., A.E., B III 441 (1783), "Troisième mémoire: Etablissement d'un consul général dans les Etats-Unis d'Amérique." See also Hill, *French Perceptions,* 66; and Godechot, "Les Relations économiques," 29–30. On the need to terminate relations with the English, see M.A.E., M.D., Etats-Unis, 2, "Considérations politiques sur le commerce," 53v.

48. On Saint Domingue's importance, see James E. McClellan, *Colonialism and Science: Saint Domingue in the Old Regime* (Baltimore: Johns Hopkins University Press, 1992), introduction and chap. 4. Barbé-Marbois served as intendant of Saint Domingue from 1784 to 1789. He was sent to French Guiana in 1797 by radical elements in the Directory and returned from exile in 1799. These biographical details were gleaned from Eugene Parker Chase, ed., *Our Revolutionary Forefathers: The Letters of François, Marquis de Barbé-Marbois, during His Residence in the United States as Secretary of the French Legation, 1779–1785* [1929] (Freeport, NY: Books for Libraries Press, 1969), 3–36. Louis-Gabriel Michaud ed., *Biographie universelle, ancien et moderne* (Paris: Delagrave et Compagnie, 1843), 3:45–53. What little is known about the relation between Barbé-Marbois and Jefferson can be found in Frank Shuffelton, "Introduction," in *Thomas Jefferson's Notes on the State of Virginia,* ed. Frank Shuffelton (London: Penguin, 1999), vii–xxxiii. See also Dorothy Medlin, "Thomas Jefferson, André Morellet, and the French Version of the *Notes on the State of Virginia,*" *William and Mary Quarterly* 35, no. 1 (1978). Documents and correspondence between Jefferson and Barbé-Marbois (but unfortunately not the

initial exchanges between the two men) can be found in Julian P. Boyd, ed., *The Papers of Thomas Jefferson* (Princeton, NJ: Princeton University Press, 1952), vols. 5–6.

49. On "unfortunate peoples," see François-Antoine Matignon de Valnais, M.A.E., Nantes, Correspondance Commerciale et Consulaire, Philadelphie, 53 (1782), "Mémoire sur le commerce entre la France et les Etats-Unis," 8v. On artisans, see Valnais, A.N., A.E., B III 441 (1781), "Mémoire sur les etats de New-Hampshire, Massachusetts-Bay et Rhode-Island"; and François de Barbé-Marbois, A.N., A.E., B III 441 (1782), "Les Anglois commercoient avec les treize etats," 7v.

50. The names of the respondents to this questionnaire are scribbled in the margins of Barbé-Marbois' document. For Barbé-Marbois' views on American religious and political culture, see Barbé-Marbois, "Les Anglois commercoient avec les treize etats," 7v and 9r (quotations). His colleague Valnais' reflections can be found in Valnais, "Mémoire sur le commerce," 9v.

51. M.A.E., M.D., Etats-Unis, 10, "Observations sur Les Etats Unis de L'Amerique," 4v; Barbé-Marbois, "Les Anglois commercoient avec les treize etats," 7v. The idea of a North–South distinction that could be commercially exploited by France is echoed in many of the consular letters and memoranda. See, e.g., M.A.E., M.D., Etats-Unis, 4, "Observations sur le commerce entre la France, ou ses colonies et les Etats-Unis," 32r–34v; and M.A.E., M.D., Etats-Unis, 4, "Obsérvations sur Les Etats-Unis de L'Amérique," 4r–6v.

52. Alexis de Tocqueville underlines the earnestness of Louis XVI's reforming intentions and the radicalism of Turgot's proposals, known collectively as the Six Edicts. See Alexis de Tocqueville, *L'Ancien régime et la révolution* (Paris: Gallimard, 1967), book 3, chaps. 4–6. For a critical account of Turgot's guild edict that also conveys a vivid sense of the chaos it unleashed, see Steven Lawrence Kaplan, "Social Classification and Representation in the Corporate World of Eighteenth-Century France: Turgot's 'Carnival,' " in *Work in France: Representation, Meaning, Organization,* ed. Cynthia Koepp and Steven Laurence Kaplan (Ithaca, NY: Cornell University Press, 1985). On the decline of reform after Turgot's Six Edicts, see Franco Venturi, *The Great States of the West,* trans. R. Burr Litchfield, vol. 1, *The End of the Old Regime in Europe, 1776–1789* (Princeton, NJ: Princeton University Press, 1991), 325; François Furet, *Revolutionary France, 1770–1880* (Oxford: Blackwell, 1992), 26; and R. R. Palmer, *The Age of Democratic Revolution: A Political History of Europe and America, 1760–1800* (Princeton, NJ: Princeton University Press, 1959), 1:450–453. For a judgment on the incompatibility of France's social structure with Turgot's reform program and the inevitability of his failure, see Edgar Faure, *La Disgrâce de Turgot* (Lausanne: Éditions Rencentre, 1961), 1–4 and 523–525.

4. Finances and the Empire of Climate

1. On genres of painting, see Thomas E. Crow, *Painters and Public Life in Eighteenth-Century Paris* (New Haven, CT: Yale University Press, 1985), introduction.

2. For a typical eighteenth-century view, see Maisoncelle, *Situation actuelle des fi-nances de la France et de l'Angleterre: Tableau comparatif, dans lequel on expose les accroissemens progressifs du revenu public & de la dette nationale dans les deux roy-aumes* (Paris: Briand, 1789), 39. Marcel Marion, *Histoire financière de la France depuis 1715* (Paris: Rousseau, 1914). For the thesis on French undertaxation and so-cial incidence, as well as Tocqueville's views, see Peter Mathias and Patrick K. O'Brien, "Taxation in Britain and France, 1715–1810: A Comparison of the Social and Eco-nomic Incidence of Taxes Collected for the Central Governments," *Journal of Eu-ropean Economic History* 5, no. 3 (1976): 634n. On the elimination of privileged ex-emption, see Michael Kwass, "A Kingdom of Taxpayers: State Formation, Privilege, and Political Culture in Eighteenth-Century France," *Journal of Modern History* 70, no. 2 (1998); and Michael Kwass, *Privilege and the Politics of Taxation in Eighteenth-Century France: Liberté, Egalité, Fiscalité* (Cambridge: Cambridge Uni-versity Press, 2000), chaps. 1–2. On the issue of administration, see Michel Mori-neau, "Budgets de l'état et gestation des finances royales en France au dix-huitième siècle," *Revue Historique* 264, no. 2 (1980): 296. Much of this apparent chaos may have been due to ministerial infighting. See Robert D. Harris, "French Finances and the American War, 1777–1783," *Journal of Modern History* 48, no. 2 (1976): 237–242; and Lionel Rothkrug, *Opposition to Louis XIV: The Political and Social Ori-gins of the French Enlightenment* (Princeton, NJ: Princeton University Press, 1965), 180. On tax efficiency, see Kathryn Norberg, "The French Fiscal Crisis of 1788 and the Financial Origins of the Revolution of 1789," in *Fiscal Crises, Liberty, and Rep-resentative Government, 1450–1789,* ed. Philip T. Hoffman and Kathryn Norberg (Stanford, CA: Stanford University Press, 1994), 267. See also J. C. Riley, *The Seven Years' War and the Old Regime in France: The Economic and Financial Toll* (Prince-ton, NJ: Princeton University Press, 1986), 66. Riley argues that the French monar-chy farmed out the taxes that were most difficult to collect. For a historiographical overview (to which the subsequent paragraphs in the text owe a number of biblio-graphic indications), see Richard Bonney, "What's New about the New French Fis-cal History," *Journal of Modern History* 70, no. 3 (1998). This literature on the state of eighteenth-century finances is used to excellent effect in David W. Carrithers, "Montesquieu and the Spirit of French Finance: An Analysis of His *Mémoire sur les dettes de l'état* (1715)," in *Montesquieu and the Spirit of Modernity,* ed. David W. Car-rithers and Patrick Coleman (Oxford: Voltaire Foundation, 2002).

3. All figures are from Morineau, "Budgets de l'état et gestation des finances," 330.

4. François Velde and David Weir, "The Financial Market and Government Debt Pol-icy in France, 1746–1792," *Journal of Economic History* 52, no. 1 (1992): 18. See also Riley, *The Seven Years' War,* 184.

5. Riley, *The Seven Years' War,* 184–186.

6. Ibid., 174. For criticisms of Riley, see Velde and Weir, "The Financial Market," 28. A similar criticism is echoed in Norberg, "The French Fiscal Crisis," 274–275.

7. On the separation of spending from taxing, see Velde and Weir, "The Financial Market," 36. David Stasavage has extended this analysis, arguing that constitu-tional checks and balances are not a sufficient condition to ensure the "credible

commitment" that leads to lower borrowing costs. Rather, he argues, cohesive parties such as England enjoyed by 1715, and the process of coalition building they demand, help to stabilize state credit. David Stasavage, *Public Debt and the Birth of the Democratic State, 1688–1789* (Cambridge: Cambridge University Press, 2003), 2–7. On taxation and the growth of revolutionary ideology, see Norberg, "The French Fiscal Crisis," 296. On the politics of privilege and taxation, see Hilton L. Root, *The Fountain of Privilege: Political Foundations of Markets in Old Regime France and England* (Berkeley: University of California Press, 1994); and Kwass, *Privilege and the Politics of Taxation,* chaps. 5–6.

8. The accession to the crown by Philip V touched off the War of Spanish Succession (1701–1713). For the identification of Bourbonism with royal economic mismanagement on both sides of the Pyrenees, with explicit references to Montesquieu's theory of climate, see M.A.E., C.P., Espagne, vol. 207 (1776), Torelly, "Observations politiques et philosophiques sur l'état de l'Espagne," ff. 166r–214v. On the Midas touch, see Plumard de Dangeul, *Remarques sur les avantages et les desavantages de la France et de Grande-Bretagne par rapport au commerce & aux autres sources de la puissance des etats* (Leiden: 1754), 101.

9. "Considérations sur le commerce d'Espagne, sur les divers moyens de le relever & sur l'interet général de l'Europe dans ce commerce," *Journal de Commerce,* May–October 1760: May: 6. Franco Venturi, *La chiesa e la repubblica dentro i loro limiti, 1758–1774,* vol. 2, *Settecento riformatore* (Torino: Giulio Einaudi, 1976), 45–64. The period after 1776 and the ascendance of Floridablanca is covered in Franco Venturi, *The Great States of the West,* trans. R. Burr Litchfield, vol. 1, *The End of the Old Regime in Europe, 1776–1789* (Princeton, NJ: Princeton University Press, 1991), 237–325. For details of these efforts in the Spanish empire, see J. H. Elliott, *Empires of the Atlantic World: Britain and Spain in America, 1492–1830* (New Haven, CT: Yale University Press, 2006), chap. 10.

10. Paul-Antoine Nolivos Saint-Cyr, *Tableau du siècle, par un auteur connu* (Geneva: 1759), 62. See the later comments by Roche-Antoine de Pellissery: "The new provinces of America, far from being considered by Ferdinand and Isabella's successors simply as related provinces that should be nurtured as markets for the agriculture and industry of the metropole, were considered by this ambitious monarch [Charles V] as the true origin of all grandeur and wealth. In consequence, Charles V disdained *political economy* and, keeping his views and his desires turned toward America, American gold and Universal Monarchy, he lost sight of the only system [i.e., political economy] that might have aided his successors in such a foolhardy enterprise." Pellissery, *Le Caffé politique d'Amsterdam,* nouvelle ed., revue et corrigée, avec des augmentations intéressantes (Amsterdam: 1778), 1:244 (original emphasis).

11. Delisle de Sales, *Vie littéraire de Forbonnais* (Paris: Fusch, 1801).

12. François Véron de Forbonnais, *Considérations sur les finances d'Espagne* (Dresden: 1753), 1–2 and 20–21.

13. Earlier criticisms of poor tax distribution made by the Marquis de Vauban (1633–1707) and Pierre le Pesant, sieur de Boisguilbert (1646–1714), are discussed in Kwass, *Privilege and the Politics of Taxation,* 224–231. The ideas on social justice among

members of the Gournay circle are widely discussed in Simone Meyssonnier, *La Balance et l'horloge: La genèse de la pensée libérale en France au XVIIIe siècle* (Paris: Editions de la Passion, 1989), but see esp. 257. Forbonnais, *Considérations sur les finances d'Espagne*, quotations on 46, 63–65, and 20–21.

14. M.A.E., M.D., Espagne 207 (1770), f. 5. This comment is reported to have been written by Marquis d'Argenson in 1755. Jean-Nicolas Démeunier, ed., *Economie politique et diplomatique*, 4 vols. (Paris: 1784–1787): 2:315. The four volumes *Economie politique et diplomatique* are volumes 44–47 of Charles-Josesph Panckoucke's *Encyclopédie méthodique ou par ordre de matières par une société de gens de lettres, de savans et d'artistes* (1782-1791), which ran to 124 volumes by 1791, continuing publication until 1832 after Panckoucke's death in 1798. M.A.E., C.P., Espagne 211 (1777), "De l'Etat actuel du gouvernement, des administrations, des finances . . . d'Espagne," ff. 8r–9v.

15. The reasoning behind this attribution is highly suggestive but can by no means be regarded as conclusive. Bibliographies point to Robinet as the author of *Considérations sur le sort et les révolutions du commerce d'Espagne*, which was supposedly published in 1761. This timing would coincide well with the typical interval for a series of articles that is subsequently issued as a book. An exhaustive search failed to turn up an example of this work, but an edited version of the *Journal de commerce* series of articles does appear later in Robinet's compendious Jean-Baptiste Robinet, *Dictionnaire universel des sciences morale, economique, politique & diplomatique, ou dictionnaire de l'homme, d'etat & du citoyen* (London: Libraires associés 1781), 18:266–330. Jean-Baptiste Robinet, "Considérations sur le commerce d'Espagne, sur les divers moyens de le relever & sur l'interet général de l'Europe dans ce commerce," *Journal de Commerce*, May 1760—January 1761: see September 1760, 22; May 1760, 3; and September 1760, 22, for quotations.

16. Jean-Baptiste Robinet, "Considérations sur le commerce d'Espagne, sur les divers moyens de le relever & sur l'interet général de l'Europe dans ce commerce," *Journal de Commerce*, November 1760, 40–41. Emphasis added. Robinet is paraphrasing Montesquieu here.

17. *HI*, 4.8, 309, 303.

18. *HI*, 8.19, 269, 307–308. Such views continued up until the revolution. See Jean-François de Bourgoing, *Nouveau voyage en Espagne ou tableau de l'etat actuel de cette monarchie: Contenant les détails les plus récens sur la constitution politique, les tribunaux, l'inquisition, les forces de terre & de mer, le commerce & les manufactures, principalement celles de soieries & de draps; sur les nouveaux établissemens, telles que la Banque de Saint-Charles, la Compagnie des Philippines, & les autres institutions qui tendent à régénérer l'Espagne; enfin; sur les moeurs, la littérature, les spectacles, sur le dernier siége de Gibraltar & le voyage de Monseigneur Comte d'Artois; Ouvrage dans lequel on a présenté avec impartialité toute ce qu'on peut dire de plus neuf, de plus avéré & de plus intéressant sur l'Espagne, depuis 1782 jusqu'à présent* (Paris: Regnault, 1789), 2:82–83.

19. Roche-Antoine de Pellissery, *Eloge politique de Colbert, qui n'a point été présenté à l'Académie Française pour le Prix de la St. Louis 1773* (Lausanne: 1775), 188–190n. Pellissery was, of course, using the earlier edition of Raynal. For a similar comparison,

not related to Raynal, see Bourgoing, *Nouveau Voyage en Espagne,* 2:7–8. Pellissery was thrown into the Bastille for his intemperate rhetoric in 1777 and only emerged eleven years later. See Simon Nicolas Henri Linguet, *Mémoires sur la Bastille* (Paris: Librarie de la Bibliothèque Nationale, 1875), 90–91. For documents pertaining to Pellissery's *embastillement,* see Frantz Funck-Brentano, *Lettres de Cachet à Paris, étude suivie d'une liste des prisoniers de la Bastille* (Paris: Imprimerie Nationale, 1903), 401. Here, the term "constitution" is being used in the sense of limited government. In this sense, absolute governments were not considered to have a constitution. Pellissery, *Eloge politique de Colbert,* 61–62.

20. The play between necessity and freedom in this vein of eighteenth-century thought has always fascinated commentators, such as Judith Shklar: "[Montesquieu's] theory of climate appeared to make human volition illusory. It was a 'hard' determinism which made it seem easy to grasp social patterns and to diagnose their malfunctions, but not to change them. Societies were natural, predictable wholes, created by automatic human responses to climate and topography." But, Shklar also observes, and here is the point: "While these forces would seem to leave no scope for deliberate political action, Montesquieu did not see them as shackles." Judith N. Shklar, *Montesquieu* (Oxford: Oxford University Press, 1987), 93–94.

21. Quotations from the *EL* come from 14.5 and 19.4. On the simplicity of despotic regimes, see *EL,* 19.4 and 5.15. D'Arcq translated this concept, as we have seen, into his six "systems of state." François Véron de Forbonnais, *Extrait du livre de l'Esprit des lois* (Amsterdam: Arkstée & Merkus, 1753), on Forbonnais trembling, 1:199–201; on colonies, 1:197–198; and on English exceptionalism, 1:175. Later, Forbonnais showed that he, too, believed in the basic idea of the general spirit and the importance of *moeurs:* "The genius or the character of a people generally has an influence upon the form of its government and, in a more specific way, on those operations, such as commerce, which belong equally to the whole nation." He also wrote, "With an understanding of the general spirit of those who govern . . . one can from this predict the end or the duration of their blindness, of the prosperity or the slow decadence of the State." François Véron de Forbonnais, "Réflexions sur la nécessité de comprendre l'étude du commerce & des finances dans celle de la politique," in *Mémoires et considérations sur le commerce et les finances d'Espagne: Avec des reflexions sur la nécessité de comprendre l'étude du commerce & des finance, dans celle de la politique* (Amsterdam: Changuion, 1761), iii and 227. At issue, it seems, is the relative composition of the general spirit and how closely its dynamics represent that of a despotism. Here Forbonnais is referring to Spain and its resemblance to France.

22. *HI,* 4.8, 319. On "overdetermination," see Georges Benrekassa, "Moeurs comme 'concept politique,' 1680–1820," in *Le Langage des Lumières* (Paris: Presses Universitaires de France, 1995).

23. Robinet, "Le Commerce d'Espagne," January 1760, 45, 21.

24. Original emphasis from the dictionnary of the Académie. Compare to the entry for "OECONOMIE ANIMALE" in Diderot and d'Alembert's *Encyclopédie:* "the order, mechanism and the ensemble of function and movements that support the lives of animals." The opposition evoked here consciously leaves aside the fact that all

constitutions, except the most positivistic ones, have a normative basis—one that often harkens back to the natural order. On shifts in the meaning of "constitution," see Olivier Béaud, "Constitution et constitutionnalisme," in *Dictionnaire de philosophie politique*, ed. Phillipe Raynaud and Stéphane Rials (Paris: Presses Universitaires de France, 1996), 118–126; Wolfgang Schmale, "Constitution, Constitutionnel," in *Handbuch politisch-sozialer Grundbegriffe in Frankreich: 1620–1820*, ed. Gerd van den Heuvel and Michael Wagner (Munich: R. Oldenbourg, 1992), 12:31–63; and G. Stourzh, "Constitution: Changing Meanings of the Term from the Early 17th to the Late 18th Century," in *Conceptual Change and the Constitution*, ed. T. Ball and J. G. A. Pocock (Lawrence: University Press of Kansas, 1998).

25. Immanuel Wallerstein, *Mercantilism and the Consolidation of the European World Economy, 1600–1750*, vol. 2, *The Modern World System* (New York: Academic Press, 1980), chap. 4; and Patrick K. O'Brien, "Inseparable Connections: Trade, Economy, Fiscal Sate, and the Expansion of Empire, 1688–1815," in *Oxford History of the British Empire*, vol. 2, ed. P. J. Marshall (Oxford: Oxford University Press, 1998).

26. See, e.g., François Véron de Forbonnais, *Recherches et considérations sur les finances de France, depuis 1595 jusqu'en 1721* (Basle: Frères Cramer, 1758), 1:2. Against the decisiveness of the Glorious Revolution, Stasavage argues that interest rates on English state debt did not stabilize until thirty years beyond this seminal event, when the Whig ascendancy was firmly in place. Stasavage, *Public Debt and the Birth of the Democratic State*, 125–129. Recently, the commonplace that France's lack of a central bank choked off capital formation has come under attack, because of the pervasiveness of private credit markets through the intermediary of notaries. See Philip T. Hoffman, Gilles Postel-Vinay, and Jean-Laurent Rosenthal, *Priceless Markets: The Political Economy of Credit in Paris, 1660–1870* (Chicago: University of Chicago Press, 2000).

27. "Considérations sur les finances & le commerce de France," *Journal de Commerce*, January 1761–June 1762: February 1761, 29.

28. Maisoncelle, *Situation actuelle*, 31–32. An earlier commentator, Moreau de Beaumont, qualified this situation as a form of "feudal anarchy." Jean-Louis Moreau de Beaumont, *Mémoires concernant les impositions et droits* (Paris: Imprimerie Royale,1768–1769), 1:4. Beaumont, former intendant of finances and royal secretary to the Company of the Indies, wrote his *Mémoires* on behalf of the crown, which was having trouble with its own *parlements* passing financial reform in the wake of the Seven Years' War and the ensuing financial disaster. In writing these historical memoirs, Moreau de Beaumont sought to uphold the *thèse royale* against partisans of local representative powers—i.e., the *parlements*. In an illuminating exposé, Keith Michael Baker discusses struggles with the *parlements* over the nature of royal power in Moreau's other writings, but without mentioning his work on taxation. See *Inventing the French Revolution: Essays on French Political Culture in the Eighteenth Century* (Cambridge: Cambridge University Press, 1990), chap. 3: "Controlling French History: The Ideological Arsenal of Jacob-Nicolas Moreau."

29. Maisoncelle, *Situation actuelle*, 32.

30. Ibid., 5. Raynal saw the same process at work: "When I see monarchs and empires furiously attacking and waging war against each other, with all their debts, with

their public funds, and their revenue already deeply mortgaged, it seems to me, says a philosophical writer, as if I saw men fighting with clubs in a potter's shop surrounded with porcelain." *HI,* 8.19, 310. Raynal is quoting David Hume's "Of Public Credit." David Hume, *Essays Moral, Political, and Literary,* ed. Eugene F. Miller (Indianapolis: Liberty Classics, 1985), 362. On the "natural edifice," see "Considérations sur les finances & le commerce de France," *Journal de Commerce,* February 1762, 18–19. On the artificial power of credit, see Jacques Accarias de Serionne, *La Richesse de l'Angleterre* (Vienna: Trattnern, 1771), 59 and 73.

31. On the Dutch capital strike against England, see R. R. Palmer, *The Age of Democratic Revolution: A Political History of Europe and America, 1760–1800* (Princeton, NJ: Princeton University Press, 1959), 1:328. French schadenfreude was balanced by alarm on the part of British observers. See, most famously, David Hume, who postulated two possibilities: "either the nation must destroy public credit, or public credit will destroy the nation. Hume, "Of Public Credit," 361.

32. These data are originally presented in table (not graph) form in Maisoncelle, *Situation actuelle,* 14–26.

33. Ibid., 23–25 and 27–30.

34. "Considérations sur les finances," February, 16. To give the reader some sense of proportion, the following figures give public sector revenue as a percentage of gross domestic product in 2005: France, 43.4 percent; the United Kingdom, 37.2 percent; Germany, 34.7 percent; the United States, 25.0 percent; Japan, 26.4 percent; Sweden, 50.4 percent; and Mexico, 19.0 percent. Source: Organisation for Economic Co-operation and Development, *Revenue Statistics: 1965–2005* (Paris: Organisation for Economic Co-operation and Development (OECD) 2006), 69, table 1.

35. Hilliard d'Auberteuil, *Tableau historique des finances de l'Angleterre, depuis le regne de Guillaume III jusqu'en 1784* (London and Paris: Couturier, 1784), 47 and 50 (quotations in this and the previous paragraph in text).

36. Ibid., 48, 64, and 136–137 (quotations in this and the previous paragraph in text). Alexander Gerschenkron, *Economic Backwardness in Historical Perspective: A Book of Essays* (Cambridge, MA: Belknap Press, 1962), 2–9. Significantly, nineteenth-century France stands as one of Gerschenkron's principal examples on the Continent, particularly in the development of its credit institutions from naught.

37. "Considérations sur les finances," February, 24, 86, and 29.

38. Central banks were established in the following countries in the following years: Holland, 1609; Sweden, 1656; England, 1694; Denmark, 1736; Prussia, 1765; and Russia, 1770. In France, a central bank was not established until 1800. Venturi, *The Great States,* 341. Among opponents of a national bank in France, see Montesquieu, *EL,* 20.10. Mirabeau the younger adduced the same logic to argue against a central bank in Spain: "According to their constitution, according to the general and particular state of things in the country where they are established, public banks can do much good or much harm." Comte de Mirabeau, *De La Banque d'Espagne dite de Saint-Charles* (1785), 4. On planting a central bank, see "Considérations sur les finances," February, 30; and March, 6, for quotation.

39. Mercier de la Rivière, *L'Ordre naturel et essentiel des sociétés politiques* (London: Jean Nourse, 1767), 38.

5. Physiocracy and the Politics of History

1. Christine Théré and Loïc Charles, "The Writing Workshop of François Quesnay and the Making of Physiocracy," *History of Political Economy* 40, no. 1 (2008). On Vauban and Boisguillbert and early agrarian reform movements more generally, see Lionel Rothkrug, *Opposition to Louis XIV: The Political and Social Origins of the French Enlightenment* (Princeton, NJ: Princeton University Press, 1965), chaps. 5 and 6. On agronomy, see André Bourde, *Agronomie et agronomes en France au xviiie siècle*, 3 vols. (Paris: S.E.V.P.E.N., 1967).

2. D'Alembert, "Discours préliminaire des éditeurs," in *Encyclopédie, ou dictionnaire raisonné des sciences, des arts et des métiers, par un société de gens de lettres,* ed. Diderot and d'Alembert (Lausanne and Berne: Sociétés Typographiques, 1781), 1:xvi.

3. Voltaire, "HISTOIRE," in *Encyclopédie, ou dictionnaire raisonné.* Karen O'Brien also cites this article to make a similar point in *Narratives of Enlightenment: Cosmopolitan History from Voltaire to Gibbon* (Cambridge: Cambridge University Press, 1997), 24.

4. On "grand passions," see "Extrait et analyse: Histoire générale de l'Asie, de l'Afrique et de l'Amérique, contenant des discours sur l'histoire ancienne des peuples de ces contrées, leur histoire moderne & la description des lieux, avec des remarques sur leur histoire naturelle, & des observations sur les religions, les gouvernements, les sciences, les arts, le commerce, les coutumes, les moeurs; les caractères &c. des nations," *Ephémérides du citoyen* 1 (1771): 213. On "disorders and chaos," see François Quesnay, "Suite du despotisme de la Chine, par M.A.: 4e," *Ephémérides du citoyen* 6 (1767): 21. On "rural [i.e., philosophical] details," see François Quesnay, "Comparaison des revenues des terres à la fin du seizième siècle, et ceux d'aujourd'hui," *Ephémérides du citoyen* 11 (1769): 79. The remark is by Dupont de Nemours in the context of an introduction to Quesnay's more "philosophical" history. For this attribution, see François Quesnay, *Oeuvres économiques complètes et autres textes,* ed. Christine Théré, Loïc Charles, and Jean-Claude Perrot (Paris: INED, 2005), 2:1145.

5. Steiner presents an excellent summary of the epistemological claims of the Physiocrats, in all of their naïveté. See Philippe Steiner, *La "Science nouvelle" de l'économie politique* (Paris: Presses Universitaires de France, 1998), 10–24. One difficulty with Steiner's account is that he does not credit the precursors (or opponents) of the Physiocrats (Linnaeus excepted) with a developed epistemology. Forbonnais, for instance, merely "slapped on" *(plaqué)* scientific notions to preexisting concerns (16). A fuller engagement with Linnaeus, and with natural history in general, may have nuanced Steiner's very clear account of the Physiocrats. Steven Kaplan remarks: "the *économistes* were impatient and complacent observers. Once they established their founding principles—imposed by reason and apprehended deductively—observation became gratuitous because an appreciation of natural law was both anterior and superior to data collection." Ferdinando Galiani, *La Bagarre: Galiani's "Lost" Parody,* edited with and introduction by Steven Laurence Kaplan (The Hague: Martinus Nijhoff, 1979), 82n. On ease of comprehension, see Nicolas Baudeau, "Première

introduction à la philosophie économique," in *Principaux économistes, deuxième partie,* ed. Eugène Daire (Paris: Librairie de Guillaumin, 1846), 656. On governance, see François Quesnay, "Tableau économique avec ses explications," in *Oeuvres économiques complètes et autres textes,* 1:439–526.

6. Eugène Daire, historian of the Physiocrats, considered this work the most faithful reproduction of Quesnay's own system. See Baudeau, "Première introduction à la philosophie économique," 335n. Contemporaries thought of Baudeau's work as a précis of Mercier de la Rivière's *Traité de l'ordre naturel & essentiel des sociétés politiques* (Paris: Desaint, 1767). See also Pierre Samuel Dupont de Nemours, "De l'origine et des progrès d'une science nouvelle [1768]," in *Collection des principaux économistes,* ed. Eugène Daire (Paris: Dessaint, 1840–1848). On Montesquieu, see ibid., 336–337. Baudeau, "Première introduction à la philosophie économique," 655. See also François Quesnay, "Lettre de M. Alpha, . . . sur le langage des science economique," *Ephémérides du citoyen* 10 (1767): 163.

7. Jean-Nicolas Démeunier, ed., *Economie politique et diplomatique,* 4 vols., *Encyclopédie méthodique ou par ordre de matières par une société de gens de lettres, de savans et d'artistes* (Paris: 1784–1787), vol. 2, article "ECONOMISTES" by Charles Grivel. For Grivel's Physiocratic connections, see C. de La Taille-Colainville, *Les Idées économiques et financières de Montesquieu* (Paris: Librairie sociale et économique, 1940), 34.

8. Dupont de Nemours, "De l'origine et des progrès," 337–338, emphasis added. Dupont, like so many other readers of Montesquieu—both sympathetic and hostile—may have been aroused by two particular passages in the *Esprit des lois,* in addition to Montesquieu's willing admission that superficial order is lacking in this same work. "I laid down principles, and then saw particular cases conform to them, as if by themselves; the histories of all nations were only the consequences of these principles" (*EL,* preface). Later on he wrote: "This subject matter is vast. In this crowd of ideas that comes to my mind, I will attend more to the order of things than to the things themselves. I must push things aside and forge ahead into the light" (*EL,* 19.1).

9. D'Alembert, "Discours préliminaire des éditeurs."

10. On Physiocratic dogmatism and enthusiasm, see Citton, "La naissance de l'économiste est un fable sans méchants." Yves Citton, *Portrait de l'économiste en physiocrate: Critique littéraire de l'économie politique* (Paris: L'Harmattan, 2000), 23. Pierre Rosanvallon, *Le Capitalisme utopique* (Paris: Editions du Seuil, 1979), 52–54. Quesnay, "Suite du despotisme de la Chine, par M.A.: 4e," 74. On "six years of despotism," see M. A. Baudot, *Notes historiques sur la Convention Nationale, le Directoire, l'Empire, et l'exil des votants* (Geneva: Slatkine, 1974), 157. Cited in Thomas E. Crow, *Painters and Public Life in Eighteenth-Century Paris* (New Haven, CT: Yale University Press, 1985), 187. On "merely historical argumentation," see Keith Michael Baker, *Inventing the French Revolution: Essays on French Political Culture in the Eighteenth Century* (Cambridge: Cambridge University Press, 1990), 84. The quote refers to Bossuet, "the greatest defender of absolutism," but speaks to precisely the same impulse in the Physiocrats, who attempted as well to protect the monarchy from the increasingly disruptive historical claims of the *parlements.*

11. Dale K. Van Kley, *The Religious Origins of the French Revolution: From Calvin to the Civil Constitution, 1560–1791* (New Haven, CT: Yale University Press, 1996), 110. For an account of the Refusal of Sacraments crisis, see 142–154.

12. The linkage between opposition to "Turgot's experiments" and the struggles between the crown and *parlement* of the 1750s and 1760s is made quite explicit by Daniel Roche, *France in the Enlightenment* (Cambridge, MA: Harvard University Press, 1998), 468–472. Quote on 473.

13. Dupont de Nemours, "De l'origine et des progrès," 347 (on sovereign authority), original emphasis. See also Quesnay, "Suite du despotisme de la Chine, par M.A.: 4e," 48. Analogous but not identical formulations may be found in the excerpts in Jean Bodin, *On Sovereignty: Four Chapters from the Six Books of the Commonwealth,* ed. and trans. Julian Franklin (Cambridge: Cambridge University Press, 1992), 11, 92, 49–50, and 103–104. For a discussion of the intellectual context that bred Bodin's distrust of divided sovereignty, see Julian H. Franklin, *Jean Bodin and the Rise of Absolutist Theory* (Cambridge: Cambridge University Press, 1973), especially chap. 4.

14. Steiner observes that the Physiocrats allowed for different economic pursuits among commercial republics and agricultural monarchies. This much is true, but these differences flow only from size and not from governmental form, social structure, *moeurs,* climate, or any of the other data Montesquieu's adherents took as basic. Steiner, *La "Science nouvelle" de l'économie politique,* 86–87. The opposition to public debate in Physiocratic thought fits uncomfortably with the thesis developed by Jürgen Habermas. For Habermas, the Physiocrats were among the leading theorists of (and participants in) the eighteenth-century public sphere. Jürgen Habermas, *The Structural Transformation of the Public Sphere* (Cambridge, MA: MIT Press, 1989), 55 and 95. Although Citton does not cite Habermas in this connection, see his pertinent comments on the contradictory Physiocratic attitudes toward public discussion in Citton, *Portrait de l'économiste en physiocrate,* chap. 4.

15. On the *Ephémérides,* see François Pellissier, "Recherche sur les 'Ephémérides du citoyen' (1765–1776) et les 'Nouvelles Ephémérides du citoyen' (1774–1776, 1788)," (master's thesis, Paris I, Sorbonne, 1978), tables 1 and 2, 33–34. The editorship of the *Journal de l'agriculture de commerce et des finances* shuttled back and forth between the hands of the Physiocrats (six years) and their enemies (three years) during the *Journal's* most vital years, from 1765 to 1774, which makes categorical judgments about its politics and methodology more difficult. See Hervé Kempf, "Le Journal d'agriculture, de commerce et de finances (1765–1783), (master's thesis, Paris I, Sorbonne, 1978), 26, annex 13, and calculations on data presented on 126–168. Kempf rightly observes a dull character to the *Journal* in the years after its revival from 1780 to 1783—which was most definitely not a period of Physiocratic ascendancy. Kempf's thematic rubrics were not readily usable for my purposes, so these calculations are based on a decomposition and retabulation of all of his data. I could not detect any clear variations in distribution of themes (in terms of themes, not politics, which, however, are clear) under different editorships.

16. The literature on Physiocracy and public opinion is immense. Steiner gives a good summary in *La "Science nouvelle" de l'économie politique,* 96–116. For the broader French context, see J. A. W. Gunn, *Queen of the World: Opinion in the Public Life of France from the Renaissance to the Revolution* (Oxford: Voltaire Foundation, 1995).

17. Pierre Samuel Dupont de Nemours, "Du Commerce & de la Compagnie des Indes," *Ephémérides du citoyen* 10 (1769): 179–180.

18. For the definitive account of *doux commerce,* see Albert O. Hirschman, *The Passions and the Interests: Political Arguments for Capitalism before Its Triumph,* 2nd ed. (Princeton, NJ: Princeton University Press, 1996). It should be noted for the sake of accuracy that the term *doux commerce* was never used by contemporaries and has only been imposed retrospectively as a way of naming this line of thought, which can be found in Montesquieu's *Esprit des lois* and, among the works of David Hume, "Of the Rise and Progress of the Arts and the Sciences (1742) in *Essays Moral, Political, and Literary,* ed. Eugene F. Miller (Indianapolis: Liberty Classics, 1985). For an important discussion of this problem in Adam Smith, see Istvan Hont, *Jealousy of Trade: International Competition and the Nation-State in Historical Perspective* (Cambridge, MA: Harvard University Press, 2005), chap. 5.

19. On stadial theory, the classic text is Ronald L. Meek, *Social Science and the Ignoble Savage* (Cambridge: Cambridge University Press, 1976), chap. 3. Meek discusses the simultaneous invention of this theory by Smith and Turgot in the 1750s, citing Montesquieu as an important influence on both thinkers. On European barbarity, see Raynal's *Histoire Philosophique et Politique des . . . deux Indes* (Amsterdam: 1770). The essays collected in Hans-Jürgen Lüsenbrink and Alexandre Mussard, eds., *Avantages et désavantages de la découverte de l'Amérique* (Saint-Etienne: Publications de l'Université de Saint-Etienne, 1994), were the replies to an essay competition sponsored by Raynal at the academy of Dijon, which asked whether the discovery of the Americas had on balance been good or bad for humanity. The response was an ambivalent "yes."

20. "Réflexions sur la réformation des finances dans plusieurs Etats d'Italie, et sur les cadastres de ces Etats," *Ephémérides du citoyen* 11 (1770): 203–205.

21. Pierre Joseph André Roubaud, "De l'Amérique," *Journal de l'agriculture, du commerce et des finances,* June 1774, 45. On debt, see "Comparaison des revenues des terres," 98. Here, this observation is used to denounce "the corrosive policies of Cardinal Richelieu."

22. In Raynal's view, feudal government was imported from Europe to America, with devastating consequences. See *HI,* 6:145. The Physiocrats also articulated this view. The term "steel frame" is Joseph Schumpeter's. See *Capitalism, Socialism, and Democracy,* 2nd ed. (New York: Harper & Brothers, 1947), 136; cited in Arno J. Mayer, *The Persistence of the Old Regime: Europe to the Great War* (New York: Pantheon Books, 1981), 12. For another statement of this view on the development of modern fiscality, see Pierre Samuel Dupont de Nemours, "Histoire de la rivalité de la France & l'Angleterre," *Ephémérides du citoyen* 2 (1771): 116–117: "The means of making revenues regenerate themselves for their profit and that of others escaped them. They could only think of seizing upon the weak to hinder

commerce, regulate industry, and to hold the two in ransom. Governments became *fiscal.*"

23. Dupont de Nemours, "Du commerce & de la Compagnie des Indes," 8:261 (original emphasis) and 8:243-244. Mirabeau defined the problem as one of an antisocial *esprit fiscal:* "*L'esprit fiscal* afin qu'on nous entende, est le contraire de *l'esprit social.*" Marquis de Mirabeau, "Eloges historiques des hommes qui dans le dernier siècle & dans celui-ci ont consacré leurs études & leurs travaux au bien de l'humanité dans le genre économique, avec une analyse politique de leurs ouvrages en ce genre," *Ephémérides du Citoyen* 3-7 (1770): 5:42, original emphasis.

24. Indeed, as Dupont de Nemours points out, any profits gained by the Compagnie des Indes during the eighteenth century were solely attributable to the tobacco monopoly granted to it by the crown—"a financial enterprise that had nothing whatever to do with the India trade." Dupont de Nemours, "Du commerce & de la Compagnie des Indes," 8:260.

25. Ibid., 8:233. For Chaussinand-Nogaret, "there was no incompatibility [save a credit shortage] between the monarchical society of the eighteenth century and development towards industrial capitalism." Dupont shows, to the contrary, a rentier class addicted to quick profits but terribly risk averse. Guy Chaussinand-Nogaret, *The French Nobility in the Eighteenth Century: From Feudalism to Enlightenment* (Cambridge: Cambridge University Press, 1985), 87, 112, and 94-101 (on overseas trading companies).

26. Roubaud worked as an editor of the *Journal de Commerce* before his "conversion" to the sect, to which his 1770 *Récréations économiques*—written as a riposte to Galiani—serves as a written testament of sorts. He worked as an editor of the *Journal de l'agriculture du commerce et des finances* and published in *Ephémérides du citoyen.* For further biographical details, see Georges Weulersse, *Le Mouvement physiocratique en France de 1756 à 1770* (Paris: Félix Alcan, 1910), 1:156. Also see Christine Théré, "Etude sociale des auteurs économiques" (Thèse de Doctorat Nouveau Régime, Université de Paris, 1990), 243. The full title of Roubaud's work is perhaps instructive: *Histoire générale de l'Asie, de l'Afrique et de l'Amérique, contenant des discours sur l'histoire ancienne des peuples de ces contrées, leur histoire moderne & la description des lieux, avec des remarques sur leur histoire naturelle, & des observations sur les religions, les gouvernements, les sciences, les arts, le commerce, les coutumes, les moeurs; les caractères &c. des nations* (Paris: Des Ventes de la Doué, 1770-1775).

27. For a classic statement, see François Véron de Forbonnais, *Elemens du commerce,* 2nd ed., 2 vols. (Leiden: 1754), as well as his article "COLONIES" in the *Encyclopédie.* The following represents how these relations were understood by practitioners of this trade: "The Discovery of America and the colonies that the Powers established there, either on the continent or on the islands, gives rise to a new employment of men, a considerably larger market for Agriculture, manufactures, and the arts, and luxury in Europe's consumption, which changes their constitution considerably by the action of Navigation and Commerce." "Mémoire du Commerce de Nantes," A.N., colonies, F^{2b} 7 (1765), f. 1r.

28. On monopoly, see Pierre Joseph André Roubaud, *Histoire générale de l'Asie, de l'Afrique et de l'Amérique* (Paris: Desvented de la Doué, 1770–1775), 13:345. On being an "object of conquest," see Roubaud, "De l'Amérique," 50–51. On Physiocracy and natural jurisprudence, see Catherine Larrère, *L'Invention de l'économie politique au XVIIIe siècle: Du droit naturel à la physiocratie* (Paris: Presses Universitaires, 1992).

29. On the "new order," see Roubaud, *Histoire générale*, 13:344; on "astonishing revolutions," see "Du Commerce des Indes," *Ephémérides du citoyen*, November 1765, 113; on the "tidal wave," see Roubaud, *Histoire générale*, 13:369; on the Europe–Indies reversal, see "Réflexions sur les principes des colonies Angloises de l'Amérique Septentrionale, touchant la liberté naturelle, les taxes de commerce & c.," *Journal de l'agriculture, du commerce et des finances,* August 1779, 149. Compare these sentiments to the following: From Raynal: "No event has been so interesting to mankind in general, and to the inhabitants of Europe in particular, as the discovery of the new world, and the passage to India by the Cape of Good Hope. It gave rise to a revolution in the commerce, and in the power of nations; and in the manners, industry, and government of the world in General" (*HI,* I.1). From Smith: "The discovery of America, and that of a passage to the East Indies by the Cape of Good Hope, are the two greatest and most important events recorded in the history of mankind. Their consequences have already been very great: but, in the short period of between two and three centuries which has elapsed since these discoveries were made, it is impossible that the whole extent of their consequences can have been seen. What benefits, or what misfortunes to mankind may hereafter result from those great events no human wisdom can foresee. By uniting, in some measure, the most distant parts of the world, by enabling them to relieve one another's wants, to increase one another's enjoyments, and to encourage one another's industry, their general tendency would seem to be beneficial. To the natives, however, both of the East and West Indies, all the commercial benefits which can have resulted from those events have been sunk and lost in the dreadful misfortunes which they have occasioned" (*WN,* 2:iv). From Marx and Engels: "The discovery of America, the rounding of the Cape, opened up fresh ground for the rising bourgeoisie. The East-Indian and Chinese markets, the colonisation of America, trade with the colonies, the increase in the means of exchange and in commodities generally, gave to commerce, to navigation, to industry, an impulse never before known, and thereby, to the revolutionary element in the tottering feudal society, a rapid development." *The Communist Manifesto* (London: Penguin Books, 2002), 220.

30. Roubaud, *Histoire générale,* 13:246, 250, 211, and 320. For other Physiocratic views of Peru, see François Quesnay, "Analyse du gouvernement des Yncas de Pérou," *Ephémérides du citoyen* 1 (1767). For a discussion of Physiocratic ideas on Peru, see Girolamo Imbruglia, *L'Invenzione del Paraguay: Studio sull'idea di comunità tra seicento e settecento* (Naples: Bibliopolis, 1983), 284–292.

31. Roubaud, *Histoire générale,* 15:62–63, 99, and 187. See also 12:130–147.

32. Royal administrators constantly worried about Frenchmen going native in the wilds of New France. For the racial element of these worries, see Brett Rushforth, "'A Little Flesh We Offer You': The Origins of Indian Slavery in New France," *William and Mary Quarterly* 60 (2003).

33. Roubaud, *Histoire générale*, 15:68 (also for the quote in the preceding paragraph in text).

34. François Quesnay, "Lettre sur l'opinion de l'Auteur de l'ESPRIT DES LOIX concernant les colonies," *Journal de l'agriculture, du commerce et des finances,* April 1766, 18.

35. Forbonnais' interest in periodization recalls Pierre-Daniel Huet, *Histoire du commerce & de la navigation des anciens* (Amsterdam: Humbert & Mortier, 1716), esp. chap. 2. Other discussions of Physiocratic views of the colonies can be found in Henri Sée, "Les économistes et la question coloniale aux xviiie siècle," *Revue d'histoire des colonies,* no. 4 (1929). Durand Echeverria, *Mirage in the West: A History of the French Image of American Society to 1815* (Princeton, NJ: Princeton University Press, 1957), chap. 7, on degeneracy theory; and Michèle Duchet, *Anthropologie et histoire au siècle des lumières: Buffon, Voltaire, Rousseau, Helvétius, Diderot,* second ed. (Paris: Albin Michel, 1995), chap. 3, on the question of the Physiocrats and slavery. Victor Riqueti Marquis de Mirabeau, *L'Ami des hommes, ou traité de population* (Avignon: 1756), part 3, 111–114. Holland, by contrast, represented a purely commercial empire. For a related discussion of Physiocracy and historical stages, see Hont, *Jealousy of Trade,* 368.

36. On the agricultural militia, see "Des Colonies françoises aux Indes Occidentales," *Ephémérides du citoyen* 5 (1766): 74. On arbitrary government, see Roubaud, *Histoire générale,* 15:189.

37. Mirabeau, *L'Ami des hommes,* part 3, 139, emphasis added. Victor Riqueti, Marquis de Mirabeau and François Quesnay, *Philosophie rurale, ou économie générale et politique de l'agriculture, réduite à l'ordre immuable des loix physiques & morales* (Amsterdam: Libraires associés,1763). For Jean-Antoine de Mirabeau's comments, see Musée Paul Arbaud, Aix en Provence, France, Fonds Mirabeau: 27 October 1753, from St. Pierre Martinique (23:17) and 10 January 1754 from Guadaloupe (23:35-36). It should be noted that the younger Mirabeau did not share his brother's laissez-faire positions at first, but his subsequent experiences in the colonies pushed him to a much different position favoring free trade between colony and metropole. Compare Mirabeau and Quesnay, *Philosophie rurale,* "Memoire sur le commerce," 124-144, with Hagley Museum and Library, manuscripts W-2 5671, "Mémoire sur les colonies," 1764 or 1765, f .302.

38. J.-P. Brissot de Warville, "Considérations sur l'indépendance des Anglo-Américains," *Journal de l'agriculture, du commerce et des finances,* April–May, 51–64; Anne-Robert-Jacques Turgot, "Mémoire sur la manière dont la France et l'Espagne devoient envisager les suites de la querelle entre la Grande-Bretagne et ses colonies (1776)," in *Oeuvres de Mr. Turgot* (Paris: Delance, 1809), 8:452.

39. As Loïc Charles reminds us, the *Tableau Economique,* the title of which translates best as "economic picture," "provided the reader with a synthetic view of Physiocratic economic theory, which could not be replicated with words." Loïc Charles, "The *Tableau Economique* as Rational Recreation," *History of Political Economy* 36, no. 3 (2004): 465. On conservation principles, see Philip Mirowski, *More Heat Than Light: Economics as Social Physics, Physics as Nature's Economics* (Cambridge:

Cambridge University Press, 1991), in economic theory in general, 101–108; and in Physiocracy in particular, 154–163.

40. On French customs zones, see Roland Mousnier, *Les Institutions de la France sous la monarchie absolue, 1598–1789,* 2nd ed. (Paris: Presses Universitaires de France, 1992), 2:410–417. Recent estimates show that 55 percent of France's urban population lived within the "five great farms" area and that the median area of France's customs zones comprised 15 percent of France's total sovereign area. Mark Dencecco, "Fragmented Authority on the European Continent, 1700–1815: A Quantitative Analysis," in *Social Science Research Network Working Papers* (2008), SSRN ID #1066705, estimates on 14. "The source of productivity growth was . . . comparative advantage, and it depended on costs of transportation and opportunities for trade with the rest of the economy. Had the French monarchy spent less on warfare and more on roads and canals, had the legal system not frustrated private efforts to improve transportation, then French agriculture might well have benefited." Philip T. Hoffman, *Growth in a Traditional Society: The French Countryside, 1450–1815* (Princeton, NJ: Princeton University Press, 1996), 204. Two works argue that guild restrictions were not as effective as commonly thought, but they nevertheless emphasize in different ways the structuring effect such restrictions had on the labor market: see Jean Jaurès, *Histoire socialiste de la révolution française,* ed. Albert Soboul (Paris: Éditions sociales, 1968), 1:133; and Michael Sonenscher, *Work and Wages: Natural Law, Politics, and the Eighteenth-Century French Trades* (Cambridge: Cambridge University Press, 1989), chap. 5. The term "legibility" comes from James C. Scott, *Seeing Like a State: How Certain Schemes to Improve the Human Condition Have Failed* (New Haven, CT: Yale University Press, 1998), chap. 1.

41. For more on labor and selfhood, see Christopher John Arthur, "Personality and the Dialectic of Labour and Property—Locke, Hegel, Marx," *Radical Philosophy* 26 (1980). Locke actually grounded the right of self-preservation in God's ownership over people, but this does not seem important to the discussion at hand. Mirabeau and Quesnay, *Philosophie rurale,* quote on 9; other discussions of co-proprietorship come at 61 and 68.

42. Smith, *WN,* 4.ix. Quoted in Rosanvallon, *Le Capitalisme utopique,* 56.

43. Pierre Samuel Dupont de Nemours, *Physiocratie, ou constitution naturelle du gouvernement le plus avantageux au genre humain* (Leiden: 1768), 80 (on two kingdoms) and 97 (on foreign merchants).

6. Center, Periphery, and *Commerce National*

1. For this and other fundamental data and insights about the structure of France's trading regime in the eighteenth century, see Jean Tarrade, *Le Commerce colonial de la France à la fin de l'ancien régime: L'évolution du régime de "l'Exclusif" de 1763 à 1789* (Paris: Presses Universitaires de France, 1972), 1:60.

2. From 1716 to 1766, exports from the French islands in America to mainland France as a ratio of metropolitan exports to the islands were around 3:2. From 1767 to 1772, this ratio shot up to 4:1. Source: calculations on official statistics from the Bureau of the Balance of Commerce, A.N., F12 242.

3. For 1768 and 1773, Tarrade provides estimates on contraband of 38.8 and 48 percent of gross production, respectively. Tarrade, *Le Commerce colonial,* 1:111. For high and low estimates of 10 and 60 percent, see Christian Schnakenbourg, *Les Sucreries de la Guadeloupe dans la seconde moitié du XVIIIe siècle* (PhD diss., economics: Université de Paris II, 1973), 118; cited in Robert Louis Stein, *The French Sugar Business in the Eighteenth Century* (Baton Rouge: Louisiana State University Press, 1988), 76n6. Reporting on the *domaine d'occident* is surprisingly variable but never out of the range of 3–5 percent. At times, the *domaine* was raised to 3.5 percent in the eighteenth century; sugar duties were usually assessed on volume, not value, and varied from port to port. Discussions of the *domaine* are found in Jean Paganucci, *Manuel historique, géographique et politique des négocians, ou Encyclopédie portative de la théorie et de la pratique du commerce* (Lyon: J.-M. Bruyset, 1762), 2:353; and Marcel Marion, *Dictionnaire des institutions de la France aux XVIIe et XVIIIe siècles* (Paris: Firmin-Didot, 1923), 184. Colonists' allegiance to France was tested during the British occupation of Martinique (1761–1763) in the final three years of the Seven Years' War. Immanuel Wallerstein defines ferment in the colonies as "antisystemic" movements but perhaps does not give enough scope to conflicts between elites. This omission is curious, since he emphasizes that the bourgeoisie "shaped the world market so as to compete effectively with bourgeoisies located in other states, and to incorporate new zones into the world-economy, thus constantly recreating new centers of peripheral production activities." Immanuel Wallerstein, *The Politics of the World Economy: The States, the Movements and the Civilizations* (Cambridge: Cambridge University Press, Editions de la Maison des Sciences de l'Homme, 1984), 20.

4. A.D., L.-Atl., C 721 (1758), "Mémoire pour la ville de Nantes; Servant de réponse à celui de Saint Malo au sujet du port Franc, Imprimé en 1737"; "Mémoires des directeurs du commerce de Guienne en réponse à celui de Saint Malo, qui demande au Roi la franchise de son port."

5. "The perfect administration of any sort is that which directs an object towards its goal; thus, the science of government in respect of the colonies consists in an understanding of their destiny. . . . [T]he colonies were founded for the utility of the metropole." A.D., L.-Atl., C 724 (1764), "Comment doit-on considérer les colonies?" Compare this to the original statement of the Exclusive regulations in 1717, which cites the need for "un commerce utile et avantageuse à notre Royaume." A.D., L.-Atl., C 724 (1717), "Edit du Roi." Minard refers to the "union sacrée" in favor of the Exclusive. Philippe Minard, *La Fortune du colbertisme: État et industrie dans la France des Lumières* (Paris: Fayard, 1998), 301.

6. François Véron de Forbonnais, "COLONIES," *Encyclopédie ou Dictionnaire Raisonné* [1753] (Geneva: Briasson, 1772), 3:648–651.

7. On the notion of chambers of commerce as the avatars of modern-day pressure groups, see Jean Tarrade, "Le Groupe de pression du commerce à la fin de l'Ancien Régime," *Bulletin de la société d'histoire moderne et contemporaine* 14, no. 13 (1970).

8. On the Council of Commerce, see David Smith, "'*Au bien du commerce*': Economic Discourse and Visions of Society in France" (PhD diss., University of Pennsylvania, 1995); and Thomas Schaeper, *The French Council of Commerce, 1700–1715: A Study*

of Mercantilism after Colbert (Columbus: Ohio State University Press, 1983), chap. 4. Not all of the port and manufacturing cities did, in fact, establish chambers of commerce following the *Arrêt* of 1701 but were content to let the *juridictions consulaires* assume some of the duties of the hoped-for chambers of commerce. In practice, then, the difference between a *juridiction consulaire* and a chamber of commerce was variable and often imperceptible; the latter term is dropped, therefore, to avoid confusion. This nomenclature is followed by other historians. The 1701 memoirs are discussed in Warren C. Scoville, "The French Economy in 1700–1701: An Appraisal by the Deputies of Trade," *Journal of Economic History* 22, no. 2 (1962). All of these memoirs were collected by the Nantes Chamber of Commerce in a bound manuscript: A.D., L.-Atl., C 894 (1701), "Mémoires concernant le commerce de France, des causes de sa décadence et des moyens de le rétablir. Dressées et envoyées par ordre du Roy à la Chambre du Commerce établie à Paris par les deputés des Provinces."

9. On "liberty and protection," see A.D., L.-Atl., C 894 (1701), Deputy of Nantes, f. 78. The complementarity of these concepts is considered in Minard, *La Fortune du colbertisme,* 300–312; Jean-Pierre Hirsch, *Les Deux rêves du commerce: Entreprise et institution dans la région lilloise (1780–1860)* (Paris: Éditions de l'École des Hautes Études en Sciences Sociales, 1991), 1–15; and Jean-Pierre Hirsch, "Les milieux du commerce, l'esprit de système et le pouvoir, à la veille de la Révolution," *Annales ESC* 30, no. 6 (1975): 1360. On the *public* and the *bien public* see A.D., L.-Atl., C 894 (1701), Deputy of Nantes, f. 172 and, e.g., ff. 24, 26, 33, 150, 178, 185–186.

10. Foreign commerce played a more controversial role, which had to be specifically theorized: "That [foreign] commerce is useful and even necessary to enrich the state, render the Prince more powerful, feared and respected by his neighbors is a principle that is not doubted. . . . But since the sole aim of merchants is to enrich themselves without minding the good of the state, their commerce may be harmful to the state even if they make considerable profits from it. It is worthy of the Council to enter into an examination as to which commerce it is advantageous for the state to protect, and which causes harm and should therefore not be tolerated. Everything that enlarges agriculture and pulls from the earth that which favors our manufactures and which facilitates the sale and transport to foreign parts and which augments our fishery and our navigation is worthwhile. It is worthy of protection; these things are equally useful to the state as they are [to] individuals." A.D., L.-Atl., C 894 (1701), Deputy of Rouen, ff. 1–2. On privilege, see A.D., L.-Atl., C 894 (1701), Deputy of Dunkirk, f. 42. Elsewhere (f. 172), Antoine Héron, the deputy of La Rochelle, explicitly contrasts commerce held by privileged companies to "public" commerce. On "facility and ease," see A.D., L.-Atl., C 894 (1701), Deputy of La Rochelle, f. 185. The word *mépris* occurs often in these memoirs, e.g., ff. 72, 73, 80, 88, 89, 91, 94.

11. A.D., L.-Atl., C 894 (1701), Deputy of Nantes, f. 149.

12. Ibid., f. 150, emphasis added.

13. A.D., L.-Atl., C 735 (1730), Directors of Guyenne, "Memoire des Directeurs de la Chambre de Commerce de Guienne sur l'estat present du commerce." The directors here had in mind the periodic uprisings against metropolitan restrictions that occasionally convulsed the islands—for instance, in Guadeloupe in 1715 and

Martinique in 1717. François du Feuquières, governor of Martinique, warmly refuted this and a similar set of accusations by the chamber of commerce of Bayonne. See A.D., L.-Atl., C 735 (1727), "Mémoire de Mr. de Feuquieres au suject du Commerce etranger qui se fait a nos Colonies et le vray moyen d'extirper ce commerce."

14. For the notion that patriotic nationalism was a spur to economic growth in the early modern period, see Liah Greenfeld, *The Spirit of Capitalism: Nationalism and Economic Growth* (Cambridge, MA: Harvard University Press, 2001), chap. 3, on France. On "sordid greed," see A.D., L.-Atl., C 735 (1726), Bayonne Chambre de Commerce, "Mémoire instructif du commerce étranger qui se fait journellement dans nos Colonies de l'Amérique." Paul Butel, *Histoire de la chambre de commerce et d'industrie de Bordeaux des origines à nos jours (1705-1985)* (Bordeaux: Chambre de Commerce et d'Industrie de Bordeaux, 1988), 45, emphasizes this aspect of the chambers' pleading.

15. On "close correspondence," see A.D., L.-Atl., C 735 (1726), Bayonne Chambre de Commerce, "Mémoir instructif du commerce étranger." Later, the émigré traveler and geographer-naturalist Volney would suggest that the Irish, English, and Germans survived their translation to America much better, thus putting these nations at an advantage in their colonization efforts. Constantin François Volney, *Tableau du climat et du sol des Etats-Unis d'Amérique, suivi d'éclaircissements sur la Floride* (Paris: Courcier et Dentu, 1803), 392. On Paris police, see A.D., L.-Atl., C 735 (1727), Nantes Chambre de Commerce, "Mémoire sur le commerce que les Etrangers font aux colonies françoises de l'Amérique et sur le moyen de l'empêcher." Paul Butel confirms this connivance, speaking of a "creolization" of the islands' governing elites over the eighteenth century. Paul Butel, *Histoire des Antilles françaises, xviie—xxe siècle* (Paris: Perrin, 2002), 131-132. Petitjean Roget emphasizes the economic necessity, for the islands, of this interloper trade as well as the complicity of the French crown in some forms of it. Jacques Petitjean Roget, *Le Gaoulé* (Fort de France: Société d'histoire de la Martinique, 1966), 497.

16. Douglas Hay uses this model to explain the mystery of the rising number of capital statutes over the eighteenth century (mainly involving offenses against property) combined with a growing number of pardons and a steady rate of executions—and a refusal to reform this seemingly contradictory situation. According to Hay, this combination of "Majesty, justice and mercy" helped to legitimate class rule. Douglas Hay, "Property, Authority, and the Criminal Law," in *Albion's Fatal Tree*, ed. Douglas Hay et al. (New York: Pantheon Books, 1975), 43 and 58. For criticism of Hay's model as unfalsifiable, see John H. Langbein, "Albion's Fatal Flaws," *Past and Present* 98, no. 1 (1983).

17. On absolutism, Mark Raeff, *The Well-Ordered Police State: Social and Institutional Change through Law in the Germanies and Russia, 1600-1800* (New Haven, CT: Yale University Press, 1983), discusses some of these paradoxical relationships in a different early modern context. Raeff shows how the state continually got in the way of the self-maintaining society it sought, through its own efforts, to create. See also H. M. Scott, *Enlightened Absolutism: Reform and Reformers in Later Eighteenth-Century Europe* (London: Macmillan, 1990), editor's introduction. Taken together, Raeff and Scott emphasize continuities between cameralist thought and enlightened

absolutism, while Raeff points out that the colonial context informed the development of both movements. For a more detailed discussion of French absolutism, see David Parker, *The Making of French Absolutism* (London: Edward Arnold, 1893). On the play of homogenization and differentiation, see Daniel Roche, *France in the Enlightenment* (Cambridge, MA: Harvard University Press, 1998), chap. 2, quote on 43. For more general reflections on the problem of space and governance, see David Harvey, *Spaces of Capital: Towards a Critical Geography* (London: Routledge, 2001), chap. 7, quote on 121. Others have been attempting to think in theoretical and historical terms about the production of differences—e.g., national and ethnic—that are, from the point of view of either liberal or Marxist orthodoxy, "incompatible with the logic of the capitalist system." See Etienne Balibar and Immanuel Wallerstein, *Race, nation, classe: Les identiés ambiguës* (Paris: La Découverte, 1997), 46–53, quote on 46. See also the discussion, with references, in the introduction to this book.

18. For the financial costs, see J. C. Riley, *The Seven Years' War and the Old Regime in France: The Economic and Financial Toll* (Princeton, NJ: Princeton University Press, 1986). On the *prise de conscience* among French elites, see, e.g., "Mémoires, recherches, observations politiques, historiques & critiques sur les guerres du commerce & principalement sur la guerre de 1672," *Journal de l'agriculture, du commerce et des finances,* June 1770. Petitjean Roget, *Le Gaoulé,* gives a good sense of the *frondeur* spirit among the planters throughout the eighteenth century. Robert Louis Stein, *The French Slave Trade in the Eighteenth Century: An Old Regime Business* (Madison: University of Wisconsin Press, 1979), 31, speaks of the "treason or benevolent neutrality" of the islanders. See also Tarrade, *Le Commerce colonial,* 1:470–472.

19. The debate on the Exclusive is discussed in some detail in Tarrade, *Le Commerce colonial,* vol. 1, chap. 8. Some of the surrounding historical detail on the debate over the Exclusive in 1765 is drawn from this work. A briefer summary can be found in Jean Meyer, Jean Tarrade, and Annie Rey-Goldzeigeur, *Histoire de la France coloniale: Des origines à 1870* (Paris: Armand Colin, 1991), 246–256. For Dubuc's memoir, see A.N., Colonies, F2b/7, piece 18 (1765), "Sur l'etendüe et les bornes des loix prohibitifs du commerce étranger dans nos colonies." On *tafias,* see the *Oxford English Dictionary:* "Origin uncertain: given in 1722 as a native name in West Indies (Labat *Voy. aux Iles de l' Amér.* III. 410 *Tafias:* 'The spirit made from sugar canes is called *guildive;* the savages and the negroes call it *tafia:* but *tafia* is also given in Malay dicts. as 'a spirit distilled from molasses.' The word appears therefore to be widely diffused in east and west.' "

20. All of these memoirs are found in the series A.N., Colonies, F2b/7. For Nantes' reaction, see F2b/7, "Mémoire du commerce de Nantes en réponse," ff. 7–8, my emphasis.

21. On "fundamental laws," see "Mémoire du commerce de Nantes en réponse," f. 9. The quotation from Montesquieu is from *EL,* 21.21. For Saint-Malo's commentary, see F2b/7, "Réponse de la Chambre du Commerce de St. Malo d'un mémoire qui a pour titre 'Sur l'étendüe & les bornes des loix prohibitives du commerce étranger dans nos colonies" (written in 1767 or 1768).

22. French products never did compete well on price but were generally considered to have an advantage in styling and workmanship. Bernard Bailyn, *The Ideological Origins of the American Revolution* (Cambridge, MA: Belknap Press, 1992), chap. 2. For the chamber of commerce's hatred of the *esprit de système* [i.e., the Physiocrats], see Hirsch, "Les milieux du commerce," 1341. Hirsch ascribes this hatred to their opposition to the 1786 Treaty of Eden, which liberalized trade between France and England. More pertinent, I think, is his hypothesis about the need for merchants and manufacturers to assert a counterideology, and a convincing form of patriotism, against the Physiocrats' "agricultural system." Hilliard d'Auberteuil, *Considérations sur l'état présent de la Colonie Françoise de Saint-Domingue: Ouvrage politique & législatif, présente au Ministre de la Marine* (Paris: Bastien, 1777), discours préliminaire, 1:18–19, 2:352–356. It is significant that this work was written in 1775 and presented to Sartine, the Minister of the Navy, in the same year as the latter convoked a "round table" in Paris in order to reconcile (yet again) metropolitan and colonial interests. Presumably, d'Auberteuil wanted to inoculate the ministers against the repetition of such arguments and the invocation of Montesquieu's authority on their behalf. The work was suppressed at the time. Sartine's roundtable is discussed in Tarrade, *Le Commerce colonial,* 1:420–448, though d'Auberteuil's work is not.

23. On Baltic trade and sobriety, see "Réponse du Commerce du St. Malo . . . ," 5r–5v. Compare to *EL,* 20.5. This anti-Physiocratic language is echoed elsewhere: "Yes, inspite of all of the systems, the utility of the colonies will always remain one of the foremost political truths. . . . [A]rguments, subtleties, metaphysical calculations, all crumble when confronted with the facts, recall the principles." A.N., Colonies, F2b/7, piece 30, 1r–1v.

24. "Réponse du Commerce du St. Malo . . . ," f. 5r. Tarrade confirms this account with reference to other sources. Tarrade, *Le Commerce colonial,* 1:121. The issue of shipping costs in the *Esprit des lois* and elsewhere in Montesquieu's oeuvre is discussed in Chapter 2 of this book.

25. Indeed, in a carton containing over thirty documents on this debate in the archives of the Ministry of the Navy, which had control over most colonial matters during the eighteenth century, in fifty pages or more, Montesquieu is the only author cited by name; see A.N., Colonies, F2b/7. On luxury, see A.N., Colonies, F2b/7, piece 26, f. 5r. The author cites *EL,* 21.6, in a marginal note. This piece is an untitled counter-response to the Chamber of Commerce of La Rochelle and is found in the back of a manuscript piece marked 25/26. On indigence, see "Réponse du Commerce du St. Malo . . . ," f. 1v. Among other arguments marshaled in favor of this conclusion was the notion that excessive wealth, and hence luxury, led to the use of slaves for luxury production and domestic labor rather than agricultural production. Ibid., 12r.

26. The remarks on this subject that are found in the *Esprit des lois* were originally written by Montesquieu in 1728 in a manuscript entitled "Considérations sur les richesses de l'Espagne." Certain elements can also be found in his *Réflexions sur la monarchie universelle.* Neither work, however, would have been available to contemporary audiences. Charles Vellay, *Montesquieu, Considérations sur les richesses de l'Espagne, précédées de la genèse de L'Esprit des loix* (Paris: J. Bernard, 1929),

1–26. "Réponse du Commerce du St. Malo . . . ," f. 22r; "Réponse de la Chambre de Commerce de la Rochelle," A.N., Colonies, F2b/7, piece 5, f. 4: "The author of the memoir states as a principle that the power of a Kingdom is exclusively the result of the number and of the wealth of its habitants. This maxim taken literally would be terribly dangerous: the annals of history present us on every page with great nations weakened by luxury."

27. "Réponse du Commerce du St. Malo . . . ," ff. 1v–2r.

28. François Quesnay, "Lettre sur l'opinion de l'auteur de l'ESPRIT DES LOIX concernant les colonies," *Journal de l'agriculture, du commerce et des finances,* April 1766; reprinted in François Quesnay, *Oeuvres économiques complètes et autres textes,* ed. Christine Théré, Loïc Charles, and Jean-Claude Perrot (Paris: INED, 2005), 2:869–879.

29. On "a world of workers," see A.D., L.-Atl., C 737 (1756), Nantes Chambre de Commerce, "Très humbles représentations du Commerce de Nantes à M. le Garde des Sceaux Ministre de la Marine, sur le commerce etranger aux colonies." For similar sentiments, see also A.D., L.-Atl., C 737 (1756), Guyenne Chambre de Commerce, "Très humble représentations des directeurs députés de la Chambre de Commerce de Guyenne à M. le Garde des Sceaux Ministre de la Marine." An element left largely unexplored in this chapter but taken up in Chapter 7 is the manner in which the chambers of commerce worked together on an issue to advance a shared agenda. The figures come from Guillaume Daudin, *Commerce et prospérité: La France au xviiie siècle* (Paris: Presses de l'Université Paris-Sorbonne, 2005), 397–398. Earlier historians also endorse this view. See Fernand Braudel, *The Wheels of Commerce,* vol. 2, Civilization and Capitalism, 15th–18th century (London: Fontana Press, 1985), who finds that the Atlantic shipping boom was responsible for the "increased modernity of Europe," 191. More recently, Robin Blackburn uses the phenomenon of New World slavery—and the circuits of European production and consumption associated with it—to solve the long-standing Marxist puzzle of "primitive accumulation." Robin Blackburn, *The Making of New World Slavery, from the Baroque to the Modern* (London: Verso, 1997). To this list should also be added Sidney W. Mintz, *Sweetness and Power: The Place of Sugar in Modern History* (New York: Penguin Books, 1985); and the excellent but curiously forgotten Ralph Davis, *The Rise of the Atlantic Economies* (Ithaca, NY: Cornell University Press, 1973).

30. The accounts of the Bureau de la Balance de Commerce, to which merchants and chambers of commerce were obliged to give information, provide abundant confirmation of the growth of colonial commerce in the years 1716–1789. (The bureau was the successor to the Council of Commerce.) A.N., F12 643, Bureau de la Balance de Commerce. These figures are gathered and printed in Ruggiero Romano, "Documenti e Prime Considerazioni intorno alla 'Balance du Commerce' della Francia dal 1716 al 1780," in *Studi in Onore di Armando Sapori,* ed. Antonio Noto (Milan: Istituto Editoriale Cisalpino, 1957). A broader discussion of these accounts can be found in Daudin, *Commerce et prospérité,* 191–203. On "branch and trunk," see A.D., L.-Atl., C 737 (1756), Nantes Chambre de Commerce, "Très humbles représentations du Commerce de Nantes à M. le Garde des Sceaux Ministre de la Marine, sur

le commerce étranger aux colonies," my emphasis. For utilitarian justifications, see A.N., A.E., BIII 441 (1777), "Mémoire sommaire." The most common alternative to *Colonie* was *Etablissement,* which has no such organic connotations, however.

31. On French fears, see Malick Ghachem, "'Between France and the Antilles': The Commercial Assimilation of the American Revolution in Saint-Domingue, 1784–1785," *Harvard Atlantic History Seminar: Working Paper Series* WP # 99026 (1999). On the politics of this *arrêt*, see Tarrade, *Le Commerce colonial,* 1:453; A.D., L.-Atl., C 737, 1784, France: Conseil d'Etat du Roi, "Arrêt du Conseil d'Etat du Roi Concernant le commerce étranger dans les Isles François de l'Amérique," my emphasis. D'Auberteuil, *Considérations sur l'état présent de la Colonie Françoise de Saint-Domingue,* echoed the same opinion, citing again Montesquieu's *EL,* 1:18–19. New historical circumstances required a different set of laws. On molasses, see John McCusker, "The Rum Trade and the Balance of Payments of the Thirteen Continental Colonies, 1650–1775" (PhD diss., University of Pittsburgh, 1970), 402 (table VI-2).

32. The directors of the Chamber of Commerce of Le Havre called it an "an insult lacking any sense whatsoever" that the metropole could not provide for colonial needs, but Paul Butel's judgment is that the colonists' claims were correct: French merchants were unable to keep up with colonial demands. Paul Butel, *L'Economie française au xviiie siècle* (Paris: SEDES, 1993), 119. A.D., L.-Atl., C 737 (1788), "Itératives observations des négociants du Havre sur l'arrêt du Conseil d'Etat du Roi, du 30 Août 1784, concernant le commerce étranger dans les Isles Françoises de l'Amérique." On the importation of slaves, Robert Louis Stein, *The French Slave Trade in the Eighteenth Century: An Old Regime Business* (Madison: University of Wisconsin Press, 1979), 46–47, affirms the importance of British slave merchants during this period. Jean-Baptiste Dubuc, *Le Pour et le contre sur un objet de grande discord, et d'importance majeure. Convient-il à l'administration de céder part, ou de ne rien céder aux étrangers dans le commerce de la métropole avec ses colonies?* (London: 1784), 1–2. For Mirabeau, see Hagley Museum and Library, manuscripts W-2 5671 (1764 or 1765), "Mémoire sur les colonies," ff. 298–302.

33. On Saint-Domingue's prosperity, see A.D., L.-Atl., C 735, Cap Français, Chambre d'Agriculture, "Copie d'un arrêté de la Chambre d'Agriculture du Cap addressé à MM les administrateurs de Saint Domingue en date du 5 Juin 1789." Jean-Baptiste Dubuc and Paul Ulric Dubuisson, *Lettres critiques et politiques sur les colonies & le commerce des villes maritimes de France, addressées à G. T. Raynal* (Geneva: 1786), 103, 13–14, and 18. The final observation is also cited by Léon Deschamps, *Histoire de la question coloniale en France* (Paris: E. Plon, Nourrit et Compagnie, 1891), 316.

34. Charles Lemesle, "Réponse à la brochure intitulée *Le Pour et le contre*" (London: 1785), 10. This pamphlet was collected by the Nantes Chamber of Commerce, and one sees its arguments trotted out by the Atlantic chambers of commerce in the ensuing four years. (Indeed, it was likely written at the behest of the Guyenne [Bordeaux region] Chamber of Commerce.) See, e.g., A. D., Gironde, C 4382, piece 26 (1788), "Nouvelles représentations des directeurs du commerce de la province de Guienne, sur l'Arrêt du Conseil du 30 Août 1784, concernant le commerce étranger

dans les Isles Françaises de l'Amérique," where the directors speak, like Lemesle, of a "chain" that "links" all the people of the kingdom. See Paul Butel, *Les négociants bordelais, l'Europe et les Isles au XVIIIe siècle* (Paris: Aubier, 1974), 378, on Lemesle's affiliation with the chamber.

35. Lemesle, "Réponse à la brochure intitulée *Le Pour et le contre,*" 26–27, emphasis added.

36. Ibid., 20. "God is a sphere whose center is everywhere and whose circumference is nowhere (Deus est sphaera infinita, cuius centrum est ubique, circumferentia nusquam)." For attributions and discussions of this expression, which is often falsely attributed to St. Augustine, see Robin Small, "Nietzsche and a Platonist Tradition of the Cosmos: Center Everywhere and Circumference Nowhere," *Journal of the History of Ideas* 44, no. 1 (1983): 90–93. For the phrase "reality of markets" and the problem of linking this to discourse, see Minard, *La Fortune du colbertisme,* 308.

37. On "general interests," see Lemesle, "Réponse à la brochure intitulée *Le Pour et le contre,*" 37. See also ibid., 61. On the "tribunal," see Chevalier de Deslandes, "Observations importantes sur la décadence du commerce maritime françois, aux colonies," in A.D., L.-Atl., C 735 (1789). The Chevalier was trying to carve out for himself a position as the head of a new *maréchaussée* in Saint Domingue, whose principal purpose would be the suppression of contraband trade.

38. On "reasonable and admissible" things, see Le Havre Chambre de Commerce, A.D., L.-Atl., C 737 (1788), "Itératives observations des négociants du Havre sur l'Arrêt du Conseil d'Etat du Roi, du 30 août 1784, concernant le commerce étranger dans les Isles Françoises de l'Amérique." On commodity prices, see Deslandes, "Observations importantes," 4. See also A.D., L.-Atl., C 735 (1789), Barbé-Marbois (intendant of Saint Domingue in 1789), "11 May, 1789, délibérations sur le nouveau régime proposé par M. le Gouverneur général pour l'admission des étrangères dans la partie du sud de la colonie." On reciprocity, see Lemesle, "Réponse à la brochure intitulée *Le Pour et le contre,*" 26. J. P. Hirsch, "Les milieux du commerce, l'esprit de système et le pouvoir, à la veille de la Révolution," *Annales ESC* 30, no. 6 (1975): 1360, discusses this conundrum. On respect for law, see also Barbé-Marbois, "11 May, 1789, délibérations sur le nouveau régime."

39. On public opinion, see Keith Michael Baker, *Inventing the French Revolution: Essays on French Political Culture in the Eighteenth Century* (Cambridge: Cambridge University Press, 1990), 170–172. Thomas E. Crow, *Painters and Public Life in Eighteenth-Century Paris* (New Haven, CT: Yale University Press, 1985), 166–180. François Furet, *Interpreting the French Revolution,* trans. Elborg Forster (Cambridge: Cambridge University Press, 1981), 30. The notion of voluntarism as a pathology of eighteenth-century political discourse that contributed to the *dérapage* of the French Revolution is a leitmotif in most of Furet's writing on the subject. See François Furet, *Revolutionary France, 1770–1880,* trans. Antonia Nevill (Oxford: Blackwell, 1988), 41–150. On the return of the repressed, see Pierre Rosanvallon, *Le Capitalisme utopique* (Paris: Editions du Seuil, 1979), 54. Michael Sonenscher also seeks to connect developments in eighteenth-century political economy with the rise of potentially radical voluntarist discourse during the revolution. See *Before the Deluge:*

Public Debt, Inequality, and the Intellectual Origins of the French Revolution (Princeton NJ: Princeton University Press, 2007), 4–11. For more on the paradoxes of the Physiocratic theory of the state, see Yves Citton, *Portrait de l'économiste en physiocrate: Critique littéraire de l'économie politique* (Paris: L'Harmattan, 2000), chap. 9. Furet echoes Rosanvallon's judgments in *Interpreting the French Revolution*, 30. In this case, Baker is attempting to correct for an overly materialist bias in Habermas's account of the rise of the public sphere and of public opinion. On law and general interest, see d'Auberteuil, *Considérations sur l'état présent de la Colonie Françoise de Saint-Domingue*, 2:360. As Wallerstein observes of a world economy divided into core and periphery, "'Nationalism'" is a mechanism both of imperium/integration and of resistance/liberation." Wallerstein, *The Politics of the World Economy*, 20.

40. On "national" credit, see A.D., L.-Atl., C 736 (1785), "Les Anglois admettent-ils, les Anglo-Américains dans leurs colonies et les autres nations ouvrent-elles leurs ports aux Etrangers?" A similar discussion can be found in Dubuc and Dubuisson, *Lettres critiques*, 70–71. An entire dossier is consecrated to the problem of debt among colonial planters: A.D. L.-Atl., C 726.

41. For Nantes' call to arms, see A. D., Gironde, C 4360 (1788, 23 July), Directors of Nantes to Guyenne Chamber of Commerce; (Cited in J. Letaconnoux, "Le Comité des députés extraordinaires des manufactures et du commerce et l'oeuvre économique de l'assemblé constituante, 1789–1791," *Annales Révolutionnaires* 6 (1913): 150n.) This effort failed, and the merchants did poorly in the general elections for representatives to the Estates General, but they did manage to exert formidable extra-parliamentary pressure by way of their *comité extraordinaire*. For other historical arguments, see A.D., Ch-Mar, La Rochelle ChC, III/1 (1788). Lille also echoed Nantes' language from the *HI* (Lille, 30 October).

42. All quotations in this paragraph come from pamphlets collected in A.D., Ch-Mar, La Rochelle ChC, III/1. For similar sentiments, also see Toulouse's pamphlet. Bordeaux and Amiens also mention feudalism and privilege.

43. A.D., Ch-Mar, La Rochelle ChC, III/1.

7. *L'Affaire des Colonies* and the Fall of the Monarchy

1. See Patrick Villiers, *Marine royale, corsaires et trafic dans l'Atlantique, de Louis XIV à Louis XVI* (Villeneuve-d'Ascq: Presses Universitaires du Septentrion, 2002), 1:204–209 and 2:494–500 for annual estimates; percentage of revenue estimates on 1:207. For the comparison between naval and war (i.e., land army) expenses as a percentage of revenue, see Michel Morineau, "Budgets de l'état et gestation des finances royales en France au dix-huitième siècle," *Revue Historique* 264, no. 2 (1980), 315 (for calculations on figures). If possible, naval accounts are even more obscure than the regular budgets of the crown as a whole, so it is safer to rely upon trends rather than upon specific figures. On this confusion, see James Pritchard, *Louis XV's Navy, 1748–1762: A Study of Organization and Administration* (Montreal: McGill-Queen's University Press, 1987), chap. 11.

2. The possibility of financial reform is broached with excessive optimism in E. N. White, "Was There a Solution to the *Ancien Régime*'s Financial Dilemma?" *Journal of*

Economic History 49 (1989). On the trend toward universal forms of taxation and its limited success, see Michael Kwass, *Privilege and the Politics of Taxation in Eighteenth-Century France: Liberté, Egalité, Fiscalité* (Cambridge: Cambridge University Press, 2000).

3. For this sobriquet, see Albert Soboul, Jean-René Suratteau, and François Gendron, *Dictionnaire historique de la Révolution française* (Paris: Presses Universitaires de France, 1989), 79. For Barnave's resistance to the charge, see Antoine Barnave, *De la Révolution et de la constitution, préface de François Furet; Introduction au texte et notes de Patrice Gueniffey* (Grenoble: Presses Universitaires de Grenoble, 1988), 131–132. (Although the editor makes a good case for changing the title of Barnave's classic work, further references to this edition will go by the more familiar *Introduction à la Révolution française*.) See also Antoine Barnave, *Œuvres de Barnave mises en ordre et précédées d'une notice historique sur Barnave* (Paris: J. Chapelle et Guiller, 1843), 2:112. The original manuscripts (ten notebooks) from which Bérenger de la Drôme largely drew the material in *Œuvres de Barnave* can be found at the Bibliothèque Municipale de Grenoble. His editorial work is heavily criticized in François Vermale, "Manuscrits et éditions des oeuvres de Barnave," *Annales historiques de la révolution française* 15 (1938). Vermale claims that no serious scholarly work can be done using la Drôme's edition because of omissions and interpellations in key passages, mainly in Barnave's *Introduction à la Révolution française*. A comparison of the sections from *Œuvres de Barnave* cited here against the original manuscript in the Bibliothèque Municipale de Grenoble (document: U.5216) showed no significant variations, so the printed edition is cited here and elsewhere.

4. Marxist reference to Barnave can be found in Jean Jaurès, *Histoire socialiste de la révolution française, édition revue et annotée par Albert Soboul* (Paris: Editions Sociales, 1968), 1:847–849. Albert Soboul, "The French Revolution in the History of the Contemporary World," in *The French Revolution: Recent Debates and New Controversies,* ed. Gary Kates (London: Routledge, 2006), 21.

5. On the "tragic hero," see François Furet and Mona Ozouf, *Terminer la révolution: Mounier et Barnave dans la Révolution française* (Grenoble: Presses Universitaires de Grenoble, 1990), 21. On the "last of the moderates," see Ran Halévi, "Feuillants," in *A Critical Dictionary of the French Revolution,* ed. François Furet and Mona Ozouf (Cambridge, MA: Harvard University Press, 1989), 350. Patrice Gueniffey re-edited Barnave's *Introduction à la Révolution française* as a way of reinforcing these judgments.

6. In a nearly two-hundred-page collection of essays on Barnave and Mounier, we find only a couple of references to these speeches. See Furet and Ozouf, *Terminer la révolution.* For Furet's views, see Barnave, *Introduction,* 12–13, from his preface. For a passing reference to distant connections in Barnave's family to colonial wealth, see François Furet and Ran Halévi, eds., *Orateurs de la Révolution française* (Paris: Pléiade, 1989), editors' introduction.

7. For these and other details on civic participation, see Isser Woloch, *The New Regime: Transformations of the French Civic Order, 1789–1820s* (New York: W. W. Norton, 1994), chap. 2; franchise figures on 66.

8. *Généralité* or *Intendance* was the administrative unit that the absolute monarchy imposed over the older provinces. Jacques Godechot, *Les Institutions de la France sous la révolution et l'empire* (Paris: Presses Universitaires de la France, 1951), 89. Among intellectual historians who have approached the question, Anthony Pagden confirms the late entrance of empire into the French political lexicon: only with the outbreak of the French Revolution did the French have to come to terms with the same set of questions that dogged the Spanish and the English, particularly after the close of the Seven Years' War. See Anthony Pagden, *Lords of All the World: Ideologies of Empire in Spain, Britain, and France* (New Haven, CT: Yale University Press, 1995), chap. 5, esp. 132–145. For a more circumstantial account of this period, see J. H. Elliott, *Empires of the Atlantic World: Britain and Spain in America, 1492–1830* (New Haven, CT: Yale University Press, 2006), chap. 10. On the supposed absence of a French empire, see James Pritchard, *In Search of Empire: The French in the Americas, 1670–1730* (Cambridge: Cambridge University Press, 2004). Although it is impeccably researched and describes the confusion of the French crown in colonial affairs in convincing detail, Pritchard's conclusions seem guided by a mistaken premise: any collection of overseas establishments that did not display the coherence and success of the British cannot be termed an empire. On administrative norms in Saint-Domingue, see James E. McClellan, *Colonialism and Science: Saint Domingue in the Old Regime* (Baltimore: Johns Hopkins University Press, 1992), 44. David Armitage, *The Ideological Origins of the British Empire* (Cambridge: Cambridge University Press, 2000), chap. 1.

9. For opposition to colonial representation, see, e.g., Pierre François Blin, a deputy from Nantes, in *AP*, 10:350–353. There are several accounts of this search for representation and the resulting ambivalence. See Gabriel Debien, *Les Colons de Saint-Domingue et la révolution: Essai sur le club Massiac (août 1789–août 1792)* (Paris: A. Colin, 1953); Yves Benot, *La Révolution française et la fin des colonies, 1789–1794* (Paris: La Découverte, 2004), chap. 5. On the question of *moeurs,* see, e.g., A.N., W 15 (1789), Procès verbaux of the Société correspondante des colons français en France, 28 August and 21 November. Quinney also emphasizes the difficulty members of the convention faced in finding a consistent definition of empire. Valerie Yow Quinney, "The Committee on Colonies of the French Constituent Assembly, 1789–91" (PhD diss., University of Wisconsin, 1967), 194–204. Debien and Benot provide fundamental accounts from which much material for this chapter has been drawn.

10. On "dissemblance," see France, *AP*, 10:348. (Later, Moreau de St. Méry would collaborate with the Committee in writing a constitutional instruction for Saint-Domingue (more on this follows in the text.) See also the comments of Cocherel, the deputy from Saint-Domingue who demanded "a constitution proper to its *moeurs*, its usages, its manufactures and its climate," A.N., D XXV 86; and A.N., W 15, Procès verbaux of the Société correspondante des colons français en France, August 28. On the question of provinces, see *AP*, 10:351. Turgot uses the term *provinces alliées,* but in a different sense, in Anne-Robert-Jacques Turgot, "Mémoire sur la manière dont la France et l'Espagne devoient envisager les suites de la querelle entre la Grande-Bretagne et ses Colonies (1776)," in *Oeuvres de Mr. Turgot* (Paris:

Delance, 1809), 8:460. Though not a merchant himself, Blin was deeply involved with colonial merchants and maintained contacts with the Club Massiac and various chambers of commerce. See A.N., W 15, Procès-verbaux, 20 November 1789; and A.D., Ch-Mar, La Rochelle ChC, Carton 19, dossier 12, letter of 21 September 1791. For La Rochefoucauld-Liancourt's words, see *AP,* 31:291. On "conditions of existence," see A.N., D XXV 89 (1791), Procès verbaux du Commission extraordinaire, 19 January–4 April 1791, meeting of 27 Jan 1791.

11. *AP,* 12:71.

12. Alexandre Lameth attended twenty of fifty-five meetings between December 1790 and September 1791 (meetings for which there are extant minutes), whereas Malouet attended fifteen. The all-time champion is nonmember Moreau de Saint Méry, who attended fifty-one meetings and intervened often and with great apparent influence. The source of this analysis is Henri Joucla, *Le Conseil supérieur des colonies et ses antécédents, avec de nombreux documents inédits et notamment les procès-verbaux du comité colonial de l'Assemblée Constituante* (Paris: Editions du Monde Moderne, 1927), 228–354. For a list of Club Massiac members, see Debien, *Essai sur le club Massiac,* 389–394.

13. On Malouet, see *AP,* 31:295. On Bayonne, see A.N., D XXV 89 (1790), Letter from Chamber of Commerce of Bayonne to Massiac, in Procès verbaux du Commission extraordinaire, meeting of 8 June. For Moreau de St. Méry, see *AP,* 25:639.

14. *AP,* 31:296, emphasis in original. Malouet discounted the possibility of reforming island sugar production to make slave labor unnecessary. In this case, one would need an intermediate social form such as feudalism to make the system work profitably. In either case, coerced labor was necessary. Blin also emphasized the colonial and metropolitan economic relationship as a "chain of dependence." See *AP,* 12:10 (2 March 1790).

15. On wariness about port cities, see A.D., Ch-Mar, La Rochelle ChC, Carton III, dossier 2: 8 September, 1789, Nairac to La Rochelle. This correspondence is printed, with an introduction, in Jean-Michel Deveau, *Le Commerce rochelais face à la Révolution: Correspondance de Jean-Baptiste Nairac* (La Rochelle: Rumeur des âges, 1989). A letter to Barnave by the Amis de la Constitution de Brest went so far as to suggest that anticolonial ministers were forming part of the counterrevolution. A.N., D XXXV 78, dossier 771, 26 April 1791. On "national principles," see A.D., Ch-Mar, La Rochelle ChC, Carton III, dossier 2, 25 August 1789, Nairac to La Rochelle, emphasis added. A letter by Camaze to Barnave restates all of these economic claims: "The loss of the colonies, which is certain if the Assembly does not revoke its decree [of 15 May]: will entail the loss of commerce and the idleness of seven million men in France. . . . [W]ill the abbé Gregoire or the National Assembly come calm them down? . . . Add to this the destruction of the Royal Navy and of the balance of power." A.N., W 12, 28 August 1791. Barnave himself put the figure at six million. See A.N., W 13, piece 58. This figure is echoed in A.D., XXV 88, dossier 842, "La conviction des faux principes," f. 4. Nairac outlines his strategy in A.D., Ch-Mar, La Rochelle ChC, Carton III, dossier 2, 25 August 1789, same to La Rochelle. On Barnave, see *AP,* 12:69–70, emphasis added.

16. A.D., Ch-Mar, La Rochelle ChC, Carton III, dossier 2, 29 August 1789, the same to La Rochelle. For historians' views on this alliance, see Debien, *Essai sur le club Massiac;* Quinney, "Committee on Colonies"; J. Letaconnoux, "Les Sources de l'histoire du comité des députés extraordinaires des manufactures et du commerce de France (1789–1791)," *Revue d'histoire moderne et contemporaine* 17 (September–October 1912); and Benot, *La Révolution française et la fin des colonies,* 47.

17. For Chilleau's decree and Barbé-Marbois' response, see A.D., L-Atl., 735 (1789), "Copie d'un decrée de la Chambre d'Agriculture du Cap addressé à MM les administrateurs de Saint-Domingue en date du 5 Juin 1789." On the campaign of vilification, see A.D., L-Atl., C 722 (1790), "Mémoire et observations du Sieur Barbé de Marbois, Intendant des Isles-sous-le-Vent en 1786, 1787, 1788 et 1789 sur une dénonciation signée par treize de MM. les Députés de Saint-Domingue, et faite à l'Assemblée Nationale au nom d'un des trois Comités de la Colonie." The broad outlines of the account in this paragraph rely heavily on Jean Tarrade, *Le Commerce colonial de la France à la fin de l'ancien régime: L'évolution du régime de "l'Exclusif" de 1763 à 1789* (Paris: Presses Universitaires de France, 1972), 2:700–712, quote on 710.

18. On free trade, see A.N., D XXV 89, Procès verbaux du Commission extraordinaire, 19 January–4 April 1791. On the dividends to patriotism, see A.N., DXXV 13, "Projet d'une coalition du commerce," not dated but most certainly during the period of the Constituent Assembly, 9 July 1789–30 September 1791. Abundant further references to the need for patriotism can be found in A.N., D XXV 78.

19. On trade, see A.N., D XXV 89, no. 12, 12 February. On *attentisme,* see the extraordinary deputies' letter of 9 March in A.N., DXXV 89. On the Massiac side, this policy is given the crudest expression early on in A.N., W15 (1789), Séances du Club Massiac, 19 September. For Barnave on unity, see Joucla, *Le Conseil supérieur des colonies,* 305.

20. Dupont's proposal to the Assembly was drawn from a memoir he wrote in 1785 as *inspecteur général du commerce,* reflecting on the decree of 1784, which softened the Exclusive. Compare Hagley Museum and Library, Manuscript W-2 4680, with *AP,* 31:280–286 (23 September 1790). Quotations on 280, 286, and again on 280.

21. For Barnave's words in the Assembly, see *AP,* 12:68–69. Seven of the thirteen original members of the Committee were either colonial deputies or had heavy interests in colonial affairs (e.g., Alexandre Lameth, among the latter category). See Edna Lemay, *Dictionnaire des constituants: 1789–1791* (Paris: Universitas, 1991). On the "second legislature," see Barnave, 25 April 1791, in Joucla, *Le Conseil supérieur des colonies,* 302. For the colonists' political machinations over this period more generally, see Debien, *Essai sur le club Massiac,* chaps. 8–10.

22. Joucla, *Le Conseil supérieur des colonies,* 340 (5 May 1791).

23. The words are those of Nairac, in his description to La Rochelle of the decree of 8 March 1790, which first announced the distinction between internal and external regimes in order to grant the colonies autonomy on the question of the status of persons.

24. On the "immensity" of the instruction, see Pétion de Villeneuve, *AP,* 27:231 (14 June 1791). Though an admittedly imprecise basis for comparison, the constitution

adopted for mainland france on 3 September 1791 contained 207 articles. Barnave's discussion is found in Joucla, *Le Conseil supérieur des colonies,* 229 (24 December 1790) and 238 (8 January 1791).

25. For Barnave on tribunals and fortifications, see Joucla, *Le Conseil supérieur des colonies,* 246 and 255. On the instruction on tribunals and fortifications, see, respectively, *AP,* 226 (title VII, § 2, article 15); and 17 (title IV, § 1, article 6).

26. Here it is important again to emphasize just how close the cooperation of colonial deputies (e.g., Moreau de St. Méry) and those with interests in the colonies (Victor Malouet) was in the drafting of this instruction: they were present at most meetings and worked collegially with Barnave. On the abolition of privileges and justice, see *AP,* 27:215 (article 7, my emphasis) and 225 (title VIII, § 2, articles 10–11), respectively. For Moreau on Jews, see Joucla, *Le Conseil supérieur des colonies,* 287 (12 February 1791). Barnave's draft of the instruction (A.N., W 13, piece 76) shows how dear the abolition of the feudal regime was to him and how uncontroversial this was for the rest of the Committee.

27. *AP,* 27:215 (titre première, articles 1–4, "bases générales"). On sovereignty, see Joucla, *Le Conseil supérieur des colonies,* 338. Barnave's drafts (A.N., W 13) of the same four articles show how difficult it was for the Committee to settle on the language that defined "national" powers, sometimes adopting *pouvoirs généraux* or even *pouvoirs speciaux.* No such difficulty of redaction presented itself in the case of the "constitutional abolition" of feudalism in the colonies.

28. Blin's discussion comes from *AP,* 5:353 (1 December 1790). On "good sense and reason," see ibid., 12:10 (2 March 1790). On Ireland's colonial status, see, among others, Armitage, *Ideological Origins,* 154–158. For an opposing view, see Sean Connolly, *Religion, Law, and Power: The Making of Protestant Ireland, 1660–1760* (Oxford: Clarendon Press, 1992). On reform and the American Revolution, see Marianne Elliott, *Partners in Revolution: The United Irishmen and France* (New Haven, CT: Yale University Press, 1982), 3–35.

29. Isser Woloch, "On the Latent Illiberalism of the French Revolution," *American Historical Review* 95, no. 5 (1990).

30. Barnave, *Œuvres,* 2:226. On English accomplishments, see *AP,* 31:253–254 (23 September 1791).

31. A.N., D XXV 89 (1791), Procès Verbaux, Special Commission, 27 February. Emphasis in original.

32. For the planetary comparison, see Barnave, *Œuvres,* 2:226. Elsewhere, Barnave recommends the federalist constitution of the United States to France as the closest thing resembling an "organized" and "elective" monarchy for modern societies. A.N., W 15, Papiers de Barnave, Cahier de Pensées et Réflexions, 2 of 2, f.105 (henceforth cited as Pensées). While many thought America and its constitution resembled an ancient republic, Barnave clearly did not: *AP,* 29:408 (11 August 1791). Charrière speaks in *AP,* 26:28 (12 May 1791).

33. On the growth of republican thought after Varennes, see Mona Ozouf, *Varennes: La mort de la royauté* (Paris: Gallimard, 2005), chap. 8. For Barnave's speech, see *AP,* 28:326–331.

34. For Barnave on Montesquieu and Rousseau, see, e.g,, A.N., W 15, Pensées, 2 of 2:, ff. 39 and 68, among others. Antoine Barnave, "Les Procès devant le tribunal révolutionnaire, 28 Novembre, 1793," in *Orateurs de la Révolution française*, ed. François Furet and Ran Halévi (Paris: Pléiade, 1989), 1:90. The subject of the history of passions in commercial society is so well explored by now that further explication would probably be redundant, but an excellent recent synthesis of this topic in the French context can be found in Céline Spector, *Montesquieu: Pouvoirs, richesses et sociétés* (Paris: Presses Universitaires de France, 2004). On the links between Barnave, Montesquieu, and the Scottish Enlightenment, see Furet's preface to Barnave, *Introduction*. See also Alison Webster, "J. Barnave: Philosopher of a Revolution," *History of European Ideas* 17, no. 1 (1993); Antoine Barnave and Emanuel Chill, *Power, Property, and History: Barnave's Introduction to the French Revolution and Other Writings* (New York: Harper & Row, 1971), editor's introduction.

35. Barnave, *Introduction*, 178–79 and 184; and *Œuvres*, 2:42–49 (quotation on 137). See also A.N., W 15, Pensées, 2 of 2, 74–75. Finally, see *AP*, 30:114 (31 August 1791): "for the average person, tranquility is more necessary than liberty. . . . [T]ranquility is the first requirement and political liberty is but an addition which makes for happiness, but which is not, strictly speaking, necessary." For "civilized" and "organized" monarchy, see A.N., W 15, Pensées, 2 of 2, ff. 81, 101, and 105.

36. Barnave, *Œuvres*, 2:202.

37. On necessary complexity, see, e.g., A.N., W 15, Pensées, 2 of 2, f. 105. For criticism of Montesquieu, see Barnave, *Introduction*, 81.

38. Emmanuel Joseph Sieyès, *Qu'est-ce que le Tiers Etat?* 3rd ed. (n.p.:1789), 45, on "available classes." On Malouet's connivance with Barnave, see Pierre-Victor Malouet, *Mémoires de Malouet* (Paris: Didier, 1868), 2:72. On the need for aristocracy, see Barnave, *Œuvres*, 2:18, 49, and 187; and Barnave, *Introduction*, 52, 92, 114, 165, and 193. For Malouet's speech, see *AP*, 29:264 and 274–278 (8 August 1791); for Barnave's speech. see *AP*, 29:365–366 (11 August 1791).

39. On "subordination," see A.N., W 13, piece 58. On artificiality and Barnave's statistics, see *AP*, 31:256–257 (23 September 1791). See also Barnave's speech of 15 May 1791, *AP*, 25:755–759. On the *moeurs* of the French population, see, in particular, A.N., W 15, Pensées, 2 of 2, ff. 68–78; and *Œuvres*, 2:181–182 and 200–202. Barnave had no doubt who was responsible for the production of wealth in modern societies: "industrial wealth belongs to the laboring class of people: its origin is work." See *Introduction*, 61.

40. *AP*, 31:257. Duval d'Epremesnil criticizes Lafayette, who advocates rights for *gens du couleur* while upholding the active/passive distinction at home (*AP*, 25:752). Moreau de St. Méry glories in this hypocrisy in *AP*, 26:10.

41. Alexis de Tocqueville, *L'Ancien régime et la Révolution* (Paris: Gallimard, 1967), book 3, chap. 3. Barnave, *Œuvres*, 2:62–63. Further discussion of the "beautiful and generous" principles of Physiocracy and free trade comes in Barnave, *Introduction*, 180. Another heated denunciation of the naïveté of his opponents comes in Barnave's defense of Raynal: Barnave, *Œuvres*, 2:149. For more on the temporary harm of free trade, see ibid., 2:208–210.

42. Edward Whiting Fox, *History in Geographic Perspective: The Other France* (New York: Norton, 1971). On France's vocation to agriculture and trade, see Barnave, *Introduction,* 180; and *Œuvres,* 2:207. On democratic revolution and commerce, see *Introduction,* 82 and 99; and *Œuvres,* 2:48 and 201. On work, see ibid., 2:6.

43. On the advances attributable to colonial commerce, see Barnave, *Œuvres,* 2:209. On "unity," see ibid., 2:201. On the colonial question and the monarchy, see Barnave, *Introduction,* 114.

44. On the link between revolutionary ideology and the slave uprising in Saint-Domingue, see Laurent Dubois, *Avengers of the New World: The Story of the Haitian Revolution* (Cambridge, MA: Harvard University Press, 2004), chap. 4. Two earlier works present a contrary view. Carolyn E. Fick emphasizes older traditions of slave rebellion in *The Making of Haiti: The Saint Domingue Revolution from Below* (Knoxville: University of Tennessee Press, 1990), chaps. 1–3; and David Patrick Geggus underlines the context of war in "Slavery, War, and Revolution in the Greater Caribbean, 1789–1815," in *A Turbulent Time: The French Revolution and the Greater Caribbean,* ed. David Barry Gaspar and David Patrick Geggus (Bloomington: Indiana University Press, 1997). Barnave was arrested on the strength of an incriminating letter found in the king's *armoire de fer* at the Tuileries Palace; during the nineteenth century, the discovery of Barnave's secret correspondence with Marie Antoinette proved definitively what Barnave's opponents could only merely suspect. My impression, upon reading this correspondence, is that Barnave was earnestly trying to save the constitutional monarchy but was being manipulated by Marie Antoinette, who negotiated with him in terribly bad faith. See Antoine Barnave and Marie Antoinette, *Correspondance secrète (Juillet 1791–Janvier 1792)* (Paris: A. Colin, 1934).

45. On the banalization of sugar consumption and its relation to revolutionary ferment, see Colin Jones and Rebecca Spang, "Sans-Culottes, *Sans café, Sans tabac:* Shifting Realms of Necessity in Eighteenth-Century France," in *Consumers and Luxury: Consumer Culture in Europe, 1650–1850,* ed. Maxine Berg and Helen Clifford (Manchester: Manchester University Press, 1999). R. R. Palmer, *The Age of Democratic Revolution: A Political History of Europe and America, 1760–1800* (Princeton, NJ: Princeton University Press, 1959), vol. 2, chap. 2. On the colonial theater, see David Barry Gaspar and David Patrick Geggus, *A Turbulent Time;* Bailey Stone, *Reinterpreting the French Revolution: A Global-Historical Perspective* (Cambridge: Cambridge University Press, 2002), chap. 4; and Laurent Dubois, *A Colony of Citizens: Revolution and Slave Emancipation in the French Caribbean, 1787–1804* (Chapel Hill: University of North Carolina Press, 2004), 84–89, for events on Martinique.

46. On Lameth, see *AP,* 12:2 (2 March 1790). On the social exclusion of the Constitution of 1791, including the "abolition" of feudalism and its contribution to the fall of the monarchy, see the account of one historian who is by no means a partisan of radical Jacobinism: Donald Sutherland, *France 1789–1815: Revolution and Counterrevolution* (New York: Oxford University Press, 1986), chap. 4. On the protracted process of the abolition of feudal dues, see John Markoff, *The Abolition of Feudalism: Peasants, Lords, and Legislators in the French Revolution* (University Park: University of Pennsylvania Press, 1996), esp. chap. 8.

47. Furet's comments in this connection are worth quoting at length: "The revolutionaries had cherished and proclaimed equality for all the French while depriving a great many of them of the right to vote or to run for office. They cherished and proclaimed liberty and yet maintained slavery in their colonies in the Antilles and elsewhere in the name of national commercial prosperity. Those who followed them made use of the timidity or inconsistency of their predecessors in an attempt to carry the Revolution forward in the name of true equality." François Furet, *The Passing of an Illusion: The Idea of Communism in the Twentieth Century* (Chicago: University of Chicago Press, 1999), 8–9.

48. On the pervasiveness of military values in the Napoleonic regime, see Alan Forrest, "The Military Culture of Napoleonic France," in *Napoleon and Europe,* ed. Philip G. Dwyer (London: Longman, 2001). Benjamin Constant, *Ecrits politiques* (Paris: Gallimard, 1997), 129–132 and 142–144 (part 1, chaps. 2 and 6).

49. François Crouzet, "Wars, Blockade, and Economic Change in Europe, 1792–1815," *Journal of Economic History* 24 (1964). For a synoptic view of these changes, see Denis Woronoff, "L'Industrialisation de la France de 1789 a 1815: Un essai de bilan," *Revue économique* 40, no. 6 (1989). See also Jeff Horn, *The Path Not Taken: French Industrialization in the Age of Revolution, 1750–1830* (Cambridge, MA: MIT Press, 2006), introduction and chap. 7. Left out of discussion here is Horn's provocative thesis about the radical "path not taken" because of Napoleonic—and, more generally, bourgeois—fear of Jacobin economic management.

Index

Absolutism, 13, 15–16, 38, 122, 164, 202; Ludovician, 38
Academies and Societies, Académie Française, 81, 263n19; Academy of Dijon, 270n19; Corresponding Society of French Colonists Residing in France ("Club Massiac"), 203; provincial, 74, 81, 82, 84; Royal Society of London, 81; Société des Amis des Noirs, 204 (*see also* Slavery). *See also* Bordeaux Academy
Acemoglu, Daron, 234n13
Adams, Julia, 16, 232n4, 234n15, 235n17
Agrarian society. *See* Society
Agronomes, 141, 267n1
Aiguillon, Anne-Charlotte de Crussol-Florensac Duchesse d', 79
Albion, 64, 197, 277n16. *See also* England
Aldrich, Robert, 237n7
Alembert, Jean le Rond d', 5, 23, 48, 80, 123, 141, 142, 143, 146, 246n8, 264n24, 267n2, 268n9
Alexander of Macedonia, 101
Althusser, Louis, 244n1, 247n16
Ameilhon, Hubert Pascal, 239n12
American Colonies. *See* Colonies of England
American War of Independence, 6, 111–112, 135–136, 185, 191, 196–197, 216, 261n2
Amiens, Peace of. *See* Peace of Amiens
Anderson, Perry, 5, 16, 232n3, 235n17, 236n20
Andrivet, Patrick, 246n9
Angleterre. *See* England
Anglophilia, 37, 72, 105, 128, 256–257n35

Anglophobia, 37, 257n35
Appleby, Joyce O., 239n10
Arcq, Philippe-Auguste de Sainte-Foix, Chevalier d', 68, 95–103, 110, 116, 157, 239n12, 253n14, 254nn15–19, 255nn22–27, 256n28, 264n21
Argenson, the Marquis d', 48, 79, 244n47, 263n14
Aristocracy and aristocrats, 2, 4, 5, 40, 49, 68, 77, 79, 125, 192, 199, 219, 220–224, 226, 236n20, 247n24, 289n38; bourgeois, 221–222, 226; equestrian, 223; feudal, 199, 223; land-holding, 199; mercantile, 221; principle of, 222; provincial, 77; republican thinkers, 247n24
Aristotle, 92. *See also* Philosophy
Armitage, David, 201, 285n8, 288n28
Arnould, Ambroise-Marie, 237n4, 259n45
Arnouville, Jean Baptiste de Machault d', 75
Aron, Raymond, 89, 245n7, 251n3
Arrighi, Giovanni, 17, 235n19
Arthur, Christopher John, 274n41
Artisans *(gens d'art)*, 59, 114, 214, 260n49
Atlantic: Atlantic world, 12–13, 74, 116, 152, 156, 162; chambers of commerce, 170, 172–173, 179, 186, 191 (*see also* Chambers of Commerce: of Bayonne; of La Rochelle; of Le Havre; of Nantes; of Saint-Malo); economy, 12, 15; empires, 183; French Atlantic world, 12, 15, 201; history, 14; Ocean, 73, 113, 159, 178, 184, 196; ports, 15, 172–173, 176, 185 (*see also* Ponant); trade and commerce, 14, 72, 116, 162, 184, 208, 228

Réaumur, René-Antoine Ferchault de, 93–94

Reform: Bourbon, 123; economic, 20, 37, 102, 116, 148, 149, 152; moderate, 3, 5, 6, 130, 165, 194, 205; political, 37; social, 91; Spanish, 123; Turgot's, 148, 260n52

Religion: French Wars of, 149; religious intolerance, 36; religious obscurantists, 90

Republic of Letters, 4, 5, 9, 23, 28, 104. *See also* Englightenment

Republicanism, 219

Revolutionary War. *See* American War of Independence

Rey-Goldzeigeur, Annie, 278n19

Richelieu, Cardinal Armand-Jean du Plessis, duc de, 244n48, 270n21

Richter, Melvin, 64, 245n7, 247n19

Rights: civil (equal), 201, 217; denial of, 204; natural, 149; political, 18, 200, 201, 204–206, 222–223; property, 106, 149; shared, 212

Riley, James C., 119–121, 261nn2,4,5,6, 278n18

Ringrose, David R., 243n41

Risteau, François, 69–70, 77, 81, 247n25, 248n26; and Montesquieu, 69–70

Rivery, Boulanger de, 69–70, 247n25

Rivière, Mercier de la, 266n39, 268n6

Robertson, John, 10, 233n9

Robinet, Jean-Baptiste, 123, 126–127, 129–130, 263nn15,16, 264n23

Robinson, James, 234n13

Roche, Daniel, 81–82, 84, 237n6

Roget, Jacques Petitjean, 238n9, 277n15, 278n18

Romano, Ruggiero, 280n30

Root, Hilton, 235n16, 262n7

Rosanvallon, Pierre, 147, 190, 274n42, 282n39, 283n39

Rosenthal, Jean-Laurent, 265n26

Rothkrug, Lionel, 240n18, 242n26, 261n2, 267n1

Rothschild, Emma, 10, 233n9, 234n12, 251n2, 252n10

Roubaud, Pierre, 154, 156–161, 167, 182, 270n21, 271n26, 272nn28–31, 273nn33,36

Rousseau, Jean-Jacques, 92, 139, 219, 252n7, 289n34; Rousseauists, 104

Ruggie, John, 235n18

Rushforth, Brett, 272n32

Russo, Elena, 258n43

Ryswick, Peace of (1697). *See* Peace of Ryswick (1697)

Saint-Cyr, Paul-Antoine Nolivos, 262n10

Saint-Maur, Marie-Marthe Dupré de, Mdm., 79

Saint Méry, Louis-Elie Moreau de, 203, 207, 213–215, 285n10, 286nn12,13, 288n26, 289n40

St. Pierre, Bernardin de, 253n12

Saint-Pierre, Charles-Irénée Castel, Abbé de, 37–41, 46, 69, 79, 85, 99, 138, 241nn20,24, 242nn26,27, 243n43, 251n46, 255n22

Sales, Delisle de, 262n11

Salter, J., 233n7, 251n2

Sartine, Antoine-Gabriel de, 279n22

Schaeper, Thomas, 275n8

Schmale, Wolfgang, 265n24

Schnakenbourg, Christian, 275n3

Schumpeter, Joseph, 270n22

Scott, Hamish M., 277n17

Scott, James C., 274n40

Scoville, Warren C., 237n3, 276n4

Secularism, 90. *See also* Religion

Sée, Henri, 238n9, 249n33, 273n35

Senarclens, Vanessa de, 246n9, 256n27

Serionne, Jacques Accarias de, 134, 246n8, 255n24

Seven Years' War (1756–1763), 5, 100, 110, 120, 135, 161, 177–178, 181, 184, 185, 197, 216, 240n16, 248n28, 255n24, 258n42, 261nn2,4,5, 265n28, 275n3, 278n18, 285n8

Shackleton, Robert, 245n6, 246n9, 248nn25,28, 249nn30,34, 250nn36,41

Shklar, Judith, 264n20

Shovlin, John, 233n8, 247n24, 253n14

Sieyès, Joseph, 221, 246n7, 289n38

Silhouette, Etienne de, 31–32, 34, 35–36, 43–47, 50, 240nn16–18, 241nn21,22,24, 242n39, 243nn40–44, 244n50

Skinner, Quentin, 241n25, 249n29. *See also* Cambridge School